JOURNAL FOR THE STUDY OF THE NEW TESTAMENT
SUPPLEMENT SERIES

26

Executive Editor, Supplement Series
David Hill

Publishing Editor
David E Orton

JSOT Press
Sheffield

WATCHWORDS

Mark 13 in Markan Eschatology

Timothy J. Geddert

Journal for the Study of the New Testament
Supplement Series 26

To my parents
George and Annie Geddert

Published by JSOT Press
JSOT Press is an imprint of
Sheffield Academic Press Ltd
The University of Sheffield
343 Fulwood Road
Sheffield S10 3BP
England

Printed in Great Britain
by Billing & Sons Ltd
Worcester

British Library Cataloguing in Publication Data

Geddert, T. J.
    Watchwords: Mark 13 in Markan eschatology
    1. Bible. N.T. Mark Critical Studies
    I. Title
    226'.306

    ISSN 0143-5108
    ISBN 1-85075-127-7

CONTENTS

Acknowledgements   9
Abbreviations   11

Chapter 1
INTRODUCTION   15

Chapter 2
A MARKAN PERSPECTIVE ON SIGNS   29
Introduction   29
I   Mark's Use of σημεῖον   30
II   Mark's Omissions of σημεῖον   34
III   The Markan Jesus and 'Objective Evidence'   40
IV   Mark and 'Objective Evidence'   47
V   Implications for Interpreting Mark 13   57

Chapter 3
A MARKAN PERSPECTIVE ON DISCERNMENT   59
Introduction   59
I   The Leaven and the Loaves (Mark 8.14–21)   61
II   The Call to Understand (7.31–8.26 in Context)   71
III   Mark's Use of βλέπω in the Light of His
     Epistemology   81
IV   βλέπω in Mark 13: Implications for Exegesis   84

Chapter 4
A MARKAN PERSPECTIVE ON DISCIPLESHIP   89
Introduction   89
I   γρηγορέω, The Doorkeeper Parable, and Gethsemane   90
II   The Four Watch Schema of the Passion Night   94
III   Implications of Mark's Four Watch Schema for
     Interpreting Mark   103

Chapter 5
MARK'S TEMPLE THEOLOGY   113
Introduction   113
I   An Overview of the Data to Be Interpreted   114
II   The 'Cleansing' of the Temple   117
III The Prophecy to Destroy and Rebuild   130
IV   The Rending of the Temple Veil   140
V   Implications for Interpreting Mark 13   145

Chapter 6
MARK'S THEOLOGY OF SUFFERING AND
    PERSECUTION   149
Introduction   149
I   The Road to Jerusalem: Via Dolorosa?   151
II   The Rejected Baptist and the Fulfilment of His Mission 155
III Jesus' Passion and the Mission of the Disciples   158
IV   Implications for Interpreting Mark 13   175

Chapter 7
MARK 13 AND MARK'S LITERARY ACHIEVEMENT   177
Introduction   177
I   Discipleship/Discernment and Mark's Literary Method   178
II   A Model for Interpreting Mark's Gospel   185
III The Literary Function of Mark 13   192

Chapter 8
MARK 13 AND THE SECRET KINGDOM   199
Introduction   199
I   The Secret Coming of the Kingdom in Mark   199
II   Mark 13.1-4 and Mark's Agenda for Mark 13   203
III The Significance of the Temple's Destruction   206
IV   The Significance of the Disciples' Suffering and
     Persecution   215

Chapter 9
MARK 13 AND THE TIMING OF THE END   223
Introduction   223
I   Judgment and Vindication: Intermediate and Final   225
II   The Destruction of the Temple and the End of the Age   231
III The Timing of the End   239
IV   A Markan Perspective for Reading Mark 13   253

SUMMARY AND CONCLUSIONS 255

Notes 259
Bibliography 317
Index of Biblical References 341
Index of Authors 349

ACKNOWLEDGEMENTS

I have frequently read long lists of acknowledgements at the beginning of a book and have sometimes wondered whether the author did any of the work. I have now written a book and will never have those thoughts again. The support and help of family and friends during the time of writing has left me with a debt of gratitude that I could never repay. Fortunately none of those who helped need settle for whatever repayment I could ever give. They will be much more richly rewarded.

Special mention must be given to two young friends whose extraordinary help in the final stages has been most remarkable. Thank you, Matthew and Andrew. I will try to help you when you are old enough to write a book.

Thanks are due to those who helped in a variety of ways along the way . . . especially to Lynn, Kathy, Conrad, Dave and Clint. I am grateful to Prof. I. Howard Marshall, who not only guided me through the research and writing, but also stood by me when the challenges along the way were not only academic. I also thank Dr. Ruth B. Edwards and Prof. G.R. Beasley-Murray for examining my Ph.D. thesis, for urging me to make some changes, and not least for recommending that my thesis be accepted. I hope they will recognize in this publication many improvements over the thesis they examined. And a special thank you to Katrina Poetker, without whose expert help and good judgment, this study would have many more deficiencies than it has.

A word of appreciation is extended to the British Commonwealth Scholarship Commission in the United Kingdom for financial support, and to family and friends in Pitmedden, Canada, and California for support in many other ways. Finally, to the first critical reviewer of this book: thanks, Gertrud, for being kind. Thanks for everything.

ABBREVIATIONS

AsSeign	*Assemblées du Seigneur* (Paris)
ASTI	*Annual of the Swedish Theological Institute* (Jerusalem)
ATR	*Anglican Theological Review* (Evanston, IL)
AusBR	*Australian Biblical Review* (Melbourne)
Bib	*Biblica* (Rome)
BibLeb	*Bibel und Leben* (Düsseldorf)
BJRL	*Bulletin of the John Rylands University Library of Manchester* (Manchester)
BR	*Biblical Research* (Chicago)
BSac	*Bibliotheca Sacra* (Dallas, TX)
BT	*Bible Translator* (London)
BTB	*Biblical Theology Bulletin* (Albany, NY)
BZ	*Biblische Zeitschrift* (Paderborn)
CBQ	*Catholic Biblical Quarterly* (Washington, DC)
CivCatt	*Civiltà Cattolica* (Rome)
ConNT	*Coniectanea Neotestamentica* (Uppsala)
CQR	*Church Quarterly Review* (London)
CTM	*Concordia Theological Monthly* (St. Louis, MO)
CurTM	*Currents in Theology and Mission* (St. Louis, MO)
DeltBibMel	*Deltion Biblikon Meleton* (Athens)
DownRev	*Downside Review* (Bath)
DunRev	*Dunwoodie Review* (New York)
ETL	*Ephemerides Theologicae Lovanienses* (Louvain-Leuven)

ETR	*Etudes Théologiques et Religieuses* (Montpellier)
EvQ	*Evangelical Quarterly* (Exeter)
EvT	*Evangelische Theologie* (Munich)
ExpTim	*Expository Times* (Banstead, Surrey)
FoiVie	*Foi et Vie* (Paris)
HeyJ	*Heythrop Journal* (London)
HorBibTheol	*Horizons in Biblical Theology* (Pittsburgh, PA)
HTR	*Harvard Theological Review* (Cambridge, MA)
HUCA	*Hebrew Union College Annual* (Cincinnati, OH)
IndJournTheol	*Indian Journal of Theology* (Calcutta)
Int	*Interpretation* (Richmond, VA)
JAAR	*Journal of the American Academy of Religion* (Chico, CA)
JBL	*Journal of Biblical Literature* (Chico, CA)
JBR	*Journal of Bible and Religion* (Brattleboro, VT)
JETS	*Journal of the Evangelical Theological Society* (Wheaton, IL)
JournTheolSAfr	*Journal of Theology for Southern Africa* (Rondebosch, S. Africa)
JR	*Journal of Religion* (Chicago)
JRAS	*Journal of the Royal Asiatic Society* (London)
JRS	*Journal of Roman Studies* (London)
JSNT	*Journal for the Study of the New Testament* (Sheffield)
JTS	*Journal of Theological Studies* (Oxford) (New series unless otherwise indicated)
LingBib	*Linguistica Biblica* (Bonn)
LouvStud	*Louvain Studies* (Louvain)
LQ	*Lutheran Quarterly* (St. Paul, MN)
LumVit	*Lumen Vitae* (Brussels)
ModChurch	*Modern Churchman* (Leominster, Herefordshire)
NedTTS	*Nederlands Theologisch Tijdschrift* (The Hague)
Neot	*Neotestamentica* (Bloemfontein, S. Africa)
NewBlackfr	*New Blackfriars* (Oxford)
NovT	*Novum Testamentum* (Leiden)
NRT	*Nouvelle Revue Théologique* (Tournai)
NTS	*New Testament Studies* (Cambridge)
PalCler	*Palestra del Clero* (Rovigo)
PerkJourn	*Perkins Journal* (Dallas, TX)
PerspRelStud	*Perspectives in Religious Studies* (Macon, GA)

ProcIrBibAssoc	*Proceedings of the Irish Biblical Association* (Dublin)
RB	*Revue Biblique* (Jerusalem)
RelLife	*Religion in Life* (Nashville, TN)
RelStudRev	*Religious Studies Review* (Waterloo, Ont.)
RestorQuart	*Restoration Quarterly* (Abilene, TX)
RevExp	*Review and Expositor* (Louisville, KY)
RevistB	*Revista Biblica* (Buenos Aires)
RevistStorLettRel	*Revista di Storia e Letteratura Religiosa* Turin
RevThom	*Revue Thomiste* (Toulouse)
RSPT	*Revue des Sciences Philosophiques et Théologiques* (Paris)
RSR	*Recherches des Sciences Religieuses* (Paris)
RTL	*Revue Théologique de Louvain* (Louvain)
RUO	*Revue de l'Université d'Ottawa* (Ottawa)
SciEccl	*Sciences Ecclésiastiques* (Montreal)
Scr	*Scripture* (London)
ScrB	*Scripture Bulletin* (Twickenham, Middlesex)
SJT	*Scottish Journal of Theology* (Edinburgh)
ST	*Studia Theologica* (Oslo)
SWJournTheol	*Southwestern Journal of Theology* (Fort Worth, TX)
TBT	*The Bible Today* (Collegeville, MN)
TheolLife	*Theology and Life* (Lancaster, PA)
ThViat	*Theologia Viatorum* (Berlin)
TijdTheol	*Tijdschrift voor Theologie* (Nijmegen)
TLZ	*Theologische Literaturzeitung* (Leipzig)
TrinJourn	*Trinity Journal* (Deerfield, IL)
TS	*Theological Studies* (Washington, DC)
TSFBull	*Theological Students Fellowship Bulletin* (London)
TSFBulletin	*Theological Students Fellowship Bulletin* (Madison, WI)
TTZ	*Trier Theologische Zeitschrift* (Trier)
TynBull	*Tyndale Bulletin* (Cambridge)
TZ	*Theologische Zeitschrift* (Basel)
USQR	*Union Seminary Quarterly Review* (New York)
VC	*Vigiliae Christianae* (Amsterdam)
VD	*Verbum Domini* (Rome)
VSpir	*Vie Spirituelle* (Paris)

ZNW	*Zeitschrift für die neutestamentliche Wissenschaft* (Berlin)
ZTK	*Zeitschrift für Theologie und Kirche* (Tübingen)

Chapter 1

INTRODUCTION

An immense amount of scholarly effort has gone into the study of Mark 13. Nevertheless, not everything that can be said, and needs to be said, has been said. This study is born out of the conviction that there is a method of studying Mark's eschatological discourse, and therefore the eschatology of Mark, which has never been thoroughly attempted. That method is to read and interpret Mark 13 in the literary and theological context of the entire Gospel in which Mark placed it.

No claim is being made that this study will answer all the questions about Mark's eschatology. Its aim is more modest. It attempts to read Mark 13 from Mark's perspective, to hear it as he intended it to be heard, and to catch glimpses of the eschatology which shaped his life and therefore his literary masterpiece. And a masterpiece it is, sometimes saying much more than appears at the surface, and often withholding precisely the information that scholars are trying so desperately to wrench from its pages. Almost every study of Mark 13 begins by saying something like, 'The Synoptic eschatological discourse bristles with problems'.[1] It surely does; but most of the problems, I am now persuaded, are the result of overlooking Mark's agenda, and trying to use his texts to carry out ours.

It is in fact only in the last few decades that a growing number of scholars have been persuaded that Mark was theologically astute enough to *have* theological perspectives and agenda worth examining. Until recently most scholars believed (and some still do) that Mark was a rather naive compiler of Jesus traditions, that his book has no overarching plan or purpose, and that it would be folly to imagine that one chapter (especially the thirteenth!) ought to be read in the

light of the other fifteen. That chapter, it has often been held, is so
out of character with the rest of the book that it must be interpreted
on its own. Some have even held that the Gospel was originally
written without it.[2]

Previous Studies

Many detailed studies of Mark 13 have appeared in this century.
Each makes unique contributions to our understanding of the
chapter, but each also fails to do what this study is aiming to do. A
brief mention of some of these is perhaps in order.

G.R. Beasley-Murray's studies[3] provide masterful evaluations of
previous attempts to analyse (or discredit) the chapter, and also
provide a way of reading Mark 13 which harmonizes with other
eschatological sayings of Jesus. No attempt is made, however, to
analyse the unique perspective of Mark and the distinctive use he
makes of the material in Mark 13.

W. Marxsen's pioneering 'redaction critical' study of Mark[4]
represents a concerted effort to hear the distinctive voice of Mark.
Moreover, Marxsen listens very carefully to Mark 13 and its unique
contribution. There are, however, two major difficulties standing in
the way of accepting his conclusions. First, most scholars would
agree that Marxsen has misread the function of Mark 13 by wrongly
interpreting the 'Galilee-symbolism' Mark employs in 14.28 and
16.7. If those two verses are not designed to urge Mark's readers to
hasten to Galilee to be ready for an imminent parousia there, then it
is highly unlikely that Mark 13 was designed to help accomplish that
function. Second, Marxsen's methodological base is too narrow. We
cannot hear Mark comprehensively if we concern ourselves almost
exclusively with those places where Mark has apparently adapted
and modified his sources.

In 1966, A.L. Moore's study of New Testament eschatology
appeared.[5] Though it did not aim to be a study of Mark 13 in the
context of Mark's Gospel, it made a major contribution by
distinguishing carefully between what Moore calls 'delimited' and
'undelimited' near expectations. The choice of terms is perhaps not
the most fortunate, but we would join Moore in insisting that unless
the distinction is observed with care, some of the subtleties of the
New Testament, and particularly of Mark 13, will be missed. The
inconsistency which scholarly literature often betrays in the use of
terms like 'imminent' is proof that for all our analysing, we

sometimes do not analyse carefully enough. Some scholars use 'imminent' to mean 'guaranteed to happen very soon' in one context and 'not guaranteed to be long delayed' in another, without differentiating between these two very different concepts. In the present study the word will be used only in the second sense, though of course it remains to be demonstrated that this has any relevance to Mark's viewpoints.

Lars Hartman's study of Mark 13[6] is an attempt to demonstrate that the eschatological discourse has its origin in a midrashic treatment of Old Testament texts, particularly from Daniel, and to sketch briefly how this midrash might have developed into the Synoptic eschatological discourse. Hartman explicitly disavows the idea that his study attempts to trace the theology of the individual evangelist.[7]

The strength of J. Lambrecht's study of Mark 13[8] is that it takes the entire chapter seriously, not only 'redactional alterations' of a source. Its weakness, from our point of view, is that it interprets Mark 13 'on its own', neither drawing on the historical and theological context which gave rise to it, nor demonstrating its meaning and function within the larger Gospel of Mark.

R. Pesch's study[9] is considered by many to be 'the magisterial work on the Markan apocalypse'.[10] However, it has been subjected to much criticism, and we would agree with those scholars who take issue with it for focusing too narrowly on redactional alterations in its attempt to understand Mark, for not demonstrating that its kingpin idea (that an apocalyptic tract lies behind the chapter) is defensible, and for viewing Mark 13 as virtually extraneous to the message of the whole Gospel.[11] It is the conviction of this study that Mark's Gospel has a much more significant plan and purpose, within which Mark 13 plays an indispensable role, than Pesch found.

Lloyd Gaston undertook a massive study of Mark 13.[12] Unfortunately, in effect he claims to understand Mark's sources better than Mark did, a claim that is rather hard to accept, especially when we consider that Mark knew what sources he was utilizing and modern scholars do not. Mark himself is not given a fair hearing in Gaston's study.

The last five books cited all made their appearance within five years (1966-70). Thereafter, no major study directed primarily at the material of Mark 13 appeared for fourteen years. It is hard to escape the feeling that scholars were getting discouraged by their inability to generate any consensus on the meaning of Mark 13, or even on the means by which that meaning was to be sought.

In 1984 two books appeared which focused directly on Mark 13, but neither took up the task assumed here. David Wenham's study[13] is not aimed at understanding the perspectives of the individual New Testament authors. It aims to reconstruct the sources they used. Egon Brandenburger's study of Mark 13[14] fails to read the chapter in its Gospel context, choosing rather to read it in the light of contemporary apocalyptic literature, as so many scholars have done before.

The scholars cited above, and many who have contributed shorter studies, have all made valuable contributions, and this study will draw heavily on those contributions. One task, however, has remained unfulfilled: the task of reading Mark 13 carefully and comprehensively in the context of Mark's Gospel.[15]

The Task that Remains Unfulfilled

Why has such a study never been undertaken? One reason is that there are other important tasks that need to be done; no scholar is to be faulted for choosing one of these rather than the one we are selecting. But other factors have also contributed. Some scholars have made faulty assumptions about Mark's literary/theological abilities. Some have over-emphasized the uniqueness of Mark 13 and therefore have been reluctant to interpret it within the context of the Gospel. Some have chosen too limited a range of exegetical tools to enable them to hear the author comprehensively. A few comments should be made about each of these factors.

Mark was a writer with a carefully considered and subtly communicated theological perspective. That conclusion has been reached by many modern scholars, and it is hoped that this study will add further support to it. Every chapter of this study helps to develop the case that Mark really did know what he was doing. And if he did, if Mark is far less of a bungling editor and far more of a theological/ literary master than earlier scholars imagined, then it is necessary to evaluate every part of Mark in terms of its meaning and function within the whole.

That includes Mark 13! It is not the 'alien intrusion' into the Gospel that many have imagined. It is not 'totally unlike anything else in Mark'.[16] It is part and parcel of the whole and must be interpreted as such. Some serious misunderstandings of Mark 13 have resulted from refusing to let the whole Gospel become the interpretative context for some of its key ideas and terms. An example is the distinction between the two key terms Mark uses to say 'watch!'—βλέπετε and γρηγορεῖτε. If their meaning is read out of a lexicon, they emerge as near synonyms. If their function is analysed in the Gospel of Mark, they can be seen to have very distinct functions, and a whole range of clues emerges as to how Mark intended Mark 13 to be understood. In each chapter of this study, remarkable insights will be gained by testing the assumption that Mark 13 'fits' in the Gospel.

A comment or two must be made about exegetical methods. There are those who would argue that if the goal of this study is to grasp the author's intentions, then this is a redaction-critical study. Unfortunately, 'redaction criticism' is a term which has meant a variety of things and should be used with caution. Many scholars speak as though 'redaction criticism' is equivalent to 'listening to the author's perspective'. That defines 'redaction criticism' in terms of its *goal*. At the same time many scholars (and sometimes the same people) say that 'redaction criticism' is 'examining the textual alterations authors have made to their sources'. That defines 'redaction criticism' in terms of its *methodology*. A term like 'redaction criticism' must not be defined both teleologically and methodologically. To do so bypasses the crucial question whether or not the proposed method is adequate to reach the desired goal. In this case it is not.

Students of Mark's Gospel are learning that no single tool is adequate to reveal the secrets of this remarkable book. If Mark has used many tools to convey his points of view—theologically loaded terms, Old Testament allusions, controlled use of key terms and concepts, structural elements, narrative progressions, and sundry other literary techniques—then it is necessary for scholars to use many tools to uncover the Markan message. We do not claim to be expert in the use of all the possible tools of exegesis. But we hope that a willingness to change from one tool to another as the medium changes, and to use several tools together when the need arises, will enable us to make progress in a study that is entirely motivated by the object of our quest, and that is to listen to Mark. *Our goal will be to uncover the intentions of the author of Mark's Gospel as they can be known by studying Mark 13 in its Gospel context*. This raises another objection that needs to be addressed.

Learning to Listen to the Author

Some literary critics insist that what we are aiming to do is impossible *in principle*. The 'author's intentions', they would insist, are not accessible via a text. These are not the appropriate objects of the readers' attention. If I understand what literary critics call 'the intentional fallacy', it is the fallacy that a text can yield *no more than* the conscious intentions of the author. It seems rather obvious that it can. It can betray information concerning grammatical conventions of which the author might well have been entirely ignorant. It can betray prejudices that the author was not consciously aware he/she had. It can allude to facts that are new and interesting to modern scholars but were so much a part of the shared knowledge of the original writer and readers that there was no original 'intention' to convey them.

But limits must be drawn. Authors are still basically in control of the communication process. They may use implied narrators and literary characters to help them make their points, but they do not create autonomous communicators and stand by helplessly as the readers are told things the author never intended them to hear. We take our stand with those equally competent literary critics who insist that it is precisely the author's conscious intentions that are the primary objects of investigation when we examine a text. We would even go so far as to say that it is misleading to speak of a *text's* meaning. Writers and speakers generate meanings; texts and speeches merely convey them.[17] We do not look *at* texts, but *through* them. A text is a medium through which an author seeks to communicate with potential readers, and it is therefore also a medium through which actual readers seek to hear what the author intended to say.

The Agenda of Mark in Mark 13

Inferences about Mark's meaning are very hazardous when based on studies which probe questions Mark was not even addressing. Studies of Mark 13 which focus heavily on sources and authorial adaptations do precisely that. We capture the author's meaning most accurately when we have learned to determine precisely which issues the author is consciously addressing and which questions the author is aiming to answer.

Since Mark communicates to his readers in large measure by allowing them to observe and overhear the interaction between the characters who feature in the story, we are obliged to listen carefully for clues as to what agenda influenced the words and actions of those characters. But we must always move beyond that concern as well. It is not our primary concern to hear what those characters say to each other. We want to determine what it is that Mark is telling his readers by recording those conversations.

Numerous scholars have been content to establish the agenda of the *disciples* in Mark 13.1-4 and imagine that they have uncovered *Mark's* agenda. But that is a fundamental confusion of categories. The disciples function as literary characters within Mark 13 and we have no assurance that their agenda is endorsed by either the Markan Jesus or by the author. Given the role of the disciples in Mark, the balance of probability is that Mark's purpose is to have the Markan Jesus criticize and correct the perspective the disciples betray. Moreover, it is even a confusion of categories to imagine that if we can establish the agenda of the Markan Jesus in 13.5-37, then we can automatically equate that with 'the intentions of the author'. It is easy to demonstrate from Mark's Gospel that at times the agenda of Jesus *within* a text is almost the opposite of the agenda Mark pursues *by means of* the text.[18] Our concern throughout will be to hear what *Mark* is saying, and we shall be listening to his characters within the narrative only because their communication with each other *within* the story is one of the tools Mark has chosen to use to help him make his points *by means of* the story.

We shall discover in due time that just as Jesus (within the story) frequently withholds information that his hearers would like him to divulge, so also Mark (in presenting his material) frequently withholds precisely that information which his readers would very much wish he had divulged. We want to learn to listen not only to what Mark intends to communicate, but to what he intends to avoid telling his readers. We shall discover that Mark, just like the Markan Jesus, expects discerning hearers/readers to grasp subtleties which others will entirely overlook. A whole field of research opens up when it is seen how carefully Mark models himself after his chief character.

We are well aware of J.M. Robinson's oft-quoted criticism of those approaches which argue not on the basis of what Mark clearly and repeatedly has to say, but on inferences drawn from matters about which Mark is silent.[19] The point is taken. Any approach which allows Markan subtleties to rule the day at the expense of his clear statements is suspect. However, to ignore Mark's less obvious clues is

also a serious error. A Gospel which highlights the subtle and
allusive character of Jesus' communication, portraying him as one
who expects some to understand while others do not ... a Gospel
with repeated calls to see more than is visible to the eyes and hear
more than is audible to the ears ... such a Gospel might well have
been written by a man who used the same techniques, and did so for
similar reasons. It bears serious consideration.

It will be our goal to address the most important and most basic
questions involved in interpreting Mark 13. If we can with some
confidence answer *these* questions from Mark's own angle of vision,
the important groundwork will be done for others to deal with the
countless subsidiary issues. In short, we want to establish the basic
framework of thought in which Mark intended his readers to
understand Mark 13. It follows that a major concern of *our* agenda is
to determine *Mark's* agenda.

Scholarly diversity on the issue of Mark's agenda can hardly be
overestimated. While one scholar argues that virtually the whole
chapter is about the destruction of the temple, the next one claims
that that issue is entirely ignored after 13.4. Many accept the more
probable view that the chapter is centrally concerned with both the
destruction of the temple and the end of the age. But among these,
one claims Mark is seeking to establish the temporal *conjunction* of
these two events and another claims that he is attempting to establish
their temporal *disjunction*. One argues that Mark is outlining the
signs by which the End will be heralded while another argues that
Mark criticizes the very notion that there can be premonitory signs.
One argues that Mark is setting up an apocalyptic timetable while
another claims he is trying to demolish all such timetables. One
argues that Mark is preparing his church to accept the fact that the
parousia might well be delayed longer than they had anticipated,
while another argues that Mark is trying to prevent that very type of
thinking. One claims that the saying on ignorance (13.32ff.) is in
tension with the main points of Jesus' answer, while another claims it
is the answer. It is clear that a great deal of care must be taken to
determine what Mark 13 is about. What is the author aiming to
accomplish? There is an almost overwhelming diversity in the
answers given to this most fundamental question.

In accounting for this diversity it becomes evident that there are
essentially two key factors:

1.   Throughout Mark 13 there are ambiguous statements,

deliberately evasive allusions, verbs without defined subjects, demonstrative pronouns without clear referents, parables without obvious interpretations, seemingly contradictory (or at least paradoxically juxtaposed) statements, and other mystifying features. Scholars have not adequately accounted for this state of affairs.

2. Mark 13 features introductory questions and a lengthy discourse which do not seem to match each other very well. Scholars have worked diligently to understand the meaning of the introduction and the meaning of the discourse. They have thereby concerned themselves with the agenda of the Markan disciples and with the agenda of the Markan Jesus. But they have not adequately sorted out the agenda of the author/redactor of both parts.

With respect to the first of these, the usual scholarly 'explanations' are: (1) Mark was a clumsy editor, (2) he used a source for purposes other than those that generated it, (3) he assumed more shared knowledge between author and reader than is possible today, or (4) he promoted a perspective which is inherently paradoxical and probably self-contradictory. When we learn to listen carefully to Markan literary subtleties we soon discover that these 'solutions' are inadequate. It is much more plausible that Mark was attempting something more subtle in Mark 13 than has usually been suspected. Perhaps he knew that the secrets of the chapter would not be disclosed unless the whole Gospel message was taken seriously as the interpretative context.

With respect to the second, the lack of concord between Mark 13.1-4 and 13.5-37 has frequently generated comments no more insightful than: (1) it proves that Mark himself composed the introductory verses, (2) it proves the discourse was inauthentic, (3) it proves Mark made the (erroneous?) association between the destruction of the temple and the end of the age, (4) it shows that Mark is relentless in his depiction of the disciples' misunderstanding. It is much more plausible that Mark is in full control of both parts of the chapter and that the introductory question(s), the answer(s) to them, and the lack of concord between those two, are all tools in Mark's hand to carry out an agenda which might well transcend the internal agenda of any one of the characters within the Markan story.

If we want to understand Mark's meaning and purposes in Mark 13, the matter of Mark's own specific agenda will need much greater clarification. How shall it be gained? It should be obvious by now that we have no intention of taking a microscope to analyse the elements of *the disciples' question(s)* in hopes thereby of firmly establishing Mark's agenda.[20] Invariably, scholars first exegete Mark 13.4 and then strain out gnats and swallow camels trying to find in Mark 13 an appropriate answer to what is asked. It is a highly dubious method of learning what Mark wanted to say. Our approach will be radically different. What is needed is to turn to the whole Gospel of Mark and test it for insights into Mark's own perspective on the issues raised in Mark 13. What is needed is not a more powerful microscope focusing on ever smaller details within Mark 13. What is needed is a network of floodlights illuminating this chapter from all over the rest of the Gospel.

By reconsidering the question of the function of Mark 13.1-4 in relation to the entire chapter, and the whole chapter in relation to Mark's theological concerns in the entire Gospel, we hope to determine the Markan agenda for Mark 13. What could be more helpful in the task of understanding Mark 13 than to determine with some confidence what it is 'about'?

It is essential to look at the whole chapter in the context of the whole Gospel from Mark's own angle of vision if we want to find answers to the key questions that so trouble those who aim to interpret Mark 13, questions like:

1. Does Mark 13 endorse 'sign-seeking' and therefore stand in complete isolation from the rest of the Gospel which shuns it, or is Mark 13 as anti-sign-seeking as anything else in the Gospel?
2. What is the relationship that Mark endorses between the destruction of the temple and the end of the age? And why is every reference to the temple, within Mark 13 and outside it, veiled in an aura of mystery?
3. What does it mean to 'watch'? Why are two different words used, and what is the significance of each?
4. Does Mark expect the End to arrive within the first generation of Christians (13.30)? Why would a key verse like 13.30 be presented in a way which leaves its message so infuriatingly ambiguous? Was Mark careless or subtle?

If we can with some confidence answer the most basic questions outlined above, we shall be in a very advantageous position to work out Mark's understanding of a whole host of subsidiary questions, like: What was being claimed by those who said, 'I am (he)'('Εγώ εἰμι)? What does it mean to stand firm 'to the end' (εἰς τέλος)? What is 'the abomination of desolation' (τὸ βδέλυγμα τῆς ἐρημώσεως)? Where does he/it stand? Who are 'the elect' (οἱ ἐκλεκτοί)? What is the meaning of the fig tree parable? The list goes on.[21]

Too many scholars have imagined that by answering *these* questions first, the overall meaning and function of the chapter can be discerned. Without even attempting to answer these specific questions first, we shall try to use the whole Gospel of Mark as the context for answering the more basic questions about Mark's agenda and his perspectives. If the overall perspective which emerges sheds light on the details that were not even under discussion, we can gain confidence that real progress has been made.[22]

Anticipating Some of our Conclusions

The vindication of our final conclusions and therefore also the retrospective justification for our initial assumptions will depend on the ability of our findings to shed light on the whole Gospel of Mark and on the place of Mark 13 within it. Our conclusions, like all conclusions, will leave some questions unanswered. We will be careful not to try to wrench from the texts answers to those questions which Mark intended to leave unanswered. We shall see that there are lots of those!

Among the theses that we will be led to defend in this study are the following:

1. Mark 13 holds an integral place in the structure and the message of Mark's Gospel. It 'fits'.
2. Mark's Gospel as a whole and Mark 13 in particular are centrally concerned with matters of 'epistemology'. All the other key themes (Christology, kingdom of God, discipleship, historical reporting, etc.) cannot adequately account for Mark's main concerns unless the issue of 'epistemology' is brought into the discussion at every level. Mark is frequently more concerned to teach his readers *how* to know than *what* to know.
3. Mark 13, like most of the Gospel, was never intended to generate a flat univocal interpretation. Interpreting Mark's Gospel is often not so much a matter of removing ambiguities

as it is explaining *why* (teleologically, not causally) they are there, and what are their implications.

It will emerge that Mark is not presenting us with a detailed road map and full colour pictures of what is to be reached at the journey's end or seen along the way. Much rather he is teaching his readers how to read the road 'signs' and pointing them to the beginning of the road. It will be up to them to make the journey if they desire understanding.

Sometimes theses are defended by attempting to move from defensible assumptions through cogent arguments to unassailable conclusions. An attempt to tune one's ear to an author seldom works like that. This study is not so much an attempt to look *at* Mark's Gospel as it is an attempt to look *along* the direction it points. Its primary goal is not to describe to the readers what we have come to see in the Gospel, but rather to guide them towards the angle of vision which has made our apprehension of Mark so much clearer than it was when the research began. The best defence for the view of Mark 13 which this study defends is the re-creation of that view in the mind of the readers. If they see the text as we see it, they can judge for themselves whether or not it commends itself as the right way to see it. It is hoped that this way of defending our theses is not wholly dissimilar to the methods chosen by Jesus and by Mark to defend theirs.

The main body of our research will consist of five chapters designed to bring insights from the larger Markan Gospel into the interpretation of Mark 13.

The first of these five studies (Chapter 2) is a study of Mark's view of 'signs'. We attempt to understand Mark's usage of (and reluctance to use!) σημεῖον ('sign') and his attitude to 'objective evidence'.

This leads us into a study of the term βλέπω ('to see/look') and its relation to the issue of epistemology in Mark's Gospel (Chapter 3). Mark 8.11-21, the most misunderstood text in Mark's Gospel (unless Mark 13 is even more misunderstood), will be studied to shed light on the meaning of the feeding accounts and on the issue of discipleship misunderstanding.

From a study of βλέπω we turn to a study of Mark's other 'watch'-word, γρηγορέω ('keep awake/watch') (Chapter 4). As we analyse its function in Mark's Gospel, we shall discover some key points about Mark's understanding of when and how the kingdom is established, and how to be prepared for its consummation.

Chapter 5 deals with Mark's 'temple theology'. Three key texts outside Mark 13 will be studied in order to determine Mark's perspective on why the temple was doomed and what the significance of its destruction would be.

Chapter 6 analyses the significance of suffering or persecution in Mark's Gospel, seeking to determine what occasions it and what issues from it. We will uncover some important clues which help us understand the significance of Mark's enigmatic final verses, and their implications for understanding Mark 13.

Throughout our study we will watch for implications that will help us interpret Mark 13, but the interpretation itself will be left mainly to the final part of our study (Chapters 7 through 9). Whether the last three chapters carry conviction will depend almost entirely on whether Chapters 2 through 6 are judged to be sound. It is in these first chapters that the foundation stones are being set in place.

A few words about assumptions are in order. In this study, no assumptions will be made, nor any conclusions defended, concerning pre-Markan sources. The assumption we make is that Mark presented his Gospel just as he did because he judged that it was the most adequate way to say whatever he wanted to say. His sources of information are not our primary concern. Though our interpretation does not lean heavily on any assumptions concerning authorship, there are no adequate reasons for denying the oldest view, that John Mark, companion of both Paul and Peter, wrote the Gospel in Rome. Surprising as it may seem, the issue of the date of Mark's Gospel is not very important in determining what Mark intended to say in Mark 13. Our interpretation is compatible with any date prior to the fall of the temple and also with a date *immediately* after it.

Perhaps our most important assumption is that Mark's Gospel (including Mark 13) is not the work of a bungling, inept, careless tradition-compiler, but of a careful, intelligent, and subtle communicator of truth . . . truth that he knew to be worthy of careful formulation, and that he hoped would elicit careful 'listening' on the part of his readers. How does one defend an assumption like this? One should not need to. The burden of proof must certainly rest on anyone who takes the opposing view, especially in the light of the enormous and wholesome impact of this Gospel on the history of humankind. If this study fails to carry conviction, there will be justification in reverting to uncomplimentary views of Mark's abilities, the virtual *opinio communis* with regard to Mark 13. I can only ask my reader to suspend judgment while I make my case.

Chapter 2

A MARKAN PERSPECTIVE ON SIGNS

Introduction

If we want to interpret Mark 13 in the context of the Gospel, where do we begin? One scholar who has attempted to interpret Mark 13 on the basis of clues from the rest of the Gospel is T.J. Weeden. Though his study is not primarily concerned with the interpretation of Mark 13, he establishes the correct procedure for doing so:[1]

> Where one began looking in the Gospel for help in interpreting chapter 13 would be the key methodological issue. The soundest methodological procedure would be to seek help in understanding the concerns of chapter 13 in that section of the Gospel where the same concerns are most likely clearly addressed.

Along with F. Busch, Weeden uses 8.34–9.1 as the interpretative key.[2] While it cannot be denied that in 8.34–9.1 we find close thematic correspondence with ch. 13,[3] a better place to begin is a few verses back in Mark 8, in the only text in Mark outside Mark 13 where the issue of 'signs' is addressed (8.11-13).[4] If one does not first investigate Mark's attitude to 'signs' and 'sign-seeking', one gets immersed too quickly in the specifics of Mark 13. Before examining Mark 13's details, it is important to learn something about Mark's broader perspective on the issue of 'signs'.

It is often claimed that Mark 13 projects an attitude to signs which is out of step with Mark's attitude in the rest of the Gospel. In actual fact, Mark's attitude to signs and sign-seeking has hardly ever been carefully examined. Perhaps Mark 13 is less out of step with the rest of the Gospel than is usually thought.

I. *Mark's Use of* σημεῖον

Previous Studies of σημεῖον *in Mark*

V.K. Robbins contributes to an understanding of σημεῖον ('sign') in Mark's Gospel by criticizing the views of Ulrich Luz and Leander Keck.[5] Robbins rightly rejects the view that the Markan usage of σημεῖον is primarily designed to combat a divine-man Christology. But Robbins is not persuasive in his argument that the main concern is errant eschatology. The texts which use σημεῖον (primarily 8.11-13 and 13.22) can be read in the way Robbins does, but we shall find support for a different way of reading them. When the Pharisees came seeking a sign (8.11-13), they betrayed a wrong epistemology, not a wrong eschatology. The broader context, as we shall see, makes it clear that according to the Markan Jesus, insight and evidence are available only to disciples who are given discernment.

The 'false christs and false prophets' in 13.22 are under the same delusion as the Pharisees. They imagine that objective proofs will suffice to defend the conclusions they are promoting. The disciples are warned against them, not merely because they promote the wrong conclusions, but because they defend their claims in unacceptable, or at least untrustworthy, ways. They are using 'signs and wonders' (σημεῖα καὶ τέρατα) as evidence of their (false) veracity, and the disciples are warned against such proofs. The issue for both the Markan Jesus and the false claimants is how 'signs' function in support of *claims* being made. The primary concern is neither false Christology nor errant eschatology; it is misguided epistemology. The Markan Jesus warns that the kind of proofs they offer are unreliable. The claims being propagated are false (i.e., they are *false* christs and *false* prophets) and the form of evidence used to defend them is not to be trusted (the signs and wonders given are 'in order to deceive' [πρὸς τὸ ἀποπλανᾶν]). The point is that the presence of objective 'signs' is no guarantee that claims are true.

An earlier study of 'Signs and Wonders' by McCasland argues that Jesus, in line with the more sophisticated Old Testament writers, shuns the idea of objective proofs by means of signs, whereas the early church generally sides with the less sophisticated Old Testament writers in clamouring for such proofs.[6] The Scriptures do indeed betray a variety of evaluations of 'sign-seeking'. However, the stance of particular writers/speakers is determined by their specific viewpoints and purposes, not their theological acumen or religious maturity.

The task of studying the Markan usage of σημεῖον, of evaluating the findings in terms of Mark's plot development and theological concerns, and of determining Mark's attitude to the whole matter of sign-seeking, is a task that remains largely unfulfilled.[7] Judgments that Mark 13 is out of step with the rest of the Gospel on the issue of 'sign-seeking' are premature.

σημεῖον—*The Range of Possible Meanings*

σημεῖον can mean many things. This is evident whether one looks at its background terms in Hebrew, its range of possible uses in Greek, or its actual usage in the New Testament. At one end of the spectrum is the 'proof' aspect, the one aspect that is particularly well outlined by Rengstorf. At times a σημεῖον clearly functions as irrefutable evidence that something is true, as an unambiguous conveyor of an item of information, or as a clear illustration of a principle. A sign of this sort functions to make a claim clear and self-evident. When used thus, there is nothing esoteric about a sign and it infallibly leads from confusion to clarity, from doubt to certainty.[8]

At the opposite end of the spectrum, σημεῖον can function as described by Kierkegaard: 'A sign is a sign only for one who knows that it is a sign, and in the strictest sense only for one who knows what it signifies'.[9] Used thus, it has hardly any evidential or public communicative value; it is an esoteric ambiguous communication that can be apprehended aright only by special insight.

On another axis altogether, the term can range in meaning all the way from a very ordinary humanly devised event which has some symbolic meaning to someone (e.g., Judas' kiss of betrayal as a σημεῖον in Matt. 26.48) to an extraordinary divinely enacted miracle which produces amazement among all on-lookers (e.g., the healing referred to in Acts 4.16).

The fact is that in the New Testament virtually anything might be called a σημεῖον, however ordinary or fantastic, however ambiguous or perspicuous, however humanly or supernaturally arranged, however divine or demonic, *provided* the action or event somehow points beyond itself so as to convey some special information or insight. This in itself indicates how hazardous it is to jump quickly to conclusions about Mark's attitude to signs in Mark 13 or in the rest of the Gospel.

σημεῖον—*The Restricted Usage of Mark*

We will be arguing that Mark's Gospel betrays a self-consciously orchestrated approach to the whole matter of 'signs'. The first evidence is that Mark uses the term in a very restricted way. It appears in only two contexts in his Gospel.[10]

In this respect his usage is in stark contrast to that of Matthew, Luke and indeed the rest of the New Testament writers, who use the term in a wide variety of ways,[11] and who match their broad range of *uses of the term* with a broad range of *attitudes to the issue* of 'sign-seeking'.[12] In Matthew and Luke, 'sign-seeking' as such is neither unequivocally endorsed nor unequivocally condemned.

When we examine precisely how and where the term appears in Mark, the contrast with Matthew and Luke is even more vivid. It appears when the Pharisees come asking for a sign and it appears in Mark 13. In both cases there are synoptic parallels and in both cases Mark's account is strikingly different from Matthew's and Luke's. With respect to the request for a sign, in Mark it is categorically refused whereas in Matthew (twice) and in Luke (once) it is not. With respect to their eschatological discourses, all three contain an opening request for a sign. Thereafter the contrast is vivid. Both Matthew and Luke utilize the term positively in Jesus' answer to indicate which events are to be taken by the disciples as σημεῖα (Matt. 24.30; Luke 21.11, 25). *Not once in Mark 13 does the Markan Jesus call an event a σημεῖον and encourage his disciples to evaluate it eschatologically.* When the term does appear in Mark's eschatological discourse (and it appears only once in Jesus' answer), it is in 13.22 to warn against being deceived by signs. The *prima facie* evidence is that Mark is purposely passing a very negative judgment on the whole matter of 'sign-seeking'.

The Pharisees are Refused a 'Sign'—Mark 8.11-13
As our next chapter will make clear, Mark 8.11-13 is part of a deliberately contrived teaching unit which not only passes a negative judgment on sign-seeking, but outlines the alternative epistemology endorsed by the Markan Jesus. For the present we will be content to observe how relentlessly Mark attacks those who come seeking signs. He portrays their request as an unmitigated distortion of the way in which Jesus' claims are to be supported and his deeds understood.

The Pharisees' request for a sign was reprehensible, according to the norms of Mark's Gospel, because:

1. *It came from the wrong people.* Pharisees are, for Mark, 'typical participants in debate'.[13] They are paradigmatic opponents; along with the Herodians (cf. 3.6) they are

responsible for the death plot on Jesus. If anyone needed persuading, they did. Jesus refused to give them the proofs they requested.

2. *It came for the wrong reason.* According to Mark, they came 'tempting him'. After 1.13 πειράζω ('to tempt') appears three times, and in each case we are told that the Pharisees come tempting Jesus (8.11; 10.2; 12.15). Mark does not spare his criticism of those who seek signs from Jesus.

3. *It came at the wrong time.* Jesus patiently proved his points and demonstrated his authority to those who had doubts about him, until they turned a blind eye and a deaf ear to him, rejected his claims, and began to plot for his life (3.6). Thereafter they would not again be treated as honest inquirers. They had missed their chance to be convinced.

4. *It came in the wrong way.* They came 'seeking a sign'. One must not overlook the Markan connotations of the otherwise innocent-sounding ζητέω ('to seek') in Mark's report of this incident. 'Whenever the verb is found it is used either with a plainly hostile reference . . . or in the bad sense of attempting to distract Jesus from his true mission'.[14] It seems not only '*sign*-seeking' but also 'sign-*seeking*' is rejected by the Markan Jesus.

5. *They expected the wrong kind of 'sign'.* It is almost certain that Mark places emphasis on 'from heaven'. Whether it defines a sign 'in the heavens' or 'out of the heavens' is less important than the fact that *they* were specifying what sort of sign they were prepared to consider adequate, and the one they specify is apparently designed to absolve them of the need for either faith or discernment.[15]

Outside Mark 13, the only time 'sign-seeking' is mentioned, the Markan Jesus categorically refuses to oblige those who want signs. In this respect, does Mark 13 fit in with the Gospel?

The Disciples are Warned against 'Sign-Givers'—Mark 13.22
Although there may be a variety of ambiguities about 13.22, one thing at least is beyond dispute: *The parading of signs is not endorsed.* Sign-giving and miracle-working in 13.22 are part of a campaign to deceive.[16] The followers of Jesus are not to be led astray by signs which are proffered as evidence that sign-givers are standing for the truth. What we have in 13.22 is really the reverse of what we have in

8.11-13. The enemies of Jesus are warned not to expect signs which
will objectively demonstrate the truth of the claims Mark endorses.
The disciples of Jesus are warned not to be led astray by signs which
are purported to demonstrate objectively the truth of the claims he
does *not* endorse.[17] Just as in Deut. 13.1f., the working of 'signs and
wonders' is here viewed as the concomitant of the false prophets.[18]
The Markan Jesus as the true divine representative refuses to give
them.[19]

While scholars have concentrated their energies trying to determine
the particular *quality* of the signs sought and given in Mark 8.11-13
and 13.22 (whether apocalyptic or 'historical', dazzling or esoteric/
symbolic), they have frequently overlooked the primary Markan
concern for the signs' *function* in relation to epistemology and
apologetics. It is not Mark's concern to focus on the nature of the
signs under discussion, but on the relationship between the giving of
signs and the apprehension of truth and meaning. It is surely not a
coincidence that Mark 8.11-13 is found linked to a context which
asks, 'Do you have eyes but not see?' (8.18), and 13.22 is embedded in
a context where Jesus' first word is the question, 'Do you see?' and
his constant refrain is 'watch!' (13.5, 9, 23, 33).

The following hypothesis seems to be supported by the data
examined thus far. It will be tested in the rest of this chapter and of
this study:

> Mark is self-consciously criticizing the idea that the important
> truths of the Gospel can be objectively demonstrated with
> persuasive effect before unbelieving eyes. Those who parade
> 'undeniable proofs' (i.e., 'signs') are deceivers. Even believers are
> not privy to the sort of evidence that dispenses with the need for
> divinely aided seeing and hearing. Without these the truth cannot
> be known and understood.

We want to demonstrate not only that Mark holds this to be true,
but that he allows his convictions to have a heavy influence on the
very means by which he communicates his views to his readers.
Having briefly examined Mark's *uses* of σημεῖον, we now turn to his
omissions of the term.

II. *Mark's Omissions of* σημεῖον

Arguments from silence are hazardous, but some kinds of silence can
also be eloquent.[20] We can establish the probability, even if not the

certainty, that the term σημεῖον appeared in Mark's sources and was deliberately dropped in order that Mark might better promote an anti-sign-seeking emphasis. If we are correct, the message conveyed by Mark's exclusions of the term corroborates the message conveyed by his inclusions, and we can rightly think of σημεῖον as a Markan technical term, used with care to make an important point.

We have already noted how restricted is the Markan usage of σημεῖον in comparison with Matthew's and Luke's. We now examine individual cases of possible omissions.

The 'Sign of Jonah' (Matt. 12.39; 16.4; Luke 11.29)

There is widespread agreement that 'the sign of Jonah' (τὸ σημεῖον Ἰωνᾶ) is either authentic or at least very early, and that Q preserved it while it was either lost in the parallel tradition or deliberately omitted by Mark.[21] Many scholars believe Mark omitted it. Why? The usual answers are that the reference was no longer understood, or that 'the sign of Jonah' would be less effective *as a sign* than the great miracles Jesus was already doing.[22] Both explanations are completely out of keeping with the immediate Markan context (8.14–21) where non-understanding is castigated, not catered to, and where the miracles most emphatically are not performing the function of objective 'signs'.

Another explanation is much more in keeping with the Markan context. Matthew's and Luke's accounts use the 'sign of Jonah' to point away from objective proofs and to focus on the need for repentance, insight and acceptance of the Christ who will die and rise. Mark points in the same direction by *omitting* the reference to the 'sign of Jonah' and using the whole pericope in a broader context which calls for the same epistemological reorientation (see Chapter 3).[23] Had they had access to such devices, Matthew and Luke would perhaps have put inverted commas around the word 'sign' (i.e., τὸ 'σημεῖον' Ἰωνᾶ) to indicate that what is provided is not precisely what was requested. Mark, because he is carefully restricting his usage of the term makes a similar point in another way.

The 'Sign of the Son of Man' (Matt. 24.30)

Matt. 24.29-35 is almost exactly the same as Mark 13.24-31 except for the significant addition to the Matthean text concerning the sign (τὸ σημεῖον) of the Son of Man in the sky and the mourning of the nations on the earth. Or is it a Matthean addition? Is it not at least as likely that Matthew has retained a reference from the tradition which

Mark deliberately dropped? Notable scholars believe that the reference is authentic[24] and/or was available to Mark in his source material.[25] Why would Mark omit it?

K. Rengstorf comments on the significance of the Matthean inclusion:[26]

> The parousia will not come directly but will announce itself first. It may be that in the background is the certainty that the last act of history will begin with a final opportunity for conversion and faith.

If this is what the additional words in Matt. 24.30 mean, or even if Mark feared someone might erroneously draw that as an implication, we can easily see why Mark would not allow them to stand. Mark disallows the view that great objective displays of God's activity are appropriate and effective means of leading the unrepentant to salvation (see IV below), and he does not allow that the last great act of history will announce its arrival ahead of time by anything which will enable calculation or final preparations (see Chapters 3 and 9).[27]

The 'Sign of the Abomination of Desolation' (Mark 13.14)
G.R. Beasley-Murray makes the interesting but highly speculative suggestion that originally the text behind Mark 13.14 said, ὅταν δε ἴδητε τὸ σημεῖον τοῦ βδελύγματος φεύγετε ... ('when you see the sign of the abomination, flee ... ')[28] citing as evidence the Greek text which is presupposed by the Syriac tradition of Matthew's Gospel. On this view, the 'sign of the abomination' would be the counterpart to the 'Sign of the Son of Man' (immediately above).

Beasley-Murray maintains that according to the tradition,[29]

> In response to the question of the disciples (v. 4) Jesus gives two signs: the ensign of the hostile army will signalise the destruction of the city, the ensign of the Son of Man will herald the redemption of his people.

There is no certainty that Beasley-Murray's reconstruction is correct, but if it is, the same reasons why Mark seems to have omitted all other indicators that objective 'signs' are available to aid in calculation and foster preparedness would explain his omission of this 'sign'. The 'abomination of desolation' (βδέλυγμα τῆς ἐρημώσεως) reference, as it stands in Mark's eschatological discourse, might well be called a 'sign' as *we* may want to use the term. It is not a σημεῖον as *Mark* uses the term, and he therefore does not call it one.

While any single suggested Markan omission might be rather tentative, and this one perhaps the most speculative of all, there is growing cumulative evidence that Mark may, at least at a number of points, have had σημεῖον in his sources and deliberately omitted it. There is more evidence still.

The 'Signs in the Sun, Moon and Stars' (Luke 21.25)

D. Wenham believes that both Luke's 'signs in the sun, moon and stars' and Matthew's 'sign of the Son of Man' are part of a pre-Synoptic eschatological discourse.[30] If both were in Mark's tradition, even if not necessarily in the form Wenham postulates, Mark has not only omitted a reference to a σημεῖον where its inclusion would have contradicted his strong 'anti-sign-seeking' stance, but also taken a series of cosmic disturbances and re-classified them as 'non-signs'.[31] Mark seems intent on precluding the idea that there can be any objectively observable signs, especially such as might seem to dispense with the necessity of prior faith in and commitment to Jesus. Premonitory signs signalling the near arrival of the parousia might well have been taken as an indication that readiness for the return of the Son of Man is, until the signs appear, not a matter of urgency. Mark has deliberately gone out of his way to avoid supplying such excuses for unpreparedness.

'There Will be Great Signs From Heaven' (Luke 21.11)

It is difficult to determine whether in Luke's mind the great signs from heaven (21.11) and the signs in the sun, moon and stars (21.25) refer to the same phenomena.[32] Whether or not they do, 21.11 and 21.25 represent separate occurrences of the *term* σημεῖον. While it is admittedly hazardous to suggest that Luke is here following a source available to Mark, it is not an impossible suggestion. If Mark did omit this reference to σημεῖα in the middle of his eschatological discourse, we have further evidence that he uses the term only to criticize the idea that signs are approved and available, omitting all other references to it.

Judas' Kiss as a Sign (Matt. 26.48)

All three Synoptic evangelists mention Judas' kiss of betrayal. Whereas Luke so constructs his account that the direct speech of Jesus makes no narrative explanation necessary (Luke 22.48), both Mark and Matthew have their narrators report that 'the betrayer arranged a "sign" with them' (Matt. 26.48, Mark 14.44). It is interesting to note, however, that whereas Matthew uses the very common and perfectly appropriate term σημεῖον, Mark uses the similar but exceedingly rare σύσσημον (a *hapax legomenon* in the New Testament).

If, on the one hand, Matthew was here following only Mark's text, the difference can easily be explained as nothing more than his attempt to substitute a much more common term for Mark's uncommon one. This does not, however, explain why Mark has his uncommon term. If it is considered 'original' (i.e., the earliest Greek form of the tradition) we are left with the possible but not altogether probable view that Mark's rare word survived all the transmission links only to be dropped at the point where Mark's text is utilized by Matthew. It is surely just as likely that Matthew has preserved the traditional term and Mark substituted another. A very plausible motive is ready at hand: Mark chose the *uncommon* term in order to avoid using σημεῖον in a sense which was at odds with the way the word functions technically in Mark's Gospel.

If, on the other hand, Matthew was following a non-Markan source alongside Mark here and found σημεῖον in that source, the probability is even greater that Mark has deliberately avoided σημεῖον at 14.44. In *any* case, it bears witness to the fact that Matthew does not restrict his usage in the way that Mark has apparently chosen to do.

A Markan omission of σημεῖον in 14.44 would have no theological significance, but it would have philological significance. If Mark is criticizing the idea that there are 'signs' available which can be evaluated objectively without the need of either commitment or special divinely given insight, and if one of the ways he makes his point is to restrict the usage of σημεῖον so as never to endorse any 'sign-seeking', then it was a stroke of genius for him to utilize σύσσημον to designate a 'sign' which required no special insight, only advance indication of its intended significance. Only prior information, no special discernment or commitment, would have been required to interpret Judas' kiss. Mark chose to avoid calling it a σημεῖον.

Evaluation

We have examined six texts in which a case can be made that Mark omitted an occurrence of σημεῖον available in his source. None of them is certain, but the cumulative evidence is that Mark has made at least some deliberate omissions. The case appears even stronger when three facts are noted:

1. Matthew retains all the Markan occurrences of σημεῖον, and Luke retains all but one.[33] The *prima facie* evidence is that Mark is the evangelist who is deliberately controlling the use and non-use of the term.

2. A single plausible theory explains all the Markan 'omissions'. Every apparent *omission* can be seen as an attempt to preserve precisely the attitude to signs that is indicated by the texts in which the term is *used*.

3. Fully half of the occurrences of σημεῖον in Luke that are not found in Mark, *and all of those in Matthew*, are in *material* that is paralleled in Mark (the Pharisaic sign-request, the eschatological discourse and the passion).[34] That is to say, the difference between Mark's usage and that of Matthew and Luke cannot be explained by the fact that the term is so frequent in their non-Markan material. Rather the *material* is common to all three synoptists. The point of divergence is the way in which they have used (or omitted) σημεῖον in that material.

It does not appear that Matthew and Luke are deliberately making points about 'sign-seeking' as such and quite certain that they are not carefully regulating how σημεῖον appears in their text. It is virtually certain that Mark is carrying out both tasks with considerable care. Is it possible that σημεῖον was a 'loaded' word for Mark in his local context and that he treated it circumspectly as a result?[35] If so then surely 13.4 would have generated considerable interest among Mark's first readers. They would have scanned Mark 13 carefully for clues as to how Mark will treat a request for a 'sign'.

We should note that for those scholars who hold that Mark utilized Matthew and/or Luke as sources, as well as for those who accept Wenham's reconstructed eschatological discourse, our argument can be strengthened immeasurably, for then we need not speculate whether or not Mark omitted references to 'signs', we can be sure he did. Yet, even without resting our case on those assumptions, it seems probable that the hypothesis we are testing is supported both by Mark's inclusions and exclusions of the term σημεῖον. This argument based on word usage needs to be tested by broader considerations of Mark's text.

III. *The Markan Jesus and 'Objective Evidence'*

Our look at 8.11-13 and 13.22 gave us a glimpse of the attitude of the Markan Jesus towards sign-seeking and sign-giving. Our look at the restricted usage of σημεῖον in Mark's Gospel gave us a glimpse of the attitude of the Gospel's author towards the same. Clearly there is a correlation between the two. In this section we intend to examine some interesting features of the story line of Mark's Gospel and observe Jesus'[36] 'tactical adjustments' in his ways of dealing with both enemies and followers. Before examining the key texts, an important question must be asked.

Does the Markan Jesus Shun Proofs in Favour of Faith?
It is frequently stated that in Mark's Gospel there is reluctance to give objective proofs *because that would somehow preclude the necessity of personal decision in response to the word of revelation.* Faith, to be genuine faith, cannot rest on adequate evidence (so the claim goes).[37] This view is sometimes seen as the only alternative to the view towards which Mark is apparently antipathetic. Either one is a 'sign-seeker' clamouring for objective proofs and endorsing them as an appropriate and effective way of winning over the unconvinced, or one shuns evidence altogether, calling for a commitment that reason cannot evaluate and that evidence cannot justify. That is a false dichotomy according to the author of Mark. He sets up his story in such a way that adequate bases for belief are available unless and until the uncommitted and the rejectors demonstrate the insincerity of their investigations and their unwillingness to live with the implications of believing Jesus. While Jesus will not oblige people with 'signs' of their choosing, he does not hold them responsible to believe without giving them a basis for doing so. It is not the case that the choice is between 'sign-seeking' and 'blind faith'.[38] The sort of evidence upon which the Markan Jesus intends faith to rest differs significantly from the sort of evidence that is portrayed in the clamouring after objective proofs, but it is evidence of a very real sort (see Chapter 3).

Virtually all Markan scholars accept that at Mark 8.27-30 we reach a turning point. Jesus relates to his disciples differently after their messianic confession than he did before. Fewer Markan scholars appreciate the way in which Mark 3.6 becomes the turning point in Jesus' relationship with his enemies. It is necessary to watch for points of continuity and discontinuity in Mark's story line if we are to correctly apprehend his portrait of Jesus and reconstruct the theological position which motivates his actions.

Nineteenth century scholars read Mark's Gospel for its clues concerning the psychological development of the historical Jesus. This is possible only if Mark's Gospel has accurately preserved an accurate chronology of historical events. Most scholars now deny that he has. We concede that Mark's Gospel provides little help in reconstructing the psychological motivations that shaped the historical Jesus' actions. What we do not concede is that we therefore have a right to ignore the chronology of Mark's *story line* in evaluating Mark's *portrait* of Jesus. We cannot treat Mark's Gospel as a 'flat book'. Mark is a capable story teller and his Gospel should be evaluated accordingly.[39]

Mark tells a developing story about the relationship between Jesus and those who reject him and finally put him to death. An examination of the way in which Jesus' relationship with his enemies changes at 3.6 is very illuminative of Mark's attitude to signs and evidence.

The Strategic Function of Mark 2.1–3.6

Although Mark 2.1–3.6 has been studied from many angles,[40] its significance in relation to Mark's epistemology has not been adequately understood. We have, in this section, precisely what many scholars deny is present in Mark's Gospel . . . the deliberate attempt to use objective proofs (verbal and visible) to persuade the unconvinced. Mark's epistemology cannot be understood properly without an adequate appreciation of: (1) how and why such evidence is given before 3.6, (2) what the decision registered in 3.6 implies concerning the ineffectiveness of the approach, (3) what changes are introduced by the Markan Jesus after 3.6.

The narrative does not justify unguarded comments that the Markan Jesus condemns the religious authorities without giving them an adequate opportunity to hear and respond.[41] On the contrary, Jesus takes the initiative to provide proofs and he responds affirmatively to requests for evidence *until the religious authorities have made up their minds to reject him*.[42]

Prior to Mark 3.6, Jesus is remarkably patient with his opponents. He is careful not to bring any hasty condemnation against them and never takes the initiative in criticizing what they are doing. He carefully defends his actions when they accuse him and he demonstrates his authority when they challenge it. In deference to them he sends the healed leper for confirmation of ritual cleanness (1.44). He proves his authority to forgive sins by doing that which is 'more difficult' (i.e., more difficult to 'say' since the truth of the statement can more easily be tested *objectively*) (2.10).[43] He explains why he offends religious scruples in his eating with 'sinners' (2.17). He explains the differences between his followers and others on the matter of fasting (2.19-22).[44] He justifies Sabbath-'breaking' by an analogy with an Old Testament precedent (2.25f). He demonstrates the fundamental difference of perspective between himself and his opponents in the matter of Sabbath healing (3.1-4), and here, though he challenges them and exhibits anger, he does so only *after* they seek occasion to act against him (3.2a).

Only *after* 3.6 does Jesus deny the Jewish leaders the evidence they seek (cf. 8.11-13).[45] After 3.6, when the Jewish leaders request signs and ask for explanations they are not obliged; Jesus rather spares no effort in exposing their hypocrisy. The stance they took in 3.6 clearly indicated that their (pretended) interest in Jesus was nothing but a sustained attempt to tempt, trap, and discredit him. They had been given evidence before 3.6; they would be given no more.

A failure to appreciate the shift in strategy at 3.6 forces commentators to set aside some of the evidence when evaluating Markan principles. M.E. Glasswell, for example, claims that Jesus' miracles are not to be evaluated for their evidential value.[46] However accurately that may summarize Jesus' approach to his opponents after 3.6, it does not accurately portray his approach before 3.6.[47] The significance of this is twofold: it tells us that Jesus *is* willing to oblige those who need evidence; and it tells us how ineffective the evidence proves to be when hearers and onlookers intend to remain neutral or opposed.[48] Mark 2.1-3.6, and particularly 2.1-12, functions to indicate the ineffectiveness of the miraculous to produce appropriate responses. Does this help us to see what purposes Mark had in mind for the material included in the early controversies?

Joanna Dewey's careful study of Mark 2.1-3.6 establishes a number of purposes Mark had in mind for 2.1-3.6.[49] What might be added to her summary is the whole issue of objective proofs of Jesus' claims. A central feature of Mark's presentation of the material in 2.1-3.6 is his portrayal of the fact that *objective displays of the miraculous and public explanations were ineffective in persuading the Jewish religious-political leadership to side with Jesus.*[50]

The Redirected Course of Action after 3.6

After 3.6 Jesus makes no effort to cater to the objections of the religious authorities. Instead of careful defences for his own way of behaving, we find exposés of *their* hypocrisy. The radically different approach can easily be detected by making a few comparisons.

The occasions for the debates between Jesus and the Pharisees in 2.23-28 and in 7.5-13 are nearly parallel, but the tone of Jesus' response is totally different. In the first case he carefully and patiently defends the actions of his disciples. In the second case he provides a scathing attack on the hypocrisy of the Pharisees and reserves explanation until after the crowds have at least joined the Pharisees, if not displaced them, as his audience (7.14).

In 11.27-33, when the religious leaders come with their pretended honest inquisitiveness, seeking from Jesus a defence for his authoritative actions, Jesus makes it clear that he would be quite willing to engage them in open debate if they were ready to drop their hypocrisy. They are not, and so Jesus remains unwilling to establish the basis of his authority any further.[51] That which he was willing to do before their rejection he is unwilling to do afterwards.

The general character of the debates in 2.1-3.6 is quite different from those in 11.27-12.44. In the former Jesus defends his own actions; in the latter Jesus criticizes theirs. In the former Jesus never initiates the conflict; in the latter he does three times (12.1; 12.35; 12.38). In the former the response of Jesus always sticks to the issue at hand; in the latter it seems always to gravitate towards the insincerity of his opponents. It would appear to be Mark's view that when the Pharisees and Herodians (representative of the spiritual and political power blocks of Israel) reject him in 3.6, they forfeit the right to be treated as honest inquirers.

After 3.6 the power centres of Israel's religious and national life appear to have no concern other than to vanquish their opponent, and they are treated accordingly. They are disqualified as Israel's leaders (see Chapter 5) and they are excluded from Jesus' close company. Since Israel's present religious leadership has rejected his offer to bring them over to his side, he will work with an alternate group of people (cf. Jesus' shift of attention to the disciples after 3.6) and prepare *them* for leadership of the renewed people of God.

At 3.6 with the shift in Jesus' 'target groups', comes also a shift in the *way* he appeals to people. The 'objective proofs' approach used before 3.6 gives way to a very different one. Now Jesus will plant seeds in receptive hearts that will germinate and, if the soil is right, eventually come to fruition (Mark 4). This approach could not even be attempted among those whose hearts were so hard (ἐπὶ τῇ πωρώσει τῆς καρδίας αὐτῶν [3.5]) the seed had no chance even of penetrating.[52]

According to all indications, Mark 3.7 is the point at which the Markan Jesus begins his efforts to demonstrate that the religious hierarchy of Israel is disqualified and in need of replacement. No fewer than five consecutive sections following 3.6 serve to establish that this is so.

Mark 3.7-12: In 3.7-12 we have Jesus withdrawing *from the synagogue*. The significance of ἀνεχώρησεν (he withdrew) (3.7) is often inadequately noted. Jesus' withdrawal is not only from his enemies but from their spheres of influence. Every reference to 'synagogues' supports this understanding of the text. Prior to 3.6 Jesus escapes from the throngs *so that* he could continue his preaching ministry 'in their synagogues' (1.35-39). After 3.6 the strategy is reversed.

Jesus does not again enter a synagogue until 6.2 where we have a perfect parallel to the events in 3.7 and a support for our interpretation of it. In the first case it is Israel's religious leaders who were given adequate evidence of Jesus' authority, both in his teaching (e.g., 2.25f.) and in his miracles (e.g., 2.10). In the second, precisely the same happens with Jesus' fellow townspeople (6.2). Both times Jesus is rejected (3.6; 6.3). Both times he ceases to appeal to them with the miraculous (8.11f.; 6.5).[53] In both cases those who should have accepted Jesus' message and his personal claims did not, and he bypasses them in favour of others (4.11f.; 6.6b). Both times rejection leads not to a curtailing of Jesus' influence but its expansion (3.7; 6.6b, 7ff.; see Chapter 6). Both times the synagogue is abandoned for open places where crowds can come for ministry (3.6f.; 6.6b, 34).

After this incident in Jesus' home town, Jesus avoids the synagogues altogether and thereafter they are mentioned only twice in Mark's Gospel: once as the place where scribes flaunt their prestigious positions (12.39) and once as the place where post-resurrection believers will be flogged (13.9). What a contrast to Jesus' ready use of synagogues as a preaching and ministry platform prior to 3.7![54]

Mark 3.13-19: The next pericope has often (and correctly) been viewed as Jesus' strategy to provide new leadership for God's people. When the significance of the strategy shift after 3.6 is clearly seen, however, it is to be noted that more is at stake than a change of personnel. Jesus is not merely substituting a group of twelve for the officialdom that has disqualified itself by rejecting him. He is taking a whole new approach to recruitment and instruction. Prior to 3.6 Jesus appeals to those already in power. Their hearts are not right, but he patiently gives them the explanations and evidence they need to lead them to a change of heart. After 3.6 there will be no more appeal to those with hard hearts (4.11-13). *Jesus will no longer attempt to make disciples out of those in authority. Hereafter he will give authority to those who are disciples.*

From now on, attachment to Jesus is a prerequisite for, not an expected result of, hearing, understanding and accepting the claims and the teaching of Jesus. Revelation will be reserved for those ready to receive. The approach to 'verification of truth' after 3.6 is totally different than the approach prior to it. They will *first* be 'with him' (μετ᾽ αὐτοῦ); thereafter they will be endowed with authority (3.14).

Mark 3.22-30: Here we find Jesus *agreeing* with the religious hierarchy that there is a division so fundamental between him and them that they must be working on opposite sides of the divine-demonic conflict. The point of disagreement is concerning who is on which side. After 3.6 it is clearly Mark's view that the religious authorities who oppose Jesus have taken their side with Satan and with Jesus' demonic opposition.[55] He will purge his kingdom of their influence just as he purged possessed people of the demonic influences that held them in bondage.[56]

Mark 3.20f., 31-35: Mark may have had a variety of reasons for drawing together the two stories that make up 3.20-35. Scholars who imagine Mark is rejecting Jesus' family (and through them leaders of the Jerusalem church)[57] often point out that the critical response of Jesus to the religious authorities (3.22-30) is, by means of the intercalation, applied also to Jesus' blood relatives. But surely the reverse is more likely. Jesus' redefinition of family in 3.34f. means that nothing except allegiance to Jesus gives one access to the special privileges of being 'around' him, not blood relationship, not Jewishness, not religious zeal, *not even expertise in Jewish religion*. The whole pericope functions not to reject his physical family, but to set before his family, his followers, his enemies (and Mark's readers!) the options: Either they join his spiritual family or they join those who will be excluded from his fellowship.[58] The two scenes drawn together in 3.20-35 are a microcosm of what is going on in the whole shift after 3.6. Together they say that former privilege means nothing; everything now depends on allegiance to Jesus.

Mark 4.1-34: The parable collection is a brilliantly composed chapter making a whole series of subtle and interrelated points. Its subtleties will be examined throughout this study. For the present we merely point out that Mark 4, more clearly than any other chapter in Mark, focuses on the three points that we are seeking here to illustrate ... that from now on rejectors will not be privileged recipients of Jesus' special instruction, that from now on Jesus invests his energies working with those who have pledged allegiance to him, and that the means by which truth is conveyed will henceforth not be by objective proofs, but rather esoteric teaching requiring special discernment.

The Turning Point: Mark 3.6

At 3.6 Jesus' opponents sealed their fate by rejecting him and beginning to plot for his life. It is as significant a turning point in Mark's Gospel as 8.27-30. At the first turning point Jesus turns his back on his rejectors and begins to work in a new way with the crowds and the disciples. At the second turning point Jesus begins the advanced course in discipleship training for those willing to walk the 'way' with him.

Morna Hooker's excellent analysis of 'the Son of Man in Mark' reaches the same conclusion:[59]

> 3.6 appears to be quite as vital a turning-point as 8.27. What Mark himself depicts is an early period during which Jesus claims authority as the Son of man and uses the phrase openly in discussion with the Jewish authorities; when they reject him he ceases to appeal to them, for their hearts are hardened, and they have no desire either to see or to hear the truth.

It is surely because Mark's story line is not always watched carefully,[60] and because Mark's interest in epistemology has so regularly been overlooked,[61] that so few have reiterated or followed up Hooker's conclusion.

It is, however, not Mark's point that Jesus learned his lesson. He did not attempt one method, find that it proved disastrous, and then scramble to find a workable alternative. At the very beginning of his ministry he calls disciples (1.16-20), he promises them a *future* preparation for ministry ('I *will* make you to become . . . ' [1.17]), and he leaves them 'waiting in the wings' until after Israel's present leaders have disqualified themselves. We have an example of a widely attested biblical procedure: Those who are under appointment by God for responsibility and privilege must be given the first opportunity to respond to a new or renewed call. Only after they have rejected and therefore forfeited their privilege can the offer and the call go out to others.[62] It is not the methodology of Jesus that is in the dock, but the moral integrity of Israel's leadership. 2.1–3.6 constitutes a genuine opportunity for conversion, but it is at the same time (since Jesus knows people's hearts [2.8, 3.5]) an exposure of their hypocrisy and hard-heartedness.

We are not claiming that everything we have said in this section is self-evident. It is a plausible way of reading Mark's story, though it will require the following section and the next complete chapter to demonstrate that it is the *correct* way of reading it. If we are on the right track, then clearly the way Mark constructed his story line supports the conclusions of the first two sections of this chapter.

To summarize: Mark's use of σημεῖον (Section I), his omissions of σημεῖον (Section II), and the way he has portrayed Jesus in his dealings with those who are given objective evidence (Section III), all support the same conclusion: 'signs' in the sense of objective proofs are an ineffective means of recruiting followers and it is inappropriate for enemies and followers alike to clamour for them.

IV. *Mark and 'Objective Evidence'*

We turn our attention back to Mark the author. He records a considerable number of miracles in his Gospel, before and after 3.6. If they are not to be thought of as 'signs' of the sort Mark seems not to favour, what role do they play? In this section we introduce a discussion of miracles by examining briefly several terms which are related to σημεῖον, suggest the primary function of miracle-reports in Mark's Gospel (especially after 3.6), introduce a discussion of Mark's 'secrecy elements' and trace out some implications of 'Markan secrecy' for Mark's task of writing a Gospel and our task of interpreting it.

The Markan Use of Terms Related to σημεῖον
There are three terms related to σημεῖον which will be mentioned here.

The first term will be treated very briefly, not because it is unimportant and not because the evidence is scanty, but rather because it will be the subject matter of the entire next chapter. The term in Mark most closely related to σημεῖον (though this may not be immediately obvious) is the term βλέπω ('to see/look'). Its usage in Mark supports the hypothesis being tested in this chapter. The call to 'see' (βλέπετε) is the Markan *alternative* to 'sign-seeking'. Characters *within* Mark's Gospel and the readers *of* the Gospel are called to have their spiritual eyes and ears opened so that they can, by a special discernment process, come to understand the real significance of that which they see and hear (and read) (see Chapter 3).

The second term, τέρας ('wonder') can also be dealt with quickly. Rengstorf suggests it can hardly be intentional that the expression 'signs and wonders' (σημεῖα καὶ τέρατα) is never used in a positive light in the Synoptics.[63] That may be so for Matthew and Luke, but it is not true for Mark. If 'signs' are not endorsed by Mark, then *a fortiori* 'signs and wonders' are not, for the combination serves to highlight the objectivity and wondrous element. The term appears in Mark only in 13.22 and whatever is said of σημεῖον in the discussion of that verse can be applied equally to the related term, τέρας.

The third term is δύναμις ('power / mighty work'), a word frequently used in Mark to designate a miracle. As noted above, V.K. Robbins studied the term along with σημεῖον. Robbins insists that Mark is not at all reluctant to present Jesus as a 'divine-man' enacting and endorsing mighty works (δυνάμεις) for their apologetic effect in demonstrating his divine authority.[64] Mark's use of the term δύναμις does not support Robbins' conclusion.

Mark utilizes a form of δύναμις ten times in the Gospel. Of these, five serve to establish the point that there is *not* presently unambiguous evidence that God is working mightily through Jesus. The five references are 9.1 (there will be a *future* manifestation of the kingdom having come in power), 12.24 (the resurrection power of God which was *not* known by the Sadducees and will be exercised in the *future*), 13.25 (the eschatological shaking of the heavenly powers in the *future*), 13.26 (the *future* coming of the Son of Man 'with great power and glory', and 14.62 (the *future* manifestation of the Son of Man seated at the right hand of the Mighty One (δυνάμεως). It is clear that in none of these cases is Mark emphasizing present visible objective displays of power by Jesus. *All five push in the opposite direction, stressing either the hiddenness of the power or the futurity of its disclosure.*

The five remaining occurrences of the term are of considerable interest. They do not support the notion that Jesus is publicly displaying his mighty miracles (δυνάμεις) for their value in verifying his claims:

1. Mark 5.30: The reader is informed that when the woman touched Jesus' cloak, power (δύναμις) went out from Jesus. There is, however, nothing in the incident which indicates that the miracle either impressed the crowds or persuaded them of anything. On the contrary, for all the references to the crowd (vv. 21, 24, 27, 30, 31), it is remarkable that the miracle is not reported to have made any impression on them at all. The reader listens in on a very private conversation between Jesus and the woman and the only comments from the 'gallery' are the comments of the *uncomprehending* disciples. Furthermore, Jesus seems to be at pains to make it clear that the 'power' went out only because she *first* believed. And finally, it is to be noted that, as the story is told, the power went out from Jesus entirely apart from any 'doing' on his part. The story hardly supports the notion that Jesus deliberately displays δυνάμεις to persuade the crowds.

2. Mark 6.2: Jesus' fellow townspeople marvel at the mighty works Jesus has been doing. The pericope makes it clear that the miracles (δυνάμεις) occasion amazement rather than insight or faith. The rejection of Jesus is eloquent testimony to the fact that great miracles are *not* of apologetic value in Mark's Gospel. The whole pericope testifies to the opposite.

3. Mark 6.5: This verse in the same context makes the corresponding point. Not only are miracles ineffective in producing faith (6.2ff.), the miracles themselves are impossible unless faith is present beforehand (6.5).

4. Mark 6.14: Again we note that those who have observed Jesus' and his disciples' miracles (δυνάμεις) may be amazed but are led neither to insight nor to faith. They completely misunderstand the nature of the power and the identity of the one who exercises it.

5. Mark 9.39: Jesus here approves of the miracle worked by one who did not follow with his disciples and himself. Jesus puts the act on the same level of significance as giving the disciples a cup of water. The disciples had apparently

misunderstood the significance of the event altogether. Nothing indicates that the miracle leads to insight or faith and in any case it is not Jesus' miracle being evaluated.

It is impossible to sustain the view that Mark reserves the term δύναμις for those mighty miracles by which Jesus gives proofs of his claims. Precisely the opposite is indicated.[65] Jesus does not work miracles for the purpose of leading from unbelief to faith. Indeed miracles are impossible unless faith is there first. Faith must be present to render a miracle possible and faith must be present that miracles might be apprehended aright. This hiddenness will remain in place until faith is turned to sight for the believers and blindness to judgment for the rest. The way in which Mark has utilized the term δύναμις supports in a remarkable way the thesis of this chapter.

What is the Function of Miracle Reports?
If we examine the effects of the miracles recorded in the Gospels on those who observed or experienced them, we can hardly be impressed with positive results. The demons of course have no doubts about the power and authority of Jesus; their response is to try if possible to escape the dire consequences for themselves (1.24; 5.7, etc.). Others, who knew his power was more than human, concluded either that Jesus was tapping Satanic power (e.g., the teachers of the law from Jerusalem, cf. 3.22) or that he must be another great one redivivus (e.g., Herod and others, cf. 6.14-16). It was Jesus' miracles which were wrongly evaluated both times. Still others were provoked to amazement, wonder, perhaps even praise, *but not to adherence to Jesus* (e.g., the crowds, cf. 2.12). The evidence is exceedingly thin that any unbeliever was ever led to faith, as Mark's Gospel defines faith, through the observation or experience of a miraculous event.[66] If we are to think of blind Bartimaeus as one who was converted as a result of being cured (10.46-52), it is significant that the triumphalist 'Son of David' language is on his lips *before* the miracle. After the miracle he follows Jesus 'on the way', and thus provides a model for those who reject triumphalist miracle-oriented Christology in favor of Mark's passion Christology.

If Mark's use of the term δύναμις reveals that the Markan Jesus does not perform miracles for their evidential value, and if the miracles recorded in Mark's Gospel do not lead to faith and following, why does Mark record them? Does he imagine the report of them will have better results among those who hear it, than the experience of them did for those present when they happened? What then is the function of miracle *reports* in the Gospel of Mark? Scholars have struggled to solve the dilemma.

E. Best argues that their primary function is to indicate the ways in which Jesus' support is offered to the Christian community.[67] H. Räisänen contends that Mark is using miracle reports to show his agreement with a *'theologia gloriae'*.[68] P.J. Achtemeier claims that the miracles are designed to point to the person who performs them, i.e., to his character and to his authoritative teaching, not to the supernatural power at work through him.[69] E. Schweizer argues that the miracles are reported to emphasize neither the deed done nor the doer, but the encounter between Jesus and those for whom miracles were performed; Mark passed on the stories to bring about the same encounter between Jesus and the reader of the account.[70] T.J. Weeden maintains that Mark is writing a polemic against the view of Jesus that is given in the first half of the Gospel; thus a Jesus viewed in terms of his miracle-working ability is foreign to Mark's conception of a true Christology.[71] L. Schenke's and U. Luz's views are rather similar to Weeden's in terms of the position Mark attacks; they differ in that they believe Mark takes a *mediating* position between a theology of glory and a theology of the cross.[72]

The very fact that so many suggestions have come forward bears testimony to the fact that it is now widely recognized that the Gospel writers, and Mark in particular, did not report the miraculous deeds of Jesus primarily in order to present an apologetic for their claims that Jesus operated under divine authority.[73]

Scholars have argued back and forth as to whether Mark 'plays up' or 'plays down' miracles in his Gospel.[74] Mark plays them neither up nor down.[75] What he does is expose their ineffectuality for apologetics and call on his readers (just as Jesus called on his followers) to discern their true significance.

Many interpreters of Mark accept some form of the conclusion Richardson reached over forty years ago:[76]

> The significance of the miracles lies in their character, or quality, or spiritual meaning, rather than in their impressiveness as mere 'wonders'. . . . As we find them in his [i.e., Mark's] Gospel, the miracle-stories are the products of profound meditation upon the significance of the person and actions of Jesus, and their interest centres in their theological rather than in their historical character.

Even this formulation of the matter, however, needs some

modification. In the first place, it sets the theological character of the
miracles *over against* the historical character. To emphasize the
theological significance of them in no way entails de-emphasizing
their historicity. If there has been profound meditation on the
significance of Jesus' person and actions, that meditation would
surely have been curtailed if it was suspected that the actions
purported to be his never happened.

In the second place, Richardson's focus on the 'meaning' of the
miracle does not quite capture Mark's concern which is frequently
focused more on the *means by which that meaning is apprehended.*
The miracles would have been reported in rather different ways if the
only concern of the evangelists had been to indicate what they mean
for the life of faith. For example, we would then expect Mark to tell
us what they mean! The way they are reported encourages us to
accept a modification of Richardson's view best represented by
scholars such as E. Lohse, H.C. Kee, and C. Brown. Each in his own
way points out that what is of concern is not merely what the miracles
mean, but the process by which that meaning is apprehended.[77]

> What is most important about these stories is not the substance of
> the miracles but the implicit epistemology: for Mark understanding
> of reality is not achieved by availability of evidence but by
> revelatory insight.

Mark is concerned to explicate a Christian epistemology.[78] We
would go so far as to claim that one of the major reasons Mark brings
forward miracle stories is to provide test cases in interpretation. He is
concerned to teach his readers how to move from the bare historical
facts to the *meaning* which the facts imply. In the following chapter it
will be demonstrated how Mark's discussion of 'the meaning of the
feedings' substantiates this suggestion.

When Does the Secrecy End?
There is an irreducible element of secrecy in Mark's Gospel. This
must be emphasized because various scholars have recognized that
W. Wrede over-systematized the secrecy elements and have tried to
demonstrate that when Wrede's tightly knit scheme is unravelled the
materials disappear. They do not. Mark 4 is sufficient on its own to
assure of this fact. Even though 8.30 and 9.9 are susceptible to
varying interpretations, they too speak of an essential secrecy which
cannot easily be erased in the interpretation of Mark's Gospel.

Because our study focuses on Markan epistemology, it will

frequently come in contact with the concealment/revelation concerns of Mark's Gospel and therefore with this secrecy theory. The majority of Markan scholars hold that 9.9 is our warrant for assuming that whatever secrecy is to be found in the Gospel has its terminus with the resurrection. A frequent spokesperson for that view is T.A. Burkill, who maintains:[79]

> It is not until Jesus has been raised from the dead that they can come to understand the mysterious meaning of the secret; for St. Mark seems to have held that the resurrection meant the end of the predetermined period of service and suffering in obscurity and the beginning of the predetermined period of enlightenment in which the gospel is openly proclaimed to the world with understanding and confidence (9.9).

There are a variety of reasons for questioning the validity of the view. We suggest the following, but will develop only the final point:

1. To rest that theory on Mark 9.9 is to load the verse with more than it can bear. All the verse indicates is that one incident is to be kept secret until the resurrection. The bulk of Markan secrecy is related not to a deliberate hiding of facts known and understood, but to a failure to understand that which is seen and heard.[80] There is no indication in Mark that the resurrection will bring full enlightenment with it.[81]

2. If it were Mark's purpose to portray the resurrection as the end of secrecy, why would he present even the resurrection account in a secretive manner, giving no explicit indications as to what the impact of it will be for believers?

3. To the extent that the passion/resurrection is enlightening, the emphasis must fall on the passion not the resurrection. It is when the centurion saw the dead Jesus, not the risen Lord, that his eyes were opened and he confessed Jesus as Son of God.

4. The parables of Mark 4 (esp. 4.21-23) indicate that there will be a final revelation of that which is now concealed. The final harvest/disclosure time matches Mark's portrayal of the parousia a great deal better than his portrayal of the resurrection.

5. Mark himself, living in the post-resurrection time writes his

Gospel out of the conviction that it is still the time of
secrecy.

The evidence for this last point is everywhere. One piece of
evidence for this is the very interest Mark shows in the secrecy
elements in the Jesus story. It is hard to account for this interest on
the assumption that it had relevance only for past history.[82]

A much more powerful body of evidence, however, is that Mark
himself practises secrecy in the very way in which he tells the story.
Numerous scholars have imagined that the secrecy theory of Mark's
Gospel is centred directly on the question of Jesus' identity (as Christ
and/or as Son of God). It is not surprising that 1.1 would, on *this*
view, seem to indicate that in Mark's view the time of open
proclamation had begun before he took up his pen. When it is
recognized that Markan secrecy is not focused centrally on Christology
but on the secret coming of the kingdom of God (cf. 4.11, see
Chapters 3 and 8), it is also recognized that the end of *that* secrecy
comes with the parousia and not the resurrection. Mark writes his
Gospel under the conviction that the kingdom is still secretly coming
even as he writes and those with eyes to see it will do so.

Mark reports secrecy, but he also practises it. It is becoming more
and more evident that Mark's Gospel features very intricate and
subtle ways of telling a story and alluding to its deeper significance.
Mark has made some of his most important points without explicit
formulation, utilizing allusion, parable, structural arrangement,
irony, paradox, and various other subtle forms of communication.
For some reason, Mark would rather speak ambiguously than
straight-forwardly. Frequently Mark's Gospel emphasizes the
cruciality of grasping a point, without telling the reader what the
point is. In Mark's Gospel we are told that there is a 'secret of the
kingdom of God' but we are not told what it is. We are told that the
meaning of the parables was openly given to the disciples, but we are
not told what the parables mean.[83] It is made abundantly clear (cf.
6.52) that 'even the deeds of Jesus were recounted by Mark from the
point of view of their parabolic function'.[84] Yet, while the parabolic
meaning of the miracles is alluded to in a variety of ways, not once is
the reader told what lessons are to be drawn from them. Perhaps
most remarkable of all is the way Mark deals with the feeding stories.
The importance of understanding their secret meaning is stressed
more than once (6.52; 8.14-21); the disciples are reprimanded for not
grasping it (8.14-21); and still *the reader of Mark's Gospel is never*

told what the feedings are considered to mean.

How does one account for all this Markan secrecy? Is Mark exceedingly inept, forgetting to tell his readers the very things he thinks are most important to know? Is it not much more likely that he is modelling himself after Jesus who also taught ambiguously, and called for understanding even when explanations were not explicitly given? If the author of Mark's Gospel *writes* under the conviction that kingdom secrecy remains in effect, clearly his Gospel should not be interpreted as though it *teaches* the opposite.

We therefore accept the minority view represented well by C.E.B. Cranfield that according to Mark:[85]

> The Messianic Secret did not come to an end with the Resurrection or the Ascension. It is continued in the life of the church. Jesus is indeed exalted now, but His church is still 'under the cross', still open to His reproach, still involved in that hiddenness and veiledness, called to share in the Messianic secret of its Lord. . . . The church cannot prove the truth of its message; it can only believe and wait and bear witness. Its testimony in the eyes of the world is sheer folly. Only those, to whom God has given the mystery of the kingdom of God, perceive as well as see and understand as well as hear.

Mark's Gospel and 'Critical Investigation'

If Mark's *message* is influenced by his conviction that kingdom secrecy is in effect right through to the parousia, our *interpretation* of the Gospel must take this into account. If Mark's *method* is influenced by the same conviction, our *means of interpreting* his Gospel must also take this into account.[86]

If this is correct, then the implications would seem to include at least the following:

1. *We must make an effort to evaluate the Gospel according to its own norms.* There are those who would insist that the only legitimate way of examining a text is from a standpoint of objective neutrality. Mark has succeeded, however, in producing a text which makes 'objective neutrality' illegitimate by definition. Mark's own message is judged false (even if the judgment is made unintentionally) by those who insist that objective neutrality must be adopted as the appropriate method of investigation.[87]

2. *We must be sensitive to the fact that Mark means more than he says.* If Mark, like Jesus, believes that special divinely-

given discernment is needed in order for the deepest truths of the Gospel to be apprehended, then we need not fear to ask regularly if perhaps more is being implied than is being said. We may wrongly apprehend the secrets, but we will not be wrong in suspecting there are secrets.

3.   *We must attempt to look along Mark's angle of vision.* The ability to construct and evaluate logical arguments is not in itself adequate to facilitate the interpretation of great literature. What is needed is the ability to gain a feel for the author's own priorities and perspectives. The danger of relying on these 'feelings' is that one is far too ready to read into Mark's Gospel all sorts of things the author never intended. But the alternative danger is equally hazardous, for an author's deepest concerns might well be hidden below the surface. In such a case, to refuse to look there is to invite misunderstanding.[88] If it is a legitimate task for scholars to attempt to think an ancient author's thoughts after him/her, we will have to broaden our view of what methods are considered acceptable for that scholarly quest.[89]

4.   *We should not consider Mark inept just because he does not provide us the answers to the questions we are asking.* If Mark *deliberately* did not answer many of the questions generated by his text, then scholars may want to criticize Mark's decisions but they should not depreciate Mark's abilities. More than anything else, an over-eagerness on the part of some scholars to pronounce Mark a clumsy redactor/author has prevented them from plumbing the depths of this amazing piece of theological literature.

A number of scholars have held that the Gospel of Mark is a carrier of 'secret messages'. We have a right to be suspicious of those suggestions when no meaningful correlation can be provided between the medium they think Mark used and the message they think he embedded under the cover of the explicit narrative. But when there is convergence between medium and message and when both propel the reader in the direction of Mark's greatest concerns, then suggestions of 'secret messages' should be taken seriously. This study, in every chapter, will suggest such 'secret messages'.

Most scholars have too quickly accepted the conclusion that Mark's interest in secrecy and esoteric teaching is modelled after apocalyptic literature (like parts of Daniel), or is an attempt to guard political immunity (like parts of Revelation), or is a device for literary effect (like the literature of William James),[90] or is a means of conveying information only to the initiated (like 2 Thess. 2.6??). A much more plausible explanation is that Mark endorses Jesus' teaching methods, and therefore also adopts them.

This chapter has ranged broadly. We began by analysing Mark's attitude to sign-seeking and ended with a discussion of Mark's esoteric teaching methods. It will require the next chapter to draw more of the threads together. Our attempt has been not so much to *prove* that Mark has written the sort of book we are claiming he wrote, but to encourage our reader to look at Mark's Gospel as we are looking at it and see if it does not come into clearer focus.

The primary text to be examined in the next chapter (8.14-21) not only functions to help *define* the sort of 'discernment' which is the Markan alternative to 'sign-seeking', it also *requires its exercise.*

V. *Implications for Interpreting Mark 13*

At this early stage only a few suggestions can be given concerning implications for interpreting Mark 13. Perhaps the following questions can suggest possibilities that lie open, awaiting acceptance or rejection on the basis of the chapters that follow.

1. Have we not already established a basis for seriously considering Mark 13.4 (the request for a sign) as an expression of the disciples' misguided expectation that Jesus will remove the veil of secrecy and enable the disciples to see in advance what only the End itself is meant to disclose?

2. If Jesus categorically refuses to give any sign at all to 'this generation' (8.12), should we not seriously consider the possibility that the ταῦτα πάντα ('these things') which 'this generation' (13.30) will live to see does not include signs?

3. Should we not seriously consider the viability of a minority opinion that within Mark 13 there are no valid 'signs' at all?[91]

4. Is it not possible that Mark 13 (like much of the rest of the Bible) concerns itself more with understanding what is happening than with facilitating predictions about the future?[92]

5. Is it not possible that what have often been called Mark 13's ambiguities and inconsistencies are in reality devices by

which Mark reveals a message more subtle than has heretofore been suspected?

6. Could Mark 13 be concerned not only with the significance of the events predicted there but also with the *means by which* that significance is apprehended?

Chapter 3

A MARKAN PERSPECTIVE ON DISCERNMENT

Introduction

The alternative to 'sign-seeking' which Mark endorses is not 'fideism' ('Just believe, don't ask for reasons!'), it is a special discernment process which turns faith into 'sight' within the context of discipleship. To make this point, Mark has taken a quite ordinary term βλέπω ('to see/look') and used it in all its occurrences as part of a subtle call to 'see' what is below the surface of events, discourses and texts.

The implications for interpreting Mark 13 are enormous: we come to see more clearly why the disciples' perspective in 13.4 is judged inadequate and we catch a glimpse of what it means to 'watch' in 13.5-33a. Moreover, we pave the way for the following chapter of our study in which Mark's other 'watchword' is analysed and contrasted with βλέπω.

The value of word studies such as those in *TDNT* is that one can learn about the *general* function of a word. The weakness is the erroneous impression sometimes left that words *always* mean what they *frequently* mean. W. Michaelis summarizes the general function for the term βλέπω:[1]

> In the NT, too, βλέπω denotes sense perception, e.g., being able to see as distinct from blindness . . . βλέπω is very much in place to denote seeing processes in the world of empirical phenomena as distinct from religious certainty, which has to do with things invisible.

He is generally correct. Such a 'merely empirical' sense is easy to find in the New Testament. With one exception, every New Testament writer who uses the term, uses it *sometimes* in a very literal, empirical sense with no concomitant suggestion of a symbolic spiritual meaning or a call to discern a hidden reality or an esoteric communication, (e.g., Matt. 15.31; Luke 24.12; John 20.5; 2 Cor. 4.18; Heb. 11.3; Rev. 9.20; etc.). The exception, we shall argue, is Mark.

Every usage of the term in Mark appears intended by the author to contribute to a carefully devised call for discernment concerning realities which lie beyond the observations of the physical senses. That is not to say that wherever the term occurs it means something spiritual rather than something physical; it is to say that every time Mark takes up the term, he uses it to contribute to a 'call for discernment' *above and beyond* whatever physical sense data are in view.

It is the task of this chapter to understand the function of βλέπω in Mark's Gospel, the relationship between physical seeing and spiritual discernment, and the alternative to 'sign-seeking' which Mark endorses as a basis for belief. That being the case, there is clearly no better place to begin our investigation than with the most misunderstood passage in Mark's Gospel, the discussion about the meaning of the feedings (8.14-21). The pericope deals with the whole issue of understanding something beyond the data available to ordinary senses, and it is sandwiched between the Pharisaic request for a sign (8.11-13) and the two-stage healing of the blind man at Bethsaida (8.22-26). The term βλέπω figures prominently in the pericope and in its immediate context. This text is ideally suited to demonstrate our present hypothesis.

Too many scholars have characterized Mark's Gospel as a series of incidents strung together 'with breathless haste, so that there is scarcely room for pause'.[2] The story itself does move quickly, especially in the first half, but the juxtaposition of one incident after another is frequently the means by which Mark calls us to pause and discern the significance of individual pericopes and the sequences in which they are placed. Mark 8.14-21 in relation to its context is an example of this.

If we can make good our claim that in this passage exegetes have been trying to wrench open the wrong doors, and if we can open the door Mark wanted us to open, we should perhaps not be surprised to find passageways which give new *entrées* into a number of adjoining pericopes. With that ambitious goal before us, we begin our examination of 8.14-21.

I. *The Leaven and the Loaves (Mark 8.14-21)*

N.A. Beck has suggested that this passage needs reclamation, by which he meant that our task is to subtract the destructive influences of *Mark's* misunderstanding and clumsy editing in order to find something of value in the pre-Markan tradition.[3] We contend that the evangelist's meaning itself is in need of reclamation. We want to hear the whole passage and grasp what Mark is trying to say.

If we are going to account for all the data, there is surely no better place to begin than with the statement that almost everyone seems content to ignore in interpreting the passage, the warning of Jesus against the leaven of the Pharisees and Herod (8.15).

How Did the Leaven Get in and Corrupt the Whole Passage?

It was W. Wrede who propounded the now incredible view that:[4]

> He [Mark] did not think through from one point in his presentation to the next. . . . Not by a single syllable does he indicate that he desires to see two facts brought into connection which he happens to tell one after the other.

Only under the influence of that erroneous assessment could a scholar of C.H. Turner's stature assign Mark 8.15 to 'parenthesis' status, and call it 'an extreme example of Mark's naïve and non-logical construction of his narrative'. He goes so far as to say that 'If the bracketed words are omitted from the sequence of the argument, everything seems plain sailing'.[5] Agreed. But if we abandon Mark as our captain we will surely end up in the wrong port! Prior to the age of redaction criticism most interpreters of 8.14-21 bracketed out 8.15.[6]

The past thirty years of Markan research have amply demonstrated that Mark is less clumsy, less illogical and a great deal more skilful than earlier scholars imagined. Contrary to Wrede's conclusion, Mark deliberately structures his accounts so that clues in the surrounding context are designed to indicate his intended meaning.[7]

Not everyone has been persuaded of this. John C. Meagher is perhaps an extreme example, maintaining that both Mark and those who preserved the traditions were extremely inept, and that only by outshining them can the modern scholar hope to recover the original meanings in the material that has survived.[8] Even among those who have a growing appreciation for Mark's abilities and his subtleties, Mark 8.15 is frequently considered the exception to the rule.

Beck, in his attempt to 'reclaim' the text, excises 8.15.[9] Others interpret the meaning of the text by adopting Turner's expedient of putting 8.15 in parentheses.[10] Sometimes an attempt is made to take the immediate context of 8.15 seriously, but it is spoiled by a rearrangement of the *larger* context.[11]

If we are going to make sense of the 8.15 and of 8.14-21, we will have to apply to this *crux interpretum* the same principles that have been employed with success elsewhere in Mark's Gospel. We will have to look for clues in the Markan context as to the meaning he intended. It would be our contention that taking the Markan context seriously requires that the warning against the Pharisees' and Herod's leaven in 8.15 be interpreted in the light of *at least* the following three concerns: the immediately preceding reference to Pharisees as representative of 'this generation'; the attitude taken in Mark's Gospel to Pharisees, Herod, and probably Herodians (with due consideration for changing attitudes in Mark's story line!); and, the function of 8.15 within 8.14-21 and its larger literary context. In my judgment, no interpretation of 8.14-21 in general, or of 8.15 in particular, has succeeded in doing all three. By far the most serious error is to assume that Mark 8.14-21 is designed to drop clues as to what Mark thinks the feedings mean. It does nothing of the sort. When the true function of 8.14-21 is understood, everything falls nicely into place, and the 'leaven allusion' is not hard to identify.

What is the Leaven of the Pharisees and Herod?
Because exegetes have overlooked the real function of 8.14-21, they have cast their net far and wide in the hopes of capturing the tropological meaning of ςύμη ('leaven'). There have been at least six different *methods* that have been used in the hopes of identifying the significance of ζύμη: (1) identifying opposite dangers represented by the Pharisees and Herod respectively; (2) identifying two differing (but not necessarily opposite) dangers which represent typical faults of the respective parties; (3) casting around for ideas on what faults the two parties had *in common*; (4) ignoring the reference to Herod and focusing on the Pharisees' greatest faults; (5) concentrating on the significance of the *imagery* in the reference to leaven; and (6) ignoring it (since the disciples did not catch on and Jesus drops the issue in frustration). With such a variety of *methods*, it is not surprising to find great diversity in the *conclusions* that are reached: false piety/godlessness (or religiosity/secularism); legalism/nationalism

(or, more generally 'bad theology'/'bad politics'); a 'wonder-worker' Christology;[12] political Messianic hopes; erroneous teaching; evil influence; hatred; pride; power; table fellowship; gradual growth in blindness; even sexual fertility!

This does not exhaust the possibilities, but enough has been said to make it clear that scholars have not been able to reach consensus on what Mark meant to convey by 'the leaven of the Pharisees and Herod'. Each of the above suggestions has *some* plausibility; each picks up on one or another clue in the Markan text. None of them, however, leads to or follows from a correct apprehension of Mark's intended meaning in 8.14-21. If the answer is to be found, it will have to be sought, not longer and harder, but in a different *way*. We contend that the same error is responsible for virtually all the (mis)identifications of Mark's intentions outlined above. Interpreters are arguing from a falsely identified 'known' to interpret what is 'unknown'.

If 8.15 is not a clumsy insertion into an unsuitable context, Mark is pointing to a contrast in 8.14-21. Almost all commentators who take Mark's contextualizing seriously imagine that what is being contrasted is 'the leaven of the Pharisees and Herod' and 'the meaning of the feedings'. The first is warned against; the second is put forward as the alternative. This is a falsely identified set of contrasting elements.

Whatever arguments are *explicitly* given by those seeking to interpret ζύμη, one gets the distinct impression that what is really being sought is an appropriate alternative to whatever they identify as 'the meaning of the feedings'. Thus, if interpreters think Mark's intended meaning for the feedings is 'Gentile inclusion', they try to demonstrate that the leaven of the Pharisees and Herod is their Jewish nationalism. If the feedings are taken to be foreshadowings of the Eucharist, then the leaven must somehow be related to either 'eating' or to an 'anti-passion theology'. If the feedings are foretastes of eschatological banqueting, then the leaven of the Pharisees is a faulty eschatology (either a misguided expectation of apocalyptic signs [8.11-13] or a failure to recognize the arrival of the eschatological age). If the feedings are thought to have primarily a Christological focus, the leaven is interpreted as a failure to recognize and accept Jesus.

The approach outlined above would be defensible if it were Mark's aim to use 8.14-21 to help the reader discover what the feedings mean, even though it would have (and in fact does have) the unfortunate result that there will be at least as many (mis)identifications of the 'leaven' as there are (mis)identifications of the 'meaning of the feedings'.

The erroneous consensus is that Mark 8.14-21 is an attempt to elucidate the 'meaning of the feedings'. In fact it is an attempt to highlight *the means by which* the feedings can be understood. The text is about epistemology. *'Leaven' is not the alternative to the meaning of the feedings which Mark endorses, but to the epistemology he defends.*[13]

Our hypothesis concerning the meaning of 8.15 in context is simple enough, and it is not entirely new. What is new is our insistence that the meaning of 8.15 in context is identical with the primary concern of Mark all the way from 7.31-8.26. Not a few scholars have found this treasure, but not realizing it was the treasure, went on searching for other objects instead of polishing the one in hand. The treasure, we insist, has more lustre and value than is usually recognized.

B.M.F. van Iersel, in his article on Mark 14.28 and 16.7, makes the following passing comment on the meaning of Mark 8.15. 'This could mean that they [the disciples] should not ask for signs but learn to understand what they see'.[14] Herein, we shall argue, is the primary concern, not only of Mark 8.15, but also of almost everything from Mark 7.31 through Mark 8.26. Mark's purpose is to show how true learning must take place, and how it contrasts with the wrong way, alluded to in the 'leaven' saying. The contrast is not between two christologies, two eschatologies, two attitudes to Gentiles, two kinds of teaching, etc. The contrast, for Mark, is between two epistemologies.

How To Interpret the Meaning of the Feedings
Before interpreting the details of the passage (i.e., trying to determine what the Markan Jesus was trying to accomplish in relation to his disciples) it is helpful to ask what Mark was aiming to accomplish in relation to his readers by including 8.14-21. Scholars inevitably gravitate to one of two answers: either Mark was trying to highlight the non-understanding of the disciples, or else he was trying to enlighten his readers concerning the real meaning of the feedings.

A surprising number of commentators adopt the first alternative *for this passage* even if they do not adopt the dubious conclusion that Mark is generally trying to discredit the disciples. V. Taylor, for example, maintains:[15]

The truth is that in Mk the saying on the leaven is ignored either because the disciples do not understand it or more probably because the writer's interest is to emphasize their failure to understand the sign of the loaves in the stories of miraculous feeding.

Since the highlighting of discipleship failure in Mark is part of a larger program to give positive discipleship teaching, it is inadequate to see 8.14-21 as if its only purpose was to highlight the disciples' blindness. In any case, such a view does not account for the details of the passage as well as the alternative reading we shall present.

If interpreters reject the 'discipleship failure' agenda for Mark 8.14-21, they invariably adopt what seems the only alternative: Mark must be attempting to drop clues for his readers so that they will be more likely to grasp 'the meaning of the feedings'. This view, however, entails the unfortunate conclusion that either Mark or else the interpreters are complete failures. We could easily present as many different ideas on what the feedings are thought to mean as we have been able to on what the 'leaven' represents.[16] The exegete is left between a rock and a hard place. Either Mark succeeds in an unworthy objective (undermining the credibility of the disciples) or he fails in a worthy one (enlightening the reader). In the first case the disciples will end up looking stupid, in the second case commentators are forced to apply the adjective either to themselves or Mark.[17] Perhaps we have been presented with a false dichotomy.

H.C. Kee moves partway towards what we consider the right approach when he comments, 'Mark, in keeping with his esoteric outlook, . . . gives only tantalizing hints to his reader of the real meaning of the miracle of feeding'.[18] We would go even further and say that he gives no hints at all. If it is once considered that the questions of Jesus in Mark 8.14-21 are designed to analyse and reveal the *nature of the problem* instead of hinting at the *answer*, it all fits. It is remarkable how many scholars have come right up to the edge of the clearing, and then immediately turned back into the jungle. A clear example is Alan Richardson who notes:[19]

> Today scholars are no longer inclined to imagine that St. Mark was merely a rather stupid recorder but imagine him as a very profound and skillful interpreter of the Gospel material. He deliberately recorded both the Feeding Miracles with a view to the development of the main theme of the first half of his Gospel, the opening of the blind eyes of the disciples.

> St. Mark pointedly emphasizes that the disciples ought to have
> understood the meaning of the sign of the broken loaves (6.52, 8.14-
> 21). They failed to do so, because 'their heart was hardened'. What
> was it that the disciples ought to have understood?

It is incredible that, after such a clear and accurate portrayal of
Mark's purposes, he asks utterly the wrong question. His final
question, 'What was it that the disciples ought to have understood?'
should rather be, 'How then were the disciples supposed to be able to
come to understand?'[20] After all, when Jesus meets blind people he
does not describe the landscape for them; he opens their eyes.

We have skirted the issue long enough. What follows is our
interpretation of the passage. Its value and its justification lie in its
ability to explain all the data that need to be explained, and in its
coherence with the whole Gospel of Mark.

A New Way of Reading Mark 8.14-21
We begin by offering a new way of reading the dialogue between
Jesus and the disciples. The disciples have obviously missed
something. Although there are textual and punctuational problems
with 8.16,[21] it is quite clear that in 8.14-16 the reader is made aware
of the disciples' inability to understand something Jesus expects
them to grasp. The material following 8.16 indicates that, whatever
else they may have failed to understand, they failed to grasp 'the
meaning of the feedings'. That they had failed to understand the full
meaning and significance of the first feeding is explicitly stated by the
narrator of Mark's story in 6.52. Apparently they have also failed to
understand the second. Their discussion about the one loaf and their
misunderstanding of the 'leaven warning' are taken by the Markan
Jesus as evidence of that.

Mark 8.18 is the point at which exegesis of this passage invariably
moves in the wrong direction. 'Don't you see?' 'Don't you hear?'
'Don't you remember?' H. Anderson comments that 'a lapse of
memory so shortly after two amazing miracles of feeding is
inconceivable!'[22] Indeed it is! *The whole point of 8.19-21 is to prove
that very point!* The quiz about the loaves and the leftovers is
designed to demonstrate that the disciples had no problem with data
recall, leaving the alternative crystal clear ... their *spiritual*
perceptions were dull. The erroneous assumption usually made is
that in the decoding of the details of the miracle the mysterious
meaning will emerge. It could be argued that by fixing on the details

of the miracle and the quantities collected, scholars are perpetuating the error for which the disciples are castigated.

Mark 8.18 is not indicating that the disciples have three problems (faulty eyes, ears, and memory). Rather it is setting out *two options*. Either their spiritual perceptions are inadequate to lead them to understanding, or else they have not retained an accurate memory of what it is that they ought to be interpreting.[23] Most modern English translations rightly take 8.18 as two parallel questions, although there are other ways of punctuating the verse. 'Do you not understand? Do you not remember?' The disciples demonstrate that their recall of the data is perfect. The real problem has thus been identified. Mark 8.19, 20 is then *not* an attempt to focus on the meaning of the feedings, but a vivid way of focusing on the nature of the disciples' problem—the problem of a good memory, but an inability to understand. They are unable to see past the data of sensory perception. They do not understand the significance. The contrast between 'data' and 'significance' is exceedingly crucial in the broader context of Mark's Gospel, as will emerge later in this chapter.

If we have correctly identified the function of vv. 19f. in the pericope, it follows that all effort to analyse the symbolic significance of the twelve (small) baskets (κόφινοι [8.19]), of the seven (large) baskets (σπυρίδες [8.20]), and therefore almost certainly of the one loaf (ἄρτος [8.14]), is misguided.[24] If the dialogue was never intended to be seen as a set of subtle hints as to the meaning of the feedings, but as an attempt to identify the disciples' problem, then we can go on to see how the author of the Gospel has *used* this pericope in its broader context. Doing so leads to the conclusion that the reading of the text which we have outlined above is not merely possible (and we think plausible); it is exceedingly probable.

If the real intended contrast is not between 'the leaven of the Pharisees' and 'the meaning of the feedings', but rather between 'the leaven of the Pharisees' and 'the right way of discerning meaning', then Mark's finesse as a writer is vindicated in this passage as in so many others in his Gospel.

Mark 8.14-21 in its Markan 'Teaching' Context
The first point to note is that Mark 8.11-13 is linked to 8.14-21 by means of 8.15. D.E. Hiebert demonstrates the close connection between the two pericopes and concludes that 'His warning against the leaven of the Pharisees is to be understood in the light of what

had just occurred'.[25] While many scholars would concur with the connection, it is only in the light of the reading of 8.14-21 given above that the significance of it can be fully apprehended. The passage is giving 'sign-seeking' and 'meaning-discernment' as the two alternative ways of apprehending and evaluating the claims and actions of Jesus. The Pharisees, who have already rejected Jesus, imagine that he will oblige them with more miracles and wonders which (at least so they were pretending) would facilitate an objective evaluation of the truth. The Pharisees did not, as Robbins believed,[26] betray an errant eschatology. They had an errant epistemology. They wanted objective data, pure and simple. They imagined that they could demand whatever sort of signs they wanted, and then maintain critical distance and draw whatever conclusions from the data happened to suit their inclinations.

When we recall the points established in the previous chapter, this passage shows its true colours. Jesus has *already* demonstrated by both deed and word (2.1-3.6) the authority he claims. They had neither 'seen' nor 'heard' because their hearts were hard. They had rejected the evidence given and were now seeking signs with evil intent. Jesus has chosen the 'other way' of recruiting leaders for a restored Israel. He will no longer appeal with objective proofs to those whose hard hearts resist both insight and commitment. He will rather spend time with those who are willing to commit themselves, and seek to lead them to insight and true discipleship.

The disciples, however, are not model pupils. Mighty works have been done in their presence, but they have done no better than to evaluate them with amazement and memorize the data for future reference. They do not understand the significance of what is happening. They are in danger of falling to the level of the Jewish religious hierarchy. They have failed to understand the first feeding (significantly because their hearts are hard [6.52, cf. 3.5]). Jesus again miraculously feeds a multitude and wishes to guide the disciples in the way of understanding. Mark has linked together three pericopes which form a single teaching unit. The disciples are confronted with two options. There is a great miracle (8.1-10), the significance of which they are called to understand. And there is a clamouring after signs (8.11-13), despite the fact that evidence has already been given and either misapprehended or ignored. 8.14-21 calls on the disciples to guard against the model provided by the Pharisees and Herod (8.15 referring to 8.11-13), and instead to discern the meaning of what they have just witnessed (8.17-21 referring to 8.1-10). The chiastic arrangement helps to tie the sequence together.

The sequence, however, must not be misunderstood. It is often claimed that the Pharisees' request is particularly misguided since Jesus has just performed the great miracle of the feeding.[27] There is no indication that they even knew about the feeding recorded in 8.1-10. Their error is to demand a sign after rejecting all the evidence *they* had already been given (see Chapter 2). The juxtaposing of the feeding account with the request for a sign is not designed primarily to re-emphasize the Pharisees' blindness. The structure is designed to display the options *before the disciples* (and the readers). Jesus is warning against 'sign-seeking'; he is pleading for 'discernment'. They must move past the data of sense perception (something the Jewish leaders were unwilling to do) so that they may, with eyes that really see and ears that really hear, discern the true significance of what is occurring around them. It becomes clear that hard-heartedness does not exclude one from Jesus' fellowship; both the disciples and the rejectors have hard hearts (cf. 6.52, 3.5). Spiritual imperception is also not grounds for exclusion; both Jesus' enemies and his disciples hear and see the words and deeds of Jesus without truly hearing or truly seeing (8.18, 4.12). The crucial condition for acceptance is whether one chooses to reject Jesus or follow him. Rejectors are rejected. Followers, however dull and unfaithful, are patiently instructed. If they follow all along the way Jesus leads, they will eventually be transformed from mere 'data-collectors' into 'meaning-discerners'. It all hinges on the decision for or against Jesus. All this, of course, sheds a great deal of light on Mark 4.

But what about the leaven of Herod? While other interpretations of the passage struggle to find something the Pharisees and Herod have in common, our interpretation has no difficulty with the question at all. In Herod's responses both to John the Baptist and to the miracle-working of Jesus (of which he is aware, though he may not observe the miracles [6.14-16]), Herod is an exact counterpart to the Pharisees. Like them he was eager to listen to God's messenger (Mark 6.20); like them he was impressed with the miracle-working of Jesus (Mark 6:14); like them he misunderstood the power behind it (6.14); like them he refused to repent of the evil of his ways in the face of clear instruction (Mark 6.18); like them he would rather have God's messenger killed than look foolish and lose authority in the eyes of others. In short, Herod was just like the Pharisees in that 'signs and wonders' were of no effect in leading to understanding, faith or repentance.[28] Anyone could see the glaring differences between the Pharisees and Herod. It took Jesus' discerning eye to identify what it was they had in common.[29] In the examples of both the Pharisees and Herod there was ample evidence that mighty works, unless they were apprehended aright, were of no value in correcting attitudes and directing actions.[30] The disciples are being warned in 8.15 lest their own hard-heartedness and lack of perception lead them along the same path. The way to avoid that disaster is to allow their eyes and ears to be opened that they might not only remember but also understand.

We are now at the point where the most remarkable confirmation for our way of reading 8.1-21 can be given. We have argued that 8.1-21 is a single Markan teaching unit which serves to identify the disciples' problem, and the danger to which it subjects them. *Mark has put around it a framework which shows how that problem is to be solved and that danger averted.* They have eyes that fail to see and ears that fail to hear; the good news is that their teacher is able to heal deaf ears (7.31-37) and open blind eyes (8.22-26)!

The misreading of 8.14-21 (see above) and preoccupations with the question of Markan sources (see below) have conspired to obscure the remarkable way in which these two parallel miracles carry forward Mark's theological concerns in this part of the Gospel and build the appropriate theological and literary bridge into the next part.

This section of Mark's Gospel is often said to contain two parallel pre-Markan miracle collections so remarkably similar that doublets are indicated. Unfortunately the parallelism is not remarkable enough that scholars can agree on where the collection begins, where it ends, how many pericopes each collection contains, etc.[31] A frequently expressed view is that the remarkably similar healing miracles (7.31-37 and 8.22-26) were the respective conclusions of the collections. The remarkable similarity is explained equally well, and Mark's purposes grasped much more clearly, on the view that Mark intends them to form a bracket around his special teaching section, pointing to the issue of deaf ears and blind eyes as the main concern of the section.[32] The miracles are parallel not only in their circumstances and in the mechanics of the cure. The function of each in the whole Gospel of Mark reveals a parallelism at a much deeper and theologically significant level.[33] When the 'hearing ears' problem is related to the parables and the 'seeing eyes' problem to the miracles, the significance of Mark's teaching unit (7.31-8.26) takes on added significance, especially in its narrative position immediately before the great turning point for the disciples (8.27-30).

II. *The Call to Understand (7.31–8.26 in Context)*

In order to relate the Markan teaching unit (7.31–8.26) to the broader concerns of Mark's Gospel, we examine the 'hearing' and 'seeing' issue from four vantage points: (1) Parables and 'Hearing Ears', (2) Miracles and 'Seeing Eyes', (3) The Messianic Confession, and (4) Mark's Epistemology (summary).

Parables and 'Hearing Ears'

M. Boucher is surely correct in her assessment that 'a correct understanding of the crucial parable chapter, Mark 4, sheds light on the entire gospel and its purpose'.[34] Yet, the complexities of Mark 4 make it almost impossible for anything both useful and adequately substantiated to be said about it in a short space. We will confine ourselves to some of the key concerns of Mark 4 as they relate to the concerns of 8.14-21. If we have correctly perceived Mark's intentions in 8.14-21, then arguing from the known (8.14-21) to the unknown (4.1-34) ought to be of benefit in understanding Mark's epistemology, the central concern of both passages.

An interesting exercise is to separate the words of Jesus in Mark 4 into two categories, (1) actual parabolic material, and, (2) everything else (introductory and concluding exhortations, comments about and explanations of parables etc.). What is revealed is that everything in the first category is arguably 'about the kingdom of God' and everything in the second is 'about spiritual perception'. Markan interpreters cannot decide whether Mark 4 is primarily about the kingdom or about true hearing. The fact is that it is about both. The insistence on the need to 'hear' aright is not merely because the message is important and urgent,[35] it is because the sort of 'kingdom' under consideration demands both hearing ears (to grasp its nature) and seeing eyes (to see the evidence of its advance).

The so-called 'interpretation' attached to the sower parable has generated a great deal of discussion, most of it centring on Mark's clumsiness and misunderstanding of the sower parable. The fact is that when Mark's purposes are clearly grasped, Mark 4.14-20 becomes a key unlocking the secrets of Mark 4.

In order to see this, it must first be noted that there is a remarkable parallelism between Mark 4.1-20 and 8.1-21.[36] The feeding miracle

(8.1-10) corresponds to the Sower parable (4.1-9.) The rejection of a sign to the Pharisees (8.11-13) corresponds to the withholding of revelation from 'those outside' (4.11-12). The discussion about the feeding (8.14-21) corresponds to the discussion about the sower parable (4.13-20). In both cases more is at stake than one miracle or one parable. The larger context of 8.1-21 is concerned to teach disciples how to apprehend the significance of miracles. The larger context of 4.1-20 is concerned to teach disciples how to understand the significance of parables.

Mark is continually criticized for failing to understand the parable of the sower and supplying an interpretation which misses its eschatological significance. No one seems to notice that it is modern interpreters, not Mark or the Markan Jesus, who characterize 4.14-20 as *the* interpretation of the Sower parable.[37] It is the Markan Jesus' attempt to instruct the disciples on how (i.e., by what means) they are to understand parables (4.13b—καὶ πῶς πάσας τὰς παραβολὰς γνώσεσθε;). Mark is less concerned with the 'answer' than with the 'means' by which answers are to be found. It is precisely what happens in 8.14-21. Just as that passage is about epistemology and not an attempt to explicate the meaning of the feedings, so also 4.13-20 is about epistemology and not an attempt to explicate fully the meaning of the sower parable. Both 8.14-21 and 4.13-20 are designed to instruct the disciples on the *means by which* true understanding is made possible.

Jesus is not saying, 'Do you not understand the parable? Here let me tell you what it means'. He is saying, 'Do you not understand the parable? Let me tell you how you can'. The disciples are clamouring for easy explanations. The Markan Jesus responds, 'What you need is not a point by point lesson on the meaning of each parable, nor on the nature of the kingdom. What you need are ears to hear its hidden message and eyes to see its hidden presence. Here is how the kingdom's seed can grow within you. . . '. Even 4.34 with its narrative comment that Jesus explained everything to his disciples is consistent with this, if we are prepared to take 4.14-20 as an example of the sort of explanations that were given. That it is possible to tie the lesson so closely to the details of the sower parable is evidence of at least three things: (1) Epistemology and eschatology are far more closely related for Mark and the Markan Jesus than is usually recognized, (2) Mark is much more concerned to commend an implicit epistemology than to describe an explicit eschatology, (3) Mark is not a clumsy editor.

When 4.13-20 is recognized as teaching on epistemology, then the Sower parable itself (4.3-8) is freed to be interpreted as a kingdom parable, the very thing the content indicates it certainly must be.[38] Has Mark then misunderstood it? Not at all. He has correctly grasped that the nature of the kingdom is such that it is intimately connected with the need for correct hearing, and therefore appropriately revealed/concealed by means of parables which require the same. It is a parable about the kingdom and it is a parable about 'the right hearing of parables'.[39]

It is surely possible that Mark (and Jesus before him) maintained that 'the nature of the kingdom' and 'the nature of true hearing' are topics which can well be combined in one parable.[40] After all, it is not only the nature of parabolic speech which requires careful listening; it is also the nature of the kingdom being proclaimed by it. Boucher raises the question whether it is the coming kingdom or the parabolic speech that is mysterious.[41] She is surely correct in insisting that it is both, and we would add *inseparably* both.

Too often Markan interpreters have been content to name some relatively simple equivalence as 'the secret of the kingom'. For example, 'the secret'

=	the fact that Jesus is the Messiah
=	the fact that the Messiah has to suffer
=	the fact that the kingdom's arrival is imminent
=	the fact that the kingdom is to appear in Galilee, etc.

No simple equivalence will do justice to Mark's view of the matter. 'The secret of the kingdom' has primarily to do with the very fact that the kingdom comes secretly. It has to do with the fact that at present only those with eyes to see and ears to hear can apprehend the nature of the kingdom and discern its advance. The secret is its secrecy.[42]

If we can avoid the pitfalls of concluding that Jesus is trying to keep non-disciples out of range of true hearing and seeing, the whole chapter demonstrates a remarkable unity, not only with itself, but with Mark's epistemology (especially in relation to 7.31-8.26). The chapter makes no claim that anyone is being consigned to the outside. What it claims is that those who *are* on the outside are being consigned to ignorance. In the light of our study of 3.6 as a crucial turning point in the apologetics of the Markan Jesus, the difficulty that some find insurmountable melts away. Jesus does not arbitrarily reject anyone. What he does is withhold revelation from those who have chosen to reject *him*. Their hearts are *already* hard (cf. 3.5), and the sower finally ceases to waste the good seed where it will not germinate. J. Lambrecht, in commenting on 3.27, makes the incredible statement that 'Nothing is said here about an intention of hardening on the part of Jesus *such as is mentioned in Mk 4.11,12*' [emphasis mine].[43] It is precisely the 'hardening' part of the Isaiah quotation that Mark *omitted*! (cf. Isa. 6.10). The religious leaders' hard-heartedness (3.5) was caused not by Jesus withholding instruction but by their own unwillingness to receive it. Their hard-heartedness was the basis of their rejecting him, not the result of his rejecting them. That Jesus ever *consigned* anyone (his family, the crowds, or his enemies) to the outside is unsupported by the text.[44]

Radical expedients (such as arguing that *all* of 4.12 is intended ironically) are not necessary, despite the final suggestion that repentance is being prevented by Jesus' withholding of revelation. That Jesus was trying to prevent repentance surely means that if those committed to a position as 'outsiders' were to see and hear any more than they already have *without becoming 'arounders'*, (3.34 and 4.10 indicate that the appropriate Markan alternative to 'outsider' is 'arounder', not 'insider') their repentance could not possibly have any more meaning or effect than it did for 'the whole Judean countryside and all the people of Jerusalem' (1.5), who 'repented' and received John's baptism and then later called for, and engineered, Jesus' death. In *that* sense 4.12c (alone) has a touch of irony in it.[45]

If our way of looking at 4.1-34 has benefited from insights into Mark's epistemology as indicated in 7.31-8.26, it is now time to repay the favours. Mark's teaching in the parable chapter sheds significant light both on the relevance of the call to 'hear' in the latter teaching unit (7.31-8.26), and on Mark's identification of 'the meaning of the feedings'.

Many indications make it clear that both the parables and the miracles of Jesus have meanings deeper than whatever appears at the surface of the empirical data.[46] Although Mark 4 puts the emphasis on *hearing* what the kingdom is like, and although the mighty works recorded thereafter put the emphasis on *seeing* the indicators of its hidden presence, the two are really inseparable.

By the time *both* hearing and sight come up for thematic discussion (7.31-8.26), we have learned that the disciples neither truly heard nor truly perceived. That the disciples' ears need some help is clear throughout the whole section from 4.34 through 7.30. It is amply illustrated in the pericope immediately following 4.1-34 in which Jesus finds the disciples harder to calm than the lake. It is also illustrated at key points in the following chapters (cf. esp. 7.17, 18).[47] It comes to a head when they do not even understand the very warning Jesus gives them concerning the need for spiritual perceptions (8.15).

All along they have also been blind. Their questioning, 'Who then is this?' (4.41), their misperception of Jesus 'that he was a ghost' (6.49), and their failure to grasp the great miracle they had just observed (6.49-52), are evidence of that. On the empirical level they had both heard the parables and seen the miracles. Had they truly *heard* the message of the parables and had they correctly *perceived* the indications that the secret kingdom was advancing in the miracles, all would have been well. As it was, both their ears and eyes needed to be healed. Eschatological prophecies were being fulfilled all around the disciples which should have convinced them that the kingdom was indeed in their midst. They had not grasped the message of the secret kingdom and they could not see its presence. The very fact that in the material that follows 7.31–8.26 the disciples are found with their ears and eyes still turned towards a kingdom with very different contours than the secret kingdom Jesus proclaims, should make it evident that 7.31–8.26 is *not* saying 'here is the point at which the disciples' ears and eyes were finally opened'. It is much rather saying 'here is how you can be made to hear and see'. When they truly hear, they will stop looking for a kingdom that proffers prestigious seats in glory (10.37). When they truly see, they will discover that the alternative kingdom Jesus proclaims is even now being established.

All this should make it clear that it is quite inadequate to focus on 'Gentile inclusion', 'eucharistic foreshadowing', 'Jesus as the new Moses', 'eschatological banqueting', etc. as *the meaning of the feedings*. What the feedings mean, for the Markan Jesus and for Mark, is that the eschatological promises are being fulfilled.[48]

The kingdom is secretly coming. Those who truly *hear* the message of the secret kingdom, and who truly *see* the significance of what is taking place around them will realize the fact. They will see that in the subduing of Satan's power (4.35-41), in the freeing of Satan's captives (5.1-20), in the healing of the sick (and acceptance of the ritually unclean [5.24b-34]), in the raising of the dead (5.21-24a; 35-43), in the feeding of the hungry (6.30-44; 8.1-10), in the 'secret epiphany' of God (6.45-56, especially v. 50 with its 'I am' [ἐγώ εἰμι]), in the extension of grace even to Gentiles (7.24-30), in the healing of deaf ears (7.31-37), and in the healing of blind eyes (8.22-26), God is fulfilling his eschatological promises. Virtually all the events of 4.35-8.26 are parabolic events, pointing beyond themselves to the kingdom in the process of coming. Did not Jesus say, '*Everything* comes in parables' (4.11)?[49] He did not say that everything is told in parables; he said everything comes that way.[50]

The parables taught that *even though* the kingdom comes without armies and fanfare, it will grow and will succeed, unstoppable by human unbelief and unhelped by human effort. The miracles taught that even at that moment it was at work.

Why is 'hearing' a crucial element in 7.31-8.26? Because unless the kingdom message of Jesus is heard aright, there can be no observation of the kingdom's hidden presence, and hence no understanding of the miracles.

Miracles and 'Seeing Eyes'
Fortunately most scholars have by now moved away from the position of Wrede and some of the form critics that Mark does not think through the connections between the pericopes he 'happens' to put consecutively.[51] It is now widely recognized that the giving-of-sight miracle (8.22-26) relates symbolically to the material before and/or after it. Yet there is little consensus on how it relates to that material.

Alan Richardson is typical of a whole group of scholars who hold that Jesus opens the eyes of the blind man in two stages to parallel the fact that he enacts the feeding miracle twice. It took two attempts to get the man to see just as it took two attempts to get the disciples to see. That they *did* see after the second feeding is evidenced by the fact that they got the messianic confession right (8.30).[52]

This view is, however, seriously at odds with what one reads in Mark. In the first place, while the messianic confession is no doubt technically correct, Mark is surely concerned to demonstrate the deficiency, not the sufficiency, of Peter's understanding. We find in Mark no congratulations of Peter for his receptivity to divine revelation, such as we find in Matt. 16. Only a command to silence separates the confession from the abrupt change of topic which leads to the mutual rebuke between Peter and Jesus. The text does not give us encouragement to believe that the disciples understood the second feeding any more than the first, and in any case there is nothing in the Christological discussion which suggests that Peter's confession was informed by insights into the feedings. As we have argued, 7.31–8.26 is not an indication of what *has* happened, but what *must* happen.

The widely held alternative view is that Peter's messianic confession corresponds with the first stage in the healing of the blind man. When the disciples have learned some further lessons concerning the place of the cross in relation to Jesus' messiahship and his kingdom message, then they can be said to 'fully see'.[53] This is a far more adequate interpretation but it is still affected by the one erroneous assumption which those in this camp share with those in Richardson's (above). They evaluate the giving-of-sight miracle and apply its symbolic significance as though the issue is *half*-sight and *full*-sight.[54] In the light of 8.14–21, a slight but important modification must be made.

The disciples' problem in 8.14–21 was that, while they had perfectly well-functioning physical senses, they did not have spiritual senses adequate to interpret the data correctly. Consider then the miracle of healing blind eyes. After the first touch by Jesus, the man saw *everything*, but *nothing* clearly. All the sense data were penetrating his organs of sight; none of it was being accurately interpreted. It is a brilliant illustration in the natural realm of the relationship between natural and spiritual seeing. At the second touch, the man did not see more people or more trees, he saw people *as* people and trees *as* trees. He apprehended correctly the significance of what he had already seen.[55]

The giving-of-sight miracle is misconstrued if it is merely described as '*half*-seeing' and '*full*-seeing'. It is rather 'seeing without understanding' and 'seeing with understanding'. It is a perfect parallel to 8.14–21 and a confirmation of our interpretation of that passage. A recognition of this illuminates Mark's intentions in the Christological discussion that follows.[56]

The Messianic Confession: To See or Not To See
R.H. Lightfoot points out some structural similarities between the giving-of-sight miracle and the pericope about Peter's confession. He draws the implication that Peter's messianic confession is paralleled to the '*full*' seeing.[57] This conclusion, however, is overturned by other indications. E. Best and many others hold to the more defensible view that it is co-ordinated with the first stage of the

healing.[58] If we recognize that the terms '*half*'-sight and '*full*'-sight need to be replaced with 'seeing without understanding' and 'seeing with understanding', then the symbolic application of this miracle to the Christological discussion becomes clear. Whereas the crowds might well be characterized as 'still blind' in their identification of Jesus as John, Elijah or a prophet, Peter's confession reveals that he can 'see' something. Jesus is indeed the Christ. Stage I of the miracle is complete.[59] But the datum needs to be *interpreted*. When Jesus begins to provide that interpretation (8.31), Peter balks. He had made a confession which was technically correct, but he had done so without any insight into the significance of what he had said. H. Conzelmann rightly notes, 'Jesus does not deny that he is the Messiah. Only the *interpretation* of the correct confession by Peter . . . is false' [emphasis his].[60]

The material from 8.31–10.45 reveals that the disciples are still not correctly understanding the kingdom, the Messiah of the kingdom, or their own roles in the kingdom. They are being taught 'along the way'.[61] The disciples continue to be recipients of Jesus' instruction, instruction which the religious authorities are denied after they reject Jesus (3.6). The disciples qualify for it, not because they are particularly perceptive, but because they have shown that they are willing to accompany Jesus on the road that leads from Galilee, the beginning of their discipleship, to Jerusalem, its goal and fulfilment. That they are utterly unprepared to understand, let alone join, Jesus in all that lies ahead does not negate the fact that they are 'with him' (3.14) and 'around him' (3.34, 4.10).[62]

Mark 8.22-26 is a transitional passage, linking the immediately preceding discussion about discernment with the immediately following discussion about Christology, but also linking the preceding chapters about the secret kingdom with the following chapters about the discipleship road. It joins 7.31-37 in forming a bracket or frame around 8.1-21 and it joins 10.46-52 in forming a bracket or frame around 8.27–10.45. For Mark 'discernment' and 'discipleship' are inseparable.[63]

The Epistemology of Mark (Summary)

We present here a synoptic view of our findings in the previous chapter and in our study of 8.14-21. In the earliest part of his Gospel Mark portrays Jesus calling disciples to accompany him, but *not* appointing them for their official ministry as leaders of the renewed

Israel until *after* those already in religious leadership have proven their unworthiness by rejecting Jesus and the message he brings. Prior to the great transition (3.6 leading to 3.14) we have the disciples waiting in the wings while Jesus appeals overtly to Israel's leadership to hear and see the nature of, and the basis for, the claims he is making as the authoritative Son of Man, the preacher of God's message of the kingdom.

Israel's religious leadership rejects Jesus and he in turn ceases to appeal to them. Having excluded themselves from his company, they are consigned to ignorance. At this point the primary concern of Jesus shifts. Instead of instructing his opponents, he exposes their hypocrisy. His positive appeals are reserved for those willing to accompany and follow him.

Along with the change in target group comes a change in teaching *methodology*. After 3.6 Jesus presents his teaching almost exclusively in parables with hidden meanings and miracles with hidden implications. Where explanations are given they are not normally exhaustive explications of Jesus' hidden meanings. They are more often appeals to listen and see, with indicators as to what barriers will have to be overcome to render that possible.

While the predestinarian emphasis in Mark 4 is sometimes overlooked, far more often it is over-estimated. When Joel Marcus says that you cannot decide to hear, indeed that 'There is no suggestion that one can alter the sort of soil one is; God's will, it must be assumed, determines that. . .'[64] he is taking a dubious interpretation of a part of the chapter to obscure almost the whole of the rest. The constant appeals to hear and understand throughout Mark 4 and the rest of the Gospel clearly confirm the viewpoint of E.E. Lemcio that 'knowledge is morally conditioned, even for the "elect"'.[65] Faithful discipleship is a condition for knowledge; but it is not a prerequisite for additional teaching. As long as Jesus' disciples remain disciples, they remain the target of Jesus' appeals to see and hear, however disobedient or imperceptive they may be.[66]

Some have argued, and no one more forcefully than J. Coutts,[67] that in Mark's Gospel the disciples who are meant to understand and are given special tutorials remain far more dull than the Pharisees and other religious leaders whose education the Markan Jesus is trying to thwart.[68] The religious leaders, however, have no understanding of the Markan Jesus' esoteric teaching concerning the secret coming of the kingdom, the meanings of the miraculous deeds, and the nature of discipleship as defined *during* (and symbolically *in terms of*) the journey through Galilee to Jerusalem. Still less do they suspect that in destroying Jesus they are in fact destroying themselves. Ambrozic is surely correct that even if the 'understanding' of the demons and enemies cannot be distinguished terminologically from the 'understanding' gradually gained by the disciples, they are nevertheless fundamentally distinct.[69]

Within the narrative of Mark's Gospel there is a constant and often subtly formulated call for the disciples to truly hear and understand. The fact that they have chosen to follow is in itself sufficient to qualify them for the calls, the esoteric teaching which is *sometimes* supplied, and most of all the miracle of divine illumination. Their part is to set aside human ways of thinking which are tied inseparably to demonic ways of thinking (8.33), and to remove the barriers that prevent the word from bearing fruit (4.15-19). Jesus exhibits immeasurable patience with those who choose for him. He consigns to ignorance those who have chosen against him. The choice for or against Jesus is the crucial factor.

We cannot summarize Mark's teaching on epistemology without indicating the extent to which Mark himself (not merely the Markan Jesus) calls for discernment. He deliberately refrains from providing simple answers to important questions. He rather uses his narrative structure, his 'technical terms', and his theological stance to call the readers to understand. Rhoads and Michie are no doubt correct that part of Mark's purpose in the two stage healing of the blind person is to call the *reader* to look a second time to see more clearly what the author is trying to say with it.[70]

At precisely those places where Mark's text *deals with* the issue of divine illumination and the concomitant calls for discernment, Mark has been most successful in dealing with his readers in the same way Jesus dealt with his disciples. Both Jesus and Mark were dismal failures if 8.14-21 was an attempt to enlighten disciples/readers concerning the meaning of the feedings. If the dialogue and the text were alike designed to call for discernment, then the task of understanding Mark goes on and on, and the degree of scholarly consensus is hardly a measure of Mark's success or failure. He has deliberately *not* made things as explicit as he could.[71]

Mark is clearly modelling himself after the Jesus he presents, and was no doubt willing to suffer the same fate as his model. Not everyone would understand him. Not everyone would even think it important to try. Some would judge him both inept and foolish.

In all this it is essential for any exegete to try to steer a course between two dangers. On the one hand, one does not want to qualify for the caustic criticism that C.S. Lewis levelled against Bultmann and his followers:[72]

> These men ask me to believe they can read between the lines of the old texts; the evidence is their obvious inability to read (in any sense worth discussing) the lines themselves.

On the other hand, neither does one want to qualify for the penetrating question of the Markan Jesus to those who could not see past the 'lines themselves', 'Do you still not understand?' (Mark 8.21). Attempting to steer a course between Scylla and Charybdis[73] seems to be the main task of modern Markan scholarship. Whatever the dangers, it is by now clear that J.M. Robinson's insistence that we must not aim to draw inferences from the way Mark orders his material ('a subject upon which Mark is silent') is misguided advice.[74]

III. *Mark's Use of* βλέπω *in the Light of His Epistemology*

We have studied Mark 8.14-21, its context, and the broader issue of 'discernment'. We are now prepared to examine how Mark has used the term βλέπω in the Gospel and particularly in Mark 13. As indicated at the beginning of this chapter, our hypothesis is that Mark has used βλέπω as a technical term. In every one of its occurrences it focuses on a discernment process that looks past externals, or else it plays a significant role in a context which has that as its primary concern. What follows is a rapid survey of all the texts outside Mark 13 which utilize the term βλέπω. Most of the texts have already been cited. The remaining ones fit the pattern remarkably well. The texts will be taken in an order which is arranged more thematically than chronologically.

1.   *Mark 8.15*: In the light of all that has been said above, very few comments need to be made here. A.M. Hunter claims that what Jesus is really saying is, 'When you see Herod and the Pharisees getting together, then look out for trouble!'[75] This is surely incorrect. βλέπετε ἀπὸ . . . is much rather an appeal to the disciples to recognize and avoid the error of the Pharisees and Herod, not to attempt to avert an external

danger.[76] The context makes it certain that it is a call for preventative discernment, not protective vigilance.

2. *Mark 8.18*: It is self-evident that the concern here is to move beyond physical sight to a discernment of the inner significance of the miracles under discussion.

3. *Mark 4.12*: Here again it is clear that the concern is with the meaning below the surface of the parables. Spiritual discernment is the issue. The text is the suitable contrast to 8.18. There disciples are urged to 'see'. Here rejectors are prevented from the same. Both the miracles and the parables contain meanings that those with unseeing eyes and unhearing ears will miss or misunderstand.

4. *Mark 8.23 and 8.24*: As argued above, and as most scholars accept, the miracle of sight-giving is intended to function symbolically in relation to the disciples' need for enlightenment.

5. *Mark 4.24*: The command 'be observant of what you hear' (βλέπετε τί ἀκούετε), aside from being a brilliant mixed metaphor, is a clear call to look beneath the surface. The disciples are to discern the inner meaning of what they hear and see. Spiritual faculties are required and to the extent that what has been given is utilized, to that extent will more be given.

6. *Mark 12.38*: This is one of two very interesting uses of βλέπω in Mark 12. Those hearing Jesus in the temple are warned, 'Watch out for (βλέπετε ἀπό) the scribes'. As in 8.15 it is obviously not only a warning against the physical danger that the presence of the scribes imposes on Jesus and those around him, even though the idiom employed can have that meaning. It is much rather a call to discern what is really happening when the scribes carry on as they do. They imagine that they can hide their threadbare pretensions beneath their flowing robes.[77] Jesus calls for a more accurate appraisal. If it is a warning, it is a warning not to approve of that which earns the divine displeasure. The first usage of βλέπω in Mark 13 demonstrates that the disciples need the admonition.

Before examining Mark 12.14 we should note that in all the usages so far examined, we see Mark (and probably his tradition before him) using a perfectly ordinary term and/or expression in a way that focuses on a discernment of inner meaning. βλέπω need not be used to focus on anything beyond empirical seeing, but for Mark it always does. βλέπετε ἀπό need not mean anything more esoteric than 'be careful of a danger'. For Mark it always does. The same is true for the idiomatic expression, 'You do not see the face' (οὐ βλέπεις εἰς πρόσωπον) in 12.14.

7. *Mark 12.14*: While the expression as used in 12.14 can mean 'You treat everyone fairly', for Mark it surely means something far more subtle and interesting. The Pharisees and Herodians are trying to flatter Jesus. They credit him with the sort of neutrality and critical distance that they are feigning in their own questioning. It is subtle irony on Mark's part that what they are crediting to Jesus, he himself is putting on the debit side of their ledger (8.15). The Markan Jesus is most emphatically *not* one who treats all people on an equal basis without 'discerning the countenance of people' (12.14).[78] He is most certainly not impartial. In effect, their flattering words convey sentiments such as, 'You do not let your audience affect the content of your teaching, you are fully and equally open with everyone. So, give us a straight-forward answer to a straight-forward question'. Jesus was decidedly not in the habit of speaking with unmistakable clarity to one and all regardless of the true nature and the motivation of their enquiries. Ironically, in the face of all this talk of open, honest communication, their very question was a trap and so was Jesus' answer. Appropriating still another level of irony, one which depends on the literal translation of the idiom, the enquirers are correct that Jesus did *not* look 'at the face'.[79] He looked past it, and his answer to the question about taxes is designed to make that point clear to them in that response. No wonder the pericope ends with the comment, 'And they were amazed at him' (12.17).

8. *Mark 5.31*: We reach the final occurrence of βλέπω outside Mark 13. A casual reading of 'you see the crowd' (βλέπεις τὸν ὄχλον) in context would perhaps give the impression that here at least there is no attempt to focus on a special discernment of inner significances. But that would be too casual a reading. Mark, who is so concerned with the issues

of true discernment and also with the disciples' difficulty in attaining it, would no doubt have seen in the disciples' attempt to call *Jesus* to a more accurate appraisal of his external environment, one more piece of evidence that the disciples could not see *past* it. Of course Jesus could see the crowds thronging. It took his discerning eye to recognize the special needs that were being met and that there was faith in the heart of the woman who touched his garment.

It is remarkable that Mark should *consistently* utilize such an ordinary term as βλέπω and also a variety of idiomatic expressions that incorporate it, in an effort to warn against lack of perception, and as a call to discern that which is real behind surface appearances. It is, we submit, one more piece of evidence that the whole issue of epistemology, and in particular the matter of gaining adequate spiritual perceptions, is a central concern of Mark from beginning to end.

It can be demonstrated that other Markan terms for 'seeing', especially compounds of βλέπω, are also used by Mark with an eye to their significance for his epistemology.[80] Yet βλέπω is the one term which is used *consistently* in this way.[81] Is it significant that not once does the narrator ever utilize the term βλέπω in relation to Jesus? He is not in need of calls for discernment. In both the places where *narrative characters* apply the term to Jesus (5.31 and 12.14), they do it in a misguided way and their comments serve only to reveal their own need for better perception. A compound of βλέπω is used of Jesus in 11.11 with some interesting implications (see Chapter 5).

If we are not on a completely false trail, we have moved into a much better position for interpreting Mark 13. In that chapter βλέπω occurs no less than five times and in ways which are remarkably similar to the various uses of the term outside Mark 13. So often interpreters of Mark 13 uncritically assume that Mark 13 *must* endorse sign-seeking; after all the disciples are called to watch (βλέπετε) for them. Mark's use of the term argues for a very different conclusion.

IV. βλέπω *in Mark 13: Implications for Exegesis*

Various explanations have been offered for the frequent and strategic positioning of the term βλέπω in Mark 13. Several scholars have suggested that Mark utilized a '"blepete" source'.[82] Pesch and others have argued that it is part of the Markan redaction.[83]

We are much more concerned with the function of the term in Mark's finished product than with its source. The two most serious errors in this respect, which reappear in almost every discussion of Mark 13, are the following:

1. The possibility that the two main terms for 'watching' in Mark 13, i.e., βλέπω and γρηγορέω, might have entirely different functions, is hardly ever seriously entertained.

2. It is often assumed without question that the repeated calls to 'watch' (either term) are indicators that Mark imagines the end will certainly come very soon, and that signs of its arrival will indicate the same.

A response to the first will be deferred until the completion of the next chapter, except to give advance notice that we will be arguing the two terms are as functionally distinct as could be imagined for two terms which are occasionally, in other literature, almost synonymous.

In response to the second, it requires only a rapid survey of the uses of the term βλέπω in Mark 13 to demonstrate that the assumption is simply erroneous. If we are going to conclude that Mark expects the end very soon, we shall have to find better arguments than those based on the Markan use of βλέπω. Not a single occurrence of the term points to the nearness of the end!

The term βλέπω is utilized indicatively in 13.2 and concerns the misplaced admiration of the disciples for the temple buildings. It has nothing to do with the near arrival of the end or with signs: neither topic has been mentioned in the chapter to this point.

The imperative βλέπετε appears four times. Twice it is a call for discernment lest disciples be deceived concerning the events and personalities purported to usher in the end of the age (13.5, 23). Once it is used in relation to the persecution of believers. Only once is it used in a context that has anything directly to do with the timing of the end (13.33 in the context of 13.32-37), and there 'watching' is the required response precisely *because of human ignorance of the timing*. Those who assume that everything in 13.32-37 is designed to say, 'Watch closely, the end may be sooner than you think!' will have to consider very carefully the argument in the next chapter that it might well mean, 'Do not fail to follow with persistence, the end may be delayed longer than you imagine, (and in the interim proleptically fulfilled in ways you cannot predict!)'. Moreover, as the next chapter will indicate, the function of the term βλέπετε in Mark 13.33 is quite unrelated to the timing question. It is a call not to 'discern the times' but to 'discern the meaning of the parable'.[84]

The points that are being made by the use of βλέπω in Mark 13 are precisely the points being made by the use of the term in the rest of the Gospel. The points are:

1. *Do not be misled by external appearances* (esp. 13.2). In the light of Mark's call for discernment throughout his Gospel and especially the close association of that call with the term βλέπω, Jesus' question surely carries the nuances: 'Indeed your eyes are taking in the beauties of the temple. But are you really *seeing*? Do you discern the significance of its present status and coming fate? Do you realize what temple-centered concerns really imply and where they will lead? The disciples could see its stones and decorations. Jesus could see its character and its doom. We have good indication from the very beginning of Mark 13 that it will be centrally concerned with the question, 'What should the believer discern in the present splendour and future devastation of this magnificent temple?'

2. *Do not be deceived by false words and misleading deeds.* In the warning concerning deceivers, βλέπετε does not mean 'avert a physical danger', nor is it merely a call to a different sort of behaviour.[85] Both in 13.5 and in 13.23 it is a call to see past the externals and recognize the deceptions that lurk beneath persuasive words and deceptive 'signs'. Both Mark 12.14 and 12.38 are appropriate parallels.[86]

3. *Discern what it means to be persecuted as a Christian.* Mark 13.9 is certainly not a warning designed to help disciples avert persecution.[87] It is an invitation to go boldly into and through the persecutions that will come in response to a person's allegiance to Christ, for therein the deepest levels of discipleship are achieved and therein the greatest opportunities to advance the Gospel are found. The Markan Jesus is calling for discernment, not self-protection. The prophecy really says, 'You will indeed be persecuted. Do not fail to discern what this means and what issues from it!' (See Chapters 6 and 8). 'The warning is, of course, to *expect* these things—*not* to try to escape them' (emphasis hers).[88] If there is any hint that the disciples are called here to self-

preservation it is in the ironic sense that their lives are saved precisely by submitting to those who would take it (13.13; cf. 8:35)!

4. *Recognize the ways in which the secret kingdom is advancing.* It requires both Chapter 4 and Chapter 6 to establish this point. The point itself is that the call for discernment in 13.33 is a call to see the kingdom established in the passion of Jesus and the call for discernment in 13.9 is a call to see it advanced in the passion of the disciples. Unless the disciples have eyes and ears for it, they will miss the point.

Those who correctly note that in Mark 13 there is a clear call for discernment and an implication thereby that true insight and knowledge are gifts from God, frequently see in this an automatic confirmation that Mark 13 is drawing on a common stock of apocalyptic ideas.[89] The fact is that this theological-epistemological perspective is just as much at home in later wisdom literature,[90] and also very much at home in Old Testament prophetic literature.[91] Moreover, it is part and parcel of a theology that runs right through Mark's Gospel emphasizing discipleship/discernment, not an apocalyptic calendar.

Chapter 2 argues that Mark 13 (like Mark's entire Gospel) is antipathetic to 'sign-seeking'. The fact that the term βλέπω occurs with some regularity in Mark 13 does not, as some have suggested, argue in the other direction. On the contrary, it confirms the point. 'Watching' is not the *means* of 'sign-seeking', it is the *alternative to it*. There is a discernment call in Mark 13, but apocalyptic signs are not to be the object of one's 'watching'.

Chapter 4

A MARKAN PERSPECTIVE
ON DISCIPLESHIP FAITHFULNESS

Introduction

In 1935, R.H. Lightfoot asserted that in Mark 13, 'There is no reference to the impending passion'.[1] There are indeed no *explicit* references. Several scholars have been impressed by this 'lacuna' and postulated explanations. R. Pesch argued that Mark 13, as a later addition, has no integral relation to the rest of the Gospel;[2] É. Trocmé argued that this Gospel originally existed without the Passion narrative.[3] Both suggestions provide an explanation, though not the correct one, for Lightfoot's insight. Fifteen years later, Lightfoot was a pioneer in highlighting the subtle and effective ways in which Mark linked Mark 13 and his Passion account even without explicit cross-referencing.[4] Most impressive of the connections is the 'four watch schema' of the passion night, Mark's apparently deliberate portrayal of the events of the passion night in terms of the four watches listed in 13.35, 'evening ... midnight ... cockcrow ... early morning' (ὀψέ ... μεσονύκτιον ... ἀλεκτοροφωνίας ... πρωΐ).

It will be the primary function of this chapter to examine Lightfoot's suggestion and analyse its implications for interpreting Mark 13.33-37, Mark's theology of the passion, Mark's view on when and how (and how many times!) the arrival of the 'eschatological Day' takes place, and various related matters, all within the context of an evaluation of Mark's intended meaning for one of the key terms meaning 'to watch'—γρηγορέω.

We continue to test our hypothesis that Mark intended Mark 13 to be interpreted in the context of the entire Gospel. The previous two chapters of our study linked Mark 13 with material preceding it; this one links it with material following it.

I. γρηγορέω, *The Doorkeeper Parable, and Gethsemane*

γρηγορέω—*An Introduction to the Term*

A. Oepke makes the point that γρηγορέω has both a literal and a figurative meaning and indicates how difficult it is to separate the two.[5] Both in the Gethsemane pericope and in the Doorkeeper parable, the only two places in Mark where the term appears, it functions on the two levels.

We have all the makings of another Markan 'technical term'. That βλέπω does not appear after Mark 13, nor γρηγορέω before it, is worth noting. That even Mark 13 is split, with the former term appearing five times in the material up to 13.33a and the latter term three times in the remainder of the chapter should provoke some reflection. What if Mark never intended the terms to be viewed as synonyms, but rather intended one term that enjoins watching (βλέπετε) to counsel correct discernment, and the other (γρηγορεῖτε) to counsel correct behaviour in the waiting time before the parousia, as we shall argue here? What if *neither* term has any connection with 'sign-seeking' or 'eschatological time-tables'? Is it significant that the entire discourse of Jesus opens with the former term (13.5) and closes with the latter (13.37)? If we can make a case that Mark deliberately selected both βλέπω and γρηγορέω as technical terms, controlled their usages, and contrasted their meanings, we will have some valuable clues as to how he intended us to understand Mark 13.

Correspondence Between the Doorkeeper Parable and the Gethsemane Account

We will be arguing that Mark intended a deliberate correlation between the time references in the Doorkeeper parable and those in the Passion account. To set the stage, we provide a brief correlation between the only two texts in Mark in which the term γρηγορέω appears, the very texts in which the connection between Mark 13 and the passion is clearest.[6] The Gethsemane account will be discussed again when we trace the four watches through the passion night.

The links between the Doorkeeper parable (13.33-37) and the Gethsemane account (14.32-42) are so remarkable that the burden of proof is surely on anyone who wants to consider them coincidental. If they are deliberate, so also, surely, is the larger pattern to which it points.

Werner Kelber sums up some of the correspondences, noting how 'watching-coming-finding-sleeping' forms a cluster of associations between the texts, and how the references to 'the hour' (ἡ ὥρα) link the passages.[7] Kelber is joined by numerous others who focus on the correspondences between the two texts.[8]

The evidence is that Mark intended the Doorkeeper parable to be correlated with the Gethsemane account: (1) no other texts in Mark can be paralleled so closely with either of these texts as these can with each other, (2) 'watching' (i.e., γρηγορέω) is not only restricted in Mark to these two texts, but is the keynote in both, (3) the threefold failure in Gethsemane to watch (14.37,40,41) is a fitting counterpart to the threefold injunction to do so (13.34,35,37), (4) 'sleeping in the crisis' is vice rather than virtue in both these texts but not elsewhere in Mark.[9]

If Mark did indeed intend that each of the two texts be read in light of the other, then this cannot fail to have significant implications. We suggest at least the following three, each of which will be examined in this chapter:

1. There may well be a better explanation than 'Markan clumsiness' for what some think is 'flawed editing' in both 13.33-37 and 14.32-42. Perhaps it is better to focus on why some of the anomalies of the texts were allowed to stand than on how they may have been produced.

2. The 'eschatological significance' of 13.32-37 must be kept in mind in evaluating Mark's meaning in 14.32-42. In what sense is Jesus' passion eschatologically significant in Mark's Gospel?

3. The 'passion-discipleship theology' of Mark, a central concern of 14.32-42, must be kept in mind in evaluating Mark's meaning in 13.33-37. In what sense is the positive model of Jesus and the negative model of the disciples in the passion exploited by Mark to clarify a picture of the sort of 'watching' that is necessary in the period that precedes the coming of the final 'Day' and 'Hour' (13.32)?[10]

Structural 'Problems' with the Doorkeeper Parable

It is widely held that Mark 13.33-37 is a combined and edited version of various other eschatological parables of Jesus. Because David

Wenham has recently dealt at length with the view of many scholars on the genesis of Mark 13.33-37, we choose to limit our discussion primarily to some comments on his views, not a rehearsal of theirs.[11] Wenham's attempt to account for the genesis of this parable ends by saying:[12]

> Our overall conclusion is that the view of Mark 13.34-36 as beginning with the parable of the talents but then switching over to the parable of the watchman works remarkably well in explaining the text as we have it, including the tensions that have so often bothered scholars.

To the objection that this makes Mark out to be an inept editor, Wenham responds, 'on almost any view of this rather difficult section Mark might have done better'.[13] How does one judge how successful Mark was without making a decision on Mark's theological aims? To determine whether or not Mark 'might have done better' must be an exegetical decision, not a source-critical one. It will be the function of this chapter to explicate and defend the following suggestions:

1. Mark's goal is to present 13.33-37 in such a way that it deliberately, albeit subtly, alludes to the immediately following passion story, especially the Gethsemane pericope.
2. Mark 13.32 is intended to have a double focus, primarily indicating ignorance about the timing of the End, but also warning that no one knows which other fulfilment(s) of the 'eschatological Day' might catch sleepers off guard in the meantime.
3. Mark intended to use a good deal of material in the Passion account to portray what it really means to obey the command, γρηγορεῖτε (watch!) and to portray models of obedience and disobedience to the command.

If we are correct then we can look for a teleological, not merely efficient cause of the 'difficulties' that Wenham is seeking to explain. The major difficulties noted by Wenham are the following:[14]

1. Mark gives the impression that he is going to tell a parabolic story, but the story never develops.
2. We are first given the impression that a man is about to go away on a long journey, but then are led to believe the crucial period of watching covers only the time period of a single night.

3. The reference to servants in the plural becomes somewhat superfluous when the focus changes to the doorkeeper in the singular.

We agree with Wenham that on *almost* any view of this rather difficult section Mark might have done better. If our suggestion concerning Mark's purpose is correct, he could scarcely have done better. That the parable never really gets told is well explained by the fact that he intends to portray the real 'parable' from 14.17–15.15.[15] That the focus shifts from a long journey to a single night is well explained by the fact that, although a long absence is in view on the primary level, Mark knows he intends to portray at a more subtle level the one crucial paradigmatic eschatologically-significant night during which one kept watch faithfully while the others all failed at their posts. That there is a shift from servants (plural) to a single servant (and specifically a doorkeeper), is explained by the fact that in the final Day and Hour there will be many servants, with Jesus playing the role of the master (ὁ κύριος [13.35]), but in the impending passion he will be portrayed as a servant, and specifically as a faithful doorkeeper. Shifts in focus may not indicate that Mark got the parables confused; they may indicate that greater care is needed in pinpointing the tropological meaning(s).[16]

The broadening of the application from 'you' (ὑμῖν) to 'everyone' (πᾶσιν) (13.37) is then not simply *expanding an audience* from four disciples to the whole group (within the story line) or from Jesus' first apostles to Mark's readers. It is *universalizing a model*: Jesus will serve as model doorkeeper for all disciples until he returns as the glorious Son of Man.[17]

Moreover, if Mark was doing what we think he was doing, we have a perfect explanation for the three different terms for 'watching' which are utilized. The major term γρηγορέω (13.34f., 37) is the one Mark is deliberately selecting for special treatment, the term he intends to load with both eschatological and passion-discipleship content. The term that precedes the 'parable' is ἀγρυπνέω (13.33), a perfect choice to focus on the major concern at the literal level. The term preceding both of these is βλέπω (13.33) a perfect choice to call the disciples (and readers) to discern in the following parable something more subtle than the obvious surface meaning.

Wenham's genetic explanation of the text may well be correct. If Mark harnessed two parables, one emphasizing the need to 'work while you wait' and the second emphasizing the need to 'stand faithful in the time of crisis', the textual anomalies are well 'explained'. But it is an explanation 'how it happened' not 'why it was done'. It is a *non sequitur* to infer that no teleological explanation need be sought if a genetic explanation has been provided. In our study of both Mark 13.33-37 and 14.32-42 and the larger Passion narrative, we accept the suggestion of W. Kelber:[18]

> What looks like a flawed text, controlled by disparate pre-Mkan (sic) traditions, may well prove to be under Mkan control, if we persist in reading the text within the Mkan theological framework.

It has occasionally been suggested that Mark deliberately introduced anomalies into the Doorkeeper parable (or at least allowed them to stand), because the meaning he intended took precedence over the coherence of the parable *as a story*. By far the most satisfying explanations for the anomalies, frequently alluded to but rarely evaluated, is the view brought forward by R.H. Lightfoot over 30 years ago:[19]

> The question has often been asked why it seems to be assumed in 13.35 that the coming of the Lord of the house will take place at night, and not by day. ... Is it possible that there is here a tacit reference to the events of that supreme night before the passion? On that *evening* the Lord *comes* for the last supper with the twelve; the scene in Gethsemane, and still more the arrest ... would take place towards midnight; Peter denies the Lord at cockcrow; and *in the morning* the chief priests with the elders and scribes, and the whole council, held a consultation, and bound Jesus, and carried him away, and *delivered him up* to Pilate. (emphasis his)

Perhaps Mark 13.33-37 is not, as Jeremias and others suggest, a parable about the passion which has been misplaced in an eschatological context. Perhaps it is an eschatological parable passed on by an editor/author with a much more profound view of the relationship between eschatology and the passion than has usually been suspected.

II. *The Four Watch Schema of the Passion Night*

Introduction
Few Markan interpreters have attempted to draw implications from Lightfoot's suggestion that Mark deliberately correlated the Doorkeeper parable with the passion night by measuring out the

events of the last night in accordance with the four watches listed in Mark 13.35. Still fewer have attempted to provide a secure footing for the suggested correlation itself. By far the strongest argument in favour of the view that Mark intended the correlation is the way he has *used* the Passion account to trace out the models of faithfulness and unfaithfulness in that crisis. His concern seems to be that post-resurrection disciples (and readers) might be instructed in the behaviour required of them as they await the return of the absent master.

There are, however, a few other arguments that are worth noting. Throughout the Gospel, Mark betrays little interest in exact time sequences. Suddenly, after 14.17, he counts the watches of the night and continues through three hour intervals right through to the burial of Jesus.[20] Furthermore, the very presence of four three-hour watches with their colloquial Roman titles is best explained as Mark's adaptation of his source to Roman readers, since traditionally the Jews marked off the night in three four-hour watches.[21] If it is a Markan adaptation both in 13.33-37 and in the Passion account, we have added reason to think he intentionally correlated them. Is Mark simply facilitating some kind of catechetical or liturgical need in the early church,[22] or is there a profound and subtly presented purpose for the pattern in relation to his overall Gospel message?

The building blocks for the following study of Mark's passion night have been set in place by many scholars. Lightfoot suggested the four watch scheme itself. Numerous scholars have noted that Mark seems to be deliberately contrasting Jesus and the disciples at various points in Mark's Passion account.[23] Several scholars have noted that discipleship failure is emphasized in each of the four watches.[24] What no one has argued is that in each of the four watches Mark is portraying Jesus as the counterpart to the disciples, succeeding exactly where they fail, and in such a way that his success atones for their failure. What seems to have been overlooked is that Mark has utilized the juxtaposing of narratives here, as elsewhere, to make subtle points above and beyond what the individual pericopes contain. And what seems to have been overlooked is that the overall teaching on discipleship which emerges provides a well-rounded definition of what it means to respond appropriately to the temptations and persecutions that post-resurrection believers (like Mark's readers)[25] would face as they awaited their absent master.

If the pattern that we shall trace is a plausible way of reading

Mark's text, there will be little need to justify the view that Mark
intended his readers to discover it. It is too meticulously crafted to be
only a figment of the readers' imaginations. While the fact that the
three-hour time intervals are counted off in the passion night as in
13.33-37 may appear to be merely a coincidental similarity, the clear
theological thread running through the entire passion night constitutes
a secure basis for accepting the 'Lightfoot Correlation' as a deliberate
Markan teaching structure, and the implications traced out in this
chapter as the reason he used that structure.

In terms of Mark's teaching methodology, we shall discover in this
chapter a phenomenon remarkably similar to that found in the
previous chapter of our study. Mark has harnessed a whole series of
incidents and presented them in such a way that each serves a
legitimate purpose within the historical narrative, and each has a
theological point of its own. But taken *together* the series demonstrates
that the whole can be greater than the sum of the parts, that the
author of the Gospel can have his own theological concerns over and
above the concerns registered in each of the incidents recorded. Has
Mark dropped subtle clues that he means more than he says? We
think so.

'In the Evening': The Fellowship Bond is Broken

Robert Fowler obviously pushes things out of proportion in
evaluating the last supper as a divorce between Jesus and his
disciples.[26] Yet we find in the upper room a very jarring collocation of
Judas' betrayal and Jesus' self-sacrificial death. Judas, for the sake of
financial gain (14.10-12), was willing to sell a righteous one; Jesus, at
the cost of his own life, was willing to buy back the guilty (10.45,
14.24).

There seems to be a deliberate attempt to focus on the fact that
both unimaginable deeds are linked to table fellowship. It is precisely
'while they were reclining and eating' (ἀνακειμένων αὐτῶν καὶ
ἐσθιόντων 14.18a) that Jesus announces the presence of a betrayer.
Moreover, the betrayer himself is identified explicitly as 'one eating
with me' (ὁ ἐσθίων μετ' ἐμοῦ 14.18b). The point is further
emphasized two verses later when Jesus identifies the betrayer as 'the
one dipping (bread) into the bowl with me' (ὁ ἐμβαπτόμενος μετ'
ἐμοῦ εἰς τὸ τρύβλιον 14.20b). There is a clear allusion to Ps. 41.9 in
which it is lamented that the closest of companions, one who has
shared table fellowship, lifts his heel against the righteous one.[27]

We must not overlook the reverse side of the picture. The table fellowship bond which the betrayer is shattering is the object of Jesus' own personal constructive concern. The institution account is not only specifically noted as taking place 'while they were eating' (ἐσθιόντων αὐτῶν 14.22), but its elements themselves are taken from the meal they shared. Indeed the very nature of the meal is to link the bond of fellowship with the act of sharing food. Thus, the heinousness of Judas' (and the other disciples') failures is accentuated by the fact that it takes place not only at table fellowship, but at the very table fellowship in which Jesus is demonstrating his own faithfulness to God and to them.[28]

D. Senior correctly notes that:[29]

> The institution account with its stress on the deep bond between Jesus and his followers and Jesus' ultimate triumph over death is a strong counterpoint to the surrounding scenes which brood over discipleship weakness and failure.

We should not imagine that Jesus and the disciples are faithful and Judas alone is unfaithful. Much rather Jesus alone is faithful, and the disciples along with Judas are unfaithful. The form of their question, 'Is it I?' (μήτι ἐγώ; 14.19b) does not indicate reflective self-probing, but utter self-confidence that they would never fail their master,[30] the one thing they *all* do, in one way or another, before the night is over. As L. Schenke has argued, the point Mark stresses in 14.18-21 is not the identification of the traitor, but the fact that he belongs to the Twelve.[31] The failure of the others will not be as heinous or irreversible as Judas', but they will be unfaithful servants nevertheless.

Their self-confidence is revealed explicitly in the debate that takes place in the temporally and topographically transitional scene on the way to Gethsemane (14.26-31). To quote Senior again:[32]

> The passover scenes conclude with predictions of desertion (v. 27) and denial (v. 30) that veer sharply from the stress on the bond between master and disciple so solemnly celebrated in the previous scene.

The disciples are confident of their ability to stand; Jesus is confident in God's faithfulness to raise him up, even though he be struck down (14.21, 25). The magnitude of Jesus' faithfulness and self-sacrifice is revealed in the fact that his self-giving and promise of renewed fellowship (14.22-24,28) are given not only with full knowledge that the disciples would defect, but also *because* of that fact.

All this takes place in the first watch (cp. 'and when evening came' [καὶ ὀψίας γενομένης 14.17a] with 'evening' [ὀψέ 13.35]). Mark 14.17-31 is not only the report of a betrayal and an instituted covenant meal. The 'evening watch' is a study in the contrast between faithfulness and unfaithfulness. It is an illustration of doorkeepers caught sleeping,[33] and of a single doorkeeper who faithfully served at his post.

To be unfaithful 'in the evening' (ὀψέ) is to hand over God's righteous person for personal gain. It is to be over-confident in one's ability to stand in the crisis. It is to break the bond of fellowship so solemnly celebrated in the covenant meals. Would any insincere or half-sincere adherents to a Christian church in a time of persecution be tempted to do any of these? Can it be doubted? Faithfulness, on the contrary, is defined as self-sacrifice for others, willingness to take the hard road of God's choosing, and confidence in God for a victorious future.

If Mark is deliberately using the Passion narrative to help define what it means to watch (γρηγορέω) in the waiting period before the consummation, then 'watching' certainly has nothing to do with watching for portents.[34] It has much more to do with faithful discipleship in a time of crisis. If there is any doubt about this last point, it should be dispelled by a quick look at the second watch of the passion night.

At Midnight: The 'Eschatological Hour' is Missed

The Gethsemane scene vividly portrays the contrast between the faithful Jesus and his unfaithful disciples. M. Dibelius pinpointed accurately the focus on contrast:[35]

> The content of the scene in Gethsemane is the contrast between the Lord who, knowing his destiny, is resigned to God's will, and the sleeping disciples. Not the torment suffered by Jesus, but his conquest of the torment, is of importance: 'Not what I will, but what thou wilt'. Otherwise, the contrast between him and the ignorant, sleeping disciples would not be complete.

Mark has been at pains to make clear throughout his Gospel that the disciples, had they been faithful, would have stayed with Jesus through his passion. They would have taken their crosses and followed (8.34-38). They would not have 'fallen away' (14.27). They would have made good on the promise, 'Even if I have to die with you, I will never disown you' (14.31b). The disciples in Gethsemane were called to pray lest they fall into temptation (εἰς πειρασμόν). In the context of Mark's thought this cannot mean that the disciples, had they prayed, would not have been asked to take up the cross; they were to pray rather that when they were tempted to be unfaithful, they would not yield.

But we are protesting too much. Surely no one would wish to deny that one of Mark's primary aims in narrating the Gethsemane incident is to portray Jesus as the one who was faithful to the will of his Father, and his disciples as those who gave in to the weakness of the flesh. He is modelling the 'watching' which they fail to practise.[36]

> In the course of this night-time Jesus is alert, watching and praying as his crisis approaches (cf. 14.34,38). But the disciples 'sleep' and are tragically unprepared (14.37,40,41).

The correlation between the Doorkeeper parable and the Gethsemane story obviously casts 'an eschatological light' on the latter. We must not, however, overlook the converse of that. The discipleship concerns so self-evident in the Gethsemane account must influence our reading of Mark's intentions in 13.33-37. To obey the command γρηγορεῖτε! in Gethsemane is to pray in the crisis, resist the weakness of the flesh, willingly submit to suffering according to God's will, and recognize that God's eschatological promises are being fulfilled, not only in spite of the suffering of his righteous one(s), but because of it. Again it is clear that 'watching' in the Doorkeeper parable has nothing to do with observing signs, with averting danger, or with knowing when. It has to do with faithful discipleship, prayer, obedience, willingness to suffer. The Hour caught the disciples sleeping and unaware in Gethsemane; it must not happen next time. Because Jesus had modelled faithful 'watching', he was prepared for the arrival of The Hour, and *therefore* recognized its advent.[37]

James and John had previously been very glib and self-confident in their insistence that they could drink the cup Jesus drinks (10.39). Peter had been equally self-confident when he promised he would be willing to die with Jesus (14.31). Jesus knows that self-confidence is inadequate if there is not faithful discipleship to match. Given the performance of precisely these three in the garden, they cannot but fail.

Linked directly to the Gethsemane scene is another temporal and topographical transitional narrative (14.43-52). Both Jesus and his disciples are now set on courses with predictable outcomes. He has watched; they have slept. He has prayed; they have not. He trusts God; they trust in the flesh. The captors arrive. Naturally the disciples strike out and flee; they have not been faithful to their discipleship obligations. Naturally Jesus willingly embraces his fate, for he has yielded to and discerned his Father's plans.

How relevant would all this be for a persecuted community? Would any be tempted to sleep instead of pray during the night when the captors were on their way? Would any lose their confidence that even through suffering, God was working out his purposes? Would any strike out at the captors? Would any be willing even to disobey their Lord to avoid capture?

Three times Jesus had prayed 'one hour' (μίαν ὥραν 14.37). Another one of the watches of the night has come and gone. With the striking of the midnight hour (deliberately not so-called, see below) Jesus stands faithful while those around him fall away. The contrast is vivid, as Mark deftly continues his double portrait and helps his readers see with ever greater clarity the meaning of true watching.

If the disciples had 'watched' in Gethsemane, they might have been ready to join Jesus in the passion. One disciple does 'follow' on the literal level; he will provide the contrast to Jesus in the next night watch.

'At the Cockcrow': Saving One's Life and Losing It
With the crowing of the cock (14.72), the perceptive reader discerns the converging of a whole series of events, motifs and themes. Another night watch has been clocked. Jesus' prophecy has been fulfilled (14.30). A Biblical model in which lower animals rebuke God's people for their unfaithfulness has been employed.[38] Peter has been awakened from his metaphorical 'slumber' to realize (along with the reader) what has happened. Peter has been unfaithful in his hour of trial, precisely while Jesus was being faithful.

The portrayal of Peter's progressive defection is employed to heighten the growing contrast between the faithful Jesus and his unfaithful 'follower'.[39] The brilliant structuring of the account, with the story of Peter's denials superimposed upon the story of Jesus' hearing before the Sanhedrin, serves to produce remarkable irony throughout the narrative. Peter is found to curse Jesus at the same time and in the same place in which Jesus makes his good confession.[40] The charge of blasphemy is laid on Jesus instead of on Peter who deserves it.[41] Jesus is mocked as a false prophet precisely while his prophecy about Peter is being fulfilled.[42] Jesus is proved a true prophet in precisely the act by which Peter is proved a false one (cf. their contrary prophecies in 14.29-31).[43]

Those who argue that here Peter caps the total defection of the twelve and puts himself out of range of restitution not only misconstrue 14.28 and 16.7, but overlook the significance of the fact that through the passion, Jesus' faithfulness is most fully expressed in the very fact that he is 'covering for' those around him who fail. They also overlook the significance of Peter's final weeping. Peter had indeed been 'caught napping', but God sent a cock to awaken him and lead him towards repentance and restitution.[44] Peter will not be punished for his blasphemy; Jesus will undeservedly take the punishment in his place. Peter will not suffer the deserved fate of a false prophet; Jesus the true prophet will suffer instead. Peter who deserves to lose his life because he is trying so hard to save it, will have it bought back by the one who will save his life precisely because he is willing to lose it.[45]

The emphasis in the narrative is on the stark contrast between Jesus and Peter. Jesus stands before the officials of the Jewish religion, sometimes in silent confidence, sometimes with a bold confession on his lips. Peter cowers before a servant girl and anonymous bystanders, stammering and lying through his teeth. It is a study in contrasts.[46]

Would anyone in Mark's persecuted community be tempted to deny their Lord when faced with questions of allegiance to Christ, either within a hostile court or in its environs? To ask the question is to answer it. Mark has deliberately used the third watch, the 'cockcrow' (ἀλεκτοροφωνίας), to fill out further the contours of the sort of faithful watching that is required until the final consummation. Jesus provides the model. Peter portrays the error into which many would be tempted to fall.

'In the Morning': No One is 'With' Jesus
P. Benoit argues that Mark had two separate 'trial' traditions among his sources. He wonders why Mark did not combine them, or at least place them side by side.[47]

Why then distinguish them as a night session and a morning session? This is a real difficulty for which, it seems to me, the critics do not provide a solution.

Might it not be argued that Mark deliberately intercalated the one story with the account of Peter's denial for the reasons given above, and deliberately reserved the other account for the morning 'watch'? Significantly the second account is introduced with the telling words 'and immediately in the early morning' (καὶ εὐθὺς πρωΐ 15.1) (cf. 'early morning' [πρωΐ 13.35]). In this final watch the tragedy of the passion night reaches its climax: none of Jesus' followers are with him any longer.

Jesus had commissioned his disciples specifically 'in order that they might be with him' (ἵνα ὦσιν μετ᾽ αὐτοῦ 3.14). They could not be sent out (ἀποστέλλω 3.14) without meeting that condition. How the paradigm was shattered through the passion night! Jesus plans a special meal '*with* his disciples' (μετὰ τῶν μαθητῶν 14.14). Jesus arrives at the supper '*with* the twelve' (μετὰ τῶν δώδεκα 14.17); there he announces that there is a betrayer in the room, 'the one eating *with* me' (ὁ ἐσθίων μετ᾽ ἐμοῦ 14.18); the betrayer is explicitly called 'one of the twelve, the one dipping (bread) into the bowl *with* me' (Εἷς τῶν δώδεκα, ὁ ἐμβαπτόμενος μετ᾽ ἐμοῦ εἰς τὸ τρύβλιον 14.20). Judas is physically '*with* him'. In no other sense are the words true. In Gethsemane Jesus takes his three closest disciples '*with* him' (μετ᾽ αὐτοῦ 14.33), but they desert their posts. In the courtyard of the High Priest, Peter is not only described as sitting '*with* the servants' (μετὰ τῶν ὑπηρετῶν 14.54); his dissociation of himself from Jesus takes the form of denying the charge: 'You also were *with* the Nazarene Jesus' (καὶ σὺ μετὰ τοῦ Ναζαρηνοῦ ἦσθα τοῦ Ἰησοῦ 14.67). By the time three watches of the night are past, not one of those who should have been '*with* him' was there. If the reader had not already been told that there would be a reunion on the other side of the passion, it would be a dark picture indeed.

Jesus recruited a band of followers to be '*with* him'. It would be their calling to replace the Jewish leadership structure that was '*against* him'. Yet, at the critical moment when the sentence is given out, Jesus finds himself alone.[48] The faithful people of God has gradually been narrowed and finally identified with the person of Jesus alone.[49] Jesus will now die in order to redeem his disciples. In each of the previous night watches his coming death was, in subtle but real ways, defined as redemptive and substitutionary. In the fourth watch an anticipatory substitution is enacted; he goes alone to his death; a sinner (Barabbas, 15.11) goes free.

Would any in the Markan community have been tempted to join with the religious and political status quo if that afforded them an opportunity to avoid the cross? Surely Mark has deliberately taken the model of Jesus as his way of showing the believers what their response should be to the various pressures that will come to bear on them, in the various watches of the night, throughout their struggling, serving and watching until the return of the Son of Man.

III. *Implications of Mark's Four Watch Schema for Interpreting Mark*

It seems certain that Mark has deliberately drawn attention to the contrast between Jesus and his disciples in the matter of faithfulness/unfaithfulness through the passion night. Jesus has taught the way of the cross, and now he walks the road alone. Those who would be his followers in the post-resurrection age will be called to model their behaviour after that of Jesus, to stand as he did in all the watches of the night.

If Mark deliberately presented the passion material according to the four watches of the night and used 13.33-37 to point to the model of Jesus, then neither Mark's passion/discipleship theology nor his eschatology should be evaluated without drawing in the implications of the four watch schema.

The Meaning of γρηγορέω

We noted in the previous chapter that distinctions have often been blurred in the interpretation of Mark's Gospel between 'ignorance', 'unfaithfulness', and 'rejection'. A failure to make a clear distinction between βλέπω and γρηγορέω is at least partly to blame.

In the first half of the Gospel, the disciples neither reject Jesus, nor are they unfaithful; they are, however, frequently ignorant of that which Jesus intends them to understand. Throughout the discipleship section (Mark 8.27–10.45, plus the transitional giving-of-sight stories, 8.22-26 and 10.46-52), they gain a great deal of understanding as Jesus makes his teaching much more plain. There are indications, however, that what they are learning is putting a strain on their willingness to be obedient.

By the time we reach the passion of Jesus, there are no more calls for discernment. The disciples have been given all the education the earthly Jesus will give them. The concern becomes one of faithfully following what they have learned. Mark 13 is the dividing point. Prior to it, the watchword is βλέπω. They are to discern meaning and truth. Subsequent to it, the watchword is γρηγορέω. They are to follow through in faithful discipleship, taking up their crosses after Jesus. It is extremely important to make a clear separation between the two terms for watching, as well as between the two concerns of Mark: (1) learning prior to the passion; (2) faithfulness through it.

It is *not* the case that the disciples' main problem in Gethsemane, or for that matter through the whole passion, was one of ignorance. It was one of disobedience and unfaithfulness. Kelber claims that the closed eyes of the disciples in Gethsemane are symbols of the fact that they fail to discern the eschatological nature of the hour.[50] However, this is to ignore a clear conceptual separation in Mark between non-understanding and non-following. It has the effect of inverting what Mark actually says. In Gethsemane they are not chided for what they fail to understand, but for what they fail to do. Jesus is no longer giving them an education in 'passion Christology'; he and they are alike being tested on what they have previously learned. Jesus, by passing the test, is demonstrating the behaviour they ought to be practising, and calling them to follow. Their failure, therefore, is defined as a failure to obey, a failure to pray, a failure to trust, a failure to follow. The problem here is not that spiritual senses are in need of sharpening; it is that the flesh is too weak.

To watch (γρηγορέω) in the unknown time before the master of the house comes back is to model oneself after Jesus. It is to be willing to die if need be rather than betray a fellow believer for personal advantage. It is to pray rather than sleep in the hour of testing, to stand and trust rather than strike and flee when the captors arrive, to make a true (even if fatal) confession rather than lie to avoid danger, to save one's life by losing it rather than losing it in a bid to keep it safe. It is resisting the temptation to play it safe, to hide in the crowd and to compromise with the authorities. To watch (γρηγορέω) is therefore *not* a discernment process; *it is to act in obedience*. Indeed, it is to act in obedience even when full knowledge is withheld.[51]

Both in Gethsemane and in the Doorkeeper parable, the commanded 'watching' is the appropriate *response* to the fact that they are ignorant of the hour; it is not a way of discerning which hour brings eschatological fulfilment. The whole point of the Doorkeeper parable seems to be that those who faithfully watch will be ready when the hour arrives, though they will be in no better position than anyone else to determine in advance which hour that will be. The very command to watch faithfully is grounded in the fact of ignorance ('watch, *because* you do not know when the time will come' [ἀγρυπνεῖτε· οὐκ οἴδατε γὰρ πότε ὁ καιρός ἐστιν 13.33]; 'watch *therefore for* you do not know . . . ' [γρηγορεῖτε οὖν, οὐκ οἴδατε γὰρ πότε . . . 13.35]).[52] The master *intends* to arrive unexpectedly. To watch (γρηγορέω) is to be instructed by the master and to obey faithfully. It is precisely the *incalculability* of the hour that motivates the required obedience.[53] Mark 13 does certainly issue repeated calls for discernment and understanding (βλέπετε—see Chapter 3). Discernment and understanding, however, are not related to the *timing* of the End. The timing itself is utterly unknown. The calls for faithful service and discipleship (γρηγορεῖτε) are grounded in that very fact.

Jesus as the Model Doorkeeper/Disciple
Another point about Mark 13.33-37 that is rarely commented on, becomes important here. *There is no indication at all in the parable that the doorkeeper is called to watch specifically for the master's arrival!* Luke, in a related passage, specifies that the goal of the watching is 'so that when he comes and knocks they can immediately open the door for him' (Lk. 12.36). No such specification is made in Mark 13.33-37.[54] The Markan parable seems to speak its message most clearly if the primary call is to be a faithful watchman *on the master's behalf* because he is away, rather than to be a faithful watchman *for his appearance* because he is returning. To be a watchman, as the parable itself makes clear, is to exercise authority (13.34) along with all the other servants, carrying out a specific responsibility during the time that the householder is away. The key concern seems to be that disciples be ever vigilant lest intruders despoil the house. The point at issue is not whether or not a disciple will be found faithfully at his post at the single and precise instant of the master's return. The point at issue is whether or not he has been faithful *right through* the long night of waiting. To be asleep at any point along the way is to become an unfaithful servant, and to fall prey to the enemy. Even a moment's sleep might permit the intruder access.[55]

From this point of view it is clear why Mark was prepared to portray Jesus throughout the passion night, not as the master of the house, but as the faithful servant, the doorkeeper who watched all through the night. While it is clear from beginning to end in Mark's Gospel that Jesus is the 'Master' and his disciples are 'servants', it is also clear that one of the roles Jesus takes on as Master is to model servanthood. This is especially so in terms of the journey from Galilee to the cross in Jerusalem. D. Dormeyer argued the same in his study of Jesus' passion.[56] Jesus walked the road to its conclusion, that thereafter his followers might do the same. He came as 'servant' the first time; they must serve him thereafter. He stood as a faithful doorkeeper the first time; he would return as the master of the house. The surface of the parable creaks a little, but it has profound depth.

Passion Theology and Eschatology
It should now be clear why those who imagine that the correlation between Mark 13.33-37 and 14.32-42 is an invitation to read apocalyptic-eschatological implications into Gethsemane and the passion are putting the cart before the horse. Reading 14.32-42 in the light of an incorrect perception of Mark 13.33-37 can only result in the obscuring of both. But if γρηγορέω in both texts is defined in terms of the behaviour of Jesus in Gethsemane and in the other three watches of the night, then it is an eschatology *highly infused with Mark's passion theology* which must be correlated with the Gethsemane pericope, not an eschatology on the lookout for signs and apocalyptic phenomena.[57] While it is certainly true that Mark wants his readers to be able to see that all their suffering is 'eschatologically oriented',[58] he also wants them to know that it is not in straining their eyes for the coming of the Son of Man, but in faithfully serving, and if necessary, suffering, that they obey the command γρηγορεῖτε.[59]

Not a few scholars have expressed the view that Mark has provided his eschatological discourse with a singularly inappropriate conclusion.[60] A correct apprehension of both βλέπω and γρηγορέω, suggests that the fit is remarkably good: the main discourse argues against sign-seeking, and the conclusion grounds faithful discipleship in the fact that the timing of the End is unknown.

When we have interpreted 13.33-37 in the light of its connection with the passion, we can take another look at the passion and observe the significance of its 'eschatological features'.

Throughout the passion narrative, and particularly in the death scene, the perceptive reader catches hints that Old Testament allusions to the 'Day of the Lord' are being utilized (cf. esp. 15.33; Isa. 13.10). Jesus' passion proleptically fulfils Old Testament eschatological expectations. It brings in the kingdom,[61] though the kingdom remains a secret kingdom and only those with eyes to see can see it.[62] T.A. Burkill comments that Mark makes no attempt to comment on the nature of the connection between the passion and the parousia, and concludes that Mark's position 'has all the appearance of being a tentative one'.[63] On the contrary, it has all the appearance of being a subtle and profound one.

The Meaning of Mark 13.32

It has often been taken for granted that there are only two alternatives concerning the meaning and function of Mark 13.32. Either it means that no one, except the Father, has any idea when the End will come, or else it means that, though the time period is bounded by a single generation and signs help determine when it is very near, the exact day and hour itself can never be pinpointed.

The primary meaning of 13.32 (interpreted in the light of 13.33) is that the timing of the final eschatological event is known only to God. However, if Mark deliberately uses 13.33-37 to point to Jesus and his way of following through with his passion as the appropriate doorkeeper/discipleship model, then one is led immediately to postulate other functions for 13.32 which supplement, without replacing, the primary one. Those who insist that Mark is saying, 'the end may be closer than you think', are probably wrong in relation to Mark's *primary* meaning, but may be correct in relation to a *secondary* one. Mark may well be saying: the Final End is incalculable and could be long delayed, but the intermediate application(s) of 13.32, equally incalculable, may be closer than imagined. Mark's comment is remarkably general when he says, 'But *concerning* that Day or the Hour no one knows' (περὶ δὲ τῆς ἡμέρας ἐκείνης ἢ τῆς ὥρας οὐδεὶς οἶδεν). Is it possible that not only the *timing* of the event is unknown? Is there also something unknown about the character of the day and hour? Or even about the way (or ways) in which it will arrive? It is well known that Augustine encouraged believers to read 13.32 as though their own personal end was in view.[64] Is it possible that, in Mark's understanding, Jesus had *his* own personal 'end' in view as well as the final End? If this seems like sheer speculation, perhaps it can be rescued from the charge by a reminder that in Gethsemane, and referring to the *passion*, Jesus says explicitly, 'The Hour has come' (ἦλθεν ἡ ὥρα 14.41),[65] and less often noted, but perhaps even more important, 'that Day' (ἐκείνη ἡ ἡμέρα), so characteristically a technical term for the day of eschatological fulfilment,[66] is utilized by Mark to refer to the *passion* (2.20)![67] 'That Day' and 'the Hour' (ἐκείνη ἡ ἡμέρα and ἡ ὥρα) may well have more than one referent. It is almost certain that they are more than simple time designations. According to Mark's narrative, the first fulfilment of 13.32 occurred but a few days after the admonition to watch was given.[68]

Mark might well have had, in addition to the primary reference to the final end, and the secondary reference to the passion of Jesus, also a tertiary reference to those within his own church who were undergoing persecution. Philip Carrington's comments are worth quoting in full:[69]

> *The idea of the advent is not fixed; it is not tied to one shape or form, or even to one event* .... What kind of coming would the Roman Christians think of as they listened to these words of Jesus in Mark's Gospel? For many of them it would be the touch of the lictor on their shoulder, or a raid on the ecclesia as it listened to the words of Christ, and a call to witness for his sake and the gospel's. For such the ordeal was sharp, the way was short, and the coming of the Son of Man immediate. Such a way of looking at it did exist in the Roman ecclesia; for in Hermas the persecutions under Domitian were regarded as a coming of the Son of God to inspect and test the building of his tower, and to approve or reject the stones which had been built into it (see Sim. ix). [emphasis his]

Vincent Taylor's insistence that 'Mark nowhere brings the teaching concerning the parousia into connection with the idea of Messianic suffering',[70] is difficult to sustain if Mark has intended the four watch schema we have outlined; it is impossible to sustain if 13.32 is itself ambivalent or even polyvalent in the ways suggested.[71]

That Mark countenances the possibility of a single prophecy finding fulfilment on various levels, should not surprise us. He opens his book by quoting one that does![72] It would be a mistake to expect Mark to denote only a single referent with every claim and description given. His religious traditions did not incline him to do so.

R.H. Lightfoot was correct when he said in 1935 that in Mark 13 'there is no reference to the impending passion',[73] that is, no *explicit* reference. He was equally correct when fifteen years later he compared Mark 13 with Mark 14 and 15 and said, 'the relationship may be closer and more subtle than was previously supposed'.[74] Mark often means more than he explicitly says. We dare not attempt to interpret Mark 13 without taking that into account.

The De-Apocalypticising of Mark 13

There is a growing tendency to see Mark 13 as an attempt to curb excessive 'apocalyptic speculation' and to promote discipleship and service, much as Paul does in II Thessalonians. Mark 13.33-37 is often thought to present a difficulty for this view. If Mark has deliberately presented the passion of Jesus as the ideal example of what it means to 'watch', then 13.33-37, far from presenting a difficulty for the view, confirms it. It is interesting that the earlier view of R. H. Lightfoot was that Mark 13 and also 16.7 raise the apocalyptic fever of the reader to 'the heights of expectation'.[75] After he noted the way in which Mark links the passion of Jesus to Mark 13,[76] his arguments fall on the other side, helping to state the case that Mark's real concern is not apocalyptic fever-raising, but faithful discipleship and service in the interim period, however short or long that period may be. We can now safely set aside any thought that Mark's concern is to teach readers how they can determine the timing of the End by the signs that precede it. His concern is to teach them how to live as faithful disciples without knowing when the End will come.

The Contrast between βλέπω and γρηγορέω

We summarize here the conclusions already reached. The 'watchword' in all of Mark 13, except in the concluding parable, is βλέπετε. The 'watchword' in the concluding parable is, in contrast, γρηγορεῖτε. There is no overlap here or in the rest of Mark's Gospel. Every occurrence of βλέπω outside Mark 13 precedes that chapter. Every occurrence of γρηγορέω outside Mark 13 follows that chapter. If the former term is a call for discernment and the latter term a call to faithful discipleship, then we find just what we should expect. The Gospel utilizes the first term in the twelve and a half chapters where the disciples are taught about the kingdom's secrecy and the need for divine illumination. It utilizes the latter term in the final chapters where we see on the one hand Jesus, working out of what has been taught, and on the other, the disciples failing to do what they should have learned. The final parable of Mark 13 is a call to learn from Jesus, learn from past mistakes, and in the unknown period before the parousia, carry out discipleship obligations faithfully.

There is only one place where the terms come close together. In Mark 13.33 we have the final occurrence of βλέπω. It is supplemented by an additional watchword, ἀγρυπνέω, calling for wakefulness, and then the terminology shifts to γρηγορέω through the remainder of the pericope and the Gospel. The term γρηγορέω, defined by its function in the Gethsemane account as illustrated through the passion night, outlines the duty of believers in the interim period before the master returns. The term which functions in the vehicle of the parable is ἀγρυπνέω; it is, after all, a parable about 'staying awake'. The term βλέπω is utilized to call for special insight into the meaning of the parable; something more subtle is being said than might at first be suspected.

If we are correct, the correlation with Mark 4.3ff. deserves comment. There an opening command to hear, (ἀκούετε), calls on the hearers/readers to 'hear' what is about to be conveyed in a parable about 'keeping one's ears open'.[77] Here an opening command to see, (βλέπετε), calls on the hearers/readers to 'see' what is about to be portrayed in a parable about 'keeping one's eyes open'. The first parable is about discernment. The second is about discipleship. Both are about the kingdom that is secretly advancing.

To hear and to see is, we recall, the very definition of true understanding, the very solution to the epistemological problem, the requirement for faithful citizenship in the secret kingdom. The matter is addressed directly in the teaching unit from 7.31–8.26, but it finds echoes throughout the Gospel.

Almost every English translation uses the same term, 'watch', for both βλέπω and γρηγορέω. An important distinction in the original text is thereby blurred.

Clues as to the Structure of Mark 13
Mark has not clumsily put together a chapter enumerating premonitory signs leading up to the Day of the Lord and then contradicted it with a call to begin watching *immediately*, since the End could well come at any moment.[78] Neither has he contented himself with deliberately juxtaposing incompatibles.[79]

The main body of Mark 13 contains an insistent call to discern the significance of the events which are predicted and to which allusion is made (13.5-23). There is no indication that discernment of an eschatological time-table or of the timing of the End is in view. The conclusion of Mark 13 defines appropriate behaviour in the time that separates the present from the End. It clearly indicates that ignorance of the End's timing is God's intention for disciples and a motivation for faithfulness.

A strong presumption is generated that while the events that *must* precede the End are taking place (13.5-23), believers must be recognizing the meaning and significance of those events *without* being deluded into thinking time charts can be constructed on the basis of them. So also the presumption is generated that at some point no more events must *necessarily* occur before the End of the Age, so that watchfulness at every instant is required, lest the unexpected arrival of the Son of Man catch disciples unfaithful at their posts. If this is correct, then 13.5-23, rather than being a catalogue of 'premonitory signs', is an indicator of the 'preparatory stages' which must occur to inaugurate the unknown time of waiting and serving. Is it possible that 13.5-23 outlines, not the final events of the post-resurrection age, but the inaugural ones? Though we have much more work to do, some pieces seem to be falling into place.

Chapter 5

MARK'S TEMPLE THEOLOGY

Introduction

Thus far the evidence seems to support the view that Mark intends the thirteenth chapter of his Gospel to contribute to an overall message calling believers to:

1. Eschew the seeking of signs and guard against those parading them (Chapter 2).
2. Discern the subtle meanings of historical events (and of Mark's text) in order to grasp theological points which are neither self-evident, nor unambiguously explained (Chapter 3).
3. Forgo calculations of eschatological timing in favour of faithful discipleship, service and suffering during the incalculable time period before the End (Chapter 4).

If we are correct, we should expect Mark to drop subtle clues in his Gospel as to precisely how one ought to interpret the significance of the main events prophesied for the time period during which the End is awaited, and faithful discipleship is practised. While there is a great diversity of events predicted for the time period covered by 13.5-23, it is clear that two sorts of events dominate: various kinds of suffering and persecution coming upon believers and/or the elect (τοὺς ἐκλεκτούς 13.20), and the event prophesied in 13.2, the fall of the temple.

It is the goal of this chapter to study *Mark's Temple Theology* and of the next to study *Suffering and Persecution*. We shall be on the lookout for clues in the broader context of Mark's Gospel which may be deliberate hints to Mark's readers, aimed at helping them apprehend aright the reasons for, and intended outcome of, these main events. If the insights we gain by examining material *outside* Mark 13 can plausibly be viewed as clues the author has dropped, enabling his reader to comprehend the meaning of the events discussed *within* Mark 13, the overall methodology adopted for this study will receive further corroboration.

What then does Mark's Gospel teach about the reasons for and the results of the destruction of the Jerusalem temple? And how do the insights help us interpret Mark 13?

I. *An Overview of the Data to Be Interpreted*

Perhaps the most important and most astonishing fact to be accounted for is that, while the temple is clearly in focus at crucial points in the last major section of Mark's Gospel, temple references are invariably wrapped in an aura of mystery. T.J. Weeden maintains that the 'mystifying features about the Temple motif ... make it difficult to fathom Mk's interest in it'.[1] In the light of what we have already learned about Mark's esoteric teaching methods, it would be more precise to say that the mystifying features about the temple motif reveal: (1) that it is a matter of great significance for Mark, (2) that a right apprehension of Mark's temple theology is essential to the message of the entire Gospel, and (3) that the *process* of discerning that theology is an essential component of what Mark understands to be the discernment-discipleship responsibility of believers.

There are three main textual units outside Mark 13 which focus on the temple. In each one there are a variety of uncertainties concerning the significance of the *details*, and in each one there are allusive structural/literary features which make the issue *as a whole* ambiguous. What then are the main mystifying features?

The first main section dealing with Mark's temple theology is the so-called 'cleansing' account (11.15-17). The short pericope generates a host of difficult questions: What exactly is meant by 'den of robbers' (σπήλαιον λῃστῶν 11.17)? What sort of vessel (σκεῦος) is not to be carried through the courtyard? Is the focus of the Isaiah quotation on *my* house? On prayer? On Gentiles? Even more difficulties arise when the pericope is examined as part of its larger context. Three pericopes seem tied to it, the 'cursing' of the fig tree (11.12-14, 20f.), the question concerning Jesus' authority (11.27-33), and the Vineyard parable (12.1-12). Each one adds to the aura of mystery surrounding the whole matter. Is the Fig Tree story intended to be a framework around the 'cleansing'? If so, in what direction does it slant the interpretation? Is the Fig Tree story 'a brief pericope, in which Mark undermines his main intent by attempting a clarifying explanation that backfires'?[2] or is it the vital clue as to Mark's real, but deliberately subtle, communication? Is the question concerning Jesus' authority an attempt to elicit from Jesus a justification for his actions in the temple? If so, what is the significance of the fact that he gives no clear answer? Is 12.1-12 the answer? Weeden's phrase, 'mystifying features', is certainly appropriate; but what is Mark's point?

The second set of texts are those referring to the prophecy of Jesus that he will destroy this temple and build another in three days (14.58; 15.29). It has been rightly said that 'Here Mark is at his most enigmatic, one might almost say his most infuriating'.[3] Again we are confronted with uncertainties in the details: What is meant by the temple 'made without hands' (ἀχειροποίητος 14.58)? What is meant by 'after three days' (διὰ τριῶν ἡμερῶν)? Does it parallel or contrast Mark's regular time notation for the resurrection, 'after three days' (μετὰ τρεῖς ἡμέρας)? Is there any significance in the fact that Mark uses two different words for 'temple' (ἱερόν and ναός)?[4] Again there are broader considerations which are even more puzzling. Why is the prophecy credited to Jesus only by false witnesses (14.57-59) and mockers (15.29f.)? Is the prophecy false on one level of reading but ironically true on another?[5] Is Mark inviting his readers to read between the lines?[6]

A third textual unit, very brief but very puzzling, is the notation that at the instant of Jesus' death the temple veil was torn (15.38). There are uncertainties concerning the details of the verse itself: Which veil is meant? Which temple is meant? Is the direction, top-bottom, part of the main point? Once again the context provides difficulties as well. Why is the report of the event interposed between two verses which obviously link closely together? Why is the significance of the event left unstated? Are we to conclude with Bultmann, Kee and others that the whole account is something of a 'literary monstrosity?'[7] Or is it an illustration of Mark's literary genius? Can anything of value be learned from further study of a verse that has been assigned more interpretations, it is probably safe to say, than any other verse in the Bible?

Every reference to the temple outside Mark 13 is puzzling. We shall show that every reference is also 'loaded', implying more than is explicitly said. The strategic placement of each of these temple texts indicates they are supremely important for Mark's message. The 'cleansing' is the occasion for the initiation of the actual death plot by the Jerusalem authorities (11.18). The prophecy to destroy and rebuild features both in the trial of Jesus and in the death scene. The rending of the temple veil is the first recorded 'result' of Jesus' expiration. In a Gospel that focuses so heavily on Jesus' passion, such collocations *must* indicate that, however puzzling the references may be, understanding them is vital. Whether interpreters consider Mark's enigmas infuriating or an exciting challenge, it would appear they have little choice but to try to unravel hidden messages, or else join those who criticize Mark as a clumsy editor.

When we turn to Mark 13, we find the same phenomenon. Here too Mark is either enigmatic and subtle in the extreme, or else careless and clumsy. Why has he not made clear which 'things' are being associated with the destruction of the temple (13.4), and whether the question of the disciples reveals a correct or incorrect linking of elements? Why is the temple not once referred to explicitly in the answer of the Markan Jesus? How do we account for an exegetical state of affairs in which some able scholars maintain that everything in 13.5-23, or even 13.5-31, is intimately related to the destruction of the temple, and equally able scholars are convinced that the destruction of the temple plays no significant part at all in those verses?

The very least that all this means is that the exegete will have to be concerned with much more than *content* in studying a pericope. Mark has given evidence over and over again that the *context* in which a pericope is placed is an essential clue as to how it is to be construed. This is undeniably the case for all the major temple references outside Mark 13. We have every reason to believe that it is also true for Mark 13 as a whole. Has Mark deliberately placed Mark 13 in an overall context designed to aid the discerning reader in understanding its main points? We have seen evidence that this is the case. We shall see additional evidence as we proceed.

This chapter will support some of our main contentions: that Mark is as much concerned with the *processes* by which one discerns the meaning of the events reported and predicted as with the bare conclusions to be reached; that historical events such as the fall of the temple are (like parables and miracles) carriers of hidden meanings; that in 'all these things' those whose eyes and ears are divinely equipped to see and hear find indications of the secret coming of the secret kingdom.

II. *The 'Cleansing' of the Temple*

Introduction

That the temple's ruin is predicted by Jesus is made unambiguously clear in 13.2, even if all the other texts about the temple leave that point uncertain. What is not unambiguously revealed is *why* the destruction of the temple is to come about. Surely neither Jesus nor Mark would be content to portray it as merely an accident of history. It is an event which somehow fits within the plans and purposes of God. In almost any interpretation of Mark's Gospel, the temple's destruction is, among other things, an act of divine judgment. If we want to understand the finer points of Mark's text, it is necessary to gain much greater precision in identifying the culprits, the crimes, the way the punishment suits the crimes, and the desired outcome of it all.

A clear majority of scholars holds that Mark's 'cleansing' account is more a disqualification than a purification, more a prophecy of destruction than a reform movement. If this consensus is correct, then our best clue as to the reason why the Markan Jesus sets his face against the temple is to be found in the direct accusation Jesus levels against 'them': 'You have made it a den of robbers' (11.17). What does it mean?

The 'Den of Robbers'

There are a number of reasons why it is difficult to determine exactly what the Markan Jesus means by the reference to the den of robbers. First, the term 'robbers' (λῃστής) itself is ambiguous, sometimes focusing on banditry and at other times referring to insurrectionism. Second, because the phrase 'den of robbers' (σπήλαιον λῃστῶν) is taken from an Old Testament quotation (Jer. 7.11), it is uncertain whether only the phrase itself, or the whole context of the quotation, is intended to be considered relevant. Third, because the phrase 'den of robbers' was already intended to be taken metaphorically when Jeremiah used it, it is uncertain whether the relevant comparison with the Mark 11 situation is the metaphor itself or the situation to which it pointed in Jeremiah's text. Fourth, since there are a large number of Old Testament texts aside from those alluded to or quoted which appear on the surface to be highly relevant to the 'cleansing' situation (and they often suggest conflicting exegetical implications),[8] it is uncertain where one ought to look for *Biblical* clues as to Mark's intentions. Fifth, because there is so much disagreement both about the historical incident behind Mark's account and also about the relevance of the terminology for a situation in the time of the Jewish war, it is uncertain where one ought to look for *historical* clues as to Mark's intentions. Sixth, since all the temple texts throughout Mark are highly ambiguous (as already indicated), it is uncertain where one ought to look for *literary* clues as to Mark's intentions. Finally, there is no consensus on which set of clues (Biblical, historical or literary) is to be given a greater number of votes at the poll. We have every reason to expect almost unlimited scholarly diversity in the interpretation of the 'cleansing' and in fact, we find this to be the case.

Alternative Explanations
A few scholars maintain that Mark has either surreptitiously slipped in (or perhaps reinterpreted) the Jeremiah quotation so that 'den of robbers' might point to the fact that the Zealots made the temple their stronghold during the Jewish war.[9] Most accept that it refers primarily to the historical event reported by Mark and that the temple authorities and/or merchants of Jesus' day are the robbers referred to by the term λῃσταί. There is a great deal of uncertainty, however, about precisely what, if anything, they were doing 'wrong'.

Were they 'nationalist rebels' because they encroached on the rights of the Gentiles? Were they at fault because they were making *secular* profit from a *sacred* institution?[10] Were their financial dealings inappropriate, not for the temple itself, but for the eschatological age Jesus was inaugurating?[11] Was the sacrificial system itself being attacked in favour of the '"pure offering" of prayers throughout the world'?[12] Is it possible that the crimes were not temple-centred at all, and that the temple becomes important only because the Jewish leaders wrongly imagined that there, i.e., in the cultus, they could find immunity for crimes committed elsewhere?[13] Or were Jewish merchants retreating into the temple *building* itself because there they could find protection after cheating Gentiles in the outer courts? Or were temple authorities cheating poor pilgrims by dishonest dealings and taking refuge in the fact that, as temple authorities, they made the rules, they determined the exchange rates, they judged which animals purchased outside the temple were unclean, etc.?[14]

Amazingly, the term for vessel (σκεῦος) used in 11.16 to indicate what must no longer be found in the temple court, is ambiguous enough to fit perfectly with nearly all of the above interpretations, as well as others that could have been supplied. It can indicate military implements, sacrificial implements, sacred vessels, merchandise, money 'bags', water pots, etc.[15]

How does one make a decision when so many possibilities lie open, each of them finding some support in the text and its Biblical and historical backgrounds? Our approach will be to postulate a solution, and then examine the various relevant contexts for confirmation.

A Suggested Solution
We suggest that the reason almost all of the above interpretations have an element of truth in them is that, while they do not identify the real problem, they focus attention on some of the results of the real problem. The real problem was not that the Jewish religious leaders were robbing the ordinary pilgrims, or the Gentiles, or the Messiah; the real problem was that the Jewish religious leaders were robbing *God*. They had been given a sacred trust. Instead of serving God, they were abusing their trust to gain wealth, power and prestige for themselves. There was a great deal of outward show of religion, but they were doing none of the things God commissioned them to do.

We claim that this understanding of their 'problem' is confirmed widely in the broader Markan narrative, and explains a number of puzzling problems in the text. In seeking support for this suggestion, the best place to begin is with the Vineyard parable.

The Vineyard Parable
Several scholars have made it unmistakably clear that the Vineyard parable is intimately connected to the temple 'cleansing' incident.[16] When it is seen how the parable functions as Jesus' answer to the authority question (see below) the point is beyond doubt. The sequence moves from the 'cleansing', to the authority question, to Jesus' parabolic answer. Mark 12.1-12 is a key piece of evidence concerning why, and under what authority, Jesus acted against the temple.[17]

We can see in the light of our findings in Chapter 2 that 12.1-12 is just the sort of 'answer' we would expect Jesus to give his enemies concerning the grounds for his authoritative action. Prior to 3.6, Jesus spoke openly concerning his authority (2.10, 28) and demonstrated it unambiguously (esp. 2.1-12). After 3.6, Jesus' approach changed. Demonstrations of his authority were directed primarily towards the disciples; they were not unambiguous 'proofs' of anything, but rather carriers of hidden meanings. Public teaching was designed both to reveal and to conceal; Jesus' enemies received nothing except parables. Jesus' behaviour in Mark 11.12–12.12 is in perfect accord with this. The 'cursing' of the fig tree functions as a demonstration of Jesus' authority (cf. 11.21); it carries a hidden meaning and is an experience reserved for the disciples. Since the religious leaders are unwilling to drop their hypocrisy, Jesus refuses to justify his authority to them.[18] When an answer is given, it is in a parable. Jesus' enemies understood that the parable was against them (a point which many modern interpreters have *not* accepted); there is no evidence that they understood its finer points.[19] The Markan Jesus did not expect them to understand, since they had not accepted his authority.[20] Discerning readers, however, are expected to understand the parable. It is my contention that unless we do we will not understand Mark's temple theology.

In the light of this clear focus on the Jewish religious leaders, it is hard to understand why so many scholars have either assumed, or argued to the conclusion that, the parable is about the transfer of election and privilege from Israel to Gentiles.[21] Are we to imagine that if the Jews had been faithful as God's tenants the Gospel would never have gone to the Gentiles? There is nothing in the parable as it stands which hints that a transfer from Jews to Gentiles is in view. Why has the parable so often been interpreted that way?

That Isa. 5 stands in the background of Mark 12.1-12 is clear, and undoubtedly accounts for part of the confusion. There it is made clear that the vineyard is Israel (Isa. 5.7), and that Israel, like the vineyard, will be the object of God's displeasure and judgment. However, Mark 12 is far from being a restatement of Isa. 5. A comparison of the two parables highlights the striking differences between them.[22] In both parables God is the owner, Israel is the vineyard, and the owner fails to obtain from the vineyard the fruit he had a right to expect. However, the *reason why* he failed in his quest for fruit is the crucial point of divergence. In the Isaiah parable, the owner did not get a harvest commensurate with his careful gardening because the vineyard itself did not produce an adequate one. In the Markan parable, the vineyard produced fruit just as desired and expected, but a blockage, the wicked tenants, prevented the owner from receiving the good fruit. In Isaiah judgment falls on the vineyard; in Mark it falls on the tenants. In Isaiah the vineyard is laid waste; in Mark the vineyard is entrusted to the care of others.[23]

It is unmistakably Israel's leadership, not Israel itself, that stands under condemnation in Mark 12.1-12.[24] Already in Isaiah there was a special focus on the leaders (cf. Isa. 3.14: 'It is you who have ruined my vineyard'). But in Isaiah the corruption did not remain among the leaders. The leadership corruption led to such serious general corruption in Israel that the whole nation was ripe for God's judgment. In Mark, by contrast, the focus remains on the leaders. It is they who are corrupt. It is they who will be judged.[25] What the Markan Jesus is doing is taking an Old Testament text referring to all Israel and adapting it to bring condemnation on Israel's leadership. It is exactly what he does in 7.6f. (cf. Isa. 29.13) and 11.17 (cf. Jer. 7.2, 11, see below). The tenants (Israel's leaders) are rejected. The vineyard (Israel) is given new tenants (new leadership) so that the good fruit produced will flow to the owner rather than to the self-serving gardeners.[26]

From this we can discern Jesus' real answer to the question concerning his authority to act against the temple. His authority derives from the fact that God sent him to receive from the tenants the fruit of the vineyard. As we might expect, Jesus' answer goes beyond the intent of the question. He not only explains why he has authority to act on God's behalf; he makes it clear why *their* authority to act on God's behalf is now being lost. They are disqualified because they are serving themselves instead of God, and are rejecting those coming to set things right.

Our overall concern is to understand Mark's temple theology. We must be careful, therefore, not to set aside the very clues which will help us to understand it. The parable itself is not temple-centred at all.[27] The parable is about the condemnation of Israel's leadership.

The parable itself features the owner coming, not to destroy the temple, but to judge and replace the tenants. If Mark or his source had wished to focus directly and explicitly on the impending destruction of the temple, the parable could have been altered so as to reflect more closely the Isaiah parable with its announcement that God would destroy the vineyard *and its walls*.[28] The issue of temple replacement is alluded to only at the end of the parable in the rejected stone saying, an allusion to which we will later return.

When it is clearly seen that the Vineyard parable is centrally about leadership corruption and disqualification, we can observe a similar emphasis in the 'cleansing' episode. It is more directly related to the temple than the Vineyard parable, but its primary concern is to reveal Jesus' reaction to the corruption of Israel's leadership, not to make a statement on the temple as such. If the Jewish leaders were robbing God, they were doing so not only in the temple but everywhere they went. We might say they robbed God, not first and foremost of that which he had a right to expect from the temple, but of that which he had a right to expect from them and from all Israel. Their misbehaviour in the temple (11.15-17) exemplified, but did not exhaust, their sinfulness.

A brief look at the broader Markan context of both the Vineyard parable and the 'cleansing' episode confirms the points established thus far.

The Broader Markan Context

That the tenants are indeed 'robbers' is confirmed throughout Mark 11 and 12. They rob the Gentiles of a place of prayer (11.17b). They rob pilgrims by their excessive profit-taking in temple trading (11.15-17). They rob widows of their houses (12.40). But most of all they rob God![29] Mark 12.13-17 makes it clear that they are (or at least pretend to be) concerned to give Caesar his due. Jesus makes it clear that if Caesar is due that which bears his image, then they owe themselves to God, for they bear his image! Jesus knows they are not paying those dues. Mark 12.28-34 highlights a shining exception to the general rule, but the one righteous scribe is clearly a foil for all the rest who would rather perform religious ceremonies than love their neighbour and who would, rather than loving God with all their heart, go so far as to plot the death of his son. Mark 12.38-40 describes the scribes in their fancy robes putting themselves in places of honour and stealing the admiration of the people. Are they not robbing God of the honour which he alone deserves? Mark 12.41-44, as we shall see, shows that even when the religious leaders are robbing the people, they are robbing God (see III below). They are taking the vintage that belongs to the owner and misappropriating it to serve themselves. It becomes clear that neither the 'cleansing' episode nor the Vineyard parable is concerned strictly with what goes on in the temple. Robbing God can take place anywhere . . . in the streets, in the market-place, in synagogues, at banquets, in financial dealings, at prayer times, and the list goes on (cf. esp. 12.38-40). The 'den of robbers' is not the exclusive scene of the crimes; it is more directly the sanctuary in which the criminals hid. Indeed, the great and final crime for which they are at last deposed (12.7-9) does not take place in the temple at all. If it is inappropriate to call 'pilgrim-fleecer', λῃσταί, the term is quite apt for those who rob God, and are willing to do violence to God's own son in the course of doing so.

When this point is accepted, then we can ask where the temple theology of Mark fits into all this. It would seem that all of Mark 11 and 12 are concerned, not so much with prefiguring the temple's destruction, as with dropping clues as to *why* the temple would be destroyed, and even more centrally, why the Jewish leaders would be deposed.

But if the main focus is on the *reasons* for the destruction of the temple, there is also a subtle focus on the *outcomes* of it. One of the ways in which this is done is by the change of imagery at the end of the Vineyard parable. The quotation in 12.10f. is not merely an incidental feature of the Vineyard parable.[30] It was essential for the imagery of the parable to be qualified lest it be thought that when the leadership replacement took place, all would remain just as before except that new leaders would do what the old ones ought to have done. No, the very fact that the son is rejected changes everything. He becomes the cornerstone for a renewed 'temple', a renewed centre and focus for the people of God as they will be in the future.[31] The quotation is from Ps. 118.22f. but not far from the surface is the thought of Zech. 10.3f., where God, because he is so concerned for the welfare of his people, directs his anger against unfaithful shepherds, predicts punishment for the leaders, and then announces that he will set up a new cornerstone.

To bring in the 'temple' concern too early is to fail to apprehend Mark's focus on the issue of leadership. But to overlook the 'temple' concern running through the entire narrative is to misread everything. The withered fig tree, although it mostly directly symbolizes the Jewish leadership probably also foreshadows the ruin of the temple. The 'cleansing', given the Markan framework, was surely viewed as a disqualification, rendering a final destruction inevitable. The mountain-moving saying could perhaps be an allusion to the destruction of the temple mount.[32] The cornerstone reference surely alludes to a renewed temple which replaces the one that is now disqualified and will eventually be destroyed. The mild anti-cult emphasis in 12.28-34 encourages us to view the temple as no longer

necessary. Those who insist that Mark 11 and 12 are concerned with
the issue of temple destruction are not mistaken. Error arises when it
is overlooked that an even more central focus is on the judgment
falling on the Jewish leaders and the reason why it was deserved.

The Jeremiah Allusion
We are now in a position to see more clearly the significance of
Mark's allusion to Jeremiah's 'den of robbers' metaphor. The
significance is not merely that, like bandits, the temple authorities
were robbing pilgrims (though they may have been doing that).
Neither is the significance merely that, as in Jer. 7, the destruction of
the temple is in view.[33] Mark may well use the 'cleansing' episode as
part of a larger prophecy that the temple will be destroyed, but the
primary relevance of Jer. 7 lies elsewhere.

Jeremiah's caustic metaphor was provoked by anti-covenantal
practices and a false reliance on the temple.[34] It is easy to forget that
Jeremiah used a *metaphor*. His real concern was neither with
brigands nor with the sanctuary they found in mountain caves. His
concern was to address the evils of a people for whom the metaphor,
though not perfectly suited, was all too apt. If we force Mark to apply
the metaphor too woodenly to the Jewish religious leaders we make
him say that all their anti-covenantal practices were done outside the
temple and their security was exclusively within it. The relevance of
Mark's utilization of the metaphor is not that it fits his situation
more perfectly than it did Jeremiah's; it is that the situation which
called forth Jeremiah's metaphor is relevantly similar to the one
Jesus faced. In Jeremiah's day 'anti-covenantal practices' were
carried out both inside and outside the temple (cf. Jer. 7.6, 9f.); the
people's (false) 'sanctuary' was both the building itself, the sacred
land, the so-called inviolable promises of God, (and in the case of the
leaders) their status as both lawmakers and judges, their prestige in
the eyes of the people, etc. (cf. Jer. 7.4, 7, 10).

With one caveat yet to be discussed, the Jeremiah reference and
the issues dealt with there are a perfect match for the situation in
Mark 11ff. There is oppression of the aliens (Jer. 7.6; cf. Mark 11.17
[and note that it was the *Gentile* court that was being used for
merchandising]). There is oppression of widows (Jer. 7.6; cf. Mark
12.40). There is the shedding of innocent blood (Jer. 7.6; cf. Mark
15.14f.), *in this place* (Jer. 7.6; cf. Mark 12.8). There is use of

deceptive words (Jer. 7.8; cf. Mark 12.13f.). There are misdemeanours leading to the crucial question whether or not they will be allowed to continue dwelling in this place (Jer. 7.7; cf. Mark 11.15). Finally, there is the explicit prediction of the temple's destruction (Jer. 7.14; cf. Mark 13.2).

We noted the major difference between Isa. 5 and Mark 12.1-12. We note now the same difference between Jer. 7 and Mark. In Jeremiah the people as a whole are condemned (Jer. 7.2).[35] In Mark, every indication is that the condemnation is reserved for the corrupt leadership. Frequent scholarly claims that Mark is rejecting Israel in favour of Gentiles are untenable.[36] Mark is careful to avoid bringing any condemnation on the people as a whole.

In all this it is clear why it is hardly appropriate to call 11.15-17 a temple 'cleansing'. It is not through a cleansing of the temple but through its disqualification, removal, and replacement (and of course the same for Israel's corrupt leaders) that God will finally be able to acquire from his vineyard the harvest it produces.

The Fig Tree Framework
Our concern will not be with the origin of the story, but with the use of it in Mark's Gospel.[37] Very few scholars, in this age of redaction- and literary-critical studies, doubt that Mark intends his readers to see the two-part story (11.12-14, 21f.) as a framework around the 'cleansing' account, designed to slant the readers' evaluation of its meaning and significance.[38] Unfortunately, however, agreeing that it is designed to help the reader understand the 'cleansing' is no guarantee that there will be agreement on what conclusions should be reached.

It will not be our goal to draw maps of all the well-trodden (though not always well-directed) paths. Our goal will be to caution against one false trail, and to encourage the avoidance of one oft-entered cul-de-sac.

The false trail is the identification of the fig tree with Israel. The fig tree is sometimes used metaphorically for Israel in the Old Testament (e.g., Hos. 9.10); the evidence is against that interpretation of the metaphor in Mark. We have seen that the larger Markan context is careful to bring condemnation only on Israel's *leadership*, not on the nation as such. Mark seems to have gone to great lengths in the rest of Mark 11-16 to show that if God failed to get his due, it was not because there were no righteous and sincere worshippers; it was because the 'fruit' the land produced was gobbled up by the faithless tenants. The fig tree is widely held to be symbolic of the temple. It may well symbolize the building itself, but if so only in *addition to* its primary referent, the religious leaders.[39]

Although uncertainty always abounds when suggestions are hazarded concerning un-cited Old Testament background texts, we will take the risk of suggesting that Hos. 9.10–10.2 has had a strong influence on the themes that dominate the main 'temple section' of Mark's Gospel (at least 11.12–13.2). It contains the following elements:

> When I found Israel, it was like finding grapes in the desert; when I saw your fathers it was like seeing the early fruit on the fig tree ... Because of their sinful deeds, I will drive them out of my house.

> I will no longer love them; all their leaders are rebellious. Ephraim is blighted, their root is withered (ῥίζας ἐξράνθη [LXX]; cf. Mark 11.20), they yield no fruit ... Israel was a spreading vine; he brought forth fruit for himself. As his fruit increased, he built more altars; as his land prospered, he adorned his sacred stones. Their heart is deceitful, and now they must bear their guilt. The Lord will demolish their altars and destroy their sacred stones (Hos. 9.10, 15b, 16, 10.1,2);

It is hard to overlook the many points of contact with Mark 11 and 12, and hard to resist the conclusion that it forms a unifying principle for the whole Markan teaching unit. In both texts fig trees and vineyards are used metaphorically. The longing is expressed in both for early figs to be found and grapes to be made available. In both are found indictments for usurping the fruitfulness of the land for selfish gain. Both mention deceitfulness. Both mention *separately* an act of driving out of God's house and a projected destruction of sacred stones. Both, significantly, are concerned with rebellious leadership.

If the Markan account deviates from the Hosea account, it is precisely in lessening the guilt of the nation and heightening the guilt of the leaders. In Hosea, the vineyard (Israel) brought forth fruit for itself; in Mark it went to the tenants. In Hosea the riches adorned the temple only; in Mark it adorned the temple and the scribes (13.1, 12.38). In Hosea Israel is deceitful; in Mark the religious authorities are deceitful.

If the present form of Mark 11 and 12 suggests influence from Hos. 9 and 10, then the immediate juxtaposing in Hos. 9.15f. of the condemnation of the leadership and the metaphor of the withered root, strongly supports our contention that the leaders are symbolized by the fig tree withered from the root. No fruit can henceforth be expected from such a tree.[40] We have seen the phenomenon before. Old Testament texts bringing condemnation on Israel are modified to restrict the blame to the leaders alone. Any close identification of the fig tree with Israel itself is a false trail. Mark 11.12-21 as a whole is not about Israel's rejection any more than is 12.1-12. It is about the rejection of Israel's self-serving leadership.[41]

Now the blind alley. How much ink has been used trying to determine whether the fig tree cursing and/or the temple 'cleansing' are 'eschatological' events? Most studies which focus on this question show little more than the fact that no one can agree on how the word 'eschatological' is most properly used. Everything reported in the New Testament is 'eschatological' in the sense that it fills out a picture, the lineaments of which were seen on the future horizon by Old Testament prophets. But horizons have a habit of moving away from the one approaching them. We see new things on a more distant horizon even as we stand in the midst of those things which appeared on the horizon from another vantage point. To ask whether a New Testament event is appropriately called 'eschatological' demands that the perspective from which one is imagined to look be clearly defined. Often it is best to avoid the term.

Is Mark attempting to link the temple's fate with the End of the age? The evidence *outside* Mark 13 is against the idea. The mere presence of a word like καιρός ('the opportune time') in the report of the fig tree cursing is no warrant at all for linking the temple issue with the End of the age. We have already seen how Mark utilizes 13.32f. (where καιρός also appears) to refer not only to the End, but also to the *passion*. Furthermore, Mark clearly uses 'Day of the Lord' imagery in his report of the death of Jesus. If there are 'eschatological associations' with the temple and its fate, then the evidence outside Mark 13 is that the associations are linked via the passion to the 'secret beginning' of the eschatological age, not to its consummation at the End. This is confirmed when it is noted that none of the references to the temple outside Mark 13 is brought into direct connection with the parousia. All of them are brought into connection with the passion. It may even be that the difficult and enigmatic phrase 'for it was not the right time for figs' (ὁ γὰρ καιρὸς οὐκ ἦν σύκων) is designed to break the sort of eschatological connection that some scholars seem intent on forging.[42] There will come a time when a fig tree in leaf will lead the observant to watch for the End (13.28f.). That time is not yet. This tree is not a pointer to the final consummation; it is along the road to the passion.

All in all, it is probably not far off target to suggest Mark has deliberately used the fig tree cursing in order to present the reader with a graphic illustration of the 'fruitlessness' of Israel's leadership, the disappointment of Jesus in finding all their religiosity to be 'nothing but leaves', and the inevitability of their utter rejection and punishment in consequence of their failure to produce. The framework around the 'cleansing' therefore slants the meaning of that event in the direction of disqualification, and that primarily of the religious leadership of Israel.[43]

That the temple will eventually be destroyed is made clear in 13.2 and there are hints of it through Mark 11-16. It would be a mistake, however, to identify temple destruction as the major concern of Mark 11 and 12, even if these chapters do help identify the reasons for and implications of the coming destruction. God will act against Israel's corrupt leadership, in part by destroying their temple, after they have sealed their fate by laying violent hands against 'the son' (12.7-9). When they kill Jesus, then God reverses the roles, disqualifies the old, resurrects Jesus, lays the cornerstone and sends out the call for those who have been taught true discipleship to come back to Jesus. A new temple is thus erected. To this matter we must return.

Whereas Jewish eschatology expected temple purification to prepare for the eschatological age, Jesus' idea of 'purification' is the setting aside of the old and the establishing of the new. Jesus 'cleansed all foods' by dealing with the matter of ritual cleanliness at the level of heart attitudes. He 'cleanses' the temple in the same way.[44] In all places, hypocrisy and greed, self-seeking and deceit are liable to God's judgment. In all places, faith, prayer, giving God his due, loving God and neighbour are the conditions for being 'not far from the kingdom of God' (12.34). What was for Isaiah only a far off dream (Isa. 56.1-8; cf. Mark 11.17) was for the Markan Jesus in the process of being fulfilled.

It is true that part of that fulfilment is the inclusion of Gentiles in the people of God. But to focus on that issue (cf. 11.17) as if it were

Mark's central concern is to mistake a part for the whole and has the same damaging effects on understanding the texts as reading Gentiles into 12.9.[45] The failure of the Jewish leaders did not consist primarily in their refusal to admit Gentiles. It consisted in their self-serving hypocrisy which prevented them from leading Israel into her eschatological role as the nucleus of a worldwide people of God.

We cannot bring this discussion of the temple 'cleansing' to a close without coming back to one of our favourite themes (and one of Mark's). We would fall short in ascertaining correctly Mark's theological views if we did not also identify a subtle but important epistemological point that he seems also to be making.

How can we be certain we are not being over-ingenious, straining to find subtle meanings where Mark never gave a minute's thought to anything particularly subtle or allusive? How can we be sure Meagher is not correct in his assessment that Mark, far from carefully working out a coherent understanding, botched the whole thing because he carelessly patched up one difficulty in such a way that he ended up making a shambles of the whole story?[46]

The fact is that Mark has dropped hints not only about his meaning but also about the fact that he is dropping hints! Almost everyone seems to have overlooked the fact that in the report of the fig tree cursing Mark has used three seemingly innocent, but probably very crucial, phrases: 'and his disciples heard him' (11.14); 'they saw' (11.20); 'Peter remembered' (11.21).[47] When we recall how the 'hearing', 'seeing', and 'remembering' references were used with such good effect in Mark 8.14–21 to call the disciples and the readers to discern more in the miracles of Jesus than meets the eye, it is hard to believe that the reference to all three here is a coincidence. Does it not invite the reader to ask whether the disciples *really* heard and *really* saw? Did they *really* understand the event?[48] Does it not invite the readers to ask the same questions of themselves?

And what about the innocent-sounding description of Jesus' 'inspection' the day he entered Jerusalem, 'and he looked around at everything' (11.11)? In Jer. 7 the same sentiment sounds ominous: '"Has this house, which bears my Name, become a den of robbers to you? *But I have been watching*!", declares the Lord'. Does Mark suggest that Jesus was able to see from the divine perspective . . . and that readers are called to do the same?

Mark not only drops hints, he drops hints that he drops hints. We can go on arguing about the *quality* of the job Mark did in embedding subtle allusions into his account, but we cannot deny that he has deliberately done so.

In his temple theology as in his whole Gospel, Mark is concerned with more than Christology, eschatology, passion theology, etc. He is also concerned with epistemology. He is trying to lead his readers to read with discernment. He deliberately does not make all his points explicit; that is his way of drawing his readers deeper into the exegetical task. He himself is doing what he portrays Jesus as doing.

III. *The Prophecy to Destroy and Rebuild*

At Jesus' trial before the Sanhedrin, it is reported that some testified falsely (ἐψευδομαρτύρουν), claiming to have heard Jesus predict *he* would destroy 'this temple' and after three days build another 'made without hands' (14.57f.). While Jesus was on the cross similar words were hurled at him in mockery (15.29). The greatest problem in interpreting Mark's intentions in this passage is that we need to determine both what the prophecy is to be taken to mean and also whether Mark wants the readers to evaluate it as a true or false report. Obviously the process is circular. The acceptability of the saying depends on its meaning and vice versa.

Is the Prophecy True or False?

Various reasons have been suggested for taking at face value the statement that, according to Mark, the testimony was false. Were the witnesses inadvertently mistaken, claiming Jesus spoke against the temple sanctuary (ναός) when in fact his actions had all been concerned with the temple precincts (ἱερόν)?[49] Were the witnesses simply lying? Was the early church embarrassed by the charge and eager to be disassociated from it? Was Mark using the charge to represent the view of his theological opponents?

Most commentators want to preserve the view that the prophecy itself is substantially one which Jesus did make or at any rate was thought by Mark to have made.[50] The problem then is to explain why it is called a false testimony. Numerous suggestions have been given: it was brought against Jesus with evil intent; it was in fact false as interpreted by the witnesses though true as Jesus had meant it; it was declared false to draw attention from it to the Christological point following; it is Mark's irony to have them reporting Jesus as speaking against the temple when in fact the witnesses were in the very act speaking against the real temple;[51] it was an attempt to lie about Jesus which failed since the claim was ironically true; the paradigm of the suffering just one (Ps. 27.12, 35.11) overrides all other considerations and makes it essential that the testimony be termed false; it is a false witness because the witnesses cannot agree on the details (time, place, etc.).[52]

It seems clear from the broader Markan context that Mark does indeed consider the prophecy to be substantially true. The old temple will indeed be destroyed (13.2). Although the point is made allusively and symbolically, Mark seems to be telling his readers that a new temple (centred in Jesus) will replace it. But if the testimony is substantially true, it is also partially false. It is true there will be a temple destruction and replacement. It is false that *Jesus* will bring this about. Mark is careful to establish this point, both in the Vineyard parable and in the death scene.[53] The prophecy concerning temple replacement is a major element in the reversal of fortunes that *God* will bring about when the wicked tenants have sealed their fate by killing the son.

Juel has argued cogently that Mark intends the 'false testimony' to be seen as false on one level but ironically true on another.[54] The arguments employed are defensible, as long as the reader is careful to substitute God for Jesus as the main actor. On no level of reading does Mark consider the prophecy completely true as it stands, with Jesus claiming to be the destroyer and rebuilder.

The reader knows that the negative half of the prophecy will be fulfilled (the temple will be destroyed [13.2]). He receives hints, but only hints, that the positive half will be fulfilled as well. It is another subtle Markan call to look below the surface of the text and find the all-important clues.

Which is the Rebuilt Temple?

Which is the temple 'made without hands'? Before looking at the options, we would do well to note carefully the following words of R.J. McKelvey:[55]

> The conception of the church as a building under construction, with no suggestion of when the work will be completed, and at the same time as a temple in which God is actually dwelling and worship is being offered, looks like a contradiction. What we have here, however, is a paradox which is basic to much New Testament

> thinking, the paradox of present possession and future hope. Like
> each of its members, the church is called to become what it is, the
> dwelling-place of God in the Spirit.

Although these words are in defence of the view that the new temple
is the church, McKelvey actually draws attention to not one but two
paradoxes: (1) the temple can simultaneously be thought of as an
individual and as a corporate entity, (2) the temple can simultaneously
be pictured as complete and also as still under construction. Both
paradoxes should be kept in mind. Add to this a reminder that we
have already found evidence in Mark that a single prophecy can have
various fulfilments at different levels, and we are ready to attempt a
reconstruction of Mark's theology of temple rebuilding.

The contrasting adjectives, 'made with hands'—'made without
hands' (χειροποίητος—ἀχειροποίητος), have been much discussed.
Is the contrast between man-made and God-made, made on earth
and made in heaven, physical and spiritual, historical and eschatological, temple suited to old order and temple suited to new order,
natural and miraculous, idolatrous and pure? Instead of attempting
the (probably impossible) task of sorting out all these options, it
seems best again to postulate a solution and test it against the wider
data of Mark's Gospel.

Since Mark has already led us to understand something of Jesus'
relation to the old temple, it is not too difficult to evaluate the
significance of the first adjective. It probably suggests something
more than simply the fact that the old temple was made with human
hands. According to the reported prophecy, the Markan Jesus has
deliberately picked up a term which Old Testament writers had used
to discredit pagan idols (e.g., Ps. 115.4; Isa. 46.6).[56] If Jesus can call
the temple a 'den of robbers' (11.17), he can also call it a pagan
idol.

It is much more difficult to determine the meaning of the second
adjective unless, in contrast to 'made with hands', it signifies the true
object of worship, or at least the place in which true worship is
brought to God. The best way of determining the meaning of the
second adjective is by first identifying the temple that is in view.

Debates go on between defenders of the two most likely
identifications for the rebuilt temple, the resurrected Jesus and the
Christian community.[57] We suggest it is both. Mark would not have
picked one over against the other. With his heavy emphasis on
leadership replacement (not merely temple replacement), Mark can

include both Jesus and the Christian community in his concept of the new temple: Jesus, because he is God's chosen replacement for the old disqualified leaders (cf. 12.10),[58] and the community, because it sides with Jesus.

We recall that according to Mark the faithful remnant of Israel was finally reduced through the passion to Jesus alone. He alone carried the destiny of the nation. With his death and resurrection he calls all people to come to him (symbolized by the confession of the centurion [15.39]), and more specifically calls back to faithfulness those who had been his followers (16.7). The community of Jesus is reborn with him at his resurrection.[59] The New Testament as a whole preserves the paradox of Jesus himself being the New Temple through which access to God is gained, and the community being the New Temple in which spiritual sacrifices are directed heavenward.

What about the fact that μετὰ τρεῖς ἡμέρας ('after three days') is used consistently of the resurrection, and διὰ τριῶν ἡμερῶν ('a little while?') is used for the predicted rebuilt temple? We noted earlier that Mark refrained from speaking of 'the midnight hour' in the Gethsemane account even though in his scheme of things he must have thought of it as such. We suggested he may not have wanted to 'over-identify' with the midnight hour lest the reader mistake the Gethsemane experience itself, and not the whole passion, for 'The Hour' of eschatological fulfilment. Could not the same motive be at work here? To have indicated that the new temple would be built μετὰ τρεῖς ἡμέρας would have 'over-identified' the temple with the resurrection alone. The phrase is ideally suited if Mark's point is to tie the building of the new temple very closely to that event, yet to suggest that the whole Christian community is part of that temple with Jesus (some joining even before the actual resurrection itself).

If we are right in adopting McKelvey's suggestion that the temple 'made without hands' can be an individual and yet a corporate entity, can be built at a particular time and yet be continuously under construction, then it is a concept perfectly suited to the kind of treatment Mark seems to be giving this material, material which is well suited to Mark's characteristically subtle form of communication.

A New Markan Teaching Unit
A feature of this study is its insistence that Mark juxtaposes

narratives in order to present subtle hints of an 'over-message' which utilizes, but goes beyond, the messages conveyed by the content of individual pericopes. Our third chapter analysed a unit focusing on discernment. Our fourth chapter analysed one focusing on discipleship. This chapter analyses three, of which two have been previously examined by other students of Mark (the story of the 'cleansing' imbedded in the story of the fig tree cursing, and the report of the torn temple veil interposed between the record of Jesus' death and the Centurion's response to it, cf. IV, below). We now offer for consideration another Markan teaching unit which has not previously been identified.

It appears that Mark has deliberately framed Mark 13 with two stories, which, read together in the context of Mark's Gospel, encourage us to view Mark 13 as a veiled account of the fulfilment of Jesus' prophecy that the old temple would be destroyed and the new one erected so that the 'fruit' might finally and fully be claimed by the rightful 'owner' of the 'vineyard'. Many interpreters have apparently suspected some sort of co-ordination in Mark's mind between the two stories of 'women who gave', the widow who gave all her living (12.41-44), and the woman who lavished her perfume on Jesus (14.1-9). Despite obvious differences, there are some features of the two stories which correspond remarkably well, either as comparisons or contrasts. Both 'givers' are women. Both make a great sacrifice. Wealth and poverty are clearly at issue in both cases. Both stories of women practising their piety by giving are linked to stories of men practising deception in order to gain (i.e., 12.41-44 is linked to 12.38-40; 14.3-9 is linked to 14.1f., 10f.). Structurally they form a pair, immediately preceding and immediately following Mark 13.

But are they really intended to form a pair? If so, is the pairing designed simply to reinforce the point that sacrificial giving is approved?[60] Or is more at stake? Is it part of a larger pattern of Markan feminism?[61] Are they used to foreshadow Jesus' death and his resurrection respectively?[62] Or is Mark concerned with a more subtle point that has not yet been adequately identified?

The biggest problem in coming to grips with Mark's intentions is the difficulty in pinning down Mark's purposes for including 12.41-44 in his account at precisely this point. 14.1-11 functions well to prepare in a number of ways for the Passion account that immediately follows: it occasions the betrayal; it performs a symbolic burial anointing; it alludes to the missionary preaching of the church beyond the resurrection.[63]

But what is the point of the story of the widow who gave her two coins? Apart from a very few commentators who evaluate it in relation to the story of the anointing, almost everyone seeks to find its real significance for Mark by examining its relation either to the text immediately preceding it, or to the one following.

It is sometimes suggested that it was linked to the preceding pericope by the catchword 'widow' (χήρα 12.40, 42), with the broader context (12.13-44) being characterized as a 'loose Markan construction by means of sequential appearances of adversaries and catchwords'.[64] More often it is held that there is a much more integral relationship between 12.38-40 and 12.41-44 than mere catchword association. Frequently it is suggested that the self-giving of the woman is being deliberately contrasted with the greed and counterfeit pity of the scribes.[65] It is sometimes related further back in the context and linked to 12.33 where true piety is defined as loving God with 'all one's strength' (i.e., 'with all one's property' according to one strand of Jewish interpretation).[66]

But what about the context following? While some have held that Mark 13 intrudes into an otherwise natural connection between 12.44 and the Passion,[67] others have suggested a variety of ways of linking 12.44 with 13.1ff. They are sometimes linked topographically, (i.e., 12.41-44 brings Jesus into the court of the women from where he exits in 13.1);[68] often in more substantial ways. Donahue hints that before Jesus functions as a prophet (Mark 13) he performs the work of a prophet, defending widows (12.41-44).[69] F.W. Danker suggests that Mark's concern is to point out that the apocalyptic woes of the End will cost the disciples no less than the woman paid, 'her whole livelihood/life' (ὅλον τὸν βίον αὐτῆς).[70] Schweizer comments that 12.41-44 illustrates the kind of discipleship which will be recompensed at the parousia.[71] A century ago Thomas Lindsay suggested there is a deliberate contrast between Jesus and his disciples. Jesus places highest value on the pittance that a sincere woman can give; the disciples place highest value on the magnificent columns of the temple.[72] Most of these suggestions are rather illuminating. Is there not a way of identifying an overall perspective which incorporates the best of them all? There is indeed. One of the keys, although itself inadequate to unlock all the doors, is A.G. Wright's attack on the consensus that Jesus' attitude to the widow who gave is one of unmitigated approval. He argues to this conclusion:[73]

> The story does not provide a pious contrast to the conduct of the scribes in the preceding section (as is the customary view); rather it provides a further illustration of the ills of official devotion. Jesus' saying is not a penetrating insight on the measuring of gifts; it is a lament. ... There is no praise of the widow in the passage and no invitation to imitate her, precisely because she ought not be imitated. ... Her contribution was totally misguided, thanks to the encouragement of official religion, but the final irony of it all was that it was also a waste.

There is no doubt that Wright's solution coheres with the Markan context far better *in some ways* than the traditional view. The appearance of 'widow' (χήρα 12.40, 42) in consecutive pericopes is surely of some significance. Does the sequence not suggest that this widow, whose whole living consisted of a mere 'two pennies' (λεπτὰ δύο), had already suffered at the hands of the rapacious scribes?[74] Is there a suggestion here that oppression of the poor is one of the key elements that motivated Jesus to 'purify' the temple in the manner he did?[75] And if the fact that she has so little to give is not bad enough, what of the fact that even the little she gave was deposited in a temple which, for all its wealth, was bankrupt? Her *entire* livelihood was utterly wasted on self-seeking religious leaders and their 'den of robbers'. Both were well-adorned (12.38; 13.1); both were also doomed (12.40; 13.2). There is indeed much cause for lament. We can hardly avoid Wright's conclusion that the woman's gift was a waste. But what about his argument that it was also misguided?

Have ordinary Bible readers and scholars alike been wrong for nineteen centuries in imagining that Jesus approved of the woman's action? Fortunately, in this case, we can have our cake and eat it too. The solution is that Jesus commended the woman for her piety and self-giving, but simultaneously condemned the religious leaders for interposing themselves between this woman and her God, grasping for themselves what was intended to be for God's glory. In that sense, Jesus' attitude would be both a praise and a lament. We can hardly overlook the perfect symmetry between this view of the matter and the Vineyard parable! The vineyard produced fruit just as the owner had hoped; but the fruit was wasted, for it never reached the owner who desired it. The tenants hoarded for themselves the precious crops.

We find evidence yet again that Jesus is condemning, not the ordinary Jew, but the religious leaders. Mark 12.41-44 joins virtually all the other material in 11.11-12.40 in revealing what the religious leaders were doing wrong. They were robbing God. The verses that immediately follow (13.1f.) indicate what will happen as a result. Disqualification of both leaders and temple is indicated. But is there also an indication of the replacement of both?

It is time to turn our eyes to Mark 14.3-9. Here we have, not the poor giving to the rich, but the rich giving to the poor, to the poorest of the poor in the first place,[76] and after his burial to all other poor. It is precisely the reversal of fortunes that is so commonly associated with eschatological fulfilment. Both women who gave are approved. However, Jesus and the Jewish authorities have precisely opposite opinions about which gift was wasted. He knows the first gift to be wasted, for though the temple into which it goes looks impressive and permanent, Jesus knows it is doomed. They are wrong in imagining that the second gift is wasted, for though the 'temple' on which it is lavished looks far less impressive, it is the one which is destined to survive. Mark has found a very subtle way of demonstrating once again for perceptive readers that there will be a replacement of both leadership and temple.

The widow who gave 'her whole livelihood/life' (ὅλον τὸν βίον αὐτῆς) is a fitting symbol for Jesus who gave his whole life as well. But tragically, and through no fault of her own, she is a fitting symbol also for Jerusalem and for its religious leaders. They had robbed her of her house (12.40). God would take away theirs as well. 'How deserted lies the city ... How like a widow is she!' (Lam. 1.1).

By contrast, the woman who anoints Jesus with her costly perfume fittingly provides a symbol for both Jesus and the new temple. That which she gave, like that which Jesus gave, was 'a fragrant offering and sacrifice to God' (Eph. 5.2). Her fame and her honour, like Jesus' own, would outlive her earthly life and be proclaimed throughout the world, and that precisely because she identified with him in his death. Taken together, Mark 12.41-44 and 14.3-9 prefigure the replacement of temples, a theme which Mark seems to have woven through his narrative.

If Jesus' attitude in 12.41-44 is bittersweet, how much more so in 14.3-9! If the religious authorities are portrayed as covertly robbing the poor and hiding their deception behind hypocritical displays of honouring God (12.40), is it a coincidence that they are also portrayed as covertly plotting against God's Son and hiding their deception behind hypocritical displays of concern for the poor (14.1,5)? In every way the earlier accusation fits the present situation, 'These people honour me with their lips, but their hearts are far from me' (7.6).

Throughout the Gospel, Mark has dropped hints that Jesus has come to bring about an inner religious renewal which would burst the outward shackles of religious scruples and observances, and set people free to worship God 'in spirit and in truth'.[77] The new wine bursts the old skins (2.22). The laws are for the benefit of people, not vice versa (2.27). Food laws are dispensible; it is inward purity that matters (7.19-23). Believing prayer, not technique, unleashes the power of God (9.23, 28f.). Love is more important than sacrifice (12.33). The culmination of it all is the final setting aside of the temple, its rituals, its demands, even its custodians; it is the new temple, the risen Jesus and his community, that will serve to mediate God's salvation to people; it is the new temple and its custodians who will, as faithful tenants, bring the harvest to God.

We have argued that Mark 12.41-44 and 14.1-9 are a matched pair designed to bring forward subtle but important points. The crucial point that we must not overlook is that Mark has taken this matched pair *and used it as the framework around Mark 13*. What are the exegetical implications?

1. *Mark 13 is to be interpreted from the perspective of 'Temple Replacement'*. It is not simply about the destruction of the old temple. It is also about the replacement of it with the new temple, Jesus and his community. That in itself suggests numerous points for consideration. If the old temple was a centre to which all nations would come (Mark 11.17) and if the new temple would expand to fill the whole world (Cf. Dan. 2.35; Mark 14.9) then perhaps Mark 13 is fundamentally concerned with the issue of breaking free from Jerusalem-centredness into worldwide mission. Perhaps Mark sees the faithful scattered from the old temple at 13.14 and regathered fully and finally into the new temple at 13.27.[78] Perhaps Mark 13 is concerned to proclaim the fact that when one gives all one has (ὅλον τὸν βίον) for the sake of the new temple it is endowed with eternal significance, as

it could never be if that same gift were brought to the old one. At any rate, the structure we have identified strongly encourages us to examine in a new light the concepts of self-sacrifice and world mission in Mark 13 and in Mark's Gospel as a whole (the very thing that will occupy our attention in the next chapter).

2. *Mark 13 is, like both 12.41-44 and 14.3-9, concerned to lead the readers out of their 'natural' way of evaluating events.* Jesus is trying to invert value systems. What appears to be a small gift is of great value. What appears to be a wasted gift is in fact a great investment. If this is a major concern of the framework around Mark 13, what of Mark 13 itself? Is it concerned to teach that what appears to be an indestructible and infinitely valuable temple is nothing of the sort? Is it saying that what appear to be signs of the End are nothing of the sort either? What if it is even saying that what appears to be evidence that Jewish apocalyptic expectations are being fulfilled, is in fact evidence of something else altogether? What if Mark 13 (as much of the rest of the Gospel) is designed to reverse the viewpoints and expectations that a pious Jew would have inherited from his religious tradition? How then should the chapter be read?

3. *Mark has a unique and pervasive, albeit subtle, way of making important theological points.* Almost every topic we study in Mark eventually leads us back to an evaluation of Markan secrecy and the esoteric communication methods used because of it. If it is true that Mark has 'used' the two pericopes (12.41-44 and 14.1-9) to say more than each one could say without the broader context, how much more confidence we should have that he has done the same with Mark 13, the extended discourse around which he has carefully designed the framework. Evidence is mounting that meanings below the surface pervade the Gospel. There are many ways to go wrong when one watches for subtleties. In the case of Mark, however, the greater danger is to overlook the deeper points and examine only the surface of the texts. The Markan Jesus expected that the events recorded would be misunderstood if dealt with that way. Mark expected the same for his Gospel. If we cannot see

past the surface, the truth remains hidden. Mark intended it that way.

We close our discussion of the prophecy to destroy and rebuild. Mark clearly accepts that the old temple will be destroyed and a new one will replace it. He does not accept that Jesus himself will act to destroy the physical temple or to exalt himself as the new. As Jesus goes his way to the cross, everything is set up for God to act. The fate of two temples is about to be decided. The custodians of each have pronounced the doom of the other. With Jesus on the cross, it seems superficially that the custodians of the physical temple will win the day. Those who have believed Jesus expect him somehow to be exalted as the cornerstone of a new temple. Are their expectations justified? Mark, in his subtle way, hints at the final resolution. He takes his final statement on the temple, the report of its veil tearing (15.38), frames it with the report of Jesus' death and the report of the Centurion's confession, and leaves the readers to work it out for themselves. It is not a coincidence that Mark has taken all three major temple statements and worked them into a context where a framework around a central report is designed to show the reader how it is all to be understood.

IV. *The Rending of the Temple Veil*

A number of uncertainties make it hard to be sure what particular point or points Mark intended to convey by juxtaposing in immediate succession the report of Jesus death (15.37), the statement that the temple veil was torn in two (15.38), and the confession of the Centurion (15.39).

Some of the uncertainty stems from the fact that it is impossible to be sure whether the inner or outer veil of the temple is intended, or for that matter whether 'veil' is not rather intended metaphorically. Even more uncertainty stems from the fact that the temple veil (either one) has a variety of distinct functions, so that the tearing of it could imply a variety of different things. But the greatest uncertainty stems from the fact that Mark makes no attempt in 15.38 to tell us explicitly what he understands to be the significance of the event. He tells us only that it happened. Any clues as to what significance he saw in it must be gleaned from the immediate and broader contexts of Mark's Gospel.

If any doubt remains that one of Mark's literary techniques is to report events without explaining their significance, and to call on the reader to discern the meaning by examining its literary relationships with surrounding material, that doubt should be removed along with the temple veil. It is difficult (though not quite impossible) to find a single scholar who does not take for granted that Mark intends to convey an unstated but important theological truth by the fact that the rending of the veil is reported in precisely the way it is.[79]

To save time and space, we will list, but not document, the various ways in which the rending of the temple veil has been understood.

The veil of the temple functioned in part to *hide from view* the most sacred parts of the temple, and specifically the presence of God. Not surprisingly, a number of interpretations of 15.38 centre on the whole matter of secrecy and revelation. It has been argued that with the death of Jesus:

1. all that hides God from view is removed (comparable to the rending of the heavens at Jesus' baptism);
2. the veil over Jesus' divine Sonship is removed (i.e., a theophany takes place);
3. the truth is revealed (concerning the significance of Jesus' death;
4. God shows his face (ripping open the curtain that he might be seen);
5. (the inverse of the preceding) the emptiness of the temple's holiest shrine is revealed (i.e., it can be seen that God was not dwelling in the physical temple).

Another function of the veil was to *enclose* that which dwelt most appropriately in a holy place. Not surprisingly, a number of interpretations centre on the matter of letting something *out*. It has been argued that at the death of Jesus:

6. God's glory flows outward to the universe;
7. the 'ex-(s)piration' of Jesus is symbolized in the Spirit of God leaving the physical temple;
8. as an act of judgment, God walks out of the Holy of Holies.

The veil also *kept out* that which had no access to the holiest parts of the temple. A number of interpretations focus on the matter of letting something *in*. It is suggested that the torn curtain symbolizes:

9. all barriers between people and God being removed;
10. Gentiles gaining access into the sanctuary (i.e., the barrier between Gentiles and God is removed); or
11. Gentiles being admitted into fellowship with Jews (i.e., the barrier between Gentiles and Jews is removed).

Less common are the following 'barrier removal' interpretations:

12. the barrier between earth and heaven is broken down in the pleroma;
13. Jesus is going through the dividing barrier and entering heaven.

The veil is intimately related to *Jewish religion*. Therefore its removal could signify:

14. the abolition of the cult (i.e., Jesus is the sacrifice; animal sacrifices are no longer needed);
15. God's rejection of the Jews;
16. the abolition of Jewish exclusiveness;
17. the obsolescence of Judaism;
18. the destruction of the old promises and old covenant;
19. the loss of significance for the temple itself.

It is sometimes emphasized that the veil is not merely *removed*; it is *torn down* (divine passive), and specifically from top to bottom. This might suggest:

20. Mark is emphasizing that in the death of Jesus, God is at work (in salvation);
21. in the coming destruction of the temple, God is at work (in judgment);
22. in the cross, i.e., in weakness and hiddenness, God himself is revealing his nature to people.

Frequently it is emphasized that the main significance of the veil is that it is *part of the temple*. Its tearing could then mean:

23. the destruction of the whole temple is being presaged;
24. the temple is rending its garments to mourn its impending doom.

At other times it is thought that Mark never intended the reference to point to the physical veil of the temple at all. It signifies the 'veil' of the *new* Temple (i.e., Jesus). Its rending might then mean:

25. Jesus has died (i.e., it is a doublet of 15.37);
26. when Jesus' body is torn, he effects reconciliation with God;
27. when Jesus' body is torn, he enters the sanctuary of God.

There are still further suggestions, not all of them implausible:

28. Since Jesus said that only when we forgive is our prayer for barrier-removal successful (Mark 11.23-25), the fact that the veil tore is evidence that Jesus forgave his enemies;
29. The powerful death cry of Jesus effects the splitting of the curtain (as a divine portent);
30. (virtually the inverse of the preceding) Since the veil covering the Holy of Holies was a sign of God's presence, its splitting is God's way of rending a previous sign useless as a sign;
31. There is a transvaluation of power and weakness (the 'life-giving' temple proves to be dead, the dead Jesus proves to be 'life-giving'; the symbol of dehumanizing power is destroyed by the powerlessness of death);
32. At the instant of Jesus' death, both temples (the old and the projected new one) are torn; the judgment of God will decide which one will be 'raised' and which 'razed';
33. The fact that the temple destruction starts when Jesus is dead proves that Jesus himself is not the temple-destroyer;
34. Mark 15.38 is part of a symbolical restatement of Mark 10.45: The Son of Man came to give his life (15.37) as a ransom (15.38) for many (15.39);
35. It is the counterpart to the soldiers dividing Jesus' clothes; God does the same with the temple's.

More than thirty interpretations for a twelve-word verse!!! It could be argued that several of the above are almost indistinguishable and should be combined, but then their places could no doubt be filled with the interpretations that escaped attention.

Some of them can be eliminated on the grounds that they are implausible, though it might be hard to generate widespread agreement on which those might be. Certainly some can be eliminated (though again it would be hard to be sure which ones) on the grounds that they are incompatible with others. Some could no doubt be seen as implications of others so that a single suggestion covers several.[80]

We would suggest that quite a few can be eliminated by noting that there is no causal link between the death of Jesus and the rending of the veil, or between the rending of the veil and the Centurion's confession. Mark is not saying that Jesus' death cry splits the veil, nor that the tearing of the veil elicits the confession. The causal link runs straight from 15.37 to 15.39 (with a cry, Jesus expired; observing, the Centurion confessed (ἰδὼν ... ὅτι οὕτως ἐξέπνευσεν εἶπεν ...).[81] The centurion was standing facing Jesus; he had no awareness of any event in the temple.[82] That being the case, the tearing of the veil must somehow function as a theological statement indicating something implied by Jesus' death, or something implicit in the Centurion's confession, or both. The fact that the theological statement is interposed directly into the cause-effect chain from 15.37 to 15.39 strongly suggests that 15.38 links theologically both backward and forward.[83] It would seem that at a minimum the structure from 15.37 through 15.39 focuses on passion theology, Christology, Gentile inclusion, temple concerns, and, of course, epistemology (the opening of 15.39 is a give-away, as also is the 'seeing' and 'hearing' irony throughout the death scene). Evidently Mark believes that somehow the temple question is relevant to all the others.

Even with the limitations imposed by our suggestions above, it is difficult to imagine how we can eliminate thirty-four of the options in order to settle on the one Mark intended. Perhaps we do not need to. The only way to account for this incredible state of affairs is to assume that Mark has a broadly conceived but subtly presented understanding of the meaning of the death of Jesus, of the implications of it for the temple, and of the outcomes that flow from the interaction of the two. Under such conditions, a very large number of the above might well be included in Mark's intentions. If he believes that Jesus' death replaces the cult as the means of access to God; if he believes that, for those who have eyes to see, the blessings of the kingdom are made available because in part 'that Day' and 'the Hour' arrive at the instant of Jesus' death; if he believes that in killing Jesus, the Jewish hierarchy has sealed its fate and occasioned the immediate redundancy and eventual destruction of the temple; if he believes that all the faults (including Gentile exclusion) of the old temple custodians are reversed by Jesus and the new temple, then many of the interpretations given above flow out either directly or indirectly from Jesus' death and are appropriately linked to the report of the rending of the temple veil.

Mark 15.38 then does not, in itself, make many new theological points, rather it makes the more general point that all those changes which have been predicted and alluded to are confirmed in the fact that Jesus has been put to death. It is the firstfruits of judgment. But it is also the firstfruits of Gentile conversion and therefore also the firstfruits of God's rebuilt temple in response to the tenants' rejection of the son and the builders' rejection of the stone (Mark 12.8-12). With the killing of Jesus the die is cast. The prophecies of Jesus will be fulfilled.

The temple 'cleansing' account focused centrally on the reason why the Jewish leaders would be judged and the temple would be destroyed. The prophecy to destroy and rebuild focused centrally on the outcomes of the temple replacement. The 'torn veil' report focused centrally on the crucial event which brings about the reversals predicted and which guarantees the fulfilment of all the predictions. All three are clothed in mystery.

V. *Implications for Interpreting Mark 13*

We have already touched on some of the implications, especially when examining the Markan framework around Mark 13 (12.41-44 and 14.1-9). At this point we will merely summarize these and suggest a few more implications, the development of which will be taken up in the last chapters of this study.

Temple Replacement: If we are right that Mark 13 is designed to lead believers to a correct evaluation of the deeper significance of the various events that transpire between the time of Jesus' resurrection and his parousia, then if the destruction of the temple is a typical example of one of those events, clearly Mark has no intention of telling his readers explicitly what conclusions they should reach. All the temple references outside Mark 13 are veiled in secrecy. All are to be interpreted with the aid of structural elements of the Markan text. When we examine Mark 13, we should be on the lookout for subtle points; we should watch to see how the juxtaposing of elements offers clues; we should look for evidence that Mark follows through on suggestions he has made in the larger context around Mark 13.

Mark's 'anti-temple' stance: Given the strong anti-temple stance of
the Markan Jesus, we can surely accept the suggestion that there is
significance in Jesus' posture on the Mount of Olives '*opposite* the
temple' (κατέναντι τοῦ ἱεροῦ 13.3).[84] Mark 13 is an anti-temple
speech; it is not a speech introduced by a few unimportant references
to the temple and then proceeding with total disregard for the temple
and its fate, as some would have it.

Mark 13 and 'Temple Theology Fulfilment': If the words and
activities of Jesus prior to the passion prefigure and predict the
destruction of the old temple and its replacement with the new, and if
the instant of Jesus' death brings about the *beginning* of all the
changes (cf. the wide variety of implications of 15.38), we should be
on the lookout for evidence that the events of the post-resurrection
age, including the temple's destruction, bring all those diverse
elements to their *fulfilment*.[85]

Flee the City: If we are right that Mark is careful to bring
condemnation on the Jewish leaders *but not on the Jewish people as
such* then the door is open to see Mark 13.14 with its warning to flee
the city as an expression of Jesus' concern for the Jewish people
living there, not only for the Christian church. If Jesus' praise for the
self-sacrificing widow is jaded by sorrow that her giving is wasted on
a doomed temple and doomed religious leaders, would we not expect
him to transmit a word of warning to pious Jews not to be seduced by
those who claim that the inviolability of the temple will be an
adequate protection against the invading Roman armies?

Gentile Inclusion: Given the concern evidenced in various places
for the inclusion of Gentiles in the new people of God, we should
pause before accepting the commonly held position that Mark 13.10
is an intrusive element weakly tied to a tightly knit literary pattern.
Perhaps it is part of a pattern as well. The mission question,
especially as it relates to the Gentiles, might prove to be more
significant in Mark 13 than is usually noted.

βλέπετε: We have argued that βλέπετε does not mean 'be careful
about' as much as 'be discerning of'. One of the things the reader is
to discern is the meaning of the fall of the old temple and its
replacement with the new.[86] We cannot be certain exactly what the
disciples in Mark 13.4 are associating chronologically or theologically
with the destruction of the temple. Our best chance of determining
what the Markan Jesus associates with it is by reading Mark 13 in the
broader context. It is there that Mark helps his readers determine

what occasions and what flows from the temple's destruction. Presumably 13.30 means all *these things* will be accomplished within one generation. It remains to be examined whether the parousia is included. Certainly our study of Mark's temple theology has given us no warrant for associating the parousia closely with anything that happens to the temple.

Parable and Allegory: Whatever Jesus did with parables, we know that Mark was prepared to interpret at least some of them allegorically. He clearly endorses an allegorical reading of the Sower parable (4.14-20) and we have seen in this chapter that the broader Markan context assumes an allegorical interpretation of the Vineyard parable.[87] Moreover, there is some evidence that Mark accepts a single point as the primary meaning of each parable, but 'uses' the parables allegorically to make subtle points to his readers, sometimes over the heads of the characters in the story. We might well give consideration to the possibility that the Fig Tree parable (13.28f.) is primarily about imminent expectation, but secondarily about something more intimately related to the imagery used in the parable itself.

Fig Tree Symbolism: If Mark has used symbols carefully and left indications as to where he accepts and where he rejects prior associations with the symbols (e.g., fig tree, den of robbers, vineyard) we should seriously consider the possibility that, according to Mark, the Fig Tree parable in Mark 13 is carefully co-ordinated in terms of its symbolism with the cursed fig tree in Mark 11. Given the fact that in both cases we have a picture of a fig tree in leaf but lacking fruit, with the first destined to *wither* and the second destined to *bear fruit*, it would be surprising in the extreme if the judgment to come on Israel's leaders and their temple would be symbolically indicated by both destinies. Given Mark's pervasive Temple Replacement theology, we should look carefully for a way of interpreting the second fig tree in relation to the *new* temple so that the stark contrast in the destinies of the two trees can be justified. If God expects no fruit from the old temple and its corrupt leadership, but expects a great harvest from the new temple centred in Jesus, the contrasting fig trees provide fitting symbols. If the judgment predicted for the Jewish leaders and their temple is associated with the withering of one fig tree, and the End of the age with the fruit-bearing of another, we should be very hesitant to accept arguments which link those two events directly together.

Chapter 6

MARK'S THEOLOGY OF SUFFERING AND PERSECUTION

Introduction

There are those who would argue that 'death' and 'resurrection' form the two-fold theme pervading Mark's Gospel. The characterization has some validity, though as we shall argue in this chapter, 'persecution' and 'vindication' might be more accurate terms.[1]

There is, however, another two-fold theme which focuses less on the narrated and implied story and more on the discourse itself. Mark's alternating emphases are often 'discernment' and 'discipleship'. We have already seen that Mark has adopted βλέπω and γρηγορέω as his technical terms for these. In the previous chapter we recognized Mark's 'temple' theme as one of the key foci for his discernment emphasis.

Mark's Gospel displays a strong emphasis on the theme of persecution. While this does not require the interpretation that Mark's community was experiencing persecution, or was in imminent danger of meeting its onslaught, the best evidence seems to support those who say that persecution was their present or expected lot.[2]

Again we shall discover that Mark has made real though subtle points by hinting that an historical narrative is not all the reader is invited to 'see' and 'hear' when working through the Markan text. Geographical and topographical entities are intended to have symbolic qualitites; the journeys that take place between them are carriers of theological/discipleship implications. We shall discover as well that Mark has again made subtle points by surreptitiously juxtaposing elements within an intentionally significant sequence without revealing the implications he apparently intends discerning readers to deduce.

If all this sounds as though we are about to embark on an ethereal journey into speculation and complicated literary analysis, let us be reminded that virtually every commentator accepts as much as we have said thus far, if only he or she accepts that Mark has taken the geographical movement of Jesus from Galilee to Jerusalem and used it to point to the 'way of life and/or death' for Christian disciples as they follow him. Let us take note also that to take an historical event and make it a paradigm for later experiences of God's people is a thoroughly Biblical way of writing. Exoduses from bondage and entrances into blessing recur in Old Testament literature, and not only when a literal journey is in view, certainly not only when the Red Sea and the Jordan River are the barriers that, apart from God's intervention, stand in the way.

Persecution was an almost continuous experience for the early church from the days of Jesus through the latest writings of the New Testament. It is clear that its presence affected the church's own understanding of the Gospel.[3] It will be our goal to determine the significance of 'persecution' in the theology of Mark's Gospel. This chapter will argue that there is a remarkably consistent pattern that runs from the passion of John, through the passion of Jesus, on to the passion of Jesus' disciples, and beyond. A study of isolated persecution texts and Markan persecution vocabulary alone is inadequate to uncover the pattern. It is embedded in the narrative structure of the Gospel. Mark encourages the reader to notice narrative juxtapositions and to draw conclusions about relationships of cause and effect, ground and implication.

It is not necessary to provide evidence for two important strands in our argument. The points have been made by others and will be assumed here. They are: (1) Mark has deliberately presented the passion of John and the passion of Jesus in such a way that the parallels between them are highlighted, and (2) Mark has very deliberately projected beyond the resurrection (especially in Mark 13, but also in 8.34-38, 10.38f., etc.) trials for Christian believers which closely parallel the passion of Jesus.

We wish to move beyond these insights by suggesting that the relationship between these various 'passions' is not merely parallelism, nor even merely foreshadowing.[4] Mark's theology of the advancing kingdom is much more like a relay race in which persecution for the sake of the Gospel is the baton passed on from each runner to the next as they take their round on the track . . . or (to stick closer to Mark's imagery), it is the cross passed on from shoulder to shoulder as new recruits travel the 'way' from Galilee to Jerusalem.

The two main sections of this chapter will deal with the 'passing of the baton' from John to Jesus, and from Jesus to the disciples. These two studies will be preceded by a section that clears up a few points essential for the understanding of Mark's viewpoint; and they are followed by suggested implications for the interpretation of Mark 13.

I. *The Road to Jerusalem: Via Dolorosa?*

It is not uncommon to read Markan commentators who speak as though in Mark's Gospel everything begins in Galilee and ends in Jerusalem, or who imagine that Mark knows of only one journey that Jesus makes from the north to the south. A careful reading of what Mark explicitly says in the narrative, and of what he projects beyond it, reveals that the alternation between Galilee and Judea is more repetitive and more significant than is usually imagined.

The Journeys of Jesus and the Disciples
The Gospel begins in Judea, not Galilee, and it ends with an arrow pointing to Galilee, not grounded in Jerusalem.[5] The Gospel reports not one but two trips by the earthly Jesus from the north to the south. He leaves Galilee at 1.9 and returns at 1.14. He leaves again at 10.1 and returns at 16.7. If the reader traces the narrated and implied story, then Mark's Gospel also speaks of two trips by the disciples from Galilee to Jerusalem. They make their first journey as they physically accompany Jesus on his *second*, and an additional journey is implied for the disciples in the post-resurrection period. They are invited to Galilee in 16.7 and it is assumed by parts of Mark 13 that they are again back in Jerusalem. All this will prove of great significance in understanding Mark's 'journey' symbolism, a motif that has intrigued many commentators, but has perhaps not yet yielded all its secrets.

The Journey Motif: The Way of Discipleship, Not to It
As the disciples literally walk behind Jesus from Galilee to Judea, they and the readers are being shown what it means truly to 'follow' Jesus on 'the way of the cross'.[6] Mark's point, of course, is not that what the disciples *did* constitutes discipleship. They are not good models. True discipleship is doing what the disciples were being *called to do*.

Even though the reader is not assured until 15.13 that Jesus will

literally die on a cross, and even though the literal cross is carried
only from 15.20 to 15.22, Mark intends his readers to think of the
whole journey from Caesarea Philippi to Jerusalem as the 'way' on
which Jesus carried his cross, and on which his followers are called to
do the same.[7] Mark has brilliantly interwoven a historical narrative
of a journey with a theological discourse on discipleship (8.27–10.45).
He has carefully tied most of the main 'discipleship lessons' explicitly
to the imagery of being 'on the way' (ἐν τῇ ὁδῷ) with, and sometimes
behind, Jesus.[8] He has then framed the whole section with the
'giving-of-sight' stories (8.22-26; 10.46-52) which call the disciples
and the readers to 'see' what is happening. It becomes clear from all
this that 'the cross' which the disciples are to carry connotes not only
martyrdom, certainly not only martyrdom on a cross; it connotes
those other 'discipleship elements' which Mark ties so closely to the
passion predictions (forfeiting 'the world' in favour of 'the soul'
[8.36f.], loyalty to the rejected Son of Man [8.38], inverted
assessments of greatness [9.33-37], finding 'glory' by way of suffering
[10.35-40], aiming at servanthood rather than lordship [10.42-44],
etc.). *The 'cross' is a way of living, not only a way of dying.*[9]

What is at the End of the Road?
One commentator has suggested that the dominant literary image of
Jesus today is that of:[10]

> . . . a lonely figure walking ahead of his puzzled and half-frightened
> disciples, speaking to them abruptly in dark riddles, with his face
> set to go up to Jerusalem.

That might well represent the perspective of the uncomprehending
disciples in Mark. It is not the perspective of the author of the
Gospel. It was precisely because the disciples could not see past the
impending trials to the glory beyond them that the disciples earned
Jesus' rebuke, 'you do not think the things of God but the things of
men' (8.33). The disciples were given the 'secret' of the kingdom
(4.11) precisely in order that they might maintain hope when the
outlook appeared grim. They were not to think that small beginnings
(4.30-32) or adverse conditions (4.3-8) would prevent the kingdom
from coming to fruition.

Mark's theology of 'the way' and of 'carrying the cross' must be
interpreted with this in mind. According to Mark, the cost of
discipleship is not exacted at the end of the journey. The whole
journey is the way of the cross. At the end is not defeat, persecution

or the passion, but vindication and glory. Jesus is not on the road to Jerusalem in order to suffer, he is on the road in order to pass through suffering into glory. A failure to realize this has caused us to misinterpret Mark's emphasis throughout the last half of his Gospel. C.E. Faw puts his finger on the problem, suggesting why the mood of Mark's Gospel is so often dominated by the idea of suffering and death:[11]

> It is interesting how scholar after scholar refers to the three predictions as 'passion announcements', 'predictions of the passion', or 'prophecies of the passion', omitting the fact that every time the death is predicted the resurrection is also predicted.

When we recognize that any suffering and persecution which might result from allegiance to Jesus is merely 'along the road', and that vindication and glory are at the end, the whole Gospel of Mark looks different. Mark 8.34-38 is not finally about losing one's life, forfeiting the world, and unashamedly joining in the Son of Man's rejection. It is finally about saving one's life, gaining one's soul, and seeing the kingdom. The dialogue with the 'rich young man' is not about the necessity of self-sacrifice, but about the means of gaining eternal life (10.17-21). The immediately ensuing dialogue with the disciples is not about how difficult and depressing is the life of following Jesus, but about how a generous repayment and finally eternal life vindicate a life of self-sacrifice and persecution (10.28-31). The disciples are not consigned to 'last' place, they are shown how they can be first; they are not consigned to slavery status, they are shown how to become great (10.43f.). If seeking glory 'along the road' is out of place (10.37f.), to give it at the end of the road is God's prerogative (10.40). The whole discipleship journey section can be viewed as a depressing call to suffering, but Mark intends it to be viewed as the secret means of gaining glory.

Much of the dramatic irony surrounding Jesus' passion is centred on the fact that Jesus' enemies imagine they can prevent Jesus' ascendancy to regal honour and authority by putting him to death, while Jesus knows that they are carrying him along the very road he himself has chosen to walk, at the end of which is his coronation.

The logic of Jesus' response to the glory-seeking sons of Zebedee is not a repudiation of the desire itself, but an explication of the fact that on the road Jesus is taking them, there is to be no glory without suffering first, and glory, when it comes will not be on human terms.

But the end of the road will bring the great reversal of fortunes that the Jews were taught to expect when the kingdom arrived.

The Kingdom's Secret: 'Defeats' Turn into Victories

The reference to 'the secret of the kingdom' (τὸ μυστήριον τῆς βασιλείας) in Mark 4.11 is not so much hinting at one particular fact about the kingdom as it is pointing toward the very nature of the kingdom itself. It is the sort of kingdom that comes with secrecy, so that only those with eyes to see and ears to hear will discern its advance. Very near the heart of this secrecy element is the fact that various events which are recorded within Mark's Gospel, and some events projected beyond it, might well appear to the untrained eye to be defeats, but in fact they are not. It is Mark's intention to help the reader recognize these seeming defeats as God-ordered advances for the kingdom.[12]

The main sections of this chapter will deal with the changes from defeat into victory that occur in the passions of John and Jesus. In each case, Mark not only indicates that vindication follows for those who are martyred, he also indicates that the very cause of the kingdom's advance is thereby furthered. The phenomenon is to be found not only in these two major 'defeats' but in virtually every minor 'defeat' along the way. Mark reports a 'setback' and immediately supercedes it, without narrative comment, by the report of a major advance. The pattern is so persistent it is hard to believe Mark did not intend it.[13] It is up to the reader to make the connection and draw the proper deductions.

In the light of this, does it surprise us when the death of Jesus itself, clearly the greatest possible 'defeat' in the eyes of those who think 'the things of men', is immediately followed without narrative comment by the report of the temple veil's tearing and the Centurion's confession? It is of a piece with Mark's theology and his methodology.[14]

Even the resurrection announcement highlights this transformation of defeat into victory. The messenger at the tomb puts emphasis on the fact that the one who has risen is 'Jesus the Nazarene *who was crucified*' (16.6).[15] The rejected one is not *replaced* by a victor; the rejected one, precisely by having been rejected, *becomes* the victor. Truly, 'defeat' itself is turned into victory, and opposition against Jesus into stepping stones advancing his cause. That is the 'secret of the kingdom'.

II. *The Rejected Baptist and the Fulfilment of His Mission*

The 'Handing Over' of John

The first announcement of John's 'passion' and the start of Jesus' ministry are very tightly connected in the narrative (1.14). The significance of this is surely not exhausted by the usual suggestions: (1) Jesus had a good sense of timing; (2) Mark is preserving the accuracy of John's prophecy that Jesus comes *after* him; (3) Mark is countering aberrant attitudes to John the Baptist within his community. The evidence of such texts as 9.11-13, 11.27-33 and 15.35f., calls us to look for deeper significance in the relationship between John/Elijah and Jesus than mere chronological succession. John's fate itself is somehow tied up with Jesus' advent. Add to that the fact that the fates of John and Jesus are so remarkably paralleled, and we have all the makings of another subtle Markan teaching structure. Elements are juxtaposed without explicit comment, but a profound theological significance seems to be attached to their co-ordination.[16]

We must certainly avoid the conclusion that Mark thinks John's ministry came to an untimely end, that his 'handing over' was a misfortune or a disaster. Mark 9.13 makes it clear that, for Mark, the ill-treatment done to John/Elijah is the very thing that he was destined according to the Scriptures to experience.[17]

Here we must recall the oft-mentioned fact that Mark has deliberately paralleled the fates of John and Jesus.[18] It is very likely that the ambiguous 'hand over' (παραδίδωμι) in 1.14 has been deliberately selected in order to further that goal.[19] Had 'into prison' been added, the parallelism would have been obscured.[20] The deliberate ambiguity is a skillful way of alluding to a parallelism which is not quite perfect, but is nevertheless important for the author. 'Just as John was Jesus' forerunner in his life, so was he in his death'.[21] Jesus' ministry is subsequent to John's; his death will follow the pattern set by John's. 1.14 clearly points in this direction. But most commentators have taken it no further.

To take the matter no further is perhaps to miss the most important point Mark is trying to make in 1.14. Mark does not only parallel the fates of Jesus and John, nor does he merely establish the fact that Jesus' ministry is subsequent to John's; he highlights the fact that *through the very fate of John the Baptist, Jesus' ministry receives the signal to go ahead*. For Mark, John completes his work precisely *by* being 'handed over'. The people have been prepared through repentance and baptism. Jesus has been prepared through his baptismal commissioning and testing. 'The Way' itself is now fully prepared with John's 'handing over'. Perhaps 'the beginning of the Gospel' (ἀρχὴ τοῦ εὐαγγελίου 1.1) is a richly endowed phrase Mark with various levels of fulfilment. Mark 1.1-14a recounts how the Gospel begins. After the preparations are complete, we see the baton being passed from John to Jesus. John has gone the way prepared for him; Jesus can now fulfil his mission in going the way prepared for him.

The 'Way' That John Prepared

'The way' (ἡ ὁδός) in 1.2f. cannot for Mark be other than 'the way of suffering', or more accurately, 'the way through suffering to glory'.[22] Perhaps Mark's reason for drawing on Mal. 3.1, but not drawing attention to that fact (the composite quotation in 1.2f. is of course credited to Isaiah who contributes the larger share) is that though the messenger does indeed come and prepare the way, he does so in a very different way than Malachi pictures, and he does it to prepare for God's presence in a different temple altogether.[23]

If 'the way' is the way through suffering, then Jesus does indeed do his purification work (Mal. 3.3) precisely by following God's messenger in 'the way' prepared for him. When it is noted exactly how 'the way' is used in the section symbolizing the passion/discipleship journey (8.27–10.45), these suggestions gain a great deal of plausibility.

Mark seems to have gone out of his way to portray the seeming 'defeat' of the Baptist as the precondition for Jesus' advent. He presented Mark 1.1-14a as John's preparation of 'the way'. He hints, by means of 1.14a, that the 'defeat' of John is the very building block on which Jesus' ministry rests, and he leaves the actual narration of John's death for a later narrative flashback, when the progress of his story about Jesus makes it more appropriate to include this story about the passion that in so many ways prefigures Jesus' own. To the report of John's passion, then, we turn our attention.

The Death of John

The positioning of the story of John's execution (coinciding with the disciples' missionary journey) has elicited comments by almost every exegete.[24] The linking of persecution and mission in Mark's Gospel suggests that we look for a theological connection. Those who have done so have almost unanimously concluded that Mark is saying mission will lead to persecution and/or death. But, is not the point rather the converse—that when God's messenger is faithful on 'the way' of suffering, the kingdom thereby advances as others take up the baton and run the next leg of the race?

So often one finds commentators reading 1.14 and 6.14-29 as though they were Mark's ominous warnings of doom.[25] 'If this is what happened to John, what better can Jesus or the community expect'? But those texts are not Mark's attempts to over-shadow his entire work with a dark cloud. They are his way of helping the discerning reader to begin to trace the silver lining, the promise of glory and vindication at the end of the road.[26] They speak of the irresistible victory of the cause for which one is called to follow 'the way'.[27] At a more immediate level, they are his way of demonstrating that, though suffering is the destined lot of those whose allegiance is with Jesus, the message they proclaim cannot be stopped by their rejection, or even by their death. 1.14 does not say, 'John's preaching led to his fate; Jesus can expect no better'. It says, 'The very death of John becomes victory in that it brings to completion the preparations for Jesus'. 6.14-29 in the context of 6.12f. and 30 does not say, 'John was beheaded for preaching repentance; the disciples can expect no better'. It says, 'Even as John's death is recounted, we observe not one but twelve messengers taking his place'.

Mark has, remarkably, used the mission of the twelve to picture the Gospel's advance after both the rejection of Jesus in Nazareth and the passion of John under Herod. Like Jesus, they go about exorcizing and healing. Like John, they preach, not the kingdom, but repentance.[28] Certainly the mission of the disciples at this point is temporary, and possibly also quite inadequate. Their real opportunity to take up the baton and run their race must await the death and resurrection of Jesus.[29] Still, the narrative juxtaposing here is part of a Markan pattern. One is rejected, but the work goes on and expands.[30] The kingdom cannot be stopped by human opposition.

Mark's whole Gospel breathes with life and hope for those who read it according to the norms Mark establishes for thinking 'the things of God'. Persecution can be a stepping stone to vindication and glory. It can also be a cause for stumbling, when those who have heard the word have shallow roots (4.17). But even then the cause of the kingdom is not set back. It will inexorably advance, however slowly, however secretly, toward its fulfilment when all the persecuted saints are gathered to the returning Son of Man. The kingdom comes 'on its own' (αὐτομάτη 4.28). Even seeming defeats are turned into

Mark has been at work establishing a 'passion paradigm'. He has shown us how it worked in the case of John and the transition from his work to that of Jesus. The passion that God's servant undergoes is neither an unforeseen tragedy, nor the goal of the road. It is a station along 'the way'. On the other side of the passion, two sorts of vindications take place ... personal vindication as the runner who completes his lap moves into the victory circle to await the final triumph ... corporate vindication as the baton is handed on to the next runner on the track in a race that cannot be lost. That is how the secret kingdom operates. We will now see how it works when Jesus' passion becomes the occasion for the disciples' ministry.

III. *Jesus' Passion and the Mission of the Disciples*

Our argument will be that just as the 'handing over' of John became the occasion for Jesus to begin his lap of the race, so also the 'handing over' of Jesus becomes the occasion for the disciples to begin theirs. If this can be established, we should seriously consider the possibility that Mark 13.9-13 suggests a new lap which begins when the disciples themselves are 'handed over', and others take up the baton for the worldwide mission.

The biggest problem is that Mark is at his most enigmatic at precisely the point where the transition from Jesus' ministry to the apostles' ministry is to take place, the point of the post-resurrection commissioning. Mark 16.7 and 16.8 are among the most difficult verses in the Gospel. If we want to understand the transition Mark envisions between Jesus' ministry and that of the apostles, the difficulties cannot be circumvented.

There are four fundamental and interlocking exegetical difficulties that we must face in dealing with Mark 16.7f: (1) the problem of the literary role Mark assigns to the apostles; (2) the problem of the authentic ending of Mark's Gospel; (3) the problem of the meaning of 'Galilee' in 16.7; and (4) the problem of identifying the meaning and significance of 16.8. Each of these would merit a longer discussion than it will be possible to include. Some widely held views will need to be dealt with rather briefly. It is hoped that the overall consistency of the final conclusions we reach will be the justification for our procedure.

Discipleship Failure in Mark's Gospel

Why does Mark highlight the failure of the disciples? An answer frequently given is that Mark is writing a polemical document and using Gospel characters as part of a sustained attack on the proponents of what he considers to be a false Christology, eschatology, or other theological view. The arguments take many forms but frequently insist that Mark is discrediting either the apostles themselves, theological opponents who trace their view to the apostles, or else theological opponents who are caricatured in the portrait Mark paints of the apostles.[31] Mark's Gospel becomes a dramatic device for intra-Christian polemics.[32] It is not possible here to evaluate the individual arguments. A general response would be that:

1. While it is undeniable that Mark highlights the failure of the disciples in his Gospel, [33] it is surely far-fetched to imagine that Mark or his church could have 'loved the Messiah and hated the Twelve'[34] if any other plausible explanation of the data can be found.[35] There are various other explanations more plausible than the one that Mark is 'assiduously involved in a vendetta against the disciples'.[36]

2. Those who focus all their attention on the disciples' failure have no plausible explanation for the positive traits that are recorded of them in Mark's Gospel.[37]

3. Some forms of the argument are quite clearly implausible. Are we to believe that Jesus repudiates the disciples because they were unable to disentangle themselves from the false theology into which Jesus himself has led them?[38] Other forms are more plausible from a literary-critical point of view, but there are also powerful literary-critical arguments opposing them.[39]

4. It is impossible to sustain the view that the disciples are repudiated, in the light of the fact that Mark 13 pictures them as defenders of the truth, in some cases guarding against the very errors they themselves once held. Their errors have been repudiated, and their theologies corrected.[40]

5. Almost all the arguments fail to distinguish between 'discipleship failure' and 'discipleship repudiation'. Apart from Judas, none of the disciples, even in their moments of darkest failure, ever contemplate repudiating their discipleship in favour of either neutrality or joining the enemy.[41]

They remain disciples, and intend to remain disciples, even when they find themselves unable or unwilling to live out all the radical demands of their calling.[42] According to Mark's theology, spiritual ignorance and moral failure on their own are not grounds for repudiation.

6.   Literary arguments defending Mark as primarily a polemicist provide far too flimsy a foundation for the various interesting 'reconstructions' of what 'really happened' in the first four decades of early church development. Where is the historical data supporting them?[43]

If the 'repudiation theory' is unacceptable, the interest Mark obviously has in the failure of the disciples needs to be explained in some other way. A very plausible explanation for Mark's interest in discipleship failure, especially Peter's, is that it was a theme of the preaching of Peter and the apostles.[44] If Peter was one of Mark's direct sources, and if Mark the author was the man who turned back on his discipleship when things got tough at Perga in Pamphylia (Acts 13.13), perhaps both the traditional level and the redactional level may have contributed to the emphasis on discipleship failure. Peter and Mark might both have reflected carefully on the seriousness of their failure and the wonder of their restoration into their Lord's service.[45] This genetic explanation does not of course rule out a teleological explanation.

The explanation defended by T.A. Burkill and E. Schweizer, is the one that so influenced W. Wrede at the beginning of the century. It is the view that, according to Mark, everyone in the Gospel is destined to misunderstand prior to the resurrection and destined to understand thereafter.[46]

The most satisfactory explanation of all, however, is that Mark, whether or not he was thinking of his own previous failures or those of Peter, is highlighting for the benefit of his readers, the magnitude of the forgiveness that is available through the death and resurrection of Jesus—even for those who have failed most seriously.[47] Throughout the first three watches of the night (see Chapter 4), while the failure of the disciples is highlighted, the building blocks are being set up for their renewal: Jesus' self-sacrifice 'for many' (14.24); Jesus' prediction of restoration (14.28); Peter's tears of repentance (14.72). If Mark highlights the disciples' failure, it is to demonstrate that such failure can be forgiven. It is Mark's way of sending a message of hope to those in his day who are prone to fail as the disciples did.[48]

While the focus is on the fact that failure can be forgiven, it is at the same time also on the fact that what the disciples failed to learn and do, Mark's readers must be careful to learn and do. The disciples are used as a *typology per contrarium*.[49] Mark's point is then twofold: The disciples failed to understand and to follow in the crisis; we must not. Yet if we do, then like them we can be forgiven and begin again.

If Mark does not view the disciples as repudiated because of their failure, but rather as invited back to their calling in consequence of the passion and resurrection of Jesus, there must be a plausible interpretation of the last two verses of Mark's Gospel which correlates meaningfully with this viewpoint.

The Authentic Ending of Mark's Gospel
There are a wide variety of difficult questions surrounding the last verses of Mark's Gospel. Because our concern is to move quickly to a discussion of 'Galilee' in Mark 16.7, we will deal rather summarily with the question of Mark's authentic ending as an issue of its own. As we shall argue, the two are related.

Scholarly consensus there is not, but in increasing measure the following five relevant points are finding scholarly support:

1. Mark 16.9-20 is a spurious ending, neither written by Mark, nor produced by making minor modifications of something he did write.[50]
2. There are no persuasive arguments demonstrating that a lost authentic ending of Mark has been substantially preserved in any of the other Gospels or in Acts.[51]
3. It is possible to end a book with γάρ.[52]
4. It is not uncharacteristic of Mark to employ the kind of literary subtleties that we must credit to him if we accept the present puzzling ending as the one he intended.[53]
5. There is only one platform which, if secure, can give a legitimate basis for concluding either that Mark wrote more, or that he intended to. That is: no plausible sense can be made of the present ending.[54]

If these five points are legitimate, and we hope this study has helped to substantiate the fourth one, then in the absence of new data, there can be no persuasive *positive* arguments in favour of a lost ending or a never-finished Gospel. The conclusion that Mark wrote (or wanted to write) more can be reached only be default, by examining all proffered interpretations of the present ending and finding them all wanting.[55]

Some interpretations, to be sure, are not acceptable. One is the view that the enigmatic ending completes a sustained attempt to discredit the apostles, the family of Jesus, the Jerusalem mother church, or someone in Mark's church cast into the role of these Gospel characters. It would be preferable to settle for an hypothetical lost ending.

There have been several unsuccessful attempts to treat most of Mark 16.1-8 as either allegory or midrash.[56] Far more successful are those interpretations which treat Mark 16.1-8 in just the way that so many other Markan texts invite us to—as a straight-forward historical narrative, but with subtle and profound theological nuances attached to it by restrained and appropriate symbolism, and especially by the juxtaposing of various contrasting and/or complementary elements.

There are various difficulties in Mark 16.1-8, but clearly the most central issues in understanding Mark's meaning involve interpreting 'Galilee' in Mark 16.7 (if it is more than purely geographical), and accounting for the fact that the women's fear and disobedience block the resurrection message from reaching the disciples (if in fact that is what Mark intends to convey).

There have, to be sure, been those who have dismissed both as pseudo-problems: Galilee is geographical *only* and the women *do* in fact (according to 16.8) report to the disciples. Neither interpretation is acceptable.

To say that Galilee is a geographical term needs to be said. Some proponents of 'symbolic' interpretations seem almost to have forgotten that. But to solve the problem of Mark's enigmatic ending by saying that it is geographical *and nothing more* is to opt for a solution which is only superficially attractive. It removes all mystery from 16.7 and thereby renders 16.8 even more difficult to deal with. If 16.7 is nothing more than an invitation to meet Jesus in Galilee (in a resurrection appearance), then how does one account for the fact that Mark ends his Gospel by saying that the message was never delivered to the disciples? One is almost forced to read Mark 16.8 as though it is saying the opposite of what it certainly seems to be saying (see below), or else to postulate a missing ending.

The missing ending solution is tolerable (though we believe unnecessary); the usual reinterpretation of Mark 16.8 is not. It is sometimes held that the women's fear is merely the natural and appropriate response to a divine messenger, and that their silence is only a refusal to chatter with folk on their way back from the tomb; Mark never intended to suggest that they did not report to the disciples. This view obviously opts for 'Markan clumsiness' over 'Markan ingenuity'. If Mark really meant that the women were over-awed by the divine messenger and hastened to obey his command, speaking to no one *except the disciples*, he certainly made his point badly. The women disobeyed out of a reprehensible fear. We shall return to this point.

What we need to do instead of reinterpreting 16.8 is to find a view of 'Galilee', which permits it to retain its geographical significance in the historical narrative, but which sees it also as the carrier of a symbolic nuance for the theological point that Mark is making by means of his resurrection report. And we need to find a way of reading 16.8 which supports that interpretation of 16.7 without making the verse say what it does not say. Somehow the fear and the disobedient silence must play a part in the message of Mark in the last two verses of his Gospel.

The Meaning of 'Galilee' in Mark 14.28; 16.7

It is not difficult to find examples throughout the Scriptures of geographical place names which have acquired associations that are frequently implied when the geographical term is cited.[57] It would not be unprecedented if Mark treated 'Galilee' in that way.

The view that 'Galilee' is not merely a geographical term but intended by the Gospel writer to point to some special theological significance associated with Galilee is an old view, as old as Augustine, Gregory the Great, and Bede. Its revival in the twentieth century began with A.M. Ramsey who suggested that, rather than signifying an actual meeting place, it signified Victory and Mission.[58] E. Lohmeyer and R.H. Lightfoot were early defenders of the view that it represented the place of the parousia of the Son of Man.

The two views, parousia and mission, have remained the most popular views to this day. At times the two views have been combined. Both views are subject to a number of criticisms.

'Galilee' as 'The Place of the Parousia'.

Arguments in defence of this interpretation[59] frequently claim that the purported Markan insertion of 14.28 and 16.7 into otherwise coherent contexts betrays his attempt to introduce parousia concerns into the text. However, 14.28

fits well into the context of 14.27-31, suggesting that discipleship renewal, not the parousia, are intended by 14.28.[60]

There are other arguments used to support the parousia interpretation but they are not persuasive. It has sometimes been suggested that the choice of vocabulary argues against a 'resurrection appearance' interpretation. The technical term for a resurrection appearance is ὤφθη not ὄψεσθε.[61] But how could the messenger at the tomb use an aorist passive to predict what the disciples would do to the risen Christ?

It is sometimes argued that Mark must have had the parousia in mind since he has little concern for the post-resurrection period. But this argument should be stood on its head. The greatest *weakness* of the Galilee—parousia connection is that it blocks out the possibilities for renewed discipleship in the post-resurrection situation, and therefore logically entails the theories of discipleship repudiation just discussed, and is subject to the same criticisms as those theories. The truth is that Mark has a great deal of interest in the period of time between the resurrection and the parousia. Primarily the discipleship-journey section (8.27-10.45), but also the rest of the Gospel, are designed by Mark to do far more than report history; he is teaching his readers what it means to be citizens of the secret kingdom, and what it means to live as faithful disciples of Jesus in the post-resurrection period. Mark and the very people he is seeking to instruct live in the time period concerning which some want to claim Mark has little interest.

It should also be considered that there is nothing whatsoever in Mark 13 which even hints that eschatological fulfilment is to take place in Galilee (despite Marxsen's use of 13.14), that the so-called 'passion predictions' uniformly predict that a resurrection, not a parousia, will follow the passion,[62] that 16.7 pictures Jesus going ahead of the disciples to wait for them, not their going ahead to wait for him, that Peter (who gets special mention in 16.7) was probably not even alive when Mark wrote, and that Galilee, far from being the scene of revelation, is the region where Jesus' messianic dignity is veiled.[63] There is little to commend the interpretation that Mark 16.7 is an announcement of an imminent parousia in Galilee.[64]

'Galilee' as 'Mission Headquarters'. The second major view of 'Galilee' is that it is, for Mark, the point of departure for the Gentile mission.[65] This is a widely held view and has advantages over the

previous interpretation. It takes seriously the post-resurrection pre-parousia period and the responsibility of the disciples to preach the Gospel during that period. It builds on what Jesus actually did in Galilee (he carried out a mission within and beyond Galilee; he did not appear as the glorious Son of Man). It takes seriously the 'journey' element in the 14.28 and 16.7 predictions. It fits neatly with 3.14 where the apostles' calling is twofold: (1) to be *with him* (during the ministry?) and, (2) to be *sent out* to preach (after the resurrection?).[66] It takes seriously the 'shepherding' imagery in 14.28 and 16.7. After the resurrection, Jesus will again be leading his disciples. It is important to notice, however, that the 'mission' interpretation features minimal continuity between the pre-passion 'journey' and the post-resurrection 'journey'. Before the passion, Jesus led his disciples on a passion/discipleship journey to Jerusalem. After the resurrection he leads them on a missionary journey through Galilee.[67]

It is precisely this discontinuity which reveals the weaknesses of this interpretation. The disciples have *not* successfully completed one journey, so that they are ready for the second. They have *not* been 'with him', so that now they can be 'sent out'. Despite the neatness with which 3.14 fits the scheme, it is probably not Mark's intention to make it fit. The whole logic of 14.28 in context, and therefore of 16.7, is that finally after the resurrection the disciples will be able to fulfil their calling, *both* to be with him and to be sent out. They utterly fail to be 'with him' during the passion (see Chapter 4). The resurrection is not the dividing line between the two responsibilities (to be with him and to be sent out); it is the start of both.

There are also other difficulties with the 'mission' interpretation. Not to be overlooked is the significant fact that the course of early church history is different from the prediction given by the messenger at the tomb. Unless 'Galilee' is *purely* symbolic and therefore the disciples can 'go to Galilee and see Jesus' without ever setting a foot outside geographical Jerusalem, the prediction that Galilee will be a centre for worldwide mission is at odds with what really happened. Furthermore, most defenders of the 'mission' interpretation of 'Galilee' have leaned heavily on the erroneous view that Mark favours a transition of election to Gentiles, at the expense of Jews.[68] Is there no way of finding *continuity* between the disciples' pre-passion and post-resurrection journeys? If Jesus' discipleship journey is the model for believers in the post-resurrection age, and if it is precisely in the context of passion/discipleship that effective mission takes place, we would do well to examine another option concerning where the risen Jesus, like a shepherd, leads his regathered flock.

'Galilee' as 'Discipleship Renewal'. If we are looking for interpretations which show most sensitivity to Mark's methods and his messages throughout the Gospel, we would do well to consider the suggestion represented here by E. Best:[69]

> Where then is he [Jesus]? In Galilee at their head. What does that mean? Listen to the story as a believer and work it out for yourself. It is like one of Jesus' own parables: the hearer is forced to go on thinking. Mark gives a clue to the way our minds should go in the word 'Galilee'. At the end we are taken back to the beginning: in 16.7 Jesus returns to Galilee whence he came in 1.9. . . . There is no resting place in the joy and triumph of the resurrection; we have always to return to the beginning in Galilee and advance forward again to the cross. It is a continual pilgrimage, and the Christ whom we follow is both the crucified and the risen Christ. In that way the story is rounded off and we realise its unity.

Best is not alone in the major part of his view as quoted above. Others have seen 'Galilee' in 16.7 as related back to 'Galilee' in 1.9 and/or 1.14, and therefore as implying a renewal of discipleship.[70] The arguments in favour of this interpretation are persuasive. The 'but' (ἀλλὰ) of 14.28 is taken seriously with its indication that after the passion things will be reversed. Jesus will be raised after being stricken; the disiples will become followers again after being scattered.[71] The travel language can be taken seriously. Jesus has gone ahead to prepare the way; in Galilee they will be regathered so that he can again (like a shepherd) lead them, and they can again (like sheep) follow (cf. 14.27f).[72] Mission is put into proper perspective; it is one of the activities of faithful disciples, not their sole preoccupation in the post-resurrection period.[73] Morna Hooker sums up this interpretation well when she says:[74]

> The invitation is to begin again. Is this why they are summoned to Galilee? Various explanations have been given for the reference to Galilee; it has been suggested that this will be the place of the parousia; or that it is the place for mission to the Gentiles. But Mark gives no hint of either idea. In his story Galilee was the place where Jesus called the disciples, trained them, taught them and

sent them out. If Jesus calls them now to follow him to Galilee, is it not because he is gathering his scattered sheep, calling each one of them once again to deny self, take up the cross, and follow him?

But here is where we must be so very careful. Numerous commentators say almost exactly what Hooker has said, and then make the erroneous assumption that the disciples have *already* walked the road of self-denial, carrying the cross.[75]

The disciples have indeed walked the road to Jerusalem in a literal physical sense. What they have failed to do is 'walk the road' in the sense of faithful discipleship. All along the way they failed both to understand and to follow aright. When the final test of discipleship came, they failed in every possible way—selling their master instead of sacrificing themselves, giving in to the flesh instead of wrestling in prayer, taking up the world's means of combat instead of dying with their leader, standing ashamed of their master instead of making a good confession, fleeing instead of following.

To imagine that the substitutionary character of Jesus' death in itself means that the disciples are deemed to have carried the cross, drunk Jesus' cup, been baptized with his baptism, or whatever, is to adopt a theology which is dubious even for Romans and utterly foreign to Mark. Jesus' faithfulness does indeed become the vehicle through which the disciples can be forgiven (see Chapter 4). Their forgiveness, however, allows them to begin again 'on the way'. It does not absolve them from the responsibility of making the journey. If the disciples are to carry out their mission when the passion and resurrection open the door to discipleship renewal, it will be in the context of doing precisely what, up to that point they have not done—take up their crosses and follow Jesus. *'Galilee' is the starting point for the discipleship road.* It is where a renewed journey to Jerusalem, carrying Christ's cross, has its beginning. It is the start of the disciples' lap around the track. The baton has now been passed on to them.[76]

That interpretation fits perfectly with what Mark and the Markan Jesus seem to have been at pains to make clear in the last half of the Gospel. To be a faithful disciple is to take up the cross and follow Jesus on the road to the passion. It is to walk from 'Galilee' to 'Jerusalem'. It is to learn the discipleship lessons which are linked with the 'on the way' symbolism. Jesus is always ahead of his failing following disciples—not only a step ahead, but a journey ahead. Now that he has completed the journey, they will be enabled to make it themselves.[77]

The present interpretation explains why the shepherd–sheep relationship is to be reinitiated, not on the road to Galilee, but after they have regathered there. We should not let modern associations with 'shepherd' crowd out the primary associations the term would have had for Mark. 'Sheep without a shepherd' in Mark are not so much 'a congregation without a minister' as 'an army without a general' or 'a nation without a king'.[78] It is thoroughly consistent with Mark's theology to suggest that the decisive moment in the kingdom's establishment came when Jesus, in the passion, was crowned king. It would be completely in line with his theology to suggest that Jesus goes back to Galilee to regather his army, from whence he will lead them in triumph into the capital city where usurpers still cling to power. There they will fight with and for him using the very weapons he used—prayer, servanthood, self-sacrifice, courageous witness, and the authoritative words and actions which come with a commission from God. In short, they will be regathered in Galilee, so that in the presence of their risen Lord, under his leadership, and in his strength, they can fulfil all the expectations that Mark's text has generated concerning their future ... drinking the cup Jesus drinks, experiencing his baptism, carrying his cross, being 'handed over', going to trial ... and in all this fulfil their mission as faithful witnesses until it is their turn to pass on the baton and go through suffering into glory. If their shepherd leads them to green pastures and still waters in Galilee, he will also lead them through the valley of the shadow of death in Jerusalem. But they have the assurance they will be with him forever.

Jesus' death is 'for many', and most immediately it is for his disciples. Because Jesus went faithfully through the passion to his glory, they can be forgiven and reinstated into their discipleship. They will not, however, be excused from making the journey themselves. Mark does not countenance any other way to glory.

We promised this chapter would not take us on an esoteric journey into unrestrained and ethereal symbol-mongering. We can now see that it has not done that. When Jesus and his disciples were on the road from Galilee to Jerusalem, their feet became dusty and their lips parched. It was a real physical journey.[79] No amount of theologizing on the part of Mark can, or was ever intended to, change that fact. That lessons were learned 'on the way' is simply good pedagogy, for Jesus and for Mark.

The journeys to be made after Easter are just as literal. The disciples will make a literal journey back to Galilee. The promise is held out that there they will meet Jesus, (and Matthew reports that they experienced just that). Mark's Gospel does not enable us to determine when they returned to Jerusalem. Unless Mark's knowledge of history stops short at the resurrection, he knows that the disciples were in Jerusalem not many weeks later. There they experienced the fulfilment of John's promise that Jesus would baptize with the Holy Spirit; there they became faithful witnesses; there they suffered as Jesus had. Mark narrates none of this. What we know for certain from the Markan text is that, if not immediately, then eventually, the disciples will be back in Jerusalem (13.14). They make literal journeys to Galilee and back again.

None of this changes if Mark decides to use the same pedagogical techniques for the post-resurrection disciples as his Jesus does for the pre-passion disciples. He portrays the meeting in Galilee, not merely as a resurrection appearance, but also as a renewal of discipleship. He portrays the return journey to Jerusalem, not merely as a travel link, but also as an opportunity for the disciples to 'take up their cross' and follow the way their master had led. Last time in Jerusalem they had failed at every turn. This time they must be faithful to their Lord, and in the power of the risen Christ they can be. It is their turn to run the track. Mark practises no unrestrained allegorizing; he teaches as Jesus taught, and the same lessons.

We are now ready to move from Mark 16.7 to Mark 16.8. It is tempting but illegitimate to slide over the difficulties of Mark's ending. He did not end with the promise of restoration in Galilee, but with the fear and silence of the women. Why? There is no easy answer, but that answer is most acceptable which does two things: (1) correlates theologically with Mark's concerns in the penultimate verse, and (2) suggests a rationale why Mark made his points in the way he did.

The Inappropriate Fear and Disobedient Silence of the Women
As already indicated, there are a number of scholars who explain Mark 16.8 as Mark's *coup de grâce* in his polemic against the disciples of Jesus. Even the women finally fail, and the disciples are deprived of a final opportunity to be rehabilitated. If the polemical interpretations of Mark are rejected, however, Mark 16.8 must fulfil a more worthy function.

It has been widely held that there is a contradiction between Mark 16.7 and 16.8, produced because one or the other was added at a later stage. Those who argue for a parousia interpretation for 'Galilee' hold that 16.7 has been the offending intruder; more often it has been claimed that 16.8 is to blame for producing the discord with which Mark's Gospel ends.

Various motives have been ascribed to the author or the tradition for adding the offending 16.8. Frequently it is suggested that the verse was added to explain the late introduction of the empty tomb story into the Gospel traditions. Alternatively it has been suggested that the added verse is an attempt to preclude all resurrection appearances, the only legitimate one being the coming of the Son of Man.[80] It has even been suggested that Mark 16.8 was added to signal to the reader that the midrashic techniques which fabricated Mark 16.1-7 had not been employed to continue the story-writing.[81]

We must now return to an earlier point and provide some basis for claiming that one widely held solution is not acceptable. It would be very attractive simply to erase the problems of Mark 16.8 by saying that the women's fear was an appropriate (or at least natural and therefore innocent) response to the fact of a divine messenger, and by understanding their silence as an indication of single-minded purpose as they ran to carry out their mission. They maintained silence with respect to others, not with respect to the disciples.[82] But this interpretation of 16.8 is hard to defend on the basis of what the verse actually says.

The women disregarded the commands of the messenger at the tomb;[83] they did not hasten to obey. On the contrary, they fled (ἔφυγον). It is the word used to characterize the flight of both the disciples and the naked young man in the garden (14.50, 52). They did not leave in respectful silence; they were disobedient out of fear. The text emphasizes not what they did, but what they did not do.[84] Even the fear itself cannot be made into the 'holy terror' that appropriately accompanied confrontation with a divine messenger.[85]

The only way we can put a positive face on the behaviour of the women is to contradict it in a continuation of the story, as the opening of the longer spurious ending does (cf. 16.10)

Some, however, have thought that the very point Mark had in mind was to emphasize the fallibility of the women's responses. It is his way of saying, 'Despite human fallibility, the resurrected Christ will be finally victorious'.[86] N.R. Petersen compares the silence of the women with Judas' betrayal, the flight of the ten, and Peter's default on his promise. It is part of the scattering. Yet it will not be determinative of the final outcome any more than the other events. Jesus will meet the disciples in Galilee.[87]

Is it not more likely that the suggestion should be reversed. It is not saying, 'Though the women fail, Jesus is victorious'. It is saying, 'Though Jesus is victorious, the women fail'.[88] The suggestion is much more in keeping with the way Mark makes his points. He juxtaposes elements and encourages the readers to work it out for themselves. Note how this interpretation of 16.8 makes it the counterpart to 16.7.

16.7 makes the point that because of the resurrection, discipleship renewal is not precluded for those who have been unfaithful in the past. 16.8 makes the point that despite the resurrection, discipleship failure is not precluded for those who have been faithful in the past.

The juxtaposition of 16.7 and 16.8 might well also be designed to say, 'Knowing is no guarantee of obedience: obedience, however, will lead to knowing'. The disciples will see if only they will obey.[89] The women, even though they have the evidence they need, will not necessarily respond in obedience.[90] Discipleship, for Mark, is something which can be, and must be, constantly renewed.

We could suggest an additional nuance: the *fact* of the resurrection changes nothing for the disciple or would-be disciple. It is *meeting* the risen Christ that makes the difference.[91] To know that it happened (as the women do) does not on its own produce a discipleship response.[92] To meet the risen Christ (as the disciples are invited to do) changes everything.

The book does not end with a closed case in terms of the obedience or disobedience of either the disciples or the women. It closes without *reporting* the obedience of either.[93] The command/invitation has gone forth. It is now up to them whether or not obedience will follow.

We have noted how Mark frequently frustrates the exegete who wants nothing but conclusions: Did the women finally tell? Did the disciples finally go? Mark himself is more concerned to teach about the *factors* which lead to correct conclusions and which induce appropriate actions. We have to allow the author of the text to establish his own priorities. Mark was evidently more concerned about his readers' discipleship than their history education; so also was his Lord.

It is remarkable how successfully Mark has managed to make his Gospel stand still at Mark 16.8. At the narrative level, the Gospel starts off running full steam; it gradually comes to a halt. The first half of the Gospel is a series of rapid snapshots of Jesus and his disciples, as they dart from event to event; the keyword is 'immediately' (εὐθύς). In the middle, everything slows down and we march with Jesus and his band along the dusty road to the south; we move steadily along a journey between definite locations. Chapters 11 and 12 slow us down further as we count out the days of Jesus' last week. With chapters 14 and 15, we find ourselves counting the watches of the last 24 hours. At the tomb, the reader is left standing still before the resurrection message. The women have fled; will they ever take up their assignment? The disciples have previously been told to make their way to Galilee (cf. 14.28);[94] will they obey? The readers are left to contemplate the alternatives. . . for the characters of the story . . . and for themselves. What will they do? Mark leaves them standing there to make their decision.[95]

We have provided a way of reading Mark 16.7f. It is not the only way the text can be read. We settle for this one instead of another because it accounts for the data of the verses themselves, it allows Mark to use terms and themes here in just the way he does throughout his Gospel, it reinforces the very lessons he has been at pains to teach, and (perhaps most importantly) it provides a rationale for why Mark would have *written* his ending the way he did. There may be several ways of reading a text, but if one of them helps understand why it was written as it was, that one is to be preferred.

If Mark's purpose had been to urge his readers to hasten to Galilee for the parousia, or to escape the coming destruction of Jerusalem, an enigmatic ending to conclude 16 chapters of history/theology is about the least appropriate way he could have made his point. If his purpose was to provide a theological basis for world mission, we should expect him to speak as unambiguously about it as the Markan Jesus does (cf. 13.10; 14.9). If it was his purpose merely to report 'what happened', why did he stop before he finished? But if it was his intention to encourage careful reflection on the nature of and bases for true discipleship and divinely aided spiritual discernment, should it surprise us if he speaks in parables and riddles? He has just spent 16 chapters telling us about the Son of God who did exactly that! A modern scholar can berate Mark (or Jesus) for using that technique throughout the Gospel; but he can hardly charge Mark with ending inappropriately or inconsistently.

Conclusion: The 'Passion Paradigm'
We have come a long way round; we are back now to an earlier question. Does Mark take the 'passion paradigm' which fits the transition from John to Jesus, and reapply it for the transition from Jesus to the disciples?

He does indeed. The very death of Jesus in the disciples' stead opens the door to their ministry thereafter—not as though they are absolved from discipleship responsibilities, but in order that, with the baton having been handed on to them, they can begin to make the journey that Jesus made before them.

We have argued that Jesus' own mission is ushered in by the passion of John the Baptist. Similarly we find the disciples' mission ushered in by the death of Jesus.[96] The 'passion paradigm' holds, and it is applied to the disciples by the 'journey paradigm'. We mentioned at the beginning of this chapter that the journeys from the north to the south were more numerous and more significant for Mark than most commentators have recognized. Jesus made the journey twice; so must the disciples. The parallels are not perfect, certainly, and nothing is to be gained by blurring the differences between Jesus and his followers. He was affirmed as God's beloved and faithful servant and Son; they needed to be forgiven for their constant failures. He stood in the time of testing; they fell.

But parallels there are, nevertheless. Both needed to make two journeys, the first for preparation and the second to carry out their ministries of service and suffering. On their first journeys, both were prepared by their predecessors and commissioned by God, both took up the new ministry at the point where their predecessors were taken away (or rather 'handed over'), and both were sent back to Galilee, preparations complete, ready for the service and suffering ahead.

Their second journeys would also be parallel, for Jesus has modelled for them what it will mean for them to 'follow'. They will serve and preach 'on the way' and will be rejected in Judea. The parallelism between those journeys is the explanation why there is such close agreement between the passion experiences predicted for the disciples in Mark 13 and those recorded for Jesus in 14–16. It is the explanation also why Mark can take the model of Jesus in his passion as the definition of 'watching' in the unknown period before the parousia (13.33-37, see Chapter 4). It is the explanation finally why despite, indeed because of, the suffering of both, the Gospel is destined to fill the world (14.9; 13.10).

There is overlap between John and Jesus and between Jesus and the disciples, but the overlap is only in the time of *preparation*. Their *ministries* are sequential, or rather cumulative. Jesus promised the 'kingdom plant' would grow by stages—'first the stalk, then the head, then the full kernel in the head' (4.28). There is continuity from stage to stage, and the precise shape of each one may vary—but all are necessary stages on the way to the harvest.

Clearly, for Mark, suffering and death are not tragedies, either personally, or in the cause of the kingdom. They are stepping stones to glory for the individual, and they become the great transition points in the successive advancement of the 'secret kingdom'.

From this point of view it can be cautiously suggested that all suffering experienced by believers as a result of their discipleship obedience is redemptive, not only that of Jesus.[97] It is of course not being suggested that for Mark all the suffering of John, Jesus and the apostles together somehow atones for sin, but then Mark does not spend much effort discussing sin-atonement. If it is true that in some way which Mark does not clearly specify, Jesus' death acquires benefit for others, and especially makes possible the forgiveness and reinstatement of those disciples who failed in the crisis, then it is true that in some sense the suffering of John acquires benefits for others as well, for it occasions the mission of Jesus; and the suffering of the disciples also acquires benefits for others, for it occasions the expanded opportunities for witness that are highlighted in Mark 13.9-13.[98]

Many scholars have pointed out the parallel between the ministries and the passions of John, Jesus and the apostles.[99] So often, however, it is viewed as something more cyclical than spiral, more like successive races around the track, than a single relay race with the baton passed on from one to the other.[100] Mark's view is thoroughly 'teleological'; each participant blazes a trail for others to follow, all heading for the final goal. In a sense, each transition is another 'beginning of the Gospel' (1.1).[101]

And if the 'passion paradigm' illumines 1.1, it also illumines 1.2f. (if we read it in the light of its source in Mal. 3). John, through his ministry and passion, prepares the way for 'the Lord'. The Lord, through his ministry and passion, purifies new Levites to serve in a new temple. They, through their ministry and passion, will see the nations come and call them blessed (cf. Mal. 3.1, 3, 12). One thing, however, is not to be forgotten: one needs to know the secret of the kingdom to recognize all this.

As many have noted, the evangelistic efforts of each of God's messengers will provoke the world's resistance.[102] Mark, however, turns that around; the world's resistance will open the door to greater evangelism.[103] Nevertheless we should not allow ourselves to slip imperceptibly into the commonly held view that mission itself, (at least if narrowly-defined as evangelistic preaching and/or kingdom proclamation) is to be the sole preoccupation of disciples during their leg of the relay. They are to be faithful disciples with all that that entails as defined by Mark's Gospel. Part of their 'mission' is to *go and tell*, part is to *be*, part is to *do*, part is to *suffer*.

IV. *Implications for Interpreting Mark 13*

The relevance of this chapter for the interpretation of Mark 13 may not be self-evident. Our goal throughout this study has been to listen carefully to Mark's overall theological viewpoint and to study his literary methods, so that when we read Mark 13 we can do it from his perspective. In that respect we can claim to have made significant advances in this chapter.

1. We have more reason than ever to conclude that Mark is a subtle theologian and careful (rather than clumsy) author. If plausible patterns can be traced in the fabric of Mark 13, we have reason to take them seriously.
2. We have provided a second focus for Mark's 'discernment' emphasis. He invites careful discernment concerning the significance of 'temple' matters (Chapter 5), but he also invites careful discernment concerning the significance of 'persecution' (Chapter 6). By nearly universal agreement, Mark 13 deals heavily in both. We ought to be ready to hear Mark more accurately.
3. We have also provided a second focus for Mark's 'discipleship' emphasis. It is a matter of 'standing firm in the crisis' (Chapter 4), but it is also a matter of allowing trials to become opportunities for mission and for 'passing the baton' to the next generation (Chapter 6).
4. We have been given a basis for viewing 13.9-13 as the

passion of the first generation of believers and their passing on of the baton to the next generation of believers who will move on in the evangelization of the world. We shall therefore need to examine other sections of the chapter to see if Mark leaves open the possibility that there will be more than one Christian generation.

5. We have come to understand something about believers' 'hope'. They are not taught to scan the heavens for indications that the Son of Man's return is immediately around the corner. They are rather taught what it means to run faithfully around the track in a race that cannot be lost. Does this not suggest that when the apostles themselves have gone 'the way' prepared for them, Mark's readers will run another lap? Perhaps more than one? We have yet to see whether 9.1 or 13.30 argue otherwise.

6. We have found no support in 16.7f. for the idea that believers are counselled to rush out of Jerusalem and Judea in order that in Galilee they might experience an imminent parousia (a not uncommon view of Mark 13.14). Therefore, the whole idea that the parousia is to be expected immediately after the crisis in Jerusalem loses some of its support.

7. 16.7 calls the disciples back to do precisely what 13.33-37 called post-resurrection disciples to do ... serve in the context of passion discipleship. From *beginning* (16.7) to *end* (13.33-37), the way of the cross modelled by Jesus is the pattern for discipleship.

8. Mark does not pick up and drop imagery carelessly. He develops symbols and paradigms in one part of his Gospel and utilizes them with effect elsewhere. We have justification for examining images in Mark 13 (like greening fig trees) in the light of their usage elsewhere.

9. And finally, Mark has pushed 'training in discipleship' right to the top of his priority list, if the evidence of his Gospel is to be taken seriously. We should be very loath to assume that Mark 13 is an unexpected deviation from the norm, and very hesitant about trying to wrench from it answers to questions which were on the periphery of Mark's interest, especially if that entails pushing his real concerns out of central focus.

Chapter 7

MARK 13 AND MARK'S LITERARY ACHIEVEMENT

Introduction

This study has attempted to analyse key terms and themes which are of central importance for the interpretation of Mark 13. We began with the hope that their elucidation in the broader Markan context would shed light on Mark's own understanding and intentions in the material of the eschatological discourse.

We have discovered along the way that the studies undertaken not only provide material relevant to the interpretation of Mark 13, but also shed a great deal of light on the Gospel as a whole. We shall discover in this chapter that they also shed a great deal of light on the literary and theological links that tie Mark 13 and the broader Gospel together.

With this chapter we begin the final part of our study. We attempt to gather our findings and focus the implications of them directly on Mark 13. We will not move immediately into an attempt to construct Mark's eschatological time-table (the usual method). It will be our plan to take our findings concerning Mark's discernment and discipleship themes and apply them to the interpretation of Mark 13. In this chapter we examine the place of Mark 13 in the larger Gospel at a structural and literary level. We want to examine how our findings affect the whole process of interpreting Mark 13. In the next, we shall examine how Mark's theology of the 'secret kingdom' informs the readers' understanding of the significance of the major events of Mark 13—suffering, temple desecration and destruction, and the return of the Son of Man.

Our final chapter will attempt to ascertain Mark's perspective on an eschatological time-table. The fact that so many different chronologies have been defended strongly suggests that more than one is consistent with the data of Mark 13. Is it possible that Mark deliberately constructed it that way?

Mark 16.7f. brings to an end the narrative of Mark's Gospel. We argued in Chapter 6 that the final two verses function as an arrow pointing the reader, the would-be disciple of the risen Christ, back to the beginning of the narrative. As the Gospel is read again in the light of Jesus' victory, the reader is instructed in the 'way' he/she has been called to go. Mark has found a way of reproducing textually exactly what he is advocating existentially. Moreover, he has brilliantly reproduced the impact of the post-resurrection message to the disciples. They too were called back to 'Galilee', back to their own beginning.

Where does that new beginning lead? We shall argue that it leads to Mark 13! It is that chapter which most clearly indicates what will be experienced by believers in the post-resurrection situation. It is that chapter which reveals how the whole story ends. All this will require that we examine the relationship between the narrative ending (16.7f.) and the implied story ending (13.24-27). Does Mark have in mind a 'model' for reading and interpreting his Gospel which helps the reader determine the significance of the particular parts?

We must reach our conclusions somewhat indirectly as we examine first some important questions about Mark's overall literary method, and then formulate a model for interpreting Mark's Gospel as a whole and Mark 13 in particular.

I. *Discipleship/Discernment and Mark's Literary Method*

The Constraints Upon Mark as Author

It is amazing that a single book, the Gospel of Mark, could be characterized in so very many different ways—from a straightforward unembellished historical narrative to a stylized caricature bordering on fiction—from an apologetic defence of the earliest kerygma to a polemic against the original preservers of the tradition—from the product of clumsy redaction to a theological and literary masterpiece.[1] How is such diversity to be explained?

Our inability to be certain about Mark's sources is part of the difficulty. This is increased by our uncertainty about the historical, sociological, and religious environments in which the book was written, and about which of those environments to consider most influential. Add to that the difficulty of reconstructing the probable shared assumptions of writer and readers nineteen centuries removed, and it is not surprising that opinions vary.

And yet the aura of mystery that pervades the Gospel of Mark seems to have a certain quality that is not fully explained by these factors alone. Nor is it fully explained by the fact that Mark's *content* includes discussions about secrecy and esoteric communication. There is something about the book itself which breeds mystery.

The best explanation for this is that Mark was writing under constraints which are usually not taken into account when analysing literature. To try to elucidate the local circumstances of an ancient writing, to analyse the language and thought forms of the day, to examine the author's sources, to reconstruct the historical events being narrated—all these are essential. Mark's Gospel, however, betrays that Mark was not merely an historian, or a theologian, or a biographer, or a preacher, or an apologist, or a literary artist. He was first and foremost a follower of Jesus. Indeed, while he may have been all or most of the above, he was *self-consciously* a Christian believer attempting to write a Gospel under the constraints which he believed were upon him as a result of that fact.

Mark, as a follower of Jesus, seems to have modelled himself after his Lord *in terms of the means by which the Gospel was communicated.* If we want to know what Mark's communication methods were, what his primary concerns were, and what procedures he believed his readers should follow in understanding him, we need to examine the communication methods of the Markan Jesus, *his* primary concerns, and the epistemology *he* endorsed. Throughout this study we have attempted to keep a conceptual difference between the way the Markan Jesus related to his hearers and the way Mark related to his readers. We have, however, a strong warrant for maintaining that the second relationship was modelled after the first. The most relevant 'constraints' on Mark as author are probably the constraints of 'discipleship' and of 'a particular epistemology'.

The Markan Jesus spoke in parables and riddles with hidden meanings (sometimes on more than one level). He avoided answering inappropriate questions.[2] He was more concerned to shape people's ways of looking than to describe the landscape for them. He believed that divine illumination would be given to those who would follow him. For his troubles he was widely misunderstood and rejected by many. He expected to be. The Gospel of Mark betrays the fact that the author held the same convictions and used the same methods. In many ways he has suffered the same fate. He also probably expected to.

Mark deliberately wrote a Gospel which was carefully designed to communicate ambiguously many of its most important concerns. We can berate him for his choice and shudder at the implications, but we cannot ignore the facts. Unless this whole study is following a completely wrong path, Mark has made many points in very subtle ways, deliberately not making them explicit for his readers. He does not leave his readers without guidance. His guidance, however, is not in the form of an explicit road map. Like the Markan Jesus, Mark functions more like a tour guide, pointing to the demands of discipleship 'along the way'.

Mark wrote to be understood: he did not subscribe to the new hermeneutic which claims a text means whatever it means to the reader.[3] But he wrote to be understood by 'qualified' readers, and the requisite qualifications were related to discipleship more than scholarship. Mark's epistemology led him to believe that the secrets of his Gospel would be revealed, not to those with superior intelligence, certainly not to those who can maintain critical distance, but to those willing to accept his guidance 'along the way' and receive the divine illumination promised for disciples of Jesus.

Mark did a matchless job of recreating in a written record what Jesus did in personal encounter.[4] 'And we should not be unduly surprised that the gospel, like its own parables, both reveals and conceals'.[5]

If Mark's 'discipleship' and 'discernment' concerns are taken with utmost seriousness, we gain valuable clues as to how Mark dealt with the whole matter of the relationship between history and theology, the locus of the greatest 'tugs-of-war' in Markan scholarship.

The Nature of the Book Mark Wrote
Mark has attempted to combine the narration of historical events with the proclamation of the Gospel. Precisely which of those two elements is highlighted, and precisely how the elements are combined are much debated. Martin Hengel rightly argues that,[6]

> The fatal error in the interpretation of the Gospels in general and of Mark in particular has been that scholars have thought that they had to decide between preaching and historical narration, that here there could only be an either-or. In reality the 'theological' contribution of the evangelist lies in the fact that he combines both these things inseparably: he preaches by narrating; he writes history and in so doing proclaims. This is to some degree the *theological* side of that *coincidentia oppositorum* which marks out

his work. At this point he has the model of Old Testament historiography before him, where this unity of narration and proclamation is often visible.

Mark needs to be defended from attacks on both sides. He is neither uninterested in the historical truth of the narration, nor is he content to present it, for what it is worth, without theological commentary.[7]

If Mark intends the whole ministry of Jesus to be a model for discipleship in the post-resurrection age (see Chapter 6), and if Mark is modelling his communication methods after those of Jesus, then it would not be unfair to describe the entire Gospel as an extended parable,[8] at least in the sense that at every point one needs to consider whether or not the mode of speech is tropical, with a primary level of meaning that links with the continuing story line of the historical narrative, and a secondary level which helps build the 'meta-message' concerning discipleship in the post-resurrection age.[9] It should not be necessary to add that 'parabolic' does not mean 'fictional'.[10]

It is universally recognized that *within Mark's Gospel* the use of parables is accompanied with an aura of mystery. Boucher's study of parable and its relation to allegory makes the point that parables can be thought of as 'mysterious' when three factors apply: (1) the speaker pronounces the parable; (2) the parable has two levels of meaning; (3) the hearer may or may not apprehend the indirect meaning.[11] Is it not plausible that the aura of mystery which hovers over the Gospel as a whole has the same explanation? If Mark's Gospel as a whole functions parabolically, then more is being said through the narrative than is being made plain. Our uncertainty about the second level of meaning is responsible for the mysteriousness of the whole Gospel.

If Mark's Gospel as a whole speaks on more than one level, we see how form and content converge in a remarkable way. The narrative ending is designed to send the disciples (within the story) back to Galilee where it all began, back so that they can make their discipleship journey over again with the victory of Christ as their presupposition and help. So also it is designed to send the readers back to the beginning so that they can re-examine the text for its claims on them in the light of the resurrection.

The Literary Techniques Mark Utilized
If Mark has done what we claim he has done, how has he done it? M.

Hengel (see above) compared Mark with Old Testament historiography in terms of its bringing together of history and theology. The comparison is fair enough, but this should not dispose us to watch for only a limited range of *methods* that Mark might have used in order to transcend a historical narration and make it also a word of proclamation. There are many ways to accomplish this. A frequently used Old Testament model is the employment of a narrative comment at the conclusion of a narrative, passing judgment on, or handing credits to, the characters whose actions have just been reported. It is a very simple method.

There are more sophisticated means that can be used. The Gospel of John, which also clearly combines historiography with proclamation, uses a variety of means, from such relatively simple devices as a historical report followed by a dialogue or monologue featuring the Johannine Jesus expounding on the symbolic meaning or application of what has just been recorded, to the somewhat more complicated device of putting an ambiguous statement (amphibole) in the mouth of Jesus, and then following it either by developing both meanings, or else by criticizing those who extracted the wrong one.[12] Luke, at least if C.H. Giblin is correct, uses a very subtle method of tropical communication by setting up typologies which suggest the applications the author wishes the reader to draw out of the narrative.[13]

Mark also has a variety of means that he adopts to turn history into proclamation:

1. One means is to have the narrator address the readers directly, sometimes sharing vitally important information that the characters in the story do not hear. Mark 1.1 (and indeed much of the introduction) is a very clearcut case. When one learns to listen to the voice of the narrator, one realizes how pervasive the narrator's influence is in guiding the reader through the story.[14]

2. Another means Mark frequently adopts is the inclusion of predictions by Jesus which relate directly to the situation of the later church. Mark 13 is the most obvious example.

3. At times one strongly suspects that Mark himself inserts an application for the later church directly into the narration of the historical event in Jesus' life. The most universally accepted case in point is Mark 7.19.[15]

4. At times, as we have argued throughout this study, Mark

sends messages to his readers by constructing 'teaching units'—by stringing together several pericopes in such a way that either the common thread linking the series together, or else the interpretative slant that one pericope puts on another, becomes the clue as to what Mark is conveying above and beyond the historical narrative.[16]

5. Another means by which Mark communicates a 'meta-message' to his readers is by the use of deliberate ambiguity. Statements are deliberately designed to mean two things, one of which is true at the narrative level, one of which is true at the discourse level in relation to the reader.[17] To *prove* that the technique is being employed may be difficult, but when the suggestion repeatedly sheds light on the author's intentions, evidence accumulates in support of the idea (see our discussion of the Markan Prologue below and our analysis of Mark 13 in Chapter 9).

We should never imagine that Mark was aiming at literary subtlety for its own sake, or was constructing cryptograms to befuddle or amuse. Mark knew that Jesus told stories with levels of meaning that were not self-evident. He believed that the whole life of Jesus had meaning and significance beyond its bare historical factuality. And he was firmly convinced that if he was careful to tell the story faithfully and drop subtle suggestions as to its significance, those who were prepared to accept the call to discipleship would find guidance through the text he wrote and the story it recorded. *Mark therefore wrote much of his Gospel on two levels at once, narrating a sequence of historical events and at the same time and with the same words, instructing readers in discernment and discipleship.* A. Stock quite rightly describes the matter thus:[18]

> Two time frames are superimposed in the narrative: that of the reader and that of the characters in the plotted narrative. . . . The superimposition of the two time frames is so handled that the reader is confronted by the same challenge to faith as were Jesus' contemporaries.

To understand how these two levels relate to each other is to understand the literary structure of Mark's Gospel. A variety of Markan interpreters have made somewhat similar claims, though we would want to distinguish our own characterization of these two levels from some others. We are not making the distinction that

Hugh Anderson attempts between a 'natural' and 'supernatural' level in the story,[19] nor the one J.M. Robinson labels as the 'human, historical language' and the 'cosmic language of God',[20] nor do we accept A.W. Mosley's theory about Jesus' public teaching and his private explanations,[21] nor are we making A.M. Ambrozic's distinction between 'unambiguous preaching' and 'esoteric teaching' levels,[22] nor would we want our 'two levels' to be thought of as strictly identical with the distinction between 'inter-character' interaction and 'narrator–reader' interaction,[23] though of course this latter distinction is important and provides one of the tools by which the author carries forward his 'meta-message'.

We are speaking about the distinction between: (1) Mark's historical narrative about the life, death and resurrection of Jesus and his interaction with other characters along the way and (2) Mark's own deliberate message to his readers (produced by a variety of means) concerning the implications and applications of the narrated story for their own situation. E. Best clearly has these two levels in mind, and rightly emphasizes their inseparability when he concludes a study of 'Jesus, Past and Present' with these words:[24]

> Mark sees the historical Jesus and the preached Christ as one and
> · the same; therefore he retells the events of the earthly life of Jesus
> at the same time as he presents him through these as son of God
> and son of man. . . . What the one who goes to the cross preaches is
> the same as what is preached through the church by the risen
> Christ. So when we hear the words of the historical Jesus and read
> of his deeds we encounter the words and deeds of the risen and
> preached Christ.

Our only suggestions would be: (1) that the words of the risen Christ through Mark are not always precisely identical with the words of the historical Jesus; at times they are new applications and implications brought to bear on a new situation; and (2) that Mark is not restricted merely to Jesus' *words* when making the historical Jesus relevant for his hearers; his ministry and his passion (and the responses these generated) also 'speak' to their situation.

In all this we must give Mark full credit not only for speaking with subtlety on two levels, but for doing so consciously and for reflecting on why and how he is doing so. We have seen evidence for this throughout and shall see more. We insist that this is what we should expect to find in a Gospel which not only highlights Jesus' parabolic speech, but which also portrays Jesus as reflecting on the purposes and methods of parabolic speech. It is what we should expect to find in a Gospel which not only teaches about a secret kingdom, but teaches about teaching about that secret kingdom.[25] J.C. Fenton sounds an ominous warning when he says that,[26]

> The clarity of the narrative sense hides at first sight the obscurity of the deeper meaning; and the ease with which the Gospels can be understood is only a cloak covering the ease with which the Gospels may be misunderstood

... which serves to warn us that it is of utmost importance to listen carefully to the whole narrative, gain a sense of Mark's priorities and methods, and interpret each part according to the role it plays in the whole.[27]

We turn then to a proposed model for interpreting Mark's Gospel as a whole, particularly pointing out the place of Mark 13 in that model. If the model stands up, we shall have gained a valuable key to be applied to the locks of Mark 13. It is our contention that this model is the logical outworking of not only the claims made in this chapter thus far, but the logical outworking of numerous points established throughout our study of Mark.

II. *A Model for Interpreting Mark's Gospel*

Consensus has not been reached in identifying the major divisions of Mark's text. Divisions at or near Mark 1.15, 3.6, 8.30, 10.52, 12.44, 13.37 and 15.47 would be widely accepted, though the exact placement of the division in almost every case is disputed.[28]

For our present purposes it is sufficient to identify breaks at or around 1.15, 12.44, and 13.37. We do not deny that there are more, but it is not essential to deal with them in the model we want to suggest. These three breaks separate Mark's text into four separate sections: the prologue (1.1-15), the main narrative (1.1-12.44), the eschatological discourse (13.1-37), and the passion/resurrection (14.1-16.8).

The Main Narrative and the Alternative Endings
At one level of reading, 1.16-12.44 is a rather straightforward account of the events of Jesus' life from the advent of his preaching/healing ministry in Galilee until he completes his controversial dialectic in Jerusalem. Many different threads are woven together into a relatively unified story with plot development moving ahead in

a variety of different ways at the same time. There is development from recruiting followers to training them, from popular acclaim to general rejection, from 'kingdom teaching' to 'passion theology', from Galilee and environs to Jerusalem. It is not strictly a biography, but it does trace the movements of the main character through various circumstances along a self-chosen path, and it does provide some insights into his motivations and expectations.

Because most of us are not very adept at listening to the voice of the narrator, nor at separating out elements of the story which are projected beyond its narrative conclusion, it is not usually self-evident that certain passages are almost without function in the developing story line at the narrative level. It needs to be drawn to our attention that the passion/resurrection narrative follows directly upon 12.44 at the level of historical reporting. Mark 13, almost in its entirety, and such passages as 8.34–9.1 and 10.39f. play their role at another level, enabling the reader to anticipate events projected into the future beyond the narrative ending.[29] The reader can almost ignore these 'prophecies' when reading Mark's text for the purpose of determining what happened to Jesus which led to his death and resurrection. The reader studies 1.16–12.44 to see how the ministry of Jesus develops, and studies 14.1–16.8 to see its logical conclusion. That is the story of Jesus that Mark tells.

We have argued, however, that Mark is not content only to report history. He is interested in telling his readers far more than merely 'what happened to Jesus'. He is concerned to teach his readers 'what will (or should) happen to disciples'.[30] Precisely because 8.34–9.1, 10.39f., and ch. 13 have only a minor role in the narrative of 'what happened to Jesus', they play the major role in the other story Mark tells, 'what will happen to the followers of Jesus after the resurrection?'[31] When readers concern themselves with that question they listen carefully for all those clues Mark gives them (prophecies of Jesus, narrative asides, clues from the narrative structure, double nuances, etc.) in order to determine what the text is designed to tell them about the lives they are to live as followers of Jesus.

The logical end of *that* story, however, is not found in 14.1–16.8; it is found in Mark 13. It is in Mark 13 that the events are plotted which will be experienced by followers of Jesus in the post-resurrection situation. A simple model helps to see the logic of Mark's narrative sequence.

Disciples' Story:	Main Body ⟶ Conclusion		
	(discourse level)		
TEXTUAL ORDER:	1.16–12.44	13.1-37	14.1–16.8
	(narrative level)		
Jesus' Story	Main Body ⟶ Conclusion		

We realize why commentators like R. Pesch at least in his earlier work can countenance the idea that the Gospel once existed without Mark 13. He is reluctant to allow Mark a free hand in stylizing story and suspicious of claims that Mark has deliberately juxtaposed elements and used other literary devices to make his own points. Pesch is not without concern about the implications for discipleship, but his approach restricts him to an examination of the explicit narrative comments and prophecies of Jesus in search of them. He has concentrated his efforts on the 'Jesus story'. Not surprisingly Mark 13.1-37 is left without a context for interpretation.

We can also understand why a scholar like E. Trocmé can countenance the idea that the Gospel once existed without a passion narrative. He has been concerned to trace Mark's *use* of the traditions in order to send a message directly to the church, and has downplayed the significance of the historical narrative in its own right. He has attempted to focus attention on the 'disciples' story'. Not surprisingly, Mark 14-16 is more easily dispensed with given this approach.

The proposal we have outlined above is not only 'a way of reading' the Gospel; it is a construction deliberately chosen by the author. The 'discipleship' and 'epistemological' constraints under which Mark operated provided him with an adequate motivation for such a writing method. Moreover, our model can be supplemented and refined so that it provides relevant clues which aid us in interpreting Mark.

If Mark 16.7f. is to be interpreted as we suggested in the preceding chapter, then we have Mark himself telling us through the narrative that readers who have come to the end of the Jesus story, must now make their way back with the disciples to the beginning in Galilee. The readers themselves must become followers of the now resurrected Christ in a life of obedient discipleship and cross-bearing. Only thus can they be led to 'see'. That is to say, just as the disciples are directed back to the place where their discipleship began, so the readers are directed back from 16.7f. to 1.16. They themselves are now recruited with the disciples by the resurrected Jesus and are called to follow the way Jesus walked. If they follow, the post-resurrection implications will be revealed to them 'along the way'. The story will no longer be merely a historical report; it will be a guide for living and for dying.

Mark 16.7f. is Mark's way of telling his readers precisely what our model suggested. The disciples' story cannot truly begin until the Jesus' story has been completed. 'The Way' is then prepared and the story can go on in the lives of followers. Mark has found a way of telling his readers that dispassionate historicism ends when readers are confronted with the resurrection. At that point a decision must be made: either readers will stop and be content with a historical narrative about Jesus, or they will join the disciples by taking up their own crosses and walking through the narrative once more, being guided by the Jesus model, living a life that also goes through suffering to vindication. The correspondence between Mark's message and his method, as well as the textual clues provided for the reader (16.7f.) are two very significant pieces of evidence that Mark would approve of the reading model that we are proposing.

The logical way of reading the story, then is something like this:

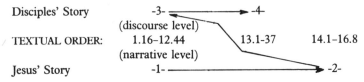

Disciples' Story	-3- ⟶ -4-
	(discourse level)
TEXTUAL ORDER:	1.16–12.44 13.1-37 14.1–16.8
	(narrative level)
Jesus' Story	-1- ⟶ -2-

16.7f. is not our only clue that Mark set up his Gospel to be read as suggested above. If Mark's theology is such that the 'journey' of Jesus from Galilee to Jerusalem typifies cross-bearing discipleship, we should find evidence, as we have, for a two-level story in 1.16–12.44. But equally, if Jesus' conduct through the passion itself is the model for the believers' conduct in their anticipated suffering, we should expect to see not merely two-level story-telling in Jesus' passion account,[32] but even more surely, cross-referencing between the two endings (chs. 13 and 14–16). But that is precisely what we have found. R.H. Lightfoot has demonstrated the connection between Mark 13 and the passion of Jesus as a whole,[33] and Chapter 4 of our study has defended the view that not only is the passion of Jesus the model for disciples in their post-resurrection suffering (13.9-13, etc.), it is also the model for all post-resurrection believers in the entire period until the return of the Son of Man (13.33-37).

Referring back to our last diagram, we would say that '-3-' is modelled after '-1-', and '-4-' is modelled after '-2-'. To be sure, Mark uses the passion narrative itself (without Mark 13) to make statements about the implied future of the story. He uses prophecy to project events into the implied future (e.g., 14.9 [world mission], 14.25 [eschatological banqueting], 14.28 [discipleship reinstatement], 14.62 [eschatological judgment], etc.); he uses symbolic events and cross-referencing to do the same (e.g., 15.18, 26 and 33-36 [Jesus' 'coronation'], 15.38 [temple destruction]), etc. But it is by means of cross-referencing between Mark 13 and the passion narrative that we see most clearly how the passion of Jesus becomes a model for discipleship in the post-resurrection age. Mark 13 is the logical end of the Markan story, for it spans the time from the resurrection to the parousia. When readers interpret Mark 13, they do so in the light of the whole Gospel, and particularly in the light of the model of faithful discipleship which is portrayed in Mark 14-16.

The Function of the Markan Prologue
We now bring into the discussion the one main section of Mark's Gospel which we have so far ignored, the 'Prologue'. Its function in Mark's Gospel provides a remarkable confirmation of the model that we are establishing.

Most commentators accept that 1.1-15 (or 1.1-13)[34] functions as a 'theological platform' for the reader. It gives the reader the information needed to understand the story. Its function is similar to that of John's prologue, and it is not entirely unlike the prologue of Job, without which the readers would be as much in the dark as the uninformed characters of the story.

But for which level of reading does it provide the theological platform? Arguments are unceasing. Those who hold that Mark's primary concern is historical read the prologue as Mark's attempt to supply essential information enabling the reader better to understand the Jesus story. Those who hold that Mark's concern is primarily kerygmatic read it as a theological commentary on the whole. Of what value is a guide if readers cannot even figure out which story it is to guide them through?

Everything depends on one's approach to a variety of puzzling questions that the prologue generates. The ambiguity and the uncertainty begin with the very first word of Mark's Gospel:[35]

> Mark 1.1 certainly holds the key to not only the meaning of this opening material but to Mark's Gospel as a whole. Unfortunately,

this key itself is locked tightly in the ambiguity of the statement
whose every word raises a crucial question.

Is the 'beginning' (ἀρχή) the prophecies and preparations
accomplished by advance messengers (Isaiah/Malachi and/or John)
or is it the work of Christ as narrated in the whole Gospel? Is the
genitive in 1.1 subjective or objective? Is the 'gospel' (εὐαγγέλιον)
Jesus' announcement of the kingdom's coming, or the evangelist's
announcement of the kerygma? What punctuation best reflects the
relationship between 1.1 and 1.2?

The puzzles, however, are not limited to the first verse. Is 'desert'
(ἔρημος) symbolic of judgment and testing, or of eschatological
preparation? Does John's similarity to Elijah highlight the latter's
prophetic or eschatological role? Is the emphasis in John's message
on his own baptism, or the one Jesus will perform? Is the author's
concern in narrating Jesus' baptism and temptation focused on the
preparation of Jesus for ministry, or the cosmic dimensions of Jesus'
victory? Does the heavenly voice commission Jesus for an impending
passion or exalt him to a position of honour? Is the temptation a
single battle Jesus needed to win to be ready for ministry or is it
something more all-encompassing in which Jesus decisively defeated
his foe? Are the wild beasts symbols of danger and Satanic attack or
indications that Jesus restores Edenic conditions and/or brings to
reality the peaceable kingdom?[36] Is 'the good news of God' (τὸ
εὐαγγέλιον τοῦ θεοῦ) equivalent to Jesus' message of the coming
kingdom, or is it the whole life, death and resurrection of Jesus? Is
the statement, 'the time has been fulfilled' (πεπλήρωται ὁ καιρός),
true because John got things ready, or because the advent of Jesus as
a whole has come? Has 'the kingdom of God' drawn close with Jesus'
coming, or been established through his victory?

Can we really believe that Mark carelessly left all these threads
hanging loose with no intention that the reader should pick them up
and weave them into a coherent pattern? (or *two* coherent patterns?)
Can we really believe that Mark provided all the data needed so that
one scholar can pick a set of answers to the questions and prove it
was Mark's concern to set the stage for Jesus' ministry, and all the
data needed so that another scholar can pick the alternative set of
answers and prove it was Mark's concern to set the stage for post-
resurrection discipleship and proclamation of the Gospel of Jesus
Christ—*and did all that without intending to do so?* I do not believe it.
It seems beyond doubt that Mark has deliberately and skilfully

written a prologue which can be read both ways, both as an introduction to the 'story of Jesus' and as an introduction to 'the story of discipleship'.[37]

The readers who come to the Gospel to learn about Jesus, read the prologue to gain insights as to what presuppositions they should take with them in reading the narrative. But Mark also writes his Gospel for those who have read *that* story to its conclusion and are sent back with the disciples to begin again. Such 'second round' readers read the prologue as the theological preparation for the journey they are about to make. They know that not only has John prepared 'the way' for Jesus, but Jesus has prepared 'the way' so that they themselves can join the disciples on the discipleship road. They now see that Mark's interest is not only in reporting Jesus' own 'good news'; Jesus himself is the 'good news' to be proclaimed. They now see that Jesus' whole ministry is the 'beginning' of the Gospel, as they themselves are affected by that Gospel. They realize that the baptism with the Holy Spirit which Jesus effects is the prerequisite for faithfulness in the post-resurrection age. They see why Jesus' Father affirms him both as the suffering servant and the exalted Son. They understand the temptation as the life-long experience of Jesus, culminated in the decisive victory Jesus won at Golgotha. They see in Jesus' victory in the 'wilderness/tomb' the effective (though secret) establishment of God's kingdom, etc.

Either we must postulate that Mark carelessly left unanswered every single question that could have been used by his readers to determine what he was really talking about, or else we must conclude that he deliberately designed the account to operate on two levels at once. The second alternative is exceedingly more probable. The way in which it correlates with the scheme we have already suggested provides evidence in both directions that we are on the right track.[38]

We would therefore redraw our diagram thus:

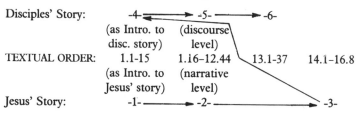

We are of course not suggesting that in Mark's mind it is sufficient to read the Gospel twice, once with each of the alternative endings. The subtleties of the Gospel rather suggest that it was designed to be heard, read and studied over and over again. What we are presenting is a model to aid us in its intepretation, not a time-table to regulate reading habits.

The model Mark chose is not a very effective means of communicating unambiguously in order to lay bare the facts for the scrutiny of dispassionate, critical investigation. But it is a remarkably good way of communicating ambiguously as Jesus did, of drawing readers into the exegetical task as Jesus drew his disciples in, of urging readers to recognize the presence of a living guide in the absence of a clear road map, of emphasizing *doing*, not merely knowing.

We have already indicated the role that Mark 13 plays in the Gospel's larger scheme. We are now ready to see how it plays that role, how its place in the Gospel illuminates its functions, and how it operates as 'the Gospel in miniature'.

III. *The Literary Function of Mark 13*

If we are right about the scheme which informs Mark's literary achievement, we can see that the Gospel is literally decapitated when Mark 13 is separated from the rest of the work and interpreted on its own as a separate literary genre. It is the logical ending of the story and intimately related both to the main narrative and to the passion and resurrection of Jesus.

Its relationship to the main narrative is one of explanation and culmination; it makes clear just what sort of road the disciple will travel in the post-resurrection age. Its relationship to the passion of Jesus is one of analogy; the disciples' passion is cast from the same mould as Jesus'. Mark 13 is the point where Mark's 'meta-message' becomes concrete, where the lessons subtly taught through Mark 1–12 and modelled in 14–16, find their historical application.

We want to look more closely at the relationship between Mark 13 and the rest of the Gospel.

Structural and Thematic Correspondences
Mark 13 is the only extended description in Mark of the actual course of events in the post-resurrection age. It should not surprise us if it betrays similarities with the course of events that led Jesus to his passion.

Briefly, the major material in Mark 1–12 could be summarized as:

1. The 'beginning' of Jesus' ministry (e.g., the first paradigmatic day in Capernaum [1.21-39]).
2. The developing conflict between Jesus (with his followers) and the officials of Jewish religion (e.g., controversies [2.1-3.6], recruitment of companions [3.13-19], identifying the real 'battle lines' [3.22-30], etc.).
3. Ministry in the context of rejection and misunderstanding (rejection even by family [3.20f., 31-35], and fellow townspeople [6.1-5]).
4. Missionary efforts beyond the borders of Israel (7.24-8.10).
5. Attempts to correct wrong concepts of Christology, eschatology, kingdom, discipleship responsibilities, etc. (e.g., 9.9-13, 10.35-45).
6. Breaking with the temple and its establishment (11.12-12.40, etc.).
7. The passion and beyond it the resurrection (14-16).

When Mark's narrative becomes explicit about the events that will occupy the attention of post-resurrection believers, the list turns out to be remarkably similar, and could be summarized as:

1. The 'beginning' (13.8) of the messianic age.
2. Developing conflict (13.9).
3. Ministry in the context of rejection (13.9-11) (even by family [13.12]).
4. Missionary outreach to all nations (13.10).
5. Guarding against wrong Christologies and eschatologies (13.5f., 21f.).
6. Making a break with the temple and its would-be defenders (13.14).
7. Predictions of a great tribulation (13.19f.) and beyond it the final vindication (13.24ff.).

It is not hard to see that the two lists, while not identical, are rather similar. A strong impression is created that the kinds of experiences that characterized the life of Jesus leading to his passion/resurrection, will also characterize the lives of those who follow him leading up to their suffering/vindication.

If the 'way' of Jesus is the model for believers in the post-resurrection age, then we have full warrant for interpreting Mark 13 in the light of the rest of the Gospel. Whatever attitudes the Markan Jesus takes in the main narrative to such things as persecution, the secret coming of the kingdom, the temple, the Gentile mission, victory beyond the passion—these attitudes disciples are to adopt in the post-resurrection age. That is to say, *Mark deliberately created his Gospel in such a way that Mark 1-12 and 14-16 function as the appropriate interpretative context for Mark 13*! When we look for clues in the rest of the Gospel in order to interpret Mark 13, we are not defeating Mark at his game; we are playing by his rules.

If post-resurrection believers will learn the lessons that the pre-passion disciples should have learned, if they adopt the attitudes the disciples should have adopted, they will not be caught off guard when they experience very much what Jesus experienced. They will be ready for the world of Mark 13, guarding against deception, standing as witnesses before officials, preaching the Gospel, standing firm in persecution, etc.[39]

If Mark has deliberately correlated Mark 13 with the rest of his Gospel, even in terms of the chapter's structure, is there not another important implication we must not overlook? Throughout Mark's Gospel the author seems deliberately to have juxtaposed elements for reasons other than geographical proximity, chronological continuity, and even topical similarity. At times elements are drawn together because they function as a unit to make a point not specifically contained in any of the individual pericopes thus linked. At times Mark was quite content to obscure the chronological order of events in his concern to place pericopes into a *theologically* meaningful arrangement.[40] The correspondences between the main Gospel narrative and Mark 13 strongly suggest that we watch for something similar in Mark 13. Perhaps Mark tried no harder to pin down exact chronological sequences in Mark 13 than elsewhere. At any rate we should always be on the lookout for indications that other concerns determined the juxtaposing of elements in the eschatological discourse.[41]

Corresponding 'Centres of Gravity'
It is instructive to notice how similar are the narrative endings of the whole Gospel (16.7f.) and of the eschatological discourse (13.33-37). Those who interpret both endings entirely differently than we do

would agree. W. Marxsen, for example, maintains that both the main narrative and Mark 13 end with the urgent call to be on the lookout for the imminent parousia.[42] We have rejected that interpretation for both texts.

The interpretations we have accepted for 16.7f. and 13.33-37 bring about an even more remarkable and a more defensible parallelism. Both 'endings' are designed to universalize the call for believers to model themselves after the cross-carrying Jesus. Mark 16.7f. sends the disciples back to the 'beginning' of the road, to take up the baton and run the race set out for them. Mark 13.33-36 pictures believers running their race in the final interim period before the parousia. What pattern are they to follow as they serve, suffer and preach? They are to 'watch' (γρηγορέω) i.e., go through their passion as Jesus went through his (see Chapter 4), being faithful in all the watches of the night as they suffer with Christ in order also to reign with him. Mark 16.7f. calls believers, along with the disciples, to the beginning of the discipleship road. Mark 13.33-36 portrays them 'watching' for its end, still doing what 16.7 called them to do. The 'disciples' story' (Mark 1-12) has transpired in the meantime. Just as Jesus' story ends with the transition to the disciples, so the 'disciples' story' ends with the transition to others who follow: 'What I say to you, I say to everyone' (13.37).

There were conditions that had to be met before either of the transfers could be made. 14.27f. predicted the conditions for the transition from Jesus to the disciples. They have now been fulfilled: the disciples have indeed 'fallen away'; the shepherd has indeed been 'struck'; the sheep have been 'scattered'; Jesus has risen. The time has come for them to be brought back together and, under the guidance of their shepherd, model their lives after his on the road to the passion.

Mark 13 outlines the conditions for the transition from the first generation of Christians to those who follow. Mark 13.5-23 predicts all the things the disciples will be called to face (προείρηκα ὑμῖν πάντα [13.23b]). When all these things have come to pass (and they will all happen in the first generation, 13.30, see Chapter 9), when the time for the return of the Son of Man is imminent, when the timing of 'that Day and the Hour' cannot be predicted, then others will be called to take up the baton for their turn on the track.

We might mention parenthetically here that this puts into analogous positions two crucial events: (1) the death and resurrection of Jesus, which are the conditions for the transfer to the disciples; and (2) the events surrounding the fall of the temple (assuming that the fall of the temple is a central feature in 13.4-23), which are the conditions for the transfer from the disciples to others. It is surely not without significance that Jesus' resurrection and the fall of Jerusalem are thus conceived by Mark as key milestones in the successive advancement of the secret kingdom. They are key transition points at which the kingdom is extended to others, the 'bridge events' which pass the baton to the next generation. The fact that they are brought together in the mysterious Markan theme of temple destruction and third day rebuilding suggests that this theme may become an important clue in the interpretation of Mark 13. We shall return to this matter in the next two chapters.

Finally, it is noteworthy that neither the resurrection of Jesus nor the parousia of the Son of Man is narrated at the very end of the respective stories in which they function as the appropriate vindication. Both are recorded *near* the end and then used as the presupposition which motivates the renewed discipleship calls with which the stories end. At the very end of both narratives the call goes out to be faithful followers of the cross-carrying Christ. According to Mark's Gospel, glory is always at the end of the road. But the report of that glory never takes centre stage as a thing in itself. It is there to provide the assurances disciples need in order to shape their attitudes and actions 'along the road'.[43] The obvious implication is that Mark's central concern is neither Christology nor eschatology. Discipleship as it is tied to passion theology forms Mark's 'centre of gravity', in the Gospel as a whole and in Mark 13.

Corresponding 'Literary Methodologies'

If our last point is accepted, namely that 13.37 is designed to focus on the transition to yet others as they begin their turn in the race, then it joins Mark 16.7f. as a call back to the beginning. If there is to be more than one post-resurrection generation, each one will be called afresh to travel the discipleship road behind Jesus, facing the events of the post-resurrection age as the first disciples did, with the model of Jesus as the permanently valid paradigm. From that point of view, Mark 13 also has its meta-message. At the narrative level (albeit as a prediction) it is the story of what the first generation will face. At another level it is the story of what every generation will face until the Son of Man interrupts the race and gathers the faithful runners together in the winner's circle.

It has frequently been urged that in Mark 13, as in all the Synoptic eschatological material, there is a double focus: one eye is on the immediate events centred around the destruction of the temple, the other is on the final events leading up to the return of the Son of Man. The 'crises' are not to be identified with each other, though the first prefigures the second. We have yet to examine whether Mark's 'time scheme' supports this interpretation. If it does, then what we find in the main narrative we find also in Mark 13. In the main narrative we have explicitly the story of Jesus and implicitly instructions for Jesus' first followers. In Mark 13 we have explicitly the story of Jesus' first followers and implicitly instructions for those who follow them. Each story becomes a typological model for believers who live after the story is told.

This chapter has focused more heavily on form than content. Mark was evidently self-consciously concerned with both. Our next chapter will focus more heavily on content as we endeavour to establish, on the basis of clues derived from the whole Gospel, what meaning Mark intends his readers to attach to the main events predicted for the post-resurrection period—the destruction of the temple, the inevitability of suffering and persecution, and (as a hermeneutical key to the whole) the advancing of the secret kingdom toward its consummation.

Chapter 8

MARK 13 AND THE SECRET KINGDOM

Introduction

The hermeneutical key to Mark's Gospel is the theology of the secret kingdom. According to Mark, discerning believers will understand the kingdom teaching of the parables, observe the kingdom's presence in the miracles and 'see' the kingdom's advance through suffering and persecution. The passion of Jesus is the centre-piece of Mark's theology of the secret kingdom; the death of Jesus is his coronation as king, and it is the day of eschatological fulfilment *par excellence*. Though the kingdom remains a secret kingdom in the post-resurrection age, though it will be revealed in judgment and salvation only at the return of the Son of Man in glory, discerning believers will be able to detect evidence of its presence and its advance if they will understand aright the significance of the events they observe and in which they participate.

This chapter examines the significance of Mark's 'kingdom theology' for the understanding of the key events that are to occur in the post-resurrection period. The two major types of events which are predicted for the post-resurrection age are: (1) the destruction of the Jerusalem temple and concomitant tribulation, and (2) various forms of suffering and persecution to be faced by believers. Both are consequences of the fact that Jesus was rejected. Both are of special significance in the advance of the secret kingdom. To understand the significance of these events is the key focus of Mark 13's insistent call βλέπετε. This chapter is concerned to determine what it was that believers were to discern in the coming of these types of events.

I. *The Secret Coming of the Kingdom in Mark*

We have already briefly touched on the 'secret kingdom' teaching of Mark as it related to Mark 4.1-34 (parables) and Mark 4.35-8.26

(miracles). We are now in a position to see more clearly just how the secret kingdom theology functions in Mark's Gospel.

Kingdom Secrecy and Christological Secrecy
It is our firm conviction that students of Mark's Gospel would have made much more progress in understanding Mark's kingdom secrecy if they were not constantly interacting with W. Wrede who set the whole discussion awry in the direction of *'Messianic Secrecy'*. It is only a slight improvement to re-label this strictly Christological approach and speak of Mark's 'Son of God' secrecy.[1] That this is a more accurate description of the Christological aspects of the secrecy is to be affirmed, but to settle for Christology itself as the focus for the secrecy is to stop short of the real goal.[2]

Mark's Gospel, while reflecting secrecy (and sometimes commanding silence) about Jesus' identity, explicitly indicates that the real secret is the secret of the kingdom of God (4.11). It is in relation to Mark's theology of the secret kingdom that all other secrecy must be evaluated. Any secrecy concerning Jesus' identity per se is linked inseparably to passion discipleship as the way of the kingdom. When disciples are able to discern the real identity of Jesus, then Jesus can move on to the more challenging agenda: he can lead them to insight and acceptance of the fact that the secret kingdom advances without present fanfare and glory, indeed often through rejection and suffering.[3] It is the *role* of Jesus as the bringer of the secret kingdom which concerns Mark (cf. 8.29-31). Any secrecy concerning his identity per se must be related to that.[4]

Mark's understanding of the kingdom is such that only in its final stages will the kingdom become publicly manifest (4.22). Until it is fully revealed, its presence is affirmed by faith, confirmed by divine illumination, and experienced while following Jesus 'along the way'. The kingdom's secret is its very secrecy. Every definition which begins 'The secret of the kingdom is *that*. . . ' falls short of Mark's intentions. The secret is not 'given' (δέδοται 4.11) by disclosing a proposition about it, but by the gracious act of God who plants seeds in the heart and causes them to grow if the soil is right.[5] Both the kingdom and its means of coming Mark pictures as 'secret' or 'hidden'.[6] If Mark's readers despair of understanding precisely *how* this sort of secret kingdom advances and grows, they are perhaps where Mark expected them to be (cf. 4.27). They are assured, however, that the secret kingdom has begun to take root and that it is advancing.

Kingdom Secrecy and Passion Discipleship

A major element of the secrecy surrounds the fact that the kingdom advances through the suffering and persecution God's representatives are called on to experience. *Jesus*, within the Gospel, speaks openly (παρρησία 8.32) about the fact that he must suffer; he speaks veiledly about the fact that thereby the kingdom advances—that thereby it will eventually become visible to those who see aright (9.1; 14.41).[7] Similarly *Mark*, by means of the Gospel, speaks openly about the fact of Jesus' passion and the coming suffering for the disciples; he speaks in a veiled way about the fact that each passion becomes a major milestone in the advancement of the secret kingdom (Mark's 'passion paradigm').

We can take it even further. Not only is the suffering/persecution, when rightly understood, seen to be a stage in the kingdom's advance, so also is the Satanic opposition which brings about that suffering/persecution. In a real sense, part of the kingdom's secrecy in Mark centres on the fact that the one with eyes to see it can watch the kingdom of Satan destroying itself!

Satan's kingdom, embodied particularly in the Jewish religious leaders, tries to deal with the 'threat' Jesus brings by putting him to death (cf. esp. 12.12). What they do not know, but the discerning reader does know, is that precisely by carrying out their designs, God carries out his. Both Satan and his henchmen (the Jewish religious leaders) lose by winning. Jesus plunders both Satan's house (3.27) and the religious leaders' (11.15-17). He predicts that Satan's house will come to an end (3.25) and he predicts the same for the Jewish leaders' (13.2). Yet not until his enemies 'succeed' in doing away with him, does his own victory take full effect (15.38f.). It is satanic to initiate and carry out the death plot (3.6 leading to 3.23-26); it is equally satanic to try to block it (8.33).[8] Satan's kingdom is indeed divided against itself.[9] It cannot possibly win.

Just as apparent defeats for God's kingdom are really secret advances, so also (and for the same reason) apparent victories for Satan's kingdom are really secret defeats. If that sounds like a 'Heads I win: Tails you lose' situation, we have probably comprehended Mark aright. It was his business to proclaim the Gospel, not give everyone a fair chance of winning. If winning depended on power, the kingdom could, at least in principle, lose. The Markan Jesus preached and inaugurated a kingdom which wins by its citizens being faithful even in death (cf. 10.42-45). It is in principle unconquerable.

There will no doubt be events which will challenge the believers' conviction that the kingdom is real and that it is advancing. It is therefore incumbent on believers that they be discerning in order to see in the events around them evidence of the secret kingdom.

Kingdom Secrecy and the Meaning of Events
Two major foci of the earlier parts of Mark's Gospel are: (1) the events which betray that the kingdom is secretly advancing, and (2) the means by which this fact is recognized.[10] The more spectacular events of Jesus' life might well appear merely 'amazing' to some, the less spectacular may appear merely 'natural', but the discerning kingdom citizen sees them as advances of the secret kingdom. The secret was not so much *how near* the kingdom had drawn, but rather *in what way* the kingdom was drawing near.[11]

According to the Markan Jesus, *everything* reveals the secret presence of the kingdom if the requisite 'seeing eyes' and 'hearing ears' are used to discern that fact. 'Everything comes in parables' (4.11). Mark takes up this perspective and passes on subtle clues that help the reader see *in what way* the kingdom advances. Whether the events in question are as mundane as welcoming a child or as spectacular as raising one from the dead, as mundane as giving a cup of water or as spectacular as calming the sea, they indicate the presence of the secret kingdom. Whether Jesus is walking on water (6.49), or on the dusty road from Galilee to Jerusalem (10.32)— whether Jesus is sharing a loaf with twelve companions (14.22), or a lunch with 5000 (6.39-44)—whether he rises early to spend the morning in prayer (1.35), or to spend eternity as the resurrected Lord (16.1-8)—the kingdom is secretly advancing. Believers should not expect unmistakable 'signs' proving this fact; they are rather called to apprehend the meaning of everything that is happening.

Whatever happens, the discerning believer is expected to be able to see God's hand at work bringing his secret purposes to fulfilment as the kingdom grows in preparation for a final harvest when all secrets will be revealed. If believers do not know *how* each event serves God's purposes, they can be assured *that* it does. Mark of course knows that God's ways are at times inscrutable even to his most faithful followers (cf. 14.34-36; 15.34). That does not excuse anyone from seeking understanding.

The decisive moment in the inauguration of the secret kingdom was the moment of Jesus' death. But neither that event nor the resurrection ended the secrecy of the kingdom. Only the parousia will do that. Mark 13 is a chapter which outlines a series of events which will happen in the post-resurrection age. The believer's responsibility is to discern the meaning of those events and see in them further evidence that the secret kingdom is alive and well. How do the main events predicted in Mark 13 betray the presence of the kingdom? The rest of this chapter will explore this question, first by returning to the question of the agenda of Mark 13, then by examining the significance of the fall of the temple and of the persecution that believers will face.

II. *Mark 13.1-4 and Mark's Agenda for Mark 13*

Mark 13.1-4 in the Light of Our Study
We suggested in our introductory chapter that there can be no a priori assumption that Mark 13.1-4 must establish the agenda of the Markan Jesus in his 'answer' (13.5-37) or of Mark in presenting the entire chapter. In the light of our findings there are many reasons for rejecting the idea that Mark 13 is an attempt to answer the question as to which sign/signs will enable the believer to chart out an eschatological time-table:

1. That view is totally inconsistent with the Markan approach to signs (σημεῖα) (Chapter 2).
2. It cuts across the grain of Mark's calls for a very different sort of discernment concerning a very different sort of 'kingdom advance' (Chapter 3).
3. It contradicts Mark's teaching that faithful discipleship in times of crisis takes place precisely when (and because) the believer is ignorant of the timing of the End (Chapter 4).
4. It is contradicted by the fact that Mark's temple theology does not focus on eschatological fulfilment but on vindication of Jesus, transfer of authority to Jesus and his disciples, and universalizing Gospel proclamation (Chapter 5).
5. It misunderstands the nature of 'passion paradigms' in Mark's Gospel; the model is a kingdom expanding ever outwards from its inauguration, not focusing ever more narrowly towards its consummation (Chapter 6).
6. It fails to read Mark 13 as the logical conclusion of Mark's discourse to readers concerning the need for discernment/ discipleship (Chapter 7).

Even while being directed at other questions, every chapter of our study has provided reasons for denying that the question of the disciples in 13.4 establishes the reader's appropriate angle of vision at the material in Mark 13.

Mark 13.1-4 in the Light of Mark's Story Line
There is at least one further reason for rejecting eschatological chronology as the focus of Mark 13, or at least for taking Mark 13.1-4 as a basis for accepting the same. We recall the arguments by N.R. Petersen, stemming primarily from a careful separation between events in the narrated story and events projected into the implied future, that the disciples are destined *not* to be finally rejected by Jesus, but to be defenders of the truths about which they were once so mistaken. A crucial point to notice, however, is that only from 13.5 onward are we truly dealing with events in the implied future of the story. Mark 13.1-4a reflects the views of the disciples in the narrated story immediately before the passion, at a time when they were most certainly 'thinking in human terms'.[12] To ignore the place of Mark 13 in Mark's story line is to make a fundamental error with disastrous consequences for the exegesis of this already difficult chapter.

Mark 13.1-4 in the Light of Mark's Secret Kingdom Theology
In the light of Mark's 'secret kingdom' theology, we can identify the primary error of the disciples in formulating the questions as they did. *They imagined that there would be a time when the need for discipleship/discernment would be obsolete, when they could live as citizens of the kingdom and not find their faith challenged by the kingdom's secrecy or their faithfulness by its widespread rejection.* Mark 13 as a whole is designed to make the point that only with the arrival of the Son of Man will the need for discernment/discipleship (in the sense of passion discipleship) end.[13] When the End arrives it will arrive in such a way that no advance preparations are possible. One must become a citizen of the secret kingdom while it still requires faith to believe in it, discerning eyes and ears to recognize it, and courageous discipleship to live out its demands.[14] Put another way, *Mark 13 as a whole is designed to show that the discipleship message of Mark's Gospel reaches its logical conclusion in Mark 13 and that the appropriate correction of the disciples' error (13.1-4) is Jesus' response (13.5-37).*
To say with grand assurance that, 'It is incontrovertible that Mark

13 as a whole is intended to be a prediction of the events immediately preceding the end and of the end itself',[15] is to misread the chapter's function in the one context where we know it belongs, Mark's Gospel. If we permit Mark's story line to influence the function of each individual part, and if we allow his theological perspectives to determine how we read his Gospel, then the one view of Mark 13 which is quite impossible is the view that it is a series of objective signs facilitating the construction of an eschatological time-table.

Much rather, Mark 13 is part and parcel with the Gospel, tracing out events that occur (here in prediction, elsewhere in narration) and dropping clues as to how the discerning believer is to evaluate them, respond to them, and especially see in them aspects of the advancing kingdom.

Mark 13.1-4 and the 'Kinds of Events' Predicted
In our study we have usually called Mark 13 an 'eschatological discourse'. It is frequently called an 'apocalyptic discourse'. Some would argue that it is most appropriately spoken of in terms of 'salvation-history'.[16] We want to express a word of caution. We need to be very careful lest we imagine that we can construct mutually exclusive definitions of the various terms and then make our interpretations of the text more precise by forcing Mark to pick one of them. History for Mark is what happens.[17] To ask whether the events predicted in Mark 13 are historical or eschatological or apocalyptic is to ask the wrong question. They are simply events the Markan Jesus believes will happen. To identify the temporal links between the various events is important, but to start labelling the events themselves by modern categories is to obscure rather than illuminate.

We join the chorus of those who insist that Mark 13 as a whole shares little in common with typical Jewish apocalyptic *as a literary genre*.[18] What we will not do is join in discussions as to whether Mark has an apocalyptic view of *history*. The imprecision of such arguments is often the root cause of the inconclusiveness of their results. If we take the events discussed in Mark 13 and prematurely slot them into precise conceptual categories, we beg questions about the temporal links between events which are difficult enough to settle without such complication. The agenda of Mark 13 is not 'to chart out an apocalyptic view of history', nor 'to define an appropriate eschatology', nor 'to write a theology of salvation history'. The agenda of Mark 13 is to call believers to discern the significance of what Jesus has predicted will come to pass.

One of those events is the destruction of the temple. What does it mean?

III. *The Significance of the Temple's Destruction*

Some scholars have queried whether Mark 13 has anything at all to say about the temple after 13.4. The question is a legitimate one, since Mark 13.5-37 does not explicitly mention the temple at all, and there are plausible ways of interpreting the whole discourse as though no interest is expressed in the Jerusalem temple after the prologue.

Any interpretation of Mark 13 which takes the view that the temple *does* feature in the 'answer' of Jesus, must provide two things: (1) a plausible suggestion as to where in Mark 13 the destruction of the temple 'fits'; and (2) an equally plausible suggestion why there are no overt indications that the destruction of the temple is under discussion. The final chapter of this study will attempt to supply the second of these, as we examine the probable reason why the temple discussion takes place under the cover of 'mystery'. At this point we will attempt to meet the first requirement.

Does Mark 13 Discuss the Destruction of the Temple?
The reasons for agreeing with the majority that Mark does have the temple's destruction in mind at 13.14ff. are at least fourfold:

1. Mark obviously endorses the prophecy of the Markan Jesus that the temple will be destroyed. That event must fit somewhere in the time period after the resurrection, the time period covered by Mark 13.
2. There are no other plausible suggestions concerning the place where 'the abomination of desolation' was to appear. There are several plausible explanations for its identification, but no real alternatives to the temple as the place where it/ he will be set up.
3. If Judeans are called to flee to the mountains, the inference is that there is war in Judea. Any war between Jews and Romans would inevitably find a focus in the temple.
4. The immediate context of Mark 13 encourages us to view it as focused on the issue of the temple.[19]

It may be objected that none of the above arguments, nor even their combined force, makes it *certain* that 13.14 and surrounding context have anything to do with the fall of the temple. We concede that it does not put the point beyond doubt. But let us not forget that *whatever* Mark 13.14 is about, it will be impossible to establish the point beyond doubt from the text itself. Mark constructed it that way. He deliberately did not tell the reader which location was being specified. He deliberately did not tell the reader which 'abomination' (βδέλυγμα) was expected. And most importantly, Mark made it quite clear that more is being implied than is being said: 'let the reader understand' (13.14).

Does the Temple's Destruction Have Any Special Significance?
If Mark 13.14ff. alludes to the events surrounding the destruction of the temple, and we accept that it does, then we should watch closely for clues in Mark 13 and in the Gospel as to what significance that event is considered to have in the development of the story, in the theology of the secret kingdom, and in relation to the end of the post-resurrection age. Clearly Mark is calling his readers to read more in the text than is being explicitly said. He speaks in riddles and he calls for reader discernment just as he does whenever the temple destruction issue arises outside Mark 13 (see Chapter 5)! The 'temple theology' developed throughout the Gospel guides the reader in discerning the significance of the temple's destruction predicted unambiguously in 13.2 and alluded to ambiguously thereafter.

The Temple and the Jewish Leaders' Rejection of Jesus
In order to trace Mark's theology of temple destruction as it informs the interpretation of Mark 13, we need to allow 13.1-4 to lead us back into the surrounding Gospel context. It is there where the relevant clues are to be found. At this point we draw on points established earlier (Chapter 5) and without a great deal of new documentation attempt to bring the whole picture into a unity.

Temple concerns pervade the Gospel from Mark 11 to the end. In the middle of that section we see the disciples admiring the grandeur and stability of the temple (13.1); Jesus counters with the statement that it will be utterly ruined (13.2). Obviously the disciples have not learned the key lessons of Mark 11 and 12. How can they hope to understand correctly what the significance will be of Jesus' trial and his passion?

The Jewish establishment held positions of power both religiously and politically. They controlled the temple and its religious functions; they supported a status quo which maintained peace with Rome. They had carved out compromise positions for themselves which they believed were acceptable both to their overlords and to God. Throughout the controversy section (11.12–12.44), we find Jesus criticizing their assumption that God was pleased with them. Their *modus operandi* was nothing less than mutiny against their real 'Overlord' (12.1-12). Their concern to pacify Caesar was blinding them to their responsibilities to God (12.13-17). Their positions were being abused for selfish gain; the majority of them loved neither God nor neighbour (12.28-34); they exploited the poor (12.38-44). As a result they would lose their commission (12.9), their lives (12.9), and their temple (13.2). They would be replaced by the one they were rejecting (12.10). He would become Israel's rightful Lord and king (12.35). Mark intends his readers to realize that there is a fundamental cleavage between Jesus and the religious leaders of Israel. With the benefit of Mark 12, the reader can with confidence confirm his suspicions that in Mark 11, Jesus was not so much cleansing the temple as disqualifying it, and along with it, the authorities controlling its affairs.

The reader who has understood Mark 11 and 12 will see a great deal more going on in Mark 14–16 than is made explicit. The religious establishment rightly viewed Jesus as a threat to their relatively secure position both religiously and politically. The trial of Jesus brings both the political and the religious elements into clear focus, and they recur at the foot of Jesus' cross. The issues are: will the Jerusalem authorities retain their political roles as leaders of national Judaism, and will Jesus be established as king in a very different sort of kingdom? Will they continue to be custodians of a physical temple or will worship be brought to God in a spiritual temple that Jesus will bring into existence? In short, who (and whose theologies) will finally survive? Jesus and the Jewish leaders obviously have contrary views. The questions all finally come down to one crucial question, 'Who operates with God's approval?' Mark is not doing investigative journalism. He has firm convictions about the answers and writes accordingly.

At the trial Jesus neither confirms nor denies that he has spoken against the temple. The reader knows that he has predicted its destruction. Jesus does, however, confirm his Christological identity and announces he will survive to be the judge of his present accusers (14.62). The accusers cry 'blasphemy!' They pretend that this justifies the death charge; the reader who adopts the views Mark is endorsing knows that in fact they are killing Jesus to protect their positions. Mark's whole emphasis on discernment is crucial here. The undiscerning—including the disciples (as evidenced by their desperate attempt to avoid and even prevent the passion)—imagine that if Jesus is killed, his cause is doomed and the religious establishment will remain in power. Jesus knows that precisely *because* the Jewish establishment puts him to death, they will be stripped of their authority and the sceptre will pass into his hands (cf. 12.7-12).

At the foot of the cross, Jesus' demise is seen by the mockers as evidence of the falsity both of his Christological affirmation and of his temple-replacement prediction. The discerning reader, however, knows the evidence is being misread and sees the irony of the whole situation. When the proleptic destruction of the temple is reported in 15.38, the discerning reader knows that the tables are already being overturned. The temple's destruction is assured. Jesus will be the centre of a rebuilt temple not made with hands.

From this Markan perspective, it is not difficult to evaluate the significance of the final destruction of the temple. It is the completion of God's judgment on Israel's leadership for rejecting Jesus. It is the proof (for those who interpret it correctly) that Jesus was right and the Jewish leaders were wrong. It is an incentive to the Christian church to move ahead boldly on the implications of Jesus' victory over his enemies (cf. 12.36).

For those who suffered as they served (13.9-12), who may have been tempted to give up when the going got tough (13.13), who were forced to make a difficult decision not to cling to the temple for security in the turbulent war years, who chose to join Jesus in abandoning the temple—for such the final collapse of the temple, for all the pain and agony it might cause, would be a vindication of the Gospel they preached and the lives they lived. It would be, for those interpreting it correctly an encouragement to see the secret kingdom still intact and progressing towards its eventual unveiling at the parousia.

Temple Destruction and the Vindication of God's Messenger
There were various intertestamental views concerning the

anticipated relationship between the Messiah and the physical
temple, as there were concerning the permanence of the temple or its
destined replacement with one even more glorious.

One of the views maintained was that the Lord would not again
allow his temple to be destroyed. We can imagine how unimpressed
Jesus would have been with that view. He was not a great defender of
the views of the elders (cf. 7.6-13), and in Mark's understanding had
no great respect for the temple and its traditions—and none at all for
its custodians.

We have every reason to believe that both Jesus and Mark were
much more influenced by the major Old Testament prophetic books
than by anonymous (or pseudonymous) intertestamental literature.
Both Jeremiah and Ezekiel bear witness to the fact that the temple
can never be considered beyond the possibility of destruction, not as
long as God's people continue to belie their calling.

It was noted in Chapter 5 how remarkably appropriate Jer. 7.14's
larger context is to the issues surrounding the temple's disqualification
in Mark 11.12-21. It is difficult to believe that Jer. 7 had no influence
on the thinking of Mark and/or his source(s).

It should also be noted how remarkably apt Ezek. 33–34 is to our
understanding of Mark's whole temple destruction theology, and its
significance for interpreting Mark 13. Again it is difficult to believe
those chapters had no influence on the material Mark presents.[20]
Almost from beginning to end, Ezek. 33 covers the same territory as
Mark's temple destruction theology. The following are some of the
more striking parallels:

1. It makes the point that when the enemy comes upon God's
    people, the innocent may die with the guilty, but the
    watchmen will be held responsible if they have failed in their
    commission (Ezek. 33.6-9; cf. Mark 12.1-12; 13.9-14; 13.33-
    37).

2. It argues that one's moral condition in the past is irrelevant;
    one's present condition determines one's destiny (Ezek.
    33.12f.; cf. Mark 2.13-17 in the context of 2.1–3.6 See
    Chapter 2).

3. It insists that no appeal to supposedly inalienable rights to
    the land are of any avail (Ezek. 33.29; cf. Mark 12.1-9): the
    land will become *desolate* on account of the *abominations* of
    the residents (καὶ ἐρημωθήσεται διὰ πάντα τὰ βδελύγματα
    αὐτῶν ἃ ἐποίησαν. Ezek. 33.29 LXX; cf. Mark 13.14.[21]

4. It argues that pretended devotion to the Lord, concern for his words and expressions of devotion count for nothing when hearts are greedy for unjust gain and lives do not live out what is heard (Ezek. 33.30-32; cf. Mark 7.6f., 12.40).

Ezekiel's warnings and reprimands are clear and unambiguous. Almost the only thing in Mark's Gospel which is as clear and unambiguous is the Markan Jesus' castigation of Israel's leadership (cf. esp. 7.6-13). Ezekiel, like a faithful watchman sounds the warnings, but nevertheless the unresponsiveness of Israel's leadership calls down God's judgment, and the city falls (Ezek. 33.21).

That it is Israel's *leadership* which is primarily responsible for the devastation of the city is made clear not only by the 'watchman' imagery, but also by the 'shepherd' imagery which follows immediately in Ezek. 34 (see Chapter 5). God's judgment is pronounced in these terms:

> I am against the shepherds and will hold them accountable for my flock. I will remove them from tending the flock . . . I myself will search for my sheep and look after them. . . . I will place over them one shepherd, my servant David (Ezek. 34.10f., 23).

What follows in Ezek. 34 fills out the whole picture. Because of the unfaithfulness of Israel, their temple is being destroyed. Because of the unfaithfulness of Israel's leaders in particular, they will be replaced by God's anointed. When he is acknowledged as shepherd, then God will make a covenant of peace, regather the flock, and bring to fruition his eschatological promises (Ezek. 34.23-29).

The consonance with Mark's theology is remarkable. Mark's Gospel draws quotations and allusions from many sources,[22] but it is hard to avoid the conclusion that Ezek. 33 and 34 undergird much of his theology of temple destruction.

It is worth noting how both chapters begin and end. Both begin with a command for the 'Son of man' to prophesy. Both end by drawing out the implications of the fulfilment of the prophecies. Ezek. 33 ends with this:

> When all this comes true—and it surely will—*then they will know* that a prophet has been among them (Ezek. 33.33; cf. 33.29).

There will be apologetic value in the fulfilment of the promise that the temple will be destroyed. It vindicates God's messenger. Ezek. 34 ends like this:

> *Then they will know* that I, the Lord their God, am with them and
> that they, the house of Israel, are my people, declares the Sovereign
> Lord. You my sheep, the sheep of my pasture, are my people, and I
> am your God, declares the Sovereign Lord (Ezek. 34.30f.).

The fulfilment of God's *ultimate* purposes also has apologetic value.
It vindicates God for the way in which he has dealt with his people.
Along the way there may have been times of doubt and uncertainty.
In the end they will know.

What a perfect model it demonstrates for interpreting Mark 13,
not only in terms of its temple destruction theology, but its whole
theology of the secret kingdom and the coming manifestation of its
victory.

Temple Destruction and the Gospel of the Secret Kingdom
When the temple is destroyed, what conclusions are discerning
believers to reach? Certainly not that the end of the age has come
upon them. That inference leans far too heavily on 13.4. Mark is not
silent about the relationship between the destruction of the temple
and the End (see Chapter 9). But far too often overlooked is the fact
that a very great deal of Mark's temple theology relates the
destruction of the temple to the *beginning* of the post-resurrection
era, not the end of it. It is this link which we must examine.

O.A. Piper speaks of Jesus' opponents and of,[23]

> ... the divine disavowal of their work as is indicated both by the
> prophecy of the destruction of Jerusalem and its Temple (Mark 13)
> and by the resurrection of Jesus.

It is quite appropriate to thus draw together these two events, for
they constitute the reversal of fortunes that God's Righteous Sufferer
anticipated when divine justice would be done. There are several
texts which, in subtle and allusive ways, point to the mutual rejection
between Jesus and the Jewish leaders, the destruction of the temple,
and the resurrection, all together (cf. esp. 12.1-12; 14.57-64). Jesus
submitted to the decision of the Jewish lower court because he knew
the judgment would be reversed in the higher divine court (14.62).
He knew that his death would be followed by his resurrection and he
knew that the misguided zeal of Israel's leaders to protect their
temple would backfire on them. Precisely by trying to protect their
temple, they would lose it. Precisely by losing his life, Jesus would
save it. Jesus' resurrection and the destruction of the temple are
legitimately considered two sides of the same coin.

The major question on which Jesus and the Jewish authorities had disagreed was, 'Who is operating under divine authority?' The resurrection and the temple's destruction settle the issue. When Jesus acted against the temple the question of his authority was raised by those who objected. Jesus gave no immediate answer, but a week later and then again four decades later, God answered. Of course Mark knows that only those who accept the message of the resurrection and confirm it by 'going and seeing' will be aware of God's verdict. Of course Mark knows that only those who can see past politics and religion to the heart of the issue will know that the destruction of the temple is God's rejection of Judaism's defenders. Yet for those with eyes to see and ears to hear, God has spoken. Both events foreshadow a greater and more visible role reversal yet to come.[24]

Jesus rises from the grave without parading proofs of his resurrection. It is left to discerning believers to confirm the reality of Jesus' resurrection (16.7). The unbelieving will have no proofs until he appears in power and glory at his parousia.

So also with the destruction of the temple. It does not provide objective unambiguous proofs that God has rejected the corrupt leaders of Israel; not, at any rate, if history goes on after the temple falls (see Chapter 9). Only the final judgment at the Son of Man's visible return brings about the final and unambiguous separation between believers and rejectors.[25]

Precisely because the destruction of the temple is so much a part of Jesus' vindication, it has significant apologetic impact for believers in their own life of faith and in their work of Gospel proclamation.[26] When Ezekiel predicted a similar event, the fulfilment functioned first and foremost as a vindication of his own position as God's messenger ('They will know a prophet has been among them' [Ezek. 33.33]). It is so also with Jesus. When his words come true, then it becomes clear that his ministry has operated under divine authority.

Mark is not suggesting that the mere presence of precognition is a stable foundation upon which to build an apologetic. He is saying that the judgment Jesus invoked on his enemies has been met with a divine response. When the temple falls, discerning believers see that Jesus has been vindicated at the expense of his enemies. They see in that event some confirmation that what they have been affirming in faith is fact. The transaction has indeed been completed. They can move ahead boldly with the task their Lord has given them, assured that if they suffer they will be vindicated. Their Lord was! The evidence they already had (he rose from the dead) is now supplemented with this new evidence (his prediction concerning judgment on Israel's rulers came true). The events are closely related to each other.

The destruction of the temple, because it provides assurance that Jesus was indeed operating under divine authority, confirms the validity of everything Jesus said and did. The believer can be assured that Jesus was indeed appointed by God to inherit the vineyard. Those Jesus appointed to be 'with him' are indeed legitimate heirs with him of that vineyard and therefore God's ordained replacement for the Jerusalem authorities who rejected Jesus. Jesus is indeed both David's son and Lord (his enemies are now under his feet). The Christian community built on Jesus is indeed the real locus for divine worship. God is indeed so concerned about including Gentiles among his people that he will remove the temple if necessary in order to make room for them (cf. 11.17).[27] What was already affirmed, ever since Jesus died and rose again (by those with eyes of faith), can now be believed and proclaimed with even greater confidence. The physical destruction of the temple is the confirmation that what the rending of the temple veil promised is indeed a reality.

It does not become a 'sign' in the Markan sense; in the strict sense it proves nothing. It will have little apologetic value for those who wish to disbelieve. Its causes and its outcomes are matters which could be disputed. However, interpreted as the Markan Jesus wants believers to interpret it, it serves to comfort and encourage believers as they suffer and proclaim, but yearn for faith to be turned to sight.

The disciples are 'on the way'. For them the destruction of the temple, for all that it is a national disaster and a tragedy for many of their compatriots, serves as a word of assurance; they have heard their Lord correctly and his word is being confirmed. It is an encouragement to continue following faithfully through difficult circumstances and to move out aggressively in the evangelization of the world.

To the issues raised by Mark 13.14ff. we shall return shortly under the topic of suffering and persecution. The fall of the temple is a judgment on the Jewish leaders and it is an interim vindication of believers who await their final vindication. But it is one more thing.

It is a test of the disciples' ability to discern and to obey. We now turn to the topic within which that will emerge with greater clarity.

IV. *The Significance of the Disciples' Suffering and Persecution*

If Mark does not speak *explicitly* about the temple in 13.5ff., that cannot be said of the issue of suffering and persecution. The theme pervades the whole chapter. No other theme brings us closer to the centre of Mark's discipleship theology, for when disciples face their own passion they are most fully modelling themselves after their cross-carrying Lord. As we have come to expect, where discipleship comes into focus, calls for discernment come with it.

In Mark 13 there are a variety of events predicted which indicate that believers will face distress, trial or persecution. It is on occasions like these, according to Mark's Gospel, that faithfulness in discipleship is most acutely tested (cf. 14.38). *In every one of the distresses forecast, we see the Markan Jesus or Mark himself dropping hints that special discernment will be needed in order that the disciples might respond to the crises as they ought.*

Without prejudicing our attempt in Chapter 9 to construct a Markan 'eschatological time-table', and without attempting to defend decisions on which sets of events are chronologically and/or theologically linked, we can isolate six clear illustrations in Mark 13 where the discipleship/discernment co-ordination can be observed. In almost every case the connection helps us to sort out Mark's intended interpretation of the event in question and sometimes even his eschatological chronology.

The Wars that Begin the Messianic Age (13.7f.)

Mark 13.7f. predicts wars and rumours of them, international strife and natural disasters. In the turbulent first few decades after the resurrection,[28] anyone who had been led to believe that such events signalled the imminent arrival of God's final Day would no doubt have found reason to allow apocalyptic speculations to reach fever pitch. Mark 13.5-8 is an attempt to put a check on such fervour. It would not be surprising if the reference to 'the beginning of birth pains' (ἀρχὴ ὠδίνων) is a deliberate attempt to utilize 'apocalyptic' language, especially in view of the fact that something similar happens in 15.33 during Jesus' passion. Mark understands Jesus' passion as his coronation; with Jesus' victory in the passion/

resurrection the messianic age itself is in gestation. It will come to full birth with the Son of Man's return. Events that immediately follow the passion/resurrection are quite appropriately termed the beginning of birth pains.

But if the wars and trials are apocalyptic events, that does not mean they signal an imminent parousia. They are but the beginning. Therefore the discernment call goes forth: 'be discerning lest someone deceive you' (βλέπετε μή τις ὑμᾶς πλανήσῃ 13.5b). The kingdom does not advance through suffering per se; it advances when God's messengers, the kingdom's citizens, take up their cross and follow. The disciples are not to imagine that the troubles they share with the world at large will fulfil the prophecies of Jesus that they too must suffer. There is reserved for them trials which are a test not only of their ability to endure suffering but of their allegiance to Jesus. These preliminary crises are to cause no distress (μὴ θροεῖσθε 13.7).[29] Others who do not know the kingdom's secret will imagine that these events signal the End. The disciple who is discerning will not be deceived.

Persecution that Gives Way to World Mission (13.9-13)
We turn next to the 'Herz- und Mittelstück' of Mark 13.[30] Very few today would challenge the conclusion that Mark 13.9-13 as a whole is structured around a threefold prediction of the disciples' 'handing-over', with v. 10 interrupting the structure in order to give notice that the church's world mission must take place 'first',[31] presumably meaning 'prior to the return of the Son of Man'.[32]

We will separate out v. 11 for individual attention in the following subsection. We do so not because it deals with a different sort of distress or takes place at a different time, but because it makes its own unique contribution to our study of the discipleship/discernment link.

M. Hooker rightly notes that,[33]

> Unlike the sufferings in 5-8, those in 9-13 are experienced specifically by Christians. The warning is, of course, to *expect* these things—*not* to try to escape them [emphasis hers],

These trials are the ones that Mark so clearly paralleled with the trials Jesus faced. They constitute the disciples' own passion (or certainly part). In the trials the disciples must respond as Jesus did. They are called to be alert, not that they might be able to escape, but that they might respond appropriately.

And right in the midst of this tightly structured pattern Mark inserts the prediction of world mission. A clearer case of Mark's 'passion paradigm' could hardly be found (see Chapter 6). The point is not that witness will inevitably lead to persecution, but that persecution will, far from defeating the cause of the church, open doors to even greater proclamation.

If we have understood that paradigm correctly, then our study begins to reap rewards here, for it prevents us from drawing wrong conclusions about Mark's chronology. The implication is surely not that the mission must be completed before the 'handing over' stops, but rather that even though the disciples are handed over by their enemies, the 'kingdom baton' will also be 'handed over' to others to take the gospel into all the world. It provides assurance for the disciples in their time of trial that the secret kingdom is still advancing. They might not survive until the coming of the Son of Man, but the cause they represent will. Indeed it will not merely survive; before the End it will cover the world.

Nevertheless, the future survival of the movement is not the only point which discerning believers will draw from 13.9-13; they are also enjoined to discern and make the most of the opportunities which the persecution itself affords them. When they stand before governors and kings, their defence will not be designed to secure their release or prove their innocence. They will use the 'witness stand' to bear a good testimony as had their Lord.[34] What will discerning disciples do in the crisis of their own 'handing-over'? They will realize they are suffering precisely what their Lord suffered. They will be encouraged by the assurance that despite their suffering (indeed even through it) the kingdom is secretly advancing. They will do their share to proclaim its gospel.

On Trial With the Holy Spirit as Advocate (13.11)
Mark 13.11 makes a more general statement about the believer's response when on trial. The surrounding verses detail the sorts of trials the believer will face. Verse 11 indicates the source of the believers' help in such trials, especially when the temptation is to try to extricate themselves from the problems through ingenuity and clever words. *Disciples will be given divine revelation when needed in order that their responses in time of crisis will be the right ones.* Jesus considered the religious leaders of Israel and other persecutors to be Satan's henchmen in opposition to God's kingdom. Against such opponents only divine help will be adequate.[35]

Only disciples are qualified recipients of divine illumination and insight and only those who are guided by such divine illumination can be faithful disciples. That twofold message pervaded so much of Mark 1-12 especially on the level of Mark's 'meta-message'. Now it is made explicit in the only sustained discourse in Mark where the discipleship of Jesus' followers in the post-resurrection situation is addressed.

When the Crisis Occurs in the Temple, Flee! (13.14ff.)
We come to a link between discernment and discipleship which may at first seem surprising or at odds with the Markan picture. In fact it is not so. Throughout Mark's Gospel, the assumption was that when disciples face times of danger and persecution, they are to trust and endure *in* the situation, not flee *from* it. Mark 13.14 turns this on its head.

The call for discernment is loud and clear. After a whole series of explicit statements outlining just what sort of trials will be experienced by the world at large (5-8) and by the disciples in particular (9-13), suddenly the Markan Jesus begins speaking in riddles. An ambiguous phrase ('the abomination that causes desolation') is used with no clear indications as to what abominates and what is made desolate; a grammatical anomaly adds to the mystery, the location is not pinpointed at all ('where it ought not to be' ὅπου οὐ δεῖ), and with the insertion of 'let the reader understand', the reader is shown that something is deliberately being left unspecified. Mark apparently believes that the disciples will be guided to identify the significance of the event when it occurs.

And when it does, surprisingly, they are to flee! Why? Why counsel flight when everywhere else in the entire Gospel flight indicates discipleship failure?

What the discerning reader must not adopt is a general principle that 'when the going gets really tough, run for your life'. That would be to contradict everything else in Mark's Gospel, and particularly the verses that immediately precede this verse.[36] The discerning believer will see that something else is going on here.

Flight to the mountains is very clearly an attempt to find safety in time of danger.[37] The call goes out not only to the believers but to all who will listen. To remain in the city is to invite disaster on oneself. To flee is to be preserved. Theologically the key point is obviously that *the temple is not inviolable*. It will not protect anyone, nor can anyone protect it. The disciples have no right or responsibility to pledge their allegiance to it or stand their ground in defending it. The Romans may be the visible enemies when the temple collapses, but Mark understands its destruction to be an act of God. It is God's response to the Jewish religious establishment for their misguided attachment to the temple, their abuse of their commission, and most centrally their rejection of their Messiah.

The disciples are to flee, not because they fear what the enemy will do, but because God desires them to absent themselves when everything stands poised for the divine judgment to fall.[38] When the judgment falls, all who will trust in themselves, their might, their leaders, their election or their temple will be judged along with the religious system they represent. All who will take their stand with Jesus will leave the temple and the city to its fate. That is why in the crises that *precede* the final abomination the Christians are *not* to flee. They are needed to proclaim the secret kingdom and rescue their compatriots from the disaster to come.

Everything hinges on one crucial question, 'On which side of the battle is God?' It was so in 30 A.D.; and it will be so in 70 A.D. If God is the defender of the city, even walls are unnecessary (cf. Zech. 2.3-6). If God comes in judgment, walls, rituals, swords, and misguided trust in the temple avail nothing (cf. Jer. 38.2). Which side Jesus was on was made clear already when he judged the temple and its custodians forty years before. If readers of Mark's Gospel have understood 11.12-21, they will also understand the reason for flight in 13.14.

It has to do with personal safety only secondarily. At the primary level it is a test of one's allegiance and source of security.[39]

> There was no necessity for the disciples to perish through misguided attachment to the doomed city (still less through a confidence in its inviolability); martyrdom for the Gospel's sake was another matter. . . . Jesus demanded the utmost renunciation for His Name and Gospel, but not for identification with the nation in its hour of doom.

Finally, if the reason for flight had less to do with safety per se than it did with one's allegiance, obviously there is a very clear focus on the whole matter of what temple-attachment *means*; that is, on what deeper theological implications reside in the act of staying in or fleeing from the place. We have all the makings here of another Markan 'meta-message' to those who live after the explicit event in view.

'Go to Galilee' was a literal command to the disciples after the resurrection. They were expected to make the physical journey. But for them, for their converts, and for Mark's readers, the command holds also a special meaning that is independent of actual pilgrimages. It is a call to discipleship, to reinstatement after failure, to renewed commitment, and to the beginning of a life of service and suffering 'on the way'.

'Flee the city' also was a literal command to those who would be present when God's judgment would fall on Jerusalem. They were expected literally to find shelter in the hills. But for them, for their converts, and for Mark's readers, the command also holds a special meaning that is independent of actual pilgrimages. It is a call to dissociate from those whom Jesus judged,[40] and to discern the kingdom's secret advances, temple or no temple, Jerusalem or no Jerusalem. The kingdom can get along well without both of them.

It is clear that unless the discernment/discipleship link is firmly held, the post-resurrection believers will be unable to be obedient when the crisis comes. They will neither understand the allusive references (13.14) nor recognize the event itself. They will not realize that suffering per se has no positive value; only when required out of allegiance to Christ is it transformed into glory. If they have not adequately comprehended the attitude Jesus had to the temple and its custodians, they will be uncertain how to respond when the sacred shrine is under threat. If they do not see the hand of God behind the Roman armies, their tears will be shed for the wrong victims. When the crisis comes, both discernment and discipleship must be operative. How else will they be able to stay and proclaim as long as possible (13.9-13), and then flee when they must (13.14)?

The Great Tribulation (13.19)

A comment or two can be made about the unprecedented and unrepeatable distress mentioned in 13.19 even without attempting to settle the question whether in Mark's chronology the reference is to an event immediately connected with the fall of the temple, an event immediately preceding the return of the Son of Man, or both of the above.

Whatever apocalyptic associations Mark attaches to the great tribulation discussed here, it is clear that false christs and false prophets capitalize on the portentous event and use it as a springboard for their own deceit, complete with signs and wonders to give themselves credibility.[41] Mark warns believers to be discerning, lest in evaluating the significance of all these things, they are led astray.

The similarity between 13.5f. and 13.21f. indicates that the danger of deception is particularly acute in times of crisis. From beginning to end, the post-resurrection period will require discipleship in the crises and discernment in the confusion.

Discipleship in the Unknown Waiting Period (13.33-37)
We will not repeat here points already made in Chapter 4. We do no more than recall that the discernment/discipleship link is firmly held together by the βλέπετε (i.e., discern!) introduction to the parable (13.33a) and the γρηγορεῖτε (i.e., remain faithful!) conclusion (13.37).

Discernment is not possible without discipleship, nor discipleship without discernment. It is this twofold theme that pervades all of Mark's Gospel and Mark 13 in a special way. We suggested above that Mark 13 has a 'meta-message' of its own. The repeated calls to 'discern' and 'be faithful' surely indicate that the 'meta-message' will be nothing other than Jesus' own prime concerns, re-applied for those who live in the time period that follows the writing of Mark's Gospel. The model of Jesus is the universally valid one from the time he prepared 'the way' until he gathers his elect to himself.

Mark's priorities are quite clear. Discerning believers are to discern the meaning of the key events in Mark 13 so that they can preach with boldness and suffer with courage, and so that they can 'see' the hidden kingdom and anticipate its final disclosure.[42] But what is the chronological link between the suffering of the saints and the End of the age? Is the 'great tribulation' brought to an end by the returning Son of Man, or does it end by the mercy of God so that mission and discipleship can go on?

Further, what about the chronological link between the fall of the temple and the End? We know that when the temple falls, then God's messenger is vindicated (cf. Ezek. 33.33). When the End of the age comes, then God's people will be delivered from danger, rejection and suffering (cf. Ezek. 34.25-30). But how does the intermediate 'secret' vindication relate to the final public one? Does Mark 13 guide the reader who joins the disciples in their curiosity about End time chronology? To these questions we now turn.

Chapter 9

MARK 13 AND THE TIMING OF THE END

Introduction

The previous chapter addressed questions very near to the centre of *Mark's* theological concerns and communication agenda for Mark 13. In this chapter we turn to the agenda which is so often near the centre of the concerns of *modern exegetes*. Mark wanted to instruct his readers on the significance of the 'secret kingdom' for their understanding of the events they were facing and would face in the post-resurrection age. Modern exegetes frequently want to eliminate the ambiguities of Mark 13 in order to construct an eschatological time-table that outlines the projected events leading up to the return of the Son of Man.

To say that it is a modern agenda to sort out Mark's eschatological time-table is not to say that no first century reader shared that concern, nor is it to say that Mark does not address the concern. First century Christians were no doubt as curious as we are about the eschatological time-table that their Lord had endorsed. They may well have hoped that Mark's inclusion of the material in Mark 13 would answer their questions. If our thesis is correct, however, Mark addressed those questions but did not provide his readers with that which they were seeking. We want to defend the thesis that Mark 13 is carefully designed to preserve an over-arching principle: *the timing of the Son of Man's return is not knowable in advance of his arrival.* In essence, our thesis in this chapter is that all the following questions receive the same answer:

1. Will there be another 'great tribulation' following the one surrounding the crisis events in Jerusalem?
2. Will there be a renewed opportunity for mission and evangelism after the fall of the temple?
3. Will the fall of the temple usher in the return of the Son of Man?
4. Will the Son of Man return in the first generation?

The answer that Mark endorses to all these questions is: 'We cannot know'. It is our conviction that Mark never intended the thirteenth chapter of his Gospel to aid readers in the task of charting out a chronology of End time events. If anything, the chapter was designed to *prevent* them from doing so, in order that they might truly live as faithful citizens of the 'secret' kingdom while waiting for its hiddenness to end and its full disclosure to vindicate their faith and reward their faithfulness.

How does one test the thesis that Mark is trying to *prevent* us from answering some questions? Our method will be to try to use the texts to answer some of those questions, and then to find an explanation for the fact that whenever we do so, we seem to run into a brick wall. If those brick walls betray the hand of a careful architect, we will have to conclude that Mark put them there to prevent his readers from taking a wrong road. Needless to say, this approach opens up considerable opportunity for arguments to become complicated and conclusions to be reached by a rather circuitous route. It is hard to know how to sort out the issues of Mark 13 when we approach it with agenda that the author apparently did not share.

It is legitimate for us to enquire what eschatological time-frame Mark endorsed, even if we can establish that it was not his primary purpose to answer the timing question that so concerned the disciples in 13.4. This legitimacy rests primarily on three factors:

1. The very fact that Mark presented the chapter in the form of a misguided question concerning time calculations, followed by a discourse designed to correct the questioners' error, is evidence that Mark had reflected carefully on the time question.
2. The chapter itself contains no shortage of terms which deal with the question of timing.[1]
3. The fact that scholars have used Mark 13 as the basis for constructing such a wide variety of eschatological time-tables, should cause us to ask what it is about Mark's perspective which motivated him to present such an indecisive answer. Is there some intentional ambiguity? Is it perhaps the very nature of his conclusions which required an indecisive statement concerning the question of timing?

We want to hear what Mark says about eschatological time-tables. And we want to be prepared to hear him say things we neither expected nor hoped he would say.

I. *Judgment and Vindication: Intermediate and Final*

In the previous chapter we argued that Mark 13 does not encourage us to affirm with confidence that the fall of the temple will immediately usher in the consummation of the kingdom and the return of the Son of Man. Does this mean that we can confidently affirm that the fall of the temple is merely an intermediate judgment of God within history to be followed by yet another judgment, a final eschatological judgment, at the end of history? Not necessarily. We want to test the thesis that Mark does not want his readers to rule out either possibility.

If we were to conclude that the fall of the temple is merely an intermediate event, and not chronologically linked to the End, we should expect to find in Mark 13 some indications as to what activities will occupy the attention of faithful disciples in the interim period between the fall of the temple and the End. It is not hard to find indications as to what those events would be. The penultimate events of history are mission (i.e., the End comes after the world mission is complete [13.10]),[2] and faithful discipleship (13.33-37; see Chapter 4). Mark's 'passion paradigm' links them firmly together. But what is the primary context for these two activities? Is it before, during or after the events surrounding the fall of the temple?

Mission and Discipleship in the Interim Period
However, if mission and discipleship are to be the penultimate events of history, one of four things is required:

1. The 'unrepeatable' tribulation (13.19) could be linked firmly to the destruction of the temple (*terminus a quo*), but separated off from the End. Then the primary context for mission/discipleship is in the interim between the tribulation and the End.
2. The 'unrepeatable' tribulation is linked firmly to the End (*terminus ad quem*), but separated off from the destruction of the temple. Then the primary context for mission/discipleship is in the interim between the destruction of the temple and the final tribulation.
3. The 'unrepeatable' tribulation spans the entire time period from the destruction of the temple to the End. Then the context for mission/discipleship is the tribulation period itself.

    4.   A single description (13.15-23, at least) points to two different fufilments, a preliminary one connected with the fall of the temple and a final one connected with the End. Then the primary context for mission/discipleship is between the first fulfilment and the second. (See discussion of 'prophetic perspective' below.)

The usual procedure would be to select one of these four, present arguments against the other three, and then defend the selected alternative as Mark's eschatological time scheme. Instead of doing this we will ask another question: How did Mark manage to present a text which seems open to all four possibilities?

A Proposal Concerning Mark's Eschatological Time-Table
The only perspective, so it seems, which makes sense of all of Mark 13 in the context of Mark's Gospel is that Mark intentionally presented the text in such a way that the reader cannot legitimately rule out any of the above options. That is to say, Mark's choice of the above options is not *one* of them, but *any* of them. Put another way, *Mark deliberately left his readers in the dark about the chronological links that are expected between the fall of the temple and the End of the age.* If we are going to defend this theory successfully, it will be essential to be able to answer two key questions:

    1.   How did Mark manage to say so very much about 'time' and not tell us the answer to the one question which we, like the disciples in 13.4, would so much like answered?
    2.   Why did he do so?

These questions will be dealt with in a variety of ways in this chapter. In the remainder of the present introductory section we aim to present a few preliminary indicators that our approach is worth pursuing.

Does Mark 13.24ff. Focus on Judgment?
One way of testing our thesis is to ask whether 'final judgment' is implied in the language of 13.24-27. *If it is*, then the key events expected at the End of the age (judgment and vindication) are *both* discussed in 13.24-27. In that case, it is plausible that 13.14ff. is not to be thought of as final judgment, but rather as an intermediate judgment within history that is theological and chronologically separate from the End. *If it is not*, it is plausible to think of the events

surrounding the fall of the temple as 'final judgment', and 13.24–27 as
the positive side of the denouement, the vindication of God's elect.

We will be arguing that judgment is neither unambiguously
included nor unambiguously excluded in the description of the final
events (13.24–27). Mark's purposes were served best by leaving the
question open.

Scholars are divided on whether or not the description of the
'cosmic convulsions' described in 13.24f. is intended to indicate
divine judgment. The language could be descriptive of judgment, but
it could also indicate the trembling of the universe at the appearance
of God.[3] Whatever the language indicates, the events themselves are
concomitant with the arrival of the Son of Man. They are not
preliminary events signalling the nearness of the parousia.[4] The
following factors seem to indicate that judgment is in view:

1. Theophany language in the Old Testament regularly includes
   judgment explicitly with it.
2. All four of the primary Old Testament texts alluded to in
   13.24f. focus unmistakably on judgment (cf. Isa. 13.10; 34.4;
   Ezek. 32.7; Joel 2.10).
3. Mark uses harvest imagery to denote the End and the
   imagery almost certainly suggests judgment (cf. esp. 4.29).[5]
4. The appearance of the Son of Man in Mark is associated
   with judgment (8.38; 14.62).

The texts alluded to in 13.24f. are taken from passages which focus
on the judgment of nations hostile to God's people.[6] Who are the
enemies of 'God's people' (i.e., the Son of Man and his elect) in
Mark's Gospel? They are clearly the religious leaders of Israel who
dispose of Jesus (15.1) and will be active when the same is done to his
followers (13.9ff.)

If Mark allows for the possibility that more than one generation
will follow Jesus (a possibility yet to be examined) then it might be
thought that the Jewish leaders are *prototypes* for whoever will be the
enemies of God's people when the Son of Man returns. If Mark does
not allow that possibility, then the objects of whatever judgment
might be in view in 13.24ff. are precisely the same as the objects of
God's wrath when he comes in judgment to destroy the temple. Are
they to be judged twice?

The unlikelihood of this scenario is what leads some commentators
to argue that although 13.24–26 could be thought to allude to

judgment, it is preferable to think of the passage as alluding primarily to a theophany in a more positive sense, *since the events surrounding the destruction of the temple already constitute God's judgment on his enemies.*

G.R. Beasley-Murray asks a pertinent question: 'Have we sufficiently taken into account that verses 14ff. actually describe *the day of the Lord on Jerusalem*?' [emphasis his].[7] In other words, has not the judgment emphasis which is normally associated with theophany language, already been dealt with before 13.24 so that in vv. 24ff. we see the 'vindication of God's elect' emphasis coming to the fore? That would take care of the problem of 'double punishment'.

The crucial question is: Does Mark envision the events surrounding the fall of the temple as final judgment, as events tied directly to the End of the age? Or are they merely historical events which are to be superseded by a greater final judgment as part of the End?

We are left with two possible scenarios:

1.   If the fall of the temple is indeed 'the day of the Lord on Jerusalem', then another final judgment is not required and the way is open to take 13.24-27 as denoting only the positive side of the final assize. It is the language of theophany and is part of the picture of the Son of Man returning to vindicate and reward his elect.

2.   If the fall of the temple is a judgment within history, but not in any sense a final judgment, then we would expect the description of the final events (13.24-27) to make room for both the negative and positive sides of the coming of God, that is to say, it denotes judgment (13.24f.) and blessing (13.26f.)

If it was Mark's purpose to avoid taking a stand on whether or not the fall of the temple was an event directly linked chronologically and eschatologically with the End, the only way he could accomplish that would be to make it uncertain whether the description of the final events (13.24-27) indicates judgment as well as blessing or just blessing. Is that not precisely what he seems to have done?

Mark 13.24f. is brilliantly ambiguous: on the one hand, it might signify the universal convulsions to be expected when God marches onto the stage. On the other hand, it might signify the judgment that falls on God's enemies. It is impossible to decide. Thus, 13.24-27 neither affirms nor denies that the events surrounding the temple's destruction constitute *the day of the Lord on Jerusalem*. That is to say, *the 'eschatological'* (to use the ambiguous word) *import of the destruction of the temple is left deliberately unspecified*. If 13.24f. is part of a campaign to prevent the reader from constructing an eschatological time-table, it plays its role well.

Is There a Time Gap Between Mark 13.23 and 13.24?
It might be imagined that even though 13.24f. does not indicate clearly whether or not the fall of the temple is an event immediately attached to the End, the question can be settled by determining whether or not there is a time gap specified between 13.23 and 13.24. If 13.24 is continuous with 13.23 then clearly the events attached to the fall of the temple are also attached to the End, and the question is settled. If 13.24 is not continuous with 13.23, then the question is also settled, but the opposite conclusion is reached. What temporal relationship is intended by 'in those days following that distress' (ἐν ἐκείναις ταῖς ἡμέραις μετὰ τὴν θλῖψιν ἐκείνην 13.24a)?

It is sometimes considered self-evident that the terms are an attempt to tie the End directly to the destruction of the temple, and/or to the accompanying tribulation (θλῖψις) and/or to the advent of false christs and false prophets. But does 'in those days following' really force the conclusion that the two time periods are closely connected? It is hard to suppress the feeling that the so-called 'self-evidency' of this is often a function of the readers' inability to project themselves back into the time perspective of the Markan Jesus. From this perspective, it seems very much less certain that 13.24a is an attempt to tie the two events closely together.[8] A growing number of scholars argue that Mark's whole point at 13.24a is to *untie* the two events, forging a time gap between them.[9] In the present state of the discussion, scholarly certainty one way or the other seems unjustified.

If the primary error of the false prophets (13.21f.) was their *false* announcement of the parousia (a conclusion they would have based on the fact of the tribulation) then Mark would be insisting the events are to be separated. A time gap between 13.23 and 13.24 would be *affirmed*.

If L. Hartman's suggestion is correct that the command to 'flee the city' is an allusion to Lot's flight from Sodom, this might well indicate that a time gap is being *denied*, at least if Luke's use of the

'Lot' motif (see Lk 17.28f.) is any guide.[10] D. Wenham's argument that Mark omitted the 'times of the Gentiles' time gap[11] would tilt the balance in the direction of continuity between 13.23 and 13.24.

Arguments focused on the phrase 'and never again shall be' (καὶ οὐ μὴ γένηται 13.19) are inconclusive. Some would insist that this addition to the quotation from Daniel is a way of indicating that life will go on after the tribulation and therefore another final eschatological tribulation is to be expected thereafter.[12] Others consider it virtually self-evident that the language (taken literally) is a clear statement that this is *the* final tribulation that first century eschatological schemes expected.

M. Hooker and W.H. Kelber try to find ways of walking the tight-rope on this question.[13] Their view is an attempt to affirm both the continuity and discontinuity of the events up to v. 23 and those following. This view does, admittedly, harmonize well with one set of interpretations of 13.28f. and 13.30. However these are very ambiguous verses (see below) and to erect a theory upon them is to build a very shaky structure indeed.

Instead of saying with Kelber and Hooker that Mark was *affirming both* continuity and discontinuity, would it not be better to say that he was *denying neither* of them? Does it not appear that Mark has presented the material in such a way that the relationship between the destruction of the temple and the End of the age is left completely uncertain? Rather than saying the two events are separated but very close, he is saying we cannot be sure either that they are separated, or that they are connected. The advantage of this alternative is that it does not rest on uncertain interpretations of 13.28f. and 13.30, it explains the ambiguous data admirably, and it harmonizes well with a great deal of evidence (see below) that this is precisely what is happening in Mark 13.

P.J. Achtemeier comments on 13.14–27 in these terms:[14]

> These verses present us with a strange tension between descriptions of events that will let us know when the end will come upon us (verses 14-20), and a warning that such an interpretation of those events is deceptive (verses 21-23).

Achtemeier's formulation really amounts to saying that Mark can legitimately use the events surrounding the fall of the temple as 'signs' indicating the nearness of the end, but if anyone else attempts the same he is labelled a false prophet. Would it not be more accurate to credit Mark with the view that the events surrounding the fall of the temple *may or may not* lead directly to the End? Is he not saying that, because it is not for us to know whether it does, any claim one way or the other is deceptive.

Perhaps Mark is neither 'clothing Jesus with a glittering apocalyptic robe'[15] nor 'stripping the [temple's] destruction of eschatological dignity'.[16] He remains uncommitted on the relationship between the temple destruction and the End. Mark is ambiguous about whether or not there is a time gap between 13.23 and 13.24, just as he is ambiguous about whether or not 13.24-26 focuses on judgment. It is therefore left completely uncertain whether the destruction of the temple constitutes 'the Day of the Lord' on Jerusalem, or whether it is one of the judgments of history, perhaps to be followed by many more before the End. We continue with our argument that the ambiguity is deliberately created by Mark, and that the resulting uncertainty for the reader is the effect Mark desired.

In order to present more evidence in support of our position, we now turn to the question from another angle.

II. *The Destruction of the Temple and the End of the Age*

Introduction

Not a few commentators have urged that Mark 13, like so many prophetic texts, has a 'dual focus'.[17] There is a 'first round' fulfilment, but the meaning of the text is not exhausted by it. We have urged that Mark's whole Gospel has a dual focus, with a primary narrative fulfilment and an implied pattern for those 'following after'. Should we expect anything different in Mark 13?

The notion of 'prophetic perspective' is often utilized to 'explain' the text, and interpretations of Mark 13 are replete with suggestions that someone either deliberately adopted such a perspective or else inadvertently fell prey to its influence. The 'prophetic perspective' phenomenon is often described using the analogies of mountain ranges and indeterminate valleys separating them.[18]

We will not be adopting a 'prophetic perspective' interpretation of Mark 13 in the sense that is usually meant, but in order to work towards the explanation that we do endorse, we must look at the varieties of ways in which the 'prophetic perspective' phenomenon is usually characterized.

The 'Prophetic Perspective'

Those who are eager to defend Jesus or Mark (or Old Testament prophets) from the charge that they erroneously identified the particular crisis they were experiencing or predicting as the one which would usher in the full and final 'Day of the Lord', often appeal to this principle. It is the nature of prophecy, so they claim, that events of two different time periods are superimposed in such a way that the description of those events does not clearly distinguish which events are immediate and which are destined for fulfilment in the more distant future.

There are at least two different ways in which this 'perspective' is described. G.B. Caird describes one of them:[19]

> The prophets looked to the future with bifocal vision. With their near sight they foresaw imminent historical events which would be brought about by familiar human causes; for example, disaster was near for Babylon because Yahweh was stirring up the Medes against them (Isa. 13.17). With their long sight they saw the day of the Lord; and it was in the nature of the prophetic experience that they were able to adjust their focus so as to impose the one image on the other and produce a synthetic picture. Yet they did not thereby lose the ability to distinguish between the two types of vision, any more than the writer of Ps. 23 lost the ability to distinguish between himself and a sheep.

The problem with this formulation of the matter is that it suggests every Old Testament prophet who prophesied concerning the Day of the Lord in relation to the crisis at hand, knew the events were of two different orders and separated in time. It would be very hard to substantiate this. Caird, apparently, would be prepared to argue to this conclusion, at least that seems to be implied by his closing analogy. The reason the Psalmist did not lose his ability to distinguish between himself and a sheep was that he knew he was not a sheep. Can we believe that when the Old Testament prophets spoke of the coming events of glory and crisis for their nation, they always knew the events would not bring in the final Day of the Lord even though they used Day of the Lord language to describe it? It would be very hard to defend the view that Caird's understanding of 'prophetic perspective' applies to Mark 13.[20]

If Jesus and Mark both knew that the destruction of the temple was not temporally linked with the End of the age, it is hard to explain why Mark 13 reached us in the form it did. It is particularly difficult to understand why they were not more successful in preventing the conclusion that 13.30 might include the parousia.

A.M. Ambrozic discusses 'prophetic perspective' as well, but with a key difference:[21]

> The prophetic perspective must not be imagined to imply that the prophets were somehow aware that their words would be fulfilled only in the distant future. Witness to it should rather be sought in the fact that their words and predictions were preserved, cherished, and eventually reinterpreted despite their non-fulfilment. ... In speaking of the prophetic perspective, we must be careful not to attribute the hindsight of the Christian church to the prophets themselves.

Whereas Caird would argue that the prophets were themselves never mistaken in the way they viewed an eschatological scenario, Ambrozic would argue that at times the predictions were technically incorrect, but that it is of the nature of the prophetic office to be susceptible to this sort of error and that their work retains value despite this fact. It seems to me that Ambrozic's view is much easier than Caird's to harmonize with the data of some of the Old Testament prophecies referred to above. Even his view, however, does not fit Mark 13. There is too much evidence that in Mark 13 we have ambiguity *deliberately* incorporated into the text (see below). The text cannot be the result of *inadvertently* superimposing two images which do not really belong together.

Caird's view better explains why Mark 13 seems to be such a carefully crafted attempt to present a well-defined view. Ambrozic's view better explains why the text does not make it unambiguously clear whether the fall of the temple and the End of the age are connected or not. Is there not a third possibility which circumvents the disadvantages of both of these alternatives?

If scholarly disagreement is, in this regard, any guide at all, it encourages the conclusion that the text does not permit the reader confidently either to affirm or to deny that (according to Mark and the Markan Jesus) *this time* the crisis of the nation *would* be the End. The best explanation for this is that Mark intended that result, and for the simple reason that he himself was also unable either to affirm or to deny that it would be.

There were a number of prophets in Old Testament literature, some of them prophesying a destruction of the temple, who linked 'Day of the Lord' motifs directly with an expected event. If he had done the same, Mark (and before him Jesus?) would have been following good precedent.[22] But by the same token, Mark had good reason to *question* whether the present crisis would be the final one. Similar crises in the past had not been final. Mark has 'played it safe'. He does not know whether this time it will be the final Day. What is more, he knows that he does not know.[23]

Ambrozic warns that we must not attribute the hindsight of the Christian church to the prophets. The warning is taken. But Mark represents the Christian church, not the prophets. There is no valid reason to deny Mark's ability to evaluate 'prophetic perspective' every bit as acutely as any scholar in the twentieth century. Perhaps he had the advantage, living closer to prophets than do modern scholars.

The link in Mark 13 between the destruction of the temple and the End is best understood by employing the notion of 'prophetic perspective', but with two key differences from the way it is usually employed. First, the term itself should not be taken to imply (with Caird) that the two events are *known* to be separated in time, nor (with Ambrozic) that the two events have been *mistakenly* superimposed. Rather 'the prophetic perspective' implies no more or less than that the two events might, but need not, be considered as one. Second, Mark should not be thought of as a victim of the 'prophetic perspective' but a master of it, enabling him to see two great events, but deliberately painting the picture in such a way that Mark's own ignorance of the temporal relationship between the events was passed on to the reader.

Mark has neither deliberately (Caird's view) nor erroneously (Ambrozic's view) looked through prophetic bifocals. It would be more accurate to say that Mark is playing the role of an optician, fitting his *readers* with bifocals! He has given us a masterpiece of prophetic literature, and boldly stayed with his conviction that the disciples' linking of the two events in 13.4 can be neither affirmed nor denied. The disciples want signs and time indicators. The Markan Jesus steadfastly refuses to give them any. Mark no doubt desired that his readers would be content to join him and his Jesus in their ignorance of End time chronology (13.32) and that they would accept the prophet's word as a call to discernment, discipleship and mission. It is all of a piece with the Gospel in which Mark 13 is included.

If the course of events subsequent to Mark's publication proves the events surrounding the temple's destruction are not the final events ushering in the parousia, then those events have the function indicated in the previous chapter; they assure believers that whatever they may yet have to face in their discipleship, God is working out his plans, vindicating Jesus and his followers, and bringing the secret kingdom ever nearer its final manifestation. If history goes on after the destruction of the temple, subsequent believers will have two sources of guidance as they go through the crises of history. They will have the model of Jesus in his passion (Mark 14-16; cf. 13.33-37), and they will have Jesus' instructions to the earliest followers on how they were to face theirs (13.5-23).

If the events surrounding the temple's destruction lead directly into the final intervention of the Son of Man, then Mark's Gospel will have served as a final encouragement to stand faithful in the crisis, to proclaim the Gospel even in the midst of suffering, and to discern as it happens how the secret kingdom is progressing towards its consummation. Whichever way history turns out, it will be one of the alternatives Mark considered possible. He wrote in such a way that the reader also can be ready for both possibilities.

By neither affirming nor denying that 13.24ff. denotes final judgment, by neither affirming nor denying that there is a time gap between 13.23 and 13.24, and by a whole host of other deliberate ambiguities (see below), Mark prevents his readers from specifying a chronology of End time events.

Further Evidence of Deliberate Ambiguity in Mark 13.5-23

Are there other polysemantic elements in Mark 13 which seem designed deliberately to avoid taking a stand on the crucial issue whether the events under discussion are 'End time events' or are merely events within an ongoing history?

There are indeed in almost every verse! Almost all the points of scholarly disagreement in Mark 13 are the result of attempting to make an exegetical decision where it is arguable that Mark has deliberately made his point in order to be ambiguous about when the End will come. Interpreters disagree because they try to force Mark into making a statement one way or the other when he was apparently trying to avoid this very thing. The following sample is drawn from 13.5-23. We shall leave the material following 13.23 for the next section.

Does v. 7 affirm or deny that the wars and rumours of wars constitute End time events? We are only told that at their arrival, 'the End is not yet'. Interpreters cannot decide if this means that the events are End time events but not the very last ones, or that they are not End time events at all. Perhaps Mark intended them not to.

When the conflicts and accompanying natural disasters are listed in v. 8, we are told 'these things are the beginning of birth pains'. Is the point that they are *not* part of the final stages since they are merely at the *beginning* of the post-resurrection period? Or is the point that once these happen the reader can be assured that now at last begin the final stages of the End time? Is an eschatological time schedule being accelerated or retarded? Scholars are divided. Perhaps Mark intended them to consider both options as possibilities.

Why is the mission mandate introduced into the period of tribulation *prior to* the mention of the events surrounding the destruction of the temple, when in fact the content of the verse makes it clear that mission is penultimate to the End itself? The position and content of 13.10 are perfectly explained if Mark could not be *sure* there would be extended opportunity to carry out the mission *after* the events predicted in 13.14ff. In order neither to affirm nor deny the expectation of an opportunity for mission afterwards, he included 13.10 *before* 13.14, but allowed the content of the verse to make it clear that mission is to be one of the primary tasks of the church right until the End, however long or short that opportunity might be after the temple falls.

The ambiguity of 'first' (πρῶτον) seems to serve the same interests. Its primary point is of course that the End will not come before the mission is complete. But when is that? St. Paul could affirm several years before the crisis in Jerusalem that 'all nations' were already receiving the good news (Rom. 1.5).[24] If Mark shared that view, then 13.10 itself does not guarantee that there will be further opportunities after the temple falls.[25] As a whole, 13.10 functions to stress the urgency of mission (since the length of the time of opportunity is unknown) and at the same time to give encouragement that whatever present trials must be faced, opportunity would be sufficient for God to bring his plans to fulfilment.[26]

When it is affirmed that 'whoever stands firm to the end (εἰς τέλος) will be saved' (13.13) which 'end' is in view? Had the definite article been included (as in 13.78) it would have indicated unambiguously that the End of the age was intended. Without it, everything is left uncertain. Is it the end of the tribulation? Is it the end of the individual's life? Or is it the End of the age? If 13.30 is taken as unambiguous evidence that the End of the age will come in Jesus' generation, then we have evidence in the text for the truth of all three possibilities; some will die (13.12), some are rescued by the divine shortening of the tribulation (13.20), some survive until the Son of Man returns (13.30). If 13.30 yields another conclusion, then perhaps every individual and every generation will experience at least one of the three alternatives, but not necessarily the same one.[27] If Mark did not know which way the prophecy would be fulfilled for those listening to the Markan Jesus, he did well in passing on the exhortation/encouragement without going beyond the evidence he had. It seems deliberately ambiguous.

What is the 'abomination of desolation' alluded to in 13.14? If it had been Mark's intention to allude to a prospective 'abomination' which would defile the Jerusalem temple, and also leave open the possibility that there might be a separate and final manifestation of satanic opposition to Christ, he could hardly have picked a more suitable phrase.[28]

Why did Mark not specify that the *temple* was in view when the abomination would be set up, saying only it would be 'where it ought not to be' (13.14)? If he intended to indicate that the prophecy would be fulfilled at least once in the Jerusalem temple, and *perhaps* also thereafter in subsequent crises wherever Satan would exert influence, the ambiguity of the text serves very effectively. 13.14 surely represents a deliberate attempt to be ambiguous about something.

If it was Mark's goal to encourage readers to be very careful in evaluating this prophetic word, neither misunderstanding its first fulfilment, nor overlooking the possibility that there might be other fulfilments, does not the inclusion of 'let the reader understand' (13.14) serve admirably as a warning?

Does not the description supplied for the great tribulation, with its very local and realistic terms, but also with its hyperbolic descriptions of unprecedented and unrepeatable horrors, suit Mark's purposes well if he was trying to prevent readers from either affirming or denying that the difficulties accompanying war in Judea were to double as a final tribulation ushering in God's eschatological Day? Might not an urgent appeal for flight but also a clear statement that only divine intervention can preserve God's elect (13.14b,20), be designed to serve the same purpose?

If Mark did not know whether the tribulation would be brought to an end *so that* history and mission could continue, or whether it would be brought to an end by the returning Son of Man, would he not have done just what he has in fact done? He has credited God with sovereignly controlling events for the benefit of the elect (13.20), but he has not said when and how God would shorten the days. If it was his purpose to leave it uncertain whether at this point the parousia occurs, then a survey of scholarly views indicates he was remarkably successful.

We could easily present other suggestions of deliberate Markan techniques for maintaining ambiguity. We have not even dipped into the riches to be found in 13.28-37. Almost every study of Mark 13 begins with a disclaimer concerning the difficulty of the chapter. It is called everything from a 'tangled skein'[29] to a 'series of enigmas'.[30] Perhaps scholars have tried so hard to eliminate the 'tangles' they have inadvertently unravelled an exquisite tapestry. Perhaps they have tried so hard to remove enigmas they have overlooked the vital clues explaining why the enigmas were put there in the first place.

Is Mark not doing in Mark 13 precisely what we saw him doing in 1.1-15? The prologue of the Gospel is a deliberate theological statement preparing the readers for *two different stories*. When read with one set of exegetical decisions, the prologue prepares the readers to understand the historical event of Jesus' human life on earth, culminating in his death and resurrection. Read with another set of exegetical decisions, it prepares the readers for the second story, the one that must be their story in the post-resurrection era (see Chapter 7).

Mark 13 does precisely the same thing with the fall of the temple. Read one way it prepares the reader to face the historical events that lead up to and include the fall of the temple. But if that event should come and go and the master of the house should remain absent still longer, then the very same chapter functions admirably as a guidebook for the unknown period following that great event. The 'first time reading' serves as a paradigm and its 'meta-message' guides the readers as they face unknown but analogous challenges in the future. Mark 16.7f. turns the readers' attention to the implied future of the Jesus story. Mark 13.37 turns the readers' attention to the implied future of Mark's story.

The readers know they are called to be discerning disciples, proclaiming the Gospel and if necessary faithfully enduring suffering and trial as Jesus did (see Chapter 4). The readers do *not* know what future abominations will call forth God's hand of judgment. They do not know how many more times God will need to shorten the days of tribulation to preserve his elect. They do not know how many more times they will need to be on guard for deceivers who claim to know more about God's timing than even the Son claimed to know. What readers can know is that once the events of 5-23 have found their first fulfilment (cf. 13.23), all that *must* precede the End has happened, and thereafter the coming of the Son of Man is imminent (i.e. not guaranteed to be delayed any longer, though by no means necessarily immediate). There have been no 'premonitory signs' facilitating calculation, but there have been 'preparatory stages' moving the secret kingdom closer to its fulfilment. What happens between 13.23 and 13.24 is God's prerogative. The discerning disciple is ready.

III. *The Timing of the End*

All of the preceding material will have to be re-evaluated if Mark 13.28-32 does not support the position adopted. In these verses Mark deals directly with the question of timing. What has he done with the question? Has he turned the whole discourse into a chronology of events with specified time periods for each phase? Or has he preserved ambiguity and uncertainty concerning possible multiple fulfilments, unknown events, and unpredictable time gaps between the completion of all necessary preliminaries (13.23) and the final intervention of God at the End of the age (13.24ff.)? We will concern ourselves here with the two key timing texts 13.30 and 13.32, and with the parable of the fig tree.

Mark 13.30: What Does the First Generation Experience?
A rehearsal of the usual arguments for and against the idea that Mark 13.30 includes the parousia among 'all these things' (ταῦτα πάντα) is unnecessary here.[31] The usual arguments based primarily on grammar (the search for referents and antecedents) and philology (the meaning of 'generation' [γενεά]) do not seem to have conclusively ruled out either option. Our intention here is not to rehearse these arguments, but rather to point out a few things that are often overlooked, to approach the question from another angle, and to defend an alternative that is normally either left out of consideration or resisted.

Mark 13.30 does not lend itself well to exegesis out of context. Unless we specify a speaker there is no way of deciding which 'generation' is in view. Unless we supply a specific context we have no way of deciding which 'things' are in view. The verse itself is a chameleon: it takes on the colours of the context in which it is placed.

Several points follow directly from this. First, 'this generation' (ἡ γενεὰ αὕτη), whatever γενεά is considered to mean, must be the generation in the relevant context of the *Markan Jesus*. Whether the logion derives from Jesus, from apocalyptic literature, from a Christian prophet speaking in the name of the resurrected Lord, or from Mark himself, makes no difference to this point.

The fact that the context alone can determine the meaning of Mark 13.30 implies, secondly, that the antecedents for 'these things' (ταῦτα πάντα) must be determined wholly from Mark 13, not from another postulated context.[32] In evaluating its antecedents according to Mark 13, we must guard against assuming that 13.4 is a valid clue. The Markan Jesus would hardly be expected to supply a date for all the things the disciples were asking about if his whole concern was to correct their perspective and assumptions. Those who insist that the verbal correspondence between 13.30 and 13.4 is of great significance should not overlook that there is also verbal correspondence between ταῦτα πάντα and an alternative antecedent: ταῦτα ('these things') in 13.29 and πάντα ('all things') in 13.23 refer to precisely the same events as each other and can together supply the antecedent for 13.30.

Fortunately Mark 13.30b contains more than demonstrative adjectives and pronouns. The declaration which is so solemnly affirmed (cf. 13.30a and 13.31) does contain *one* noun. Unfortunately its meaning is very much disputed. Is it possible that 'generation' (γενεά) is deliberately ambiguous?

The best defence of the view that it means anything other than 'contemporaries' (or possibly 'evil contemporaries') has been given by E. Lövestam.[33] He argues primarily on the basis of Old Testament usage that previous 'generations' (i.e., evil people) have passed away, like 'the generation of the flood' and 'the generation of the wilderness', but the righteous who were not truly a part of the evil generation (e.g., Noah, Joshua) escaped God's judgment and therefore outlived the 'evil generation'. Mark 13.30 is Jesus' word to his followers (who do not belong to the present evil generation) that they will *not* outlive the present evil generation. In this view 13.30 serves to indicate that the Old Testament pattern will *not* be followed this time. The implication therefore is precisely the opposite of the way Mark 13.30 is usually understood. It is usually taken to mean that the first century followers of Jesus *will* live until the judgment falls on Jesus' enemies. Lövestam's view makes it deny precisely this point. All it says, according to this view, is that evil people will continue to live as long as Jesus' followers. The implication is that 13.30 is hardly a word about the timing of God's judgment or vindication at all; it is a description of the circumstances in which the believers will be living during the entire interim from Jesus' day to the Son of Man's Day.

If Lövestam's definition of γενεά were to stand, what would the statement mean in the broader context of Mark's Gospel? It is not insignificant, as Lövestam himself points out,[34] that 'this generation' (ἡ γενεὰ αὕτη) in Mark 8.11f. is doing precisely what the wilderness generation was doing. The Old Testament wilderness generation, despite the fact that mighty miracles were being done in the wilderness, challenged God's appointed leader, 'tempted' God, and demanded proofs that God was in their midst. The correspondence with Mark 8.11f. is exact. The Pharisees, representative of ἡ γενεὰ αὕτη (cf. 8.12), knew that Jesus had been performing great miracles (some even in the wilderness), yet they came tempting him and seeking signs.

If we were to grant Lövestam's *connotation* for ἡ γενεὰ αὕτη we would be able to specify the *denotation* of the phrase in the Markan context. It denotes the Jewish religious leaders who were opposing and rejecting Jesus, the very ones who would be punished for their sins in the destruction to come on the temple! An argument which begins by denying that γενεά must *mean* 'contemporaries', ends up affirming that some of Jesus' contemporaries are *specified* by the denoter, and leads to conclusions far from those Lövestam himself reached.

Interpreting Mark 13.30 in its Mark 13 context along the lines indicated above suggests this meaning: Christians will not outlive the Jewish religious leaders. If the destruction of the temple is the event in which Jesus' evil opponents are to be judged, two implications follow: (1) the destruction of the temple falls on the generation of Jesus' contemporaries (since it is they who will be punished), and (2) this event is simultaneous with the End of the age (since there can be no intermediate judgment if Christians will not outlive 'the evil generation').[35]

But is Lövestam's definition for γενεά to be accepted? It is not without problems when applied to Mark's context. Perhaps the greatest problem is to explain why the disciples are invited/urged to flee the city when the crisis comes there. If 13.30 is designed to say that it will not be possible to escape the present evil generation, why does 13.14 seem to make precisely the opposite point? While it is undeniable that ἡ γενεὰ αὕτη normally describes evil people, it usually also signifies 'contemporaries'; after all, the 'generation of the flood' and the 'generation of the wilderness', while they may have been wicked, were still a literal generation.

It would seem that if the idea of 'wickedness', regularly associated with ἡ γενεὰ αὕτη, is being highlighted, then the proper inference is not that they are not contemporaries, but rather that judgment rather than blessing is to be understood by 'all these things'. In that case 13.30 might well be saying: 'This very generation, the one guilty of the sins under consideration, will suffer the punishment for its own sins'. In the context of Mark 13, the verse would then mean that the judgment on the Jewish leaders (that is, the destruction of the temple, etc.) will fall on the very individuals who rejected Jesus. This way of looking at it finds support from our suggestion that Ezek. 33 and 34 influenced Mark in his temple destruction theology (cf. Ezek. 33.1-20). Whether the End of the age is then also included in the thought of 13.30 depends on whether the judgment on Jerusalem is considered an element of final judgment or not, the very issue Mark 13 will not allow us to settle.

If the idea of 'wickedness' is *not* being highlighted by γενεά, the meaning of 13:30 must be determined on the basis of the usual arguments that attempt to pin down the antecedents for 'all these things' (ταῦτα πάντα). Those arguments are quite inconclusive. How then will the issue be settled? There are two more points that can be made before we make a decision.

First, those exegetes who would insist that the inclusion of 13.30 *after* 13.24-27 forces us to understand 13.24-27 to be included in ταῦτα πάντα, underestimate the extent to which Mark's text 'doubles back' temporally.[36] It does so at least three times in the section from 13.24-37 (v. 28 doubles back after v. 27, v. 33 does after v. 32, and v. 37 does after v. 36). It *may* do it several times in 5-23 as well.[37] It would not be uncharacteristic of Mark 13 if 13.30 represented a doubling-back. 13.29 brings the End into view and then 13.30 reverts back to the events preceding the End.

Second, if Mark's Jesus had intended to indicate that the generation of his contemporaries would live to see the parousia, is it not surprising that he left the subject of the verb ὄψονται ('they will see') in 13.26 unspecified and that the verb itself is in the third person? Throughout Mark 13.5-23 the disciples are addressed in the second person, with two very important exceptions: (1) it is not specified that it will be the disciples who will be carrying out the mission that is penultimate to the end (13.10); and, (2) the third person is utilized when discussing the tribulation that follows the flight from the city. In the first case the author seems to have taken precautions against taking a stand on who would be alive to complete the missionary task prior to the parousia. In the second case two motivations might have been at work: (1) the Judeans (third person) are being invited to flee along with the apostles (a view which harmonizes well with the call to preach prior to their flight); and (2) the text is not taking a stand on whether the unrepeatable tribulation has a future focus beyond the present crisis.[38] Both the rule and the exceptions substantiate the overall view we are taking, and the unspecified subject of the verb in 13.26 (ὄψονται) fits this perfectly. Mark is not taking a stand on whether the disciples will be present to see the Son of Man returning.[39]

Does 13.30 then include the parousia among 'these things' or does it not? To borrow someone else's phraseology and apply it to a new context:[40]

> When exegetes have been divided for so long a time with regard to
> so serious a question we may safely assume that in the text itself
> there are reasons to favor an opinion for or against.

The best solution is to conclude that Mark, although he knew his readers wanted to pin down a date for the parousia, refused to give them a basis for fixing it. He set a limit of one generation from the time of Jesus (40 years?) for the destruction of the temple, but employed deliberate ambiguity to prevent the reader from either affirming or denying that the parousia would take place within that generation.

It might be asked why Mark did not place 13.30 *before* 13.24-27 if the only thing he wanted clearly to *affirm* was that the judgment on the Jewish leaders would precede the end of the present generation. But that would not have served his purposes. He did not want to affirm confidently that the parousia would occur in the first generation, but neither did he want to deny that it would be so. To do either would have involved going beyond the knowledge he had, and equally as serious, would have undercut his emphasis on faithful discipleship *because of* ignorance of timing (see 13.32-37 and next subsection). Mark is very insistent (cf. esp. 13.33-37) that the disciples of Jesus themselves, as well as any possible future generations (13.37), must be prepared for the possibility that the End could come at any time. To have placed 13.30 before 13.24-27 could easily have left the impression that the first generation would not experience the parousia and was therefore exempt from constant readiness for it. Positioning 13.30 after 13.24-27 was required by Mark's discipleship concerns, and this in turn necessitated that 'all these things' (ταῦτα πάντα) be left ambiguous; the parousia may or may not be included. All of this implies that Mark must have been prepared to credit the Markan Jesus with ignorance about the timing of the End. Clearly he was (13.32). All in all, it seems that Mark 13.30 is as hard to define as anything in Mark 13. It is not the case that 'This statement of Our Lord's needs little explanation for its understanding. It simply requires grace to be received'.[41]

The best solution is to accept a suggestion that is hardly ever considered, but which seems to fit perfectly into the chapter and the Gospel as we have been learning to read them. *Mark 13.30 guarantees that the Jewish leaders will be punished, but it deliberately does not take a stand on whether or not this implies that the End of the age will come upon Jesus' contemporaries.* It achieves this ambiguity by specifying neither the precise connotation nor the precise denotation of 'generation' (γενεά),[42] by leaving ambiguous which things would be fulfilled within the generation in question, by not making it clear whether there is a temporal doubling back, and by supplying a context which does not allow the reader either to affirm or deny with confidence that the parousia is included in its perspective.

If it seems undesirable to settle for such a conclusion, what of the alternatives? Can we really believe that Mark's first readers would have easily solved all the problems that contemporary scholars find so puzzling? Can we really believe that Mark was as inept as he would have to have been if he thought he was speaking clearly and unambiguously throughout Mark 13? Can we believe that he would formulate a statement carelessly and then follow it with 13.31? Why should we hesitate to accept that he would put highly ambiguous statements in the mouth of the Markan Jesus, when that is what has been going on throughout the Gospel? We might have preferred if things had been said less ambiguously. On the basis of Mark 4, 8.14-21 and numerous other Markan texts, it is clear that Mark did not share our preferences.

Some exegetes look to Mark 9.1 for help in interpreting 13.30. There is, however, not much help to be gained from it.[43] Whereas Mark 8.38 undoubtedly refers to the parousia, it is not certain that 9.1 does. The change of topic from 'Son of Man' to 'kingdom of God' certainly puts the matter in doubt, as does the fact that 9.1 predicts a 'sighting' of the kingdom, not its consummation (especially in the light of Mark's 'discernment' teaching).

It is not possible to determine Mark's understanding of 9.1 without taking seriously the connection he has forged between it and the Transfiguration account. Many scholars cannot believe Mark intended the transfiguration experience itself to be the fulfilment of 9.1.[44] I do not think that the possibility can be ruled out. But even if that is not considered acceptable, the possibility can hardly be ruled out that whatever is being unveiled or prefigured by the Transfiguration constitutes the kingdom having come with power. Recent studies have clearly shown that in the context of Mark's Gospel no simple arrow can be drawn from the Transfiguration to *one* specific event, be it an unveiling of Jesus' hidden glory, the passion, the resurrection, the giving of the Holy Spirit, the exaltation of Jesus, the parousia, or whatever.[45] Rather, the Transfiguration account points to a complex of events and subsumes them all under 'the secret kingdom' which some of Jesus' contemporaries will be granted to 'see'.

Time and space prevent us from dwelling at length on all the complicated issues involved in interpreting either the Transfiguration ('the glory and the despair of New Testament commentators'),[46] or Mark 9.1 which is illuminated by it. We can here merely state our convictions that:

1. Mark is deliberately using the context of 9.1 to disengage it from any specific time frame.[47]
2. Mark is using the Transfiguration account in its context to point to the passion of Jesus as a first and sufficient fulfilment of the promise of 9.1, for those with eyes to see it.[48]

If Mark 9.1 aids us at all in interpreting Mark 13.30, it is by giving us a second example of a text in Mark which might erroneously be thought to pin down the timing of the parousia, but which Mark has skilfully used to further his own concerns about discipleship and discernment, while leaving the reader in the dark (as he was) concerning End time chronology.

Mark 13.32f.: No One Knows When

If Mark 13.30 does not state definitively that the return of the Son of Man is to occur within the generation of Jesus' contemporaries, then we are free to take Mark 13.32 at full face value.

When it is noted that 'That Day' (ἡ ἡμέρα ἐκείνη) and 'The Hour' (ἡ ὥρα) are technical terms for the Day of the Lord, it can be seen that Mark 13.32 says only that there is *something* about 'That Day' or 'The Hour' which is known only to the Father. It is *concerning the final eschatological events* (περὶ δὲ τῆς ἡμέρας ἐκείνης ἢ τῆς ὥρας) that humans, angels and the Son alike share ignorance. Without 13.33 we could not be sure that one of the main unknown features is the timing (οὐκ οἴδατε πότε ὁ καιρός ἐστιν)[49].

If 'That Day' and 'The Hour' specify the event itself, then the particle δέ in 13.32 can be given its adversative force: 'Concerning the time of judgment on the Jewish religious leaders, a *terminus ad quem* of one generation has been foretold (13.30). Concerning the arrival of the Eschatological Day, on the contrary, no one knows about that except God' (13.32f.).[50]

This makes 13.33 a key verse. It not only confirms that the timing of the final eschatological event is totally unknowable (not only in terms of the precise day and hour within a limited time period),[51] but it also grounds the discipleship call in that pervasive ignorance.

We should not underestimate the significance of the claim that no one, not even the Son, knows the time of the End's arrival. This makes it clear that neither the implied narrator of the Markan Gospel, who otherwise is consistently cast as an omniscient intrusive narrator, nor the character who delivers the discourse of 13.5-37 knows the timing of the End. Commentators frequently agree with the Markan Jesus that he did not know, but have interpreted the chapter as though he in fact did not know but thought he did know. 13.32 is not a statement by Mark's narrator that Jesus did not know, it is the Markan Jesus' own declaration of ignorance. He knew he did not know! It is hard to find a stronger motivation for interpreting Mark 13 along the lines that we are here suggesting. It is quite misguided to see clues as to when the End will come when the only two literary characters (Jesus and the implied narrator) who could be counted on to guide us reliably towards the right answer are self-confessedly ignorant of the answer.[52]

Mark 13.32f. should be used as a controlling exegetical principle for all of Mark 13. In a chapter with many unknowns, the clearest statement of all is that the time of the end is unknown. That clear statement must not be weakened by allowing an interpretation of the rest of the chapter to rob it of its force. V. Taylor turns the exegetical influence around by 'establishing' that Mark 13 as a whole encourages apocalyptic forecasts, and then using this as evidence that Mark eliminates the anti-speculation emphasis otherwise present in 13.32, a verse which 'threatens the apocalyptic edifice'.[53] The whole chapter makes much more sense if we accept that the note of total and complete ignorance with which Mark 13 ends has really served as the silent presupposition of the whole chapter. Discerning discipleship is the burden of the whole chapter and the whole Gospel. Mark 13 ends by grounding the discipleship call firmly in the fact of 'eschatological ignorance': 'Be discerning, keep awake, *for* (γάρ) you do not know when the time will come' (13.33).[54] The last verse expands the applicability of the command: 'What I say to you, I say to everyone, watch!' (13.37). Mark does not know how many generations will take up the baton and run the course before the race is declared finished and won.

The Fig Tree Parable
As we near the completion of our study we turn at last to the one short parable which is often taken to be unambiguous evidence either that Mark 13 as a whole is designed to guide the reader towards firm conclusions about the timing of the Son of Man's return, or else that Mark was not able to put together a self-consistent discourse.[55] Unambiguous evidence? We shall see.

G.R. Beasley-Murray questioned in 1957:[56]

> How could Jesus, while yet employing sobriety of language, have conveyed to his disciples the prudence of observing 'signs of the times' more clearly than he has done in this parable?

If we can apply that question, not to Jesus, but to the Markan Jesus within the context of Mark's Gospel, the following answers could be suggested:

1. He could have made the point non-parabolically. Parables in Mark are not designed to be unambiguous communication devices.
2. He could have avoided using 'fig tree imagery' to make his point, imagery which has already been used symbolically in Mark's Gospel, and in a context where the meaning is not made explicit.

3. He could have indicated which things are denoted by 'these things' in the application of the parable.
4. He could have indicated what or who should be recognized as 'near' when 'these things' are observed to have happened.
5. He could have made it clear whether 'near' means that it will happen very soon in time or that it stands in close spatial proximity. 13.28 suggests the former, but 13.29 suggests the latter.[57]
6. He could have indicated what it is about the relationship between seeing leaves and the certain arrival of summer (the *tertium comparationis*) that illustrates the eschatological point being made. There are more plausible options than might be immediately obvious (e.g., certainty, temporal proximity, both of the above,[58] opportunity for fruit, inevitability of harvest, etc.).
7. He could have helped the reader decide whether the main verb in v. 29 is indicative or imperative. It makes a great difference whether Mark's point is to call for understanding (with no guarantee that it will be achieved) or is to announce an inevitable result of simple observation.
8. He could have indicated whether he intends the details of the parable to have symbolic value, and if so what value.[59]
9. In particular, he could have given some indication whether θέρος suggests 'summer' or 'summer fruit-bearing' or 'summer harvest' or even 'harvest-judgment'.[60]

W.R. Telford is quite justified in claiming that the parable 'is fraught with difficulties. ... The words and syntax of verses 28 and 29 are extremely puzzling and their precise meaning is obscure'.[61]

If some interpreters insist that the meaning is plain they have to contend with the evidence of the literature that this text has generated more diversity in interpretation than any other in the whole thirteenth chapter of Mark. It is usually taken as an unexamined assumption that all the ambiguities must be removed and that the parable must be forced to make a straightforward statement about signs and their effect on time calculations. When pressed into service in this way, forced to do a task for which it was not designed, it is not surprising if it should appear somewhat incompetent. One does not need to rehearse all the arguments and counter-arguments used to debate about which 'unambiguous' message it conveys. The effect of the arguments is to cancel each other out and render the usual alternatives unproven.

As in our discussion of 13.30, we here intend only to point out a few issues which are often overlooked, and then make a suggestion concerning Mark's real intentions.

Strictly speaking, the parable (or simile) has a slight ellipsis. Greening fig trees do not cause summer to arrive, nor do they cause people to know it will arrive. It is only *awareness* of a fig tree's greening which can have any effect on one's expectations. When the similitude is applied (13.29) it is made clear that the function of the parable is not to make a statement about the cause and effect relationship between two *objective events* nor about their temporal proximity. It is talking about the relationship between *seeing* something and *knowing* something.[62]

In the Markan context this is of great significance, especially when it is recalled that in the other 'parabolic' fig tree event (11.12-14, 20f.) 'seeing', 'hearing', and 'remembering', the very terms Mark employs with such effect in presenting a theology of discernment, were used to urge the reader to grasp the point which was not obvious at the surface of the text (see Chapter 5). It is of even greater significance if Mark is using material in Mark 13 to call disciples to discern the real significance of the historical events which were being illegitimately seized as foundations for an eschatological time-table (see Chapter 8).

In Mark's context we have every reason to suspect that the unspecified subject of ἐγγύς ἐστιν ('. . . is near') is in fact near before that nearness is recognized,[63] and that the fact of its nearness in no way suggests that the actual arrival will not have to be awaited, perhaps for a very long time.[64]

The opening of the 'parable' is significant. The Markan Jesus does not quite call it a parable in the usual sense of the term. On the contrary, he says, 'From the fig tree learn the veiled meaning' (μάθετε τὴν παραβολήν 13.28).[65] Is it possible that the 'veiled meaning' refers, as so often in Mark, to a deeper level of communication which takes up as symbols the elements of the parable itself?

It is very difficult to believe that Mark did not intend some sort of co-ordination between the fig tree budding parable and the fig tree cursing event.[66] The similarities are remarkable indeed:

1. The 'cursing' of the fig tree in Mark 11 was intended by Mark to indicate the disqualification of Israel's leadership,

and concomitant with that, to prefigure the temple's destruction. In view of the fact that this is precisely the meaning Mark seems to be investing in the main events of 13.5-23, it is quite possible that 'these things' in the fig tree parable link it symbolically with the earlier event narrated in chapter 11.

2. If this 'contextual' connection is not impressive enough, consider the co-ordination of content: both deal with fig trees, in both the tree stands in leaf, in both there is expectation of fruit, in both it is presently lacking. But here the comparison turns to contrast. One tree is cursed for failing in its task: the other (one expects) goes on to bear fruit. In the first case, 'it was not the right time for figs'; in the second, 'you know that summer is near'.

It is remarkable that so few commentators have considered the possibility that two complementary events are being alluded to, the first of which brings forth God's wrath and his judgment, the second of which furthers his eschatological purposes and prepares for the final Day.[67] It would not be uncharacteristic of Mark to co-ordinate the message of a parable with special lessons to be learned from an event of Jesus' life. The same happens when the parables of Mark 4 are co-ordinated with the miracles of Mark 5-8 (see Chapter 3), and even more significantly when the parable that concludes Mark 13 is co-ordinated with the events of Jesus' passion (see Chapter 4).

What conclusions should be drawn from these correlations? Surely not the conclusion Telford draws, that both in Mark 11 and in Mark 13 the fig tree serves to generate imminent eschatological expectation and to highlight the signs by which it is fostered.[68] On the contrary, the withered fig tree in chapter 11 speaks of the disqualification of Israel's unfaithful leaders and the destruction of their temple. But can we seriously credit Mark with using the image of a withering fig tree to presage the temple's destruction in Mark 11, and using a fig tree getting ready to produce fruit as a picture of the very same event in Mark 13? Far better not to correlate them at all than to have them used in opposite ways to make the same point. We are left with two options—either we abandon the idea there is any intended co-ordination between the two uses of fig trees, or we abandon the idea that 'these things' (corresponding to the fig tree's greening) refers to the destruction of the temple per se. The latter course is to be followed. All we need to do is suggest a slight modification of the usual interpretation of the parable and it fits the situation very well.

The greening of the fig tree represents the event accompanying the disqualification and destruction of the temple, namely its replacement with the new temple. The Jewish religious leaders are disqualified (the withering of the fig tree [11.20]); Jesus and his followers replace them as leaders of God's people (the greening of the fig tree [13.28]). This new 'temple' will perform the eschatological function of incorporating into the people of God believers from all nations. In this way, preparations will be complete for God's final Day (cf. 13.10).[69]

Does this mean that 13.28f. is not about the destruction of the temple of Jerusalem after all? By no means. When it is realized that the parable is not about 'the event' but about 'seeing the event' everything falls nicely into place. The event itself is the destruction of the temple. But what the discerning believer 'sees' is more than just the destruction of a building, the dispossession of a people, and the collapse of a nation. Discerning believers 'see' in this event that God's judgment has fallen on those who have rejected Jesus. They 'see' in this event vindication for Jesus' claim that he, with his followers, would replace the Jewish leaders, and that a temple rebuilt without hands would be the locus of God's eschatological fulfilment.[70] They 'see' God bringing his secret kingdom to fruition (see Chapter 8).

Thus we come right back to the conclusion most often defended for the fig tree parable. When 'these things' (i.e., all the events narrated in 13.5-23 and particularly the destruction of the temple) are seen to have occurred, then the disciple can be assured that everything stands ready for God to bring his purposes to fulfilment.[71] But we come back to this consensus somewhat wiser. We come realizing that 'these things' are not 'premonitory signs' that can be easily recognized, but are 'preparatory stages' which must be discerned carefully in the light of Jesus' and Mark's theology of temple destruction and replacement. We come realizing that Mark has presented a brilliant parable designed to teach in subtle ways the very lessons that Mark 13 is all about, enabling discerning readers, like discerning disciples, to catch glimpses of the way God is fulfilling his purposes.

Mark has used both 'temple' imagery (one destroyed and another built) and 'fig tree' imagery (one withered and another turning green)

to symbolize the way in which God sets aside unfaithful leaders and
rebuilds with Jesus and his followers. It will be the responsibility of
the post-resurrection disciples to bear fruit, the very thing Israel's
leaders did not do.

Because discerning readers have already been taught that the
outcome of faithfulness in trial is mission, and that in any case
mission is the penultimate event which is interrupted by the coming
of the Son of Man, they will be inclined to read the parable with this
in mind. Fruit-bearing is the proper function of a healthy fig tree;
'fruit-bearing' will also be the primary preoccupation of disciples
who take their role as the 'new fig tree' seriously. Fruit is borne as
disciples serve and suffer in faithfulness to the one who went 'the
way' first, and as they thereby prepare for others to do the same after.
It is borne by those who understand the implications of their calling,
and who know that any possible future suffering will result in greater
opportunities for others to take up the baton.[72]

What the parable will not tell them is how long the fruit-bearing
season will last before he who is near steps onto the stage (or if an
impersonal subject is adopted, before that which is near becomes a
reality). Nothing in the parable, like nothing in the chapter, is
designed to specify when the Son of Man will return. The term ἐγγύς
(near) certainly does not help to specify a time frame, especially in
the context of Mark's Gospel where the same occurrence of the term
can mean several things on different levels of textual reading (cf. 1.15
and the discussion in Chapter 7).

The image change at the end of the parable certainly does not help
answer the question concerning the time of his/its arrival,[73]
especially in the light of the facts that: (1) it redirects 'near' (ἐγγύς)
from a temporal significance to a spatial one; and, (2) it moves the
reader on to the final parable of the chapter[74] where the whole point
is that the faithful watchman does not know how long it will be
necessary to stand at the door before the master appears.

Even the imagery in the vehicle of the parable does not settle the
question concerning the timing of the End. If it is too pedantic to
interpret 13.32 as leaving only the exact 'day' and exact 'hour'
uncertain, it is also too pedantic to imagine that 13.28 limits the time
gap to one 'season'. It is very natural to take the parable to mean that
at some unpredictable time during the summer, he/it will arrive.
Until that happens, and no one knows when it will, God's appointed
fig tree must be about its business of bearing fruit. When it is 'the

right time' (ὁ καιρός cf. 13.33 and 11.13) the master wants to find the desired fruit. That the great in-gathering (cf. 13.27) will occur in the *immediate* aftermath of the destruction of the temple is neither affirmed nor denied. It is not for believers to know. Their task is to bear fruit in mission and faithful discipleship.[75]

In the light of everything that Mark's Gospel has taught us about the coming of the secret kingdom, it is hanging far too much weight from the slender branches of a budding fig tree to let this brilliantly ambiguous and subtle parable overrule everything else in Mark 13 and 'prove' that Mark was after all interested in fostering End time calculation.

We close this section by insisting that we have not twisted and turned the parable of the fig tree into something which, contrary to its natural reading, says nothing about the advance of God's programme and the way in which observation of it alerts the reader to the imminence of its culmination. The parable says precisely that. It assures the discerning reader that when the temple has fallen the Son of Man may arrive at any time. That is not the whole meaning of the parable, but that most obvious surface meaning is not denied by seeing it more deeply. What the parable refuses to do is make claims about how long the final eschatological event can remain 'imminent'. Mark would no doubt have been quite unprepared to imagine that two millenia might pass without the harvest interrupting the summer of fruit-bearing. His text, however, carefully crafted to prevent time calculations, is not thereby falsified.[76]

IV. *A Markan Perspective for Reading Mark 13*

One of the key issues in interpreting Mark 13 is establishing the author's perspective on the relationship between the destruction of the temple and the End of the age.[77] Traditionally there have been four main 'solutions':

1. Mark supports the idea that the destruction of the temple is to be considered a major event of eschatological fulfilment, the implication being that the End of the age will follow directly after.
2. Mark criticizes that very view, insisting that the two events are to be eschatologically and temporally separated.
3. Mark was a careless or incapable redactor who did not know how to compile traditions without presenting a confusing

and contradictory picture; though he may have held one or the other view, the chapter is so self-contradictory that the contemporary reader cannot make out which was his view.

4.   Mark, and before him Jesus, was 'victim' of a 'prophetic perspective' phenomenon; the portrait of the two events has been, either deliberately or inadvertently, presented in such a way that they are tied together more closely than they should have been. Fortunately we have hindsight to figure out what should have been said.

The biggest challenge facing those who would settle for one of the above interpretations is to account for the fact that the same data on which they base their conclusions can also be harnessed to support all three of the other alternatives. If our solution is the correct one, it is easy to see why they all arose. They arose because modern readers have been trying to force Mark to make a decision he never made. They arose because readers resist the conclusion, despite 13.32, that Mark refused to take a stand on the temporal relationship between the events, and that he tried to prevent his readers from taking a stand as well.

Mark 13 was presented with great care so as not to permit the exegete to conclude either that the End would follow immediately upon the crisis that surrounds the temple's destruction, or that it would not. The End would be 'imminent' after that event, but could remain so for generations. The readers are left in ignorance as to whether their generation will be the final one or not. They are not left with an artificial sense of uncertainty about the timing that rests wholly on their own exegetical uncertainty. They are left with an uncertainty which was deliberately cultivated by the author of the text.

Mark 13 is no doubt a 'happy hunting ground for scholars with a flair for ingenuity'.[78] The findings of our study suggest that a very great deal of ingenuity should be attributed to the author of the text itself, and behind him, depending on how much he took over from traditions, the early church and her Lord.[79] If our conclusions about Mark's perspectives and his writing methods are substantially correct, then perhaps the most important lesson that Markan scholars can learn from it is that Mark is due a great deal more respect as a theologian and a literary artist than many of us have given him. Perhaps he deserves to be accounted our teacher rather than merely an object of our criticism.

Mark 13.32-37, sometimes considered to be inconsistent with the rest of the chapter, is in fact the prism through which the whole chapter is to be read. Its message is not fully summed up either by 'Look carefully, the End may be closer than you think', or by 'Keep looking unfailingly, the End may be delayed longer than you expect'. Its message is rather that, whether the interval be short or long, what is required in the meantime is faithful discipleship and mission, discerning ears and eyes to detect God at work, and unfailing confidence that the kingdom, still hidden, is destined to be revealed. Discerning disciples not only see, but participate in, a kingdom come with power. Those alive at the End of the age will see it come with great power and glory. In the meantime Jesus' followers suffer and serve and pass on the baton to those who follow after. It is not for them to know how many laps the race will go on. It is their responsibility only to run faithfully their leg of the race.

SUMMARY AND CONCLUSIONS

Mark has written a remarkable Gospel. On the simplest level it is the story of Jesus from his baptism to his resurrection. The first half of the story features Jesus moving about Galilee and its neighbouring territories, healing, teaching, working miracles and combatting human and demonic enemies. The second half features Jesus travelling south, instructing his disciples on the way, and finally facing his enemies and dying at their hands in Jerusalem. He rises again and is expected to return in glory to judge his enemies and gather his elect.

The story itself captivates the imagination and challenges the assumptions and lives of all who read and study it. But Mark was not content simply to tell the story. He has produced a literary masterpiece which, while deceptively simple on the surface, has intrigued scholars and lay people alike with its mystery and ambiguity.

Mark's story is carefully designed to communicate a profound theology and to challenge would-be followers of Jesus. The theology of Mark's Gospel centres around the 'secret kingdom' which comes without objective proofs of its presence. The challenge is for Jesus' disciples to learn to 'see' and 'hear' that which goes beyond the data available to the senses.

Throughout Mark's Gospel, subtle clues enable the discerning reader to grasp points that Mark is intending to communicate, but is deliberately not making explicit. Through a variety of literary techniques, veiled clues, carefully controlled word usage, and carefully contrived deliberate ambiguity, Mark embeds profound theological reflections in the stories he tells. Juxtaposing narrative elements without comment but with deliberate intent to influence the readers' interpretations is a favourite Markan technique. In all this Mark is modelling himself after the Markan Jesus who also speaks ambiguously, calls for hearers to grasp points not made explicitly, and firmly believes that divine illumination will bring committed disciples to the understanding they need. Jesus used parables and miracles alike to teach and to give glimpses of the kingdom he is proclaiming. Mark is similarly creative and subtle in the ways he gives his readers glimpses of the message he proclaims.

To read Mark's Gospel as though it were a series of unrelated historical glimpses into the life and ministry of Jesus is to miss its most profound truths. Each element of the story must be read in the light of all the others and with a careful concern for its position within the story line and its function within the Markan discourse.

Mark 13 is an integral part of Mark's Gospel. In many ways it is the Gospel's centrepiece, not displacing the passion and resurrection at the centre, but joining them. Mark 13 teaches disciples how the passion and resurrection of Jesus influence their own discipleship in the post-resurrection age. The passion of Jesus is the model for faithful discipleship in the crises of life. The resurrection of Jesus provides the assurance and the strength that disciples need in order to remain faithful to their Lord, when on the surface it appears that their enemies may triumph and when the kingdom gives little unambiguous evidence of its continuing presence and its glorious destiny.

Mark's eschatological discourse is a response to a request for a sign, and by implication, a request for an eschatological time-table accompanied by unambiguous evidence that God's programme is staying on course. It is a response, but does not provide what the disciples desired. In Mark's Gospel seeking signs is considered reprehensible (8.11-13). Signs are given only by false christs and false prophets, and the disciples are warned not to be misled (13.22). Instead of providing signs, the Markan Jesus teaches his disciples to live with uncertainty about the timing. He teaches them to discern carefully the meaning of what is happening, the significance of current events for the establishment of the secret kingdom, and the opportunities that crisis situations offer for the spread of the Gospel. Mark 13 is a call to understand, but it is also a call to live faithfully when understanding is absent.

Among other events referred to in Mark 13, two great events stand out: the fall of the temple and the end of the age. Did Mark think the first would lead directly into the second? Modern scholars have argued back and forth whether or not Mark expected the fall of the temple to usher in the consummation. They have tried desperately to eliminate the ambiguities of Mark 13 and settle the issue once and for all. The evidence seems to indicate that Mark was trying to produce the very uncertainty which has troubled scholars, and that he deliberately incorporated the very ambiguity which scholars want to eliminate.

Mark himself did not know when the End would come. What he knew was that in his own time (i.e., within one generation of Jesus; cf. [13.30]), all would be ready so that delay could no longer be guaranteed. His concern was to turn his readers' attention away from sign-seeking and in the direction of understanding and obedience.

The destruction of the temple is a profoundly important event in the scheme of Mark 13, and indeed of the whole Gospel. The Jewish religious leaders are pictured in the Gospel as men who have abused their trust, robbed God of his due, and used their positions and influence to enhance their own reputations and line their pockets. They do away with Jesus to protect the privileges and responsibilities which they rightly conclude Jesus has come to take from them. The die is cast when they put Jesus to death. Their destiny is to perish, and the temple on which they lean for security, and in which they invest their hopes, is destined to be replaced by Jesus and his community. To understand rightly the significance of the temple's destruction is not to draw conclusions about the timing of the End, but to discern that God is continuing to vindicate Jesus and his followers at the expense of those who have rejected the Son. But none of this temple destruction theology is made explicit. Every reference to the temple within and outside Mark 13 is veiled in mystery. Disciples are called to discern the meaning of it all. Mark's readers are called to do the same.

Throughout Mark's Gospel there is a concentration of attention on the twin and inseparable themes of 'discernment' and 'discipleship'.

In Mark 13 two 'watchwords' are utilized (βλέπετε and γρηγορεῖτε) calling believers to understand the significance of the events they experience and to serve (and if necessary, suffer) faithfully in the unknown time period before the return of the Son of Man.

The message of Mark 13, as of Mark's entire Gospel, is that merely collecting information is not sufficient. There must be understanding, and the prerequisite for understanding is faithful discipleship. Instead of giving easy answers, both the Markan Jesus and Mark himself teach disciples how to qualify for divinely-aided understanding, how to discern the meaning of what they see and hear, and how to follow faithfully 'along the way'. Those who would wait until all the facts are available and all the questions settled before deciding whether or not to make a commitment will never reach the destination to which Mark desires to lead his readers.

And where does Mark want to lead his readers? He wants to lead them on the same road that Jesus led his disciples. He wants to lead them from their own 'Galilee' (where they first hear the call to discipleship) to their own 'Jerusalem' (the place where their discipleship is tested and consummated). He wants to lead them on the journey of faithful discipleship, carrying the cross of Christ. He wants to lead them through faithful mission, through their own passion, and on to the glory beyond. John prepared Jesus' way; Jesus prepared the disciples' way; they in their turn prepare for those who follow. Each time the baton is passed on, the race is one lap nearer completion, but no one knows when the Son of Man will gather his faithful runners into the victory circle and pronounce the race finished and won.

Mark does not countenance any easy way to glory. Without both discernment and discipleship the secret kingdom cannot be experienced, the Lord cannot be followed, and the Gospel cannot be apprehended. That is the challenge. The example and the victory of Jesus make both discernment and discipleship a possibility. That is the good news.

NOTES

Notes to Chapter 1

1. D. Wenham, '"This generation will not pass. . . "' (1982), p. 127.
2. E.g., R. Pesch, *Naherwartungen: Tradition und Redaktion in Mk. 13* (1968).
3. *Jesus and the Future* (1954), and *A Commentary on Mark 13* (1957).
4. The original German edition of *Mark the Evangelist* (1969) appeared in 1956 under the title, *Der Evangelist Markus: Studien zur Redaktionsgeschichte des Evangeliums.*
5. *The Parousia in the New Testament.*
6. *Prophecy Interpreted* (1966).
7. *Ibid.*, p. 206.
8. *Die Redaktion der Markus-Apokalypse* (1967).
9. *Naherwartungen: Tradition und Redaktion in Mk. 13* (1968).
10. W. Kelber, *The Kingdom in Mark* (1974), p. 109, note 1.
11. Pesch goes so far as to say that 'würde Kapitel 13 im Evangelium fehlen, der Leser würde hier keine Lücke bemerken' (*Ibid.*, p. 65).
12. *No Stone on Another* (1970).
13. *The Rediscovery of Jesus' Eschatological Discourse* (1984).
14. *Markus 13 und die Apokalyptik* (1984).
15. For a more detailed evaluation of scholarly literature on Mark 13, the reader is invited to consult my unpublished dissertation, 'Mark 13 in its Markan Interpretative Context' (Aberdeen University, 1986).
16. M.D. Hooker, 'Trial and Tribulation in Mark xiii' (1982), p. 78.
17. For a detailed examination of the issues, see E.D. Hirsch, *Validity in Interpretation* (1967), and G.B. Caird, *The Language and Imagery of the Bible* (1980).
18. As an example, consider Mark 3.11, 12. It is the agenda of the Markan Jesus to *conceal*, and of the author to *reveal*, what the demons were saying about Jesus.
19. *The Problem of History in Mark* (1957), p. 12.
20. As, for example, Ambrozic would have us do. Cf. '. . . to understand his [Mark's] answer, we must understand his [Mark's] question. For that reason we must examine vs. 4 more closely' (*The Hidden Kingdom* [1972], p. 225).
21. Desmond Ford provides a good summary of the unanswered questions concerning Mark 13. Cf. *The Abomination of Desolation in Biblical*

Eschatology (1979), pp. 60f. Cf. also D. Wenham, 'Recent Study of Mark 13' (1975), pp. 6f.

22. '... the test of any theory being that it not only solves the problem which led to its formulation, but is found to shed light on other problems which were not under consideration at the time' (P. Carrington, *The Primitive Christian Calendar* [1952], p. 14).

Notes to Chapter 2

1. *Mark—Traditions in Conflict* (1971), p. 99.

2. *Zum Verständnis der synoptischen Eschatologie* (1938), pp. 38ff. Cf. also M.D. Hooker, *The Son of Man in Mark* (1967), p. 156. ('The whole of chapter 13 is thus an elaboration of the theme found in 8.34-38').

3. See Weeden's listing of the thematic correspondences (*Ibid.*, p. 99).

4. Cf. K. Kertelge, *Die Wunder Jesu im Markusevangelium* (1970), pp. 23ff.

5. '*Dynameis* and *Sēmeia* in Mark' (1973).

6. S.V. McCasland, 'Signs and Wonders' (1957), p. 152.

7. O. Linton's study of the various Biblical and first century conceptions of 'signs' is a direct challenge to those who imagine that the 'sign from heaven' requested by the Pharisees referred originally to a miracle 'of a higher order', 'un prodige extraordinaire', 'ein von den sonstigen Wundertaten Jesu unterschiedenes Wunder', etc. ('The Demand for a Sign from Heaven' [1965], p. 115). He seems more concerned at times to defend the Pharisees for their request than Jesus for his refusal. In any case it has hardly any relevance for a study of Mark since Linton himself concludes that 'possibly already Mark has the idea that the "sign from heaven" was 'un prodige extraordinaire' (*Ibid.*, p. 129).

K. Rengstorf's article on signs in *TDNT* is useful in tracing the various ways in which σημεῖον can be used, but it has little value in determining the specific Markan attitude to sign-seeking.

8. K.H. Rengstorf, *TDNT*, VII, p. 206.

9. Cited by C. Brown, *Miracles and the Critical Mind* (1984), p. 135.

10. It is taken for granted in this study that Mark 16.17, 20 can be omitted from a discussion of *Markan* usage. The attitude to σημεῖα in the longer ending is totally inconsistent with Markan usage despite the contrary claims of W.R. Farmer (*The Last Twelve Verses of Mark* [1974], pp. 102f.).

11. Matthew uses the term to signify such widely diverse things as Judas' betrayal kiss (26.48) and 'the sign of the Son of Man in heaven' (24.30). Likewise, Luke's usage ranges from the cradle of Jesus as a σημεῖον for the shepherds (2.12) to the signs 'from heaven' (21.11) and 'in sun and moon and stars' (21.25).

12. Throughout the New Testament there are positive evaluations of the

idea that signs and wonders are given to authenticate the claims of Jesus and the apostles (cf. Acts 2.43; 4.30; 5.12; 6.8; 14.3; 15.12; Rom. 15.19; 2 Cor. 12.12; Heb. 2.4.) (cf. K. Kertelge, *Die Wunder Jesu im Markusevangelium* [1970], pp. 28ff.) and alongside these statements, hints of a much more restrained approach to 'signs' and even indications that they are not to be sought (esp. 1 Cor. 1.22) (cf. T. Snoy, 'Les miracles dans l'évangile de Marc' [1972], p. 466).

13. R. Bultmann, *The History of the Synoptic Tradition* (1968), p. 52.

14. R.P. Martin, *Mark: Evangelist and Theologian* (1972), p. 168. Of the eight Markan usages of ζητέω (apart from this one), it is used four times to indicate that Jesus' enemies were seeking opportunities to arrest and kill him (11.18; 12.12; 14.1, 11), all clearly with malicious intent. It is used once with similar effect to report the search for evidence against him (14.55). The three remaining usages are 1.36 where Simon and his companions convey the crowd's attempt to detain Jesus, 3.32 where the crowds convey Jesus' family's attempt to detain Jesus, and 16.7 where the young man at the tomb chides the women for their inappropriate and misplaced search for the body of Jesus. (Cf. G. Hebert, 'The Resurrection-Narrative in St. Mark's Gospel' [1962], pp. 69f.). While malicious intent is not necessarily indicated by any of these last three reports, all are clearly misguided and negatively evaluated by Mark. When we interpret the Markan purposes for the larger context of 8.11-13 we will see clearly that it is precisely in their '*seeking* a sign' that the Pharisees are most out of step with the purposes of Jesus.

15. Q. Quesnell makes the interesting suggestion that in the Markan framework the ἀπὸ τοῦ οὐρανοῦ of 8.11 must be read in terms of the ἐξ οὐρανοῦ of 11.30 (*The Mind of Mark* [1969], p. 253). This plausible suggestion would have some interesting implications. The Pharisees would then be feigning honesty here and Jesus exposing their real dishonesty in 11.30. They would be aiming at an objective test of Jesus' authority without making a decision about John's; they would be trying to bypass the need for moral conditioning (John's baptism) in the task of evaluating God's working. Neither in Mark 8.11-13 nor in 11.27-33 will Jesus oblige those who imagine that one's spiritual condition is irrelevant to the search for truth and the evaluation of those who make truth claims. 'It is a difficult and demanding thing to find the right kind of assurance, and the Pharisees were asking for it cheaply and on their own terms' (C.F.D. Moule, *The Gospel According to Mark* [1965], p. 61).

16. Mark 13.22 is a remarkable departure from the norm, since miracle-working was a central ingredient in Jewish eschatological literature. Cf. H.C. Kee, *Community of the New Age* (1977), p. 27.

17. This correlation demonstrates how wrong R. Meye's assessment is when he argues that what the false prophets are doing is mimicking the sign-giving methods of the Markan Jesus. On the contrary, they are doing precisely what the Markan Jesus refuses to do. (Cf. 'Psalm 107 as

"Horizon"' [1978], pp. 4f.) C.E.B. Cranfield rightly *contrasts* the sign-givers and Jesus: 'One characteristic of the false Messiahs and false prophets is specially mentioned. Unlike the true Messiah, they will not be at all reluctant to show signs and wonders. They will appeal to outwardly spectacular results and exploit to the full the natural craving of the disciples to escape from the painful paradoxes and tensions and indirectness of faith into the comfortable security of sight' ('St. Mark 13' [1953], p. 301).

18. R.P. Martin, *Mark: Evangelist and Theologian* (1972), p. 172.

19. It is of course not true that everywhere in the Bible 'signs and wonders' are taken as indicators of false prophecy. G.B. Caird probably assesses correctly the real significance of the Deut. 13.1f. reference to 'signs and wonders' when he says, 'God had deliberately left open the possibility of error to provide a test of his people's loyalty; if they were loyal, they would be able to distinguish the false prophet from the true' (*The Language and Imagery of the Bible* [1980], p. 218).

20. J.M. Robinson, 'The Literary Composition of Mark' (1974), p. 13.

21. Cf. V. Mora, *Le signe de Jonas* (1983), pp. 117f. ('Avons-nous ici un écho de ses paroles et de ses pensées? Notre réponse est affirmative').

22. E. Schweizer, *The Good News According to Mark* (1970), p. 158; N. Perrin, *Rediscovering the Teaching of Jesus* (1976), pp. 192f. A recent suggestion by J. Swetnam is that Mark omitted it because he does not present the resurrection (i.e., 'the sign of Jonah') as a 'sign' ('No Sign of Jonah'. [1985], p. 127.) There is very much to be said for this. See discussion following.

23. Cf. A.E.J. Rawlinson, *St. Mark* (1949), p. 258; C.E.B. Cranfield, *The Gospel According to St. Mark* (1977), p. 259.

24. E.g., G.R. Beasley-Murray, *Jesus and the Future* (1954), p. 259.

25. E.g., D. Wenham, *The Rediscovery of Jesus' Eschatological Discourse* (1984), pp. 318-20.

26. *TDNT*, VII, p. 237.

27. This does not mean that Mark necessarily disagrees with what he finds in his source. What he does by omitting the reference to 'the sign of the Son of Man in heaven' (if that is what he has done) is to prevent his readers from drawing unacceptable implications from it.

28. Cf. *Jesus and the Future* (1954), pp. 255-58. He reaffirms his view in *A Commentary on Mark 13* (1957), p. 70.

29. *Ibid.*, p. 93.

30. *The Rediscovery of Jesus' Eschatological Discourse* (1984), p. 323. Cf. pp. 308ff.

31. Many commentators have noted that Mark does not view the cosmic disturbances of 13.24f. as premonitory signs indicating the near arrival of the end, but has rather presented them as accompanying phenomena which indicate the character of the end as a theophany (either in salvation or judgment or both) (see Chapter 9).

32. The opening of 21.12 ('but before all these things') obscures the chronological order of events in Luke 21 and thus makes a decision on this rather difficult.

33. The one that Luke omits is 13.22. This exception is interesting in the light of Mark's and Luke's respective attitudes to signs (and wonders). Luke is quite ready to cite them as appropriate indicators of the veracity of true witnesses (cf. Acts 2.22, 43; 4.30; 5.12; 6.8; 14.3; 15.12). A Lukan inclusion of Mark 13.22 might well have given his readers the impression that objectively observable signs and wonders are after all not trustworthy indicators of the truth—a view Luke could scarcely afford to let stand, but precisely the point that Mark is at pains to drive home.

34. Luke uses σημεῖον three times in material not paralleled in Mark, twice in the birth narratives (2.12, 34) and once when Herod desires a sign from Jesus (23.8).

35. Note Caird's insistence that words can have evocative power, not only sense and reference (*The Language and Imagery of the Bible* [1980], p. 84). Perhaps σημεῖον had that power for Mark and/or his first readers.

36. In the discussion following, 'Jesus' should be taken to mean 'the Markan Jesus' even where this is not specified. We are not making claims about the historical Jesus' interaction with his environment, but rather about the way Mark has chosen to present his story.

37. William Lane echoes the views of many scholars when he says, 'Theologically, the demand for unmistakable proof that God is at work in Jesus' ministry is an expression of unbelief . . . The call for a sign is a denial of the summons to radical faith which is integral to the gospel' (*The Gospel According to Mark* [1974], p. 278).

38. Note, e.g., the oft-quoted analogy E. Schweizer introduces of a husband hiring a private detective to gather proof of his wife's faithfulness (*The Good News According to Mark* [1970], p. 159). Schweizer is no doubt correct that his attempt to find proof would destroy the very love he was seeking to establish. However, if the husband would be wrong in initiating *that sort of* test, the wife would surely be just as wrong if she deliberately withheld all demonstrations of her love in order to gain certainty that her husband's trust was *genuine*.

39. Many charges that Mark has been inconsistent would be dropped if those making them realized that Mark never intended to picture Jesus unaffected by those around him behaving on an unchanging manner from the beginning of the Gospel to the end. It is hazardous to make over-generalized statements about what the Markan Jesus does or does not do. We cannot adequately understand the attitude of the Markan Jesus to 'objective evidence' unless we observe and account for changes along the way. Even R.P. Martin's otherwise excellent treatment of the issue of 'evidence' is marred by an inadequate appreciation of Mark's story line. It is false that 'The Jesus of Mark rejects every petition which is directed to him that he

should declare himself and show his hand . . . he refused to declare himself in the way that his enemies, accusers and friends would have desired' (*Mark: Evangelist and Theologian* [1972], pp. 206f.). However true that might be for certain parts of Mark's Gospel, it is false for 2.1-12.

40. Scholars have focused their attention on pre-Markan sources, the structure of the passage, its fore-shadowing function, its apologetic function, its Christology and its ethical implications. They have not studied the passage adequately in terms of the one issue which we shall insist was central to Mark's concern, the issue of epistemology and the verification of truth claims.

41. Cf. e.g., T.L. Budesheim, 'Jesus and the Disciples in Conflict with Judaism' (1971). It might still be objected that Jesus is unfair since he condemns Jewish leaders *as a class* on the basis of rejection by a few representatives. (Cf. esp. J.C. Weber, 'Jesus' Opponents in the Gospel of Mark' [1966], p. 218). Mark's Gospel counters that charge as well by making it clear that there are exceptions to the rule (15.43) and by showing how Jesus treats those not typical of their class (12.34).

42. Cf. U. Luz, 'The Secrecy Motif and the Marcan Christology' (1983), p. 76.

43. 'Jesus . . . sought to give a visible proof of His authority and ability to grant the invisible (and therefore unverifiable) act of forgiveness by performing the act of healing that was equally God's prerogative and impossible for an ordinary man' (I.H. Marshall, 'St. Mark' [1974], p. 113).

44. It is not clear who questioned Jesus concerning fasting practice but it is not improbable that they were religious leaders or accomplices sent by them to trap Jesus. It is noteworthy that Jesus treated them as though they were honest inquirers even though it is probable that the question itself was designed as a trap. Cf. J.B. Muddimann, 'Jesus and Fasting' (1975), p. 278.

45. This goes a long way toward alleviating the difficulties of 4.10-12, except for those who wrongly interpret the 'outsiders' as those who would like to be followers if only they knew how they could.

46. 'The Use of Miracles in the Markan Gospel' (1965), p. 155.

47. Those who insist that in 2.1-12 Mark has compromised his theology are trying too hard to turn a story into a systematic theology textbook. Mark is not undermining his secrecy theory in 2.10, 28. (Cf. H. Räisänen, *Das 'Messiasgeheimnis' im Markusevangelium* [1976], pp. 144ff.; A. Richardson, *The Miracle-Stories of the Gospels* [1942], p. 103). On the contrary, he is telling a story which will reveal why the secrecy has a place.

48. The best response that is generated from the crowds is amazement and praise to God. It is quite clear that these responses are not considered adequate in the Markan narrative. That numinous awe is not endorsed as an appropriate response in the Markan narrative has been demonstrated often. Cf. J.M. Robinson, *The Problem of History in Mark* (1957), pp. 70-72; R.P. Martin, *Mark: Evangelist and Theologian* (1972), pp. 165, 171-73; D.

Rhoads, and D. Michie, *Mark as Story* (1982), p. 135; W. Swartley, *Mark: The Way for All Nations* (1981), p. 48. All that comes from the opponents is rejection (3.6), misinterpretation of the miracles that are given (3.22; 6.14), and a clamouring for more 'signs' (8.11-13).

49. She claims that 2.1-3.6 urges the readers to choose between the two irreconcilable responses to the message of the kingdom, accepting the way of Jesus and the new life of the kingdom or choosing the old way of the Jewish leaders. It introduces them, furthermore, to themes and motifs developed later in the Gospel (Son of Man Christology, discipleship as enthusiastic response to Jesus, the Jewish leaders' rejection of Jesus, the theme of life and death, etc.) Cf. *Markan Public Debate* (1980), pp. 194f.

50. There can be no doubt that Jesus' claims were not attractive to those with vested interests in the prestige and power that went along with religious and political authority. He claimed (and demonstrated!) the right to take on the prerogatives of the religious leaders: declaring divine forgiveness (2.1-12), determining ritual and moral acceptability (2.16f.), regulating fasting practices (2.19f.) and Sabbath activities (2.27), etc. They had a difficult choice to make at 3.6. They chose wrongly and would thereafter suffer the consequences.

51. 'Jesus macht seine Antwort von der Beantwortung der Gegenfrage ganz abhängig' (J. Kremer, 'Jesu Antwort auf die Frage nach seiner Vollmacht' [1968], p. 131). This is true in a double sense: he is unwilling to engage in debate unless they prove their sincerity first, and his answer will have no positive effect unless they first accept John's call for cleansing and preparation.

52. If their hearts change, they can still be brought into the kingdom. On the whole this does not happen. Of the whole religious and political leadership structure of Israel, only Joseph of Arimathea and an unnamed scribe are either waiting for the kingdom of God (15.43) or not far from it (12.34).

53. There is much to be said for Swartley's suggestion that the reason their lack of faith prevented Jesus from doing many miracles was that, having rejected the evidence Jesus had already given (i.e., lacking faith), Jesus could not appeal to them in *that way* anymore. Cf. W. Swartley, *Mark: The Way for All Nations* (1981), p. 85.

54. Until Mark 3.6, synagogues appear to have been a regular place for teaching and ministry (cf. 1.21, 3.1, and especially the summarizing statement in 1.39). It is not impossible that 'leaving the synagogue' and 'entering the house' are ideals that Mark envisions for Christians in the post-resurrection situation. Cf. G. Gaide, 'De l'admiration à la foi' (1974), pp. 39ff.

55. Note J.C. Fenton's assessment of the significance of 1.21-28. 'There is a contrast between his teaching with authority and the teaching of the scribes; on the other hand, there is a conflict between himself and an unclean

spirit. That is to say he faces Judaism with a new teaching, and he threatens the demons with destruction. It *will become clear* that these are not two separate activities, but two aspects of the one coming of the kingdom of God. . . . Mark seems to identify the kingdom of Satan with the Judaism of Christ's time' [emphasis mine] ('Destruction and Salvation' [1952], pp. 56f.). It does 'become clear', indeed in the very first meeting between Jesus and his opponents after 3.6!

56. D.J. Doughty points out significant parallels between 1.21-28 and 3.1-6 (where Jesus 'again entered the synagogue' [cf. 1.21; 3.1]). Whereas the crowds acclaim Jesus throughout 1.21-3.6, the Pharisees reject him. Whereas the crowds considered the miraculous as evidence of Jesus' divine authority, the Pharisees did not ('The Authority of the Son of Man' [1983], p. 180). What he overlooked was the even more significant parallelism, that both the demons and the religious authorities clearly recognized that their own positions of authority were jeopardized by Jesus' authoritative teaching with miracle-working power to back it up. In Mark's mind the religious authorities are the allies of Satan, and with the coming of the stronger one, they were destined to be stripped of their authority and power. Not forever would Jesus cater to their feigned 'honest searching'. After 3.6 their hypocrisy would be exposed at every turn.

57. Cf. W.H. Kelber, *The Kingdom in Mark* (1974), pp. 26ff., 145.

58. To join Jesus' spiritual family, however, his physical family will have to make a fundamental shift. They had been demanding that Jesus leave *his* fellowship and enter *their* charge (ἐξῆλθον κρατῆσαι αὐτόν [3.21]). Jesus invites them to reverse their priorities and join his circle.

59. *The Son of Man in Mark* (1967), p. 179.

60. It is undeniable that there is a major tactical adjustment at 8.31 ('and he began to teach them that . . . ' (even though there is disagreement over precisely what it was that triggered the changed course). Why then have so few scholars suspected there might well be other such tactical adjustments along the way? The point that D.D. Duling makes for 8.27−10.52 is just as true for 2.1-3.6. 'Today, redaction critics stress that this transitional section is crucial not for the messianic consciousness of Jesus, but for the theology of *Mark* ('Intepreting the Markan "Hodology"' [1974], p. 7).

61. Mark's Gospel has been seen to *function* as an apologetic document in a variety of ways, but very rarely has anyone suspected that Mark himself is not merely 'doing apologetics' but 'analysing apologetics'. Our study will find a great deal of evidence that Mark is at least as interested in the *means by which* truths are apprehended and verified as he is about explicating the truths that readers should grasp.

62. The close analogy between the way the Markan Jesus treats the Jewish leadership and the way other New Testament writers deal with the transition from Jewish privilege to Gentile opportunity has led many scholars to reach the disastrous conclusion that Mark's Gospel favours a transition from

Jewish Christianity to Gentile Christianity. How false that interpretation is and how distorting its effects are on the interpretation of numerous passages will be shown in Chapter 5.

63. σημεῖον, *TDNT*, VII, p. 241. Note the many positive evaluations of σημεῖα καὶ τέρατα in Acts.

64. 'Dynameis and Semeia in Mark' (1973), pp. 8, 19.

65. 'In this age the *dunamis* is veiled but it can be 'seen' by those who have the eyes of faith' (cf. A. Stock, *Call to Discipleship* [1982], p. 77).

66. R.H. Lightfoot, *The Gospel Message of Saint Mark* (1950), p. 37. 'It is clear that for Mark the miracles did not compel belief in Jesus and ought not now to be used as if they might' (M.E. Glasswell, 'The Use of Miracles in the Markan Gospel' [1965], p. 160).

67. 'The Miracles in Mark' (1978), p. 550. He frequently indicates their 'spiritual implications'.

68. *Das 'Messiasgeheminis' im Markusevangelium* (1976), pp. 107f. Cf. also J.A. Wilde, 'The Social World of Mark's Gospel' (1978), p. 55, where it is (incredibly) claimed that 'Mark is attracted to the present, pragmatic comfort afforded by the same thaumaturgy that many Pentecostals, Charismatics, and other religious healers and their patients find attractive'.

69. 'Person and Deed: Jesus and the Storm-Tossed Sea' (1962), p. 170. Cf. also '"He Taught Them Many Things"' (1980), pp. 479f.

70. *The Good News According to Mark* (1970), pp. 20f.

71. *Mark—Traditions in Conflict* (1971), esp. p. 161.

72. L. Schenke, *Glory and the Way of the Cross* (1972), p. 55; U. Luz, 'The Secrecy Motif and the Marcan Christology' (1983), p. 88.

73. This motive cannot be *entirely* ruled out. One of the reasons miracles are reported in Mark's Gospel is surely that by so doing Mark is able to help make his case that Jesus was no ordinary man making unsupportable claims about the divine authority under which he operates. Incredibly Alec McCowen insists that the greater the miracle performed the more surely 'Jesus emerges as an ordinary man' (*Personal Mark* [1984], p. 87). In Mark's Gospel Jesus both speaks and acts with divine authority and it is part of Mark's purpose to make this clear to his reader. 'The Rabbis taught, and nothing happened. Jesus taught, and all kinds of things happened' (T.W. Manson, *Jesus the Messiah* [1961], p. 35) Nevertheless, Mark had other and more primary purposes in reporting miracle stories.

74. M.E. Glasswell is typical of those who jump from the correct insight that Mark does not focus on the mere factuality of miracles as historical events to the invalid inference that Mark must be playing down the historicity of them in favour of Gospel proclamation. Cf. Glasswell, *Ibid.*, p. 156.

75. Cf. T. Snoy, 'Les miracles dans l'évangile de Marc' (1973), p. 100.

76. *The Miracle-Stories of the Gospels* (1942), pp. 22, 100. This view is not true for all the biblical writers. While it is true that many parts of both the

Old and the New Testaments do betray a reluctance to focus on miracles as 'wonders' (cf. esp E.J. Tinsley, 'The Sign of the Son of Man' [1955], p. 298), elsewhere it is precisely the wondrous aspect which is highlighted. Cf. Dan. 4.2f.; 6.27; Mic. 7.15; Jer. 32.20f. Cf. H.C. Kee, *Community of the New Age* (1977), p. 256; C.F.D. Moule, *Miracles* (1965), p. 236; W.A. Beardslee, *Literary Criticism of the New Testament* (1970), p. 25.

77. H.C. Kee, *Community of the New Age* (1977), p. 58.

78. When this is noted, texts like 6.52 and 8.17-21 betray their real significance. They are not included as part of a Markan attack on the disciples. They are included as part of Mark's call for his readers to look more deeply into the texts than the disciples did in the situations reported.

79. *New Light on the Earliest Gospel* (1972), p. 6.

80. This is the point Strecker seems to have overlooked in his defence of Wrede's view of the theory. Cf. 'The Theory of the Messianic Secret in Mark's Gospel' (1983), p. 60.

81. A.M. Ambrozic, *The Hidden Kingdom* (1972), p. 29.

82. H. Anderson notes that 'The Evangelist has been careful to try to preserve the ambiguity inherent in Jesus' ministry. Not everyone around can see and understand in it the signs of the presence of the kingdom of God. ... It is thus made clear that the actualisation of the reign of God in Jesus' word and deed is certainly not a matter that everyone can immediately grasp' (*The Gospel of Mark* [1976], p. 125).

83. The only exception is really the exception that proves the rule. The explanation Mark appends to the sower parable is not so much a *disclosure* of its meaning as a *call to* apprehend its meaning using the elements of the story to point out *the conditions* on which understanding depends (see Chapter 3).

84. R.P. Martin, *Mark: Evangelist and Theologian* (1972), p. 114; cf. R.P. Meye, *Jesus and the Twelve* (1968), p. 214.

85. 'St. Mark 4.1-34' (1952), pp. 64f.

86. E.C. Hoskyns and F.N. Davey reached the radical conclusion that modern critical method is adequate only to explicate the New Testament message, not to make a judgment on its truth (*The Riddle of the New Testament* [1947], pp. 223, 226). If Mark and the Markan Jesus are correct, this must be radicalized further still, for it would then follow that not only is historical critical investigation unable to adjudicate on whether the claims are true or false, it is also incapable of discovering fully even the nature of the claims on which a judgment of truth or falsity must be made.

87. B.W. Bacon provides a suitable example of the model to be avoided. He quite explicitly says that in order to safeguard the right of scholars to approach the texts with complete scientific objectivity, we must rule out in advance any hypothesis which would render the Gospels inaccessible to the methods we want to use. Cf. *The Gospel of Mark* (1925), p. 69.

88. J.W. Sider's comments on parable interpretation are equally applicable
to all of Mark's Gospel: 'Jesus [and Mark, we might add] could make a
symbol mean what he chose, but responsible exegetes cannot do likewise
without real danger of becoming as creative as Jesus the author was. The
only premise from which symbolic exegesis follows logically is that the
exegete knows what is going on in the author's mind; that is sometimes true,
but in the nature of symbols it is hard to be sure when.... What if
interpreters do get sidetracked by details? Literary critics have to take the
risk with literature much more complex than any parable. If they fail we
blame the interpreters, not the method. Fear of mistaking a part of a parable
for the whole should make exegetes consider all the parts carefully, not
proceed as if they did not exist' ('Proportional Analogy in the Gospel
Parables' [1985], p. 21).
89. Cf. B.D. Chilton, 'The Transfiguration' (1980), p. 116. Chilton also
criticizes those who attempt to treat the New Testament as though it were
designed to suit modern scientific tools.
90. Commenting on one of James' novels, T. Todorov maintains: 'The
secret is by definition inviolable, because it consists in the very fact that it
exists. The quest of the secret must never finish, because it is identical with
the secret itself' ('The Structural Analysis of Literature', in D. Robey,
Structuralism: An Introduction [1973], p. 101). We shall see that this is not
irrelevant to a proper understanding of Markan secrecy and of Mark 4.11 in
particular.
91. Cf. A.B. Kolenkow, 'Beyond Miracles, Suffering and Eschatology'
(1973), p. 170.
92. C.F.D. Moule, *Miracles* (1965), p. 238.

Notes to Chapter 3

1. *TDNT* V, pp. 343f.
2. A. Menzies, *The Earliest Gospel* (1901), p. 26.
3. N.A. Beck, 'Reclaiming a Biblical Text: The Mark 8.14-21 Discussion
about Bread in the Boat' (1981).
4. *The Messianic Secret* (1971), p. 132.
5. 'Markan Usage' (1925), p. 150.
6. Cf. e.g. C.L. Mitton, *The Gospel According to St. Mark* (1957), p. 61.
('The warning about "leaven" in 8.15 has, however, no clear link with the
surrounding verses').
7. See especially the work of P.J. Achtemeier. 'Mark is ... creative
enough to give the reader hints about how he thinks the material is to be
understood. By bracketing one tradition within another, he tells us he thinks
they share some point, clearer, usually, in one of them than the other. By
repetition of vocabulary ... he calls our attention to what he thinks belongs

together' ('Mark as Interpreter of the Jesus Tradition' [1978], p. 346). 'Such arrangements and juxtapositions constitute a major hermeneutical device of the author of this earliest Gospel, and careful attention to them is an indispensable aid to understanding that Gospel' (*Mark* [1975], p. 26). What Mark does with Jesus traditions is not wholly dissimilar to what the scribes were doing to Old Testament texts, drawing two or more together and allowing their combination to yield new insights.

8. Cf. *Clumsy Construction in Mark's Gospel* (1980). Not surprisingly, Mark 8.14-21 figures prominently in Meagher's attempt to discredit Mark (p. 77). See also p. 59 where this text is described as 'another brief passage in which he employs standard devices of elaboration in a manner that leads to nearly total mystification and the complete obfuscation of what was probably the main point of his source'.

9. 'Reclaiming a Biblical Text' (1981), p. 55.

10. Cf. e.g., 'One must account for the fact that verses 16-21 seem to be quite unconnected with warning about the leaven and relate obviously to the disciples' lack of bread' (H. Anderson, *The Gospel of Mark* [1976], p. 200). 'If vs. 15 is put into parenthesis, vs. 16 makes better sense, because it then follows vs. 14' (E. Schweizer, *The Good News According to Mark* [1970], p. 39). 'This isolated saying of Jesus is freely associated with the foregoing because of the association of yeast and bread. It breaks the natural sequence of vv. 14 and 16; yeast does not figure in the rest of the passage' (E.J. Malley, 'The Gospel According to Mark' [1968], p. 39).

11. W. Lane rightly notes that, 'the intimate connection between Ch. 8.14-21 and the preceding verses determines the context for interpretation of verse 15' (*The Gospel According to Mark* [1974], p. 280). Unfortunately he has already rearranged the larger context by taking 8.11-13 out of its Markan interpretative context and by reading it as though it appeared in 3.22-30 (p. 276). To rearrange Mark's text is the surest way of misreading his intentions.

12. Did Jesus imagine the disciples were about to request that the one loaf in the boat be multiplied to feed them? (cf. W. Hendriksen, *New Testament Commentary: Mark* [1975], p. 320).

13. Mark has often been called inept. Is it because scholars have wrongly assumed Mark intended to answer all the questions generated by his text? 'What do the parables mean?' 'What is the secret of the kingdom?' 'What is the meaning of the feedings?' 'What are the signs of the end of the age?' Mark has not been very successful if he intended to answer those questions. But if he did not, we need to seek Mark's agenda more carefully and not upbraid him for failing to accommodate himself to ours.

14. '"To Galilee" or "in Galilee" in Mark 14.28 and 16.7?' (1982), p. 369.

15. *The Gospel According to St. Mark* (1953), p. 366.

16. F. Kermode can perhaps be forgiven for his comment that, 'although

this passage has been subjected to the intense scrutiny of the commentators, no one, so far as I know, has improved on the disciples' performance' (*The Genesis of Secrecy* [1979], p. 47). J.D.M. Derrett comments, 'If they [the disciples] felt foolish, what of us?' (*The Making of Mark, I* [1985], p. 142).

17. J.C. Meagher comments sarcastically about the disciples: 'Poor blockheads, they don't get it. Uneasily, the reader may also note that he himself is just as much in the dark, despite his post-resurrection advantage over the puzzled disciples'. Meagher puts the blame on Mark (*Clumsy Construction in Mark's Gospel* [1980]. p. 77).

18. *Community of the New Age* (1977), p. 111. Kee is unusually sensitive to Mark's esoteric teaching methods, although we believe he is in error in relating this to 'apocalypticism'.

19. 'The Feeding of the Five Thousand' (1955), p. 144.

20. M.E. Glasswell likewise veers off into a discussion of Christology just when he had set the stage to grasp Mark's teaching on epistemology; cf. 'The Use of Miracles in Mark's Gospel' (1965), pp. 158f.

21. See C.E.B. Cranfield, *The Gospel According to St. Mark* (1965), p. 261.

22. *The Gospel of Mark* (1976), p. 202.

23. To a writer (and readers) well versed in the Old Testament, v. 16 would hardly have sounded like the spelling out of a three-fold problem. It would have sounded like the delineation of two options, something like this: 'Do you have the spiritual perception problem which the Old Testament prophets so often encountered among recalcitrant Israel? or do you not even remember what happened?' A recognition that 8.18a is a direct allusion to Jer. 5.21 and/or Ezek. 12.2 as well as an indirect allusion via Mark's text to the Isaianic background of Mark 4.12, makes it quite clear that the focus here is on spiritual imperception. The secondary alternative (a faulty memory) is ruled out by the following quiz. It is interesting that even God's chosen servant is charged with spiritual imperception (Isa. 42.18f.), further supporting our contention that Mark is not here attempting to discredit the disciples.

24. It is well known that almost all interpretations of the feedings which focus on Gentile inclusion make use of number symbolism in one way or another. But are the Gentiles fed in both feedings (G.H. Boobyer), only in the second (many scholars), or in a postulated later feeding with 3000 present (to make up 12,000) (B.E. Thiering)? Are they fed on the seven loaves of the second feeding (most scholars), the one loaf in the boat (D. Senior), or on the crumbs left over (M. Hooker)? Commonly the numbers 'four' and 'seven' (of the second feeding) are taken to point somehow to Gentiles. But is Mark thinking of seven deacons? seven Noachide laws? seven(ty) nations? There are hardly two interpreters who agree. The variety of different ways that numbers are used to hint at 'Gentile inclusion' is characteristic of the scholarly confusion surrounding this whole passage.

L.W. Countryman, in a recent article rightly rejects Jew-Gentile concerns as central to the passage. Taking his clue from the broader Markan context, he rightly relates 8.14-21 to Mark's epistemology. However, he is so much under the influence of the consensus that the numbers have to be decoded, that he manages to use them to fit his theory. The theory itself is much more plausible than the evidence he uses to defend it. 'How Many Baskets Full?' (1985), pp. 643-55.

25. *Mark: A Portrait of the Servant* (1974), p. 197.

26. '*Dynameis* and *Sēmeia* in Mark' (1973). See Chapter 2.I.

27. Cf. e.g., R. Meye, *Jesus and the Twelve* (1968), p. 69.

28. There are many more parallels between the passion of John the Baptist and Jesus, some of which will prove very important in Chapter 7. The ones given above show the almost exact parallelism between the Pharisees and Herod *in the matter of epistemology*.

29. Cf. R. Schnackenburg, *The Gospel According to St. Mark*, *I* (1971), p. 142. ('In their *unbelieving rejection* of Jesus the Pharisees and Herod were in agreement in spite of all differences' [emphasis his]). Cf. also R. Wolff, *The Gospel According to Mark* (1969), p. 58.

30. Cf. J. Marcus, 'Mark 4.10-12 and Marcan Epistemology' (1984), p. 569. We could go even further in relating 8.15 to Mark's overall concerns if it is legitimate to consider the Herodians as implicated along with Herod. It is not impossible that the original reading in 8.15 is 'of the Herodians' (τῶν Ἡρῳδιανῶν), but this is a minority and probably incorrect reading. (Cf. H. Anderson, *The Gospel of Mark* [1976], p. 200). But even if we read 'Herod' in the text, Mark might have had Herodians in mind along with the Pharisees. It is surely significant that the Pharisees and Herodians join hands precisely at 3.6 (where the reader is vividly shown that objective proofs presented to opponents can lead only to rejection, not conversion) and at 12.13-17 (where they *pretend* neutrality and objectivity while really trying to further their hostile designs). Jesus endorses only that kind of 'epistemology' which depends on prior commitment, which understands what is given rather than designing one's own tests, and which requires spiritually perceptive faculties in order to function.

31. Arguments for and against such collections are abundant. Cf. e.g., N. Perrin and D.C. Duling, 'The Gospel of Mark: The Apocalyptic Drama' (1982), p. 235; T. Suriano, 'Eucharistic Reveals Jesus' (1972), p. 644; E.S. Johnson, 'Mark viii. 22-26' (1979), p. 374.

32. It is not difficult to find scholars who see one or the other miracle as symbolically related to the disciples' problem of non-understanding. (Cf. e.g., D.E. Nineham, 'St. Mark's Gospel' [1957], p. 270). However, invariably the miracle of healing ears is seen in relation to the first feeding miracle and the miracle of giving sight in relation to the second; cf. e.g., A. Richardson, *The Miracle-Stories of the Gospels* (1942), pp. 82f. Richardson imagines that the restoration of hearing is comparable to the half-sight indicated in 8.22-26, so

that after the first feeding the disciples saw only partially, and it took a second miraculous feeding to give them full sight. But surely Mark's point is that they remembered well the sense data for *both* feedings, but the meaning of both was beyond their grasp. Cf. also H. Anderson, *The Gospel of Mark* (1976), p. 203; F.J. Matera, 'Interpreting Mark' (1968), p. 130.

33. G. O'Mahoney is quite correct when he points out that 'Jesus healed a man's hearing, and the healing had two facets: the man heard, then he heard so as to speak. He healed a man's blindness, and the healing was in two stages: the man saw, then he saw and made sense of what he saw' ('Mark's Gospel and the Parable of the Sower' [1978], p. 1765 [sic]).

34. *The Mysterious Parable* (1977), p. 42.

35. Cf. A.M. Ambrozic, *The Hidden Kingdom* (1972), p. 134. ('The ten references to 'hearing' which occur in the parable chapter clearly indicate the importance of what is being taught and the urgency of the message').

36. Cf. Ambrozic, *Ibid.*, p. 69f. D. Nineham, *The Gospel of St Mark* (1963), p. 211.

37. Cf. W. Lane, *The Gospel According to Mark* (1974), p. 156.

38. That the Sower parable is 'about the kingdom' has been asserted by many scholars, especially those who argue that the appended interpretation is not authentic. Cf. especially J. Jeremias, *The Parables of Jesus* (1963), p. 150. ('The interpretation misses the eschatological point of the parable'). Even V. Taylor is prepared to blame Mark and his sources for a 'loss of perception' concerning the real significance of the Sower parable; cf. *The Gospel According to St. Mark* (1953), p. 258.

39. Cf. M. Boucher, *The Mysterious Parable* (1977), p. 46; H.H. Graham, 'The Gospel According to St. Mark' (1976), p. 48.

40. 'Whether the interpretation of the Sower comes from Jesus or from the church, only a doctrinaire addiction to the one-point theory could persuade us that it is not what Jesus meant' (G.B. Caird, *The Language and Imagery of the Bible* [1980], p. 166). J.W. Sider considers the 'one-point addiction' the 'most pernicious part of Jülicher's legacy to a century of interpretation ('Nurturing our Nurse' [1982], p. 17; cf. also G.R. Beasley-Murray, *Jesus and the Kingdom of God* [1986], p. 129). J. Lambrecht believes that Mark himself framed the Sower parable with the calls to hear, possibly because the concern with hearing is so central in the interpretation he supplied ('Redaction and Theology in Mk. IV' [1974], p. 302). If it is Mark who added the framework, then we should consider very seriously D. Daube's suggestion that it does not mean simply 'this is important, so listen' but that Mark is rather drawing attention to a hidden meaning (*The New Testament and Rabbinic Judaism* [1956], p. 432).

41. *The Mysterious Parable* (1977), p. 44.

42. Cf. F. Kermode, *The Genesis of Secrecy* (1979), p. 143.

43. *Parables of Jesus* (1978), p. 179.

44. See especially P.S. Minear's analysis of λαός ('people') and ὄχλος

('crowd') in Mark's Gospel, with his evidence that the 'crowds' get very favourable treatment. They are certainly not consigned to 'outsider' status against their desires; cf. 'Audience Criticism and Markan Ecclesiology' (1972), esp. pp. 80-82. C.F.D. Moule's interpretation of Mark 4 has much to commend it. He rightly denies that Jesus is deliberately keeping outsiders as outsiders. Unfortunately he is content to consider the 'arounders' as a 'chance company' when Mark makes it clear that they are defined as those who choose to do the will of God (3.34f) ('On Defining the Messianic Secret in Mark' [1978], pp. 245-47).

45. It is quite clear that Mark did not intend the whole Isaiah quotation to be taken ironically, even if those scholars are correct who think that Isaiah and/or Jesus intended it that way (cf. C.A. Moore, 'Mark 4.12' [1974], p. 341).

46. 'Mark 4.12 adds further dimension to the concept of parable: not only what is heard is not perceived by 'those outside', but also what is seen is not perceived. This implies that the action as well as the teachings of Jesus function parabolically for Mark' (P. Patten, 'The Form and Function of Parable' [1983], p. 254). Cf. also The Entrevernes Group, 'Signs and Parables' (1978), pp. 233f.

47. It is noteworthy that the context for the Isa. 29.13 quotation in Mark 7 focuses clearly on spiritual perceptions: 'In that day the deaf will hear the words of the scroll, and out of gloom and darkness the eyes of the blind will see' (13.18).

48. It is hard to be certain how many of the suggested identifications of 'the meaning of the feedings' occurred to Mark. If the most basic meaning was 'the eschatological promises are being fulfilled', then a number of the other suggestions can be subsumed under the primary concern. There is no need to trace complex sea-crossing patterns or subtle symbolic allusions in the number of left-over baskets to make the point. If a very general meaning, such as the one suggested, was in the minds of at least some of the early church's apostles and preachers as they used the story of the feedings in sermons, it is not hard to see how some of the details of the story might have acquired allusions to various different aspects of the fulfilment of eschatological expectations. The fact that the story appears six times in the Gospels is eloquent testimony to the fact that it was an oft-told tale. Cf. T. Suriano, 'Eucharist Reveals Jesus' (1972), p. 643; D. Nineham, *The Gospel of St. Mark* (1963), pp. 23f.

49. Cf. U.W. Mauser, *Christ in the Wilderness* (1963), pp. 120f.

50. G.R. Beasley-Murray, 'Eschatology in the Gospel of Mark' (1978), p. 44.

51. R.H. Lightfoot was one of the earliest to recognize that there is a great deal of interpretation implied in Mark's text by the positioning of pericopes in relation to each other (*History and Interpretation in the Gospels* [1935], p. 57).

52. Cf. A. Richardson, 'The Feeding of the Five Thousand' (1955), p. 145.

53. Cf. e.g., E. Best, 'The Miracles in Mark' (1978), p. 545, and A.M. Ambrozic, *The Hidden Kingdom* (1972), p. 89. ('Throughout the section 8.27–10.52, which is devoted primarily to their instruction, the disciples show that the scales have not yet fallen from their eyes').

54. Cf. E. Best, 'Discipleship in Mark' (1970), p. 325.

55. Apart from those who have commented on this miracle from a medical point of view, few have adequately distinguished the two stages. G. Walker finds a modern parallel in people who have had operations to remove bilateral congenital cataracts ('The Blind Recover Their Sight' [1975], p. 23). J.K. Howard argues that more is at stake than 'merely the healing of an oracular lesion'. The miracle is 'functional as well as anatomical'. ('Men as Trees, Walking' [1984], p. 169). *Both* clearly point out the difference between 'collecting sense data' and 'understanding what one sees'.

56. Cf. esp. R. Beauvery, 'La guérison d'un aveugle à Bethsaîde (Mc 8, 22-26)' (1968), p. 58.

57. *History and Interpretation in the Gospels* (1935), pp. 90f. Cf. also D.J. Hawkin, 'The Symbolism and Structure of the Marcan Redaction' (1977), p. 104; R. Meye, *Jesus and the Twelve* (1968), pp. 70f., and many others.

58. Cf. 'Peter in the Gospel According to Mark' (1978), pp. 549f.

59. Both the religious teachers (3.22) and Herod (6.16) had made different inferences from what they had seen and heard. They were still blind along with the others who misidentified Jesus (8.28).

60. 'History and Theology in the Passion Narratives' (1970), p. 184. Cf. also R.A. Edwards, 'A New Approach to the Gospel of Mark' (1970), pp. 334f.; M. Boucher, *The Mysterious Parable* (1977), p. 82.

61. The threefold passion prediction, the consistent pattern of following each prediction with an evidence of discipleship misunderstanding, and that with corrective teaching, demonstrates that the Markan teaching concern is carefully threaded through the narrative. Cf. D.J. Hawkin, 'The Incomprehension of the Disciples' (1972), p. 496; P.J. Achtemeier, 'An Exposition of Mark 9.30-37' (1976), p. 180; J.L. Bailey, 'Perspectives on the Gospel of Mark' (1985), p. 22, and many others.

62. They qualify for further instruction, and there is hope that some day they shall see and hear aright. Morna Hooker correctly states, 'If the necessity for suffering and rejection arises from his authority, then it is clear that they can be explained only to those who recognize that authority' (*The Son of Man in Mark* [1967], p. 111).

63. A. Paul argues that 10.46-52 is itself a treatise on discipleship ('Guérison de Bartimée' [1972], p. 51). It is fascinating that in the first half of Mark's Gospel, where the concern is heavily focused on 'discernment', Mark uses 'discipleship' pericopes as transitional sections (e.g., 1.14-20, 3.7-19, 6.1-7, etc.) and in the latter half of the Gospel, where the concern is heavily

focused on 'discipleship', Mark uses 'discernment' pericopes as transitional sections (8.22-26 and 10.46-52). A number of scholars have argued that Mark uses *summary statements* in a transitional way so that the discipleship-oriented texts immediately following start a new unit. It is, however, quite clear that in each case the discipleship material is closely linked to the summaries and can be viewed as providing a transition along with the summaries (1.16-20 is tied to 1.14,15; 3.13-19 is tied to 3.7-12; 6.7 is tied to 6.6b, etc). See the argument by Achtemeier that 'Mark located the story [10.46-52] in his gospel where he did, not because the reference to the Son of David prepares the way for the triumphal entry, but because this story, together with the account of the healing of the blind man in 8.22-26, form an *inclusio* to set off a major section of Mark's gospel on the meaning of discipleship' ('"And he followed him"' [1978], p. 115). Cf. also J. Dewey, *Markan Public Debate* (1980), p. 23, and many others for the viewpoint that the two stories of healing blind men frame the midsection of the Gospel. A. Stock quite rightly notes that, 'What Jesus does at the beginning and end of the trip, open the eyes of blind men, he is in effect trying to do all along his way to the city' (*Call to Discipleship* [1982], p. 136). Cf. also Stock, 'Hinge Transitions in Mark's Gospel' (1985), p. 28. C.W. Hedrick calls 8.22-26 a 'transitional giving of sight story' ('The Role of Summary Statements' [1984], p. 289), thus indicating that 8.22-26 functions structurally in relation to what precedes and what follows. A Kuby quite appropriately maintains that the first half of Mark deals with the disciples' 'Nichtbegreifen' and the second half with their 'Mißverständnis' ('Zur Konzeption des Markus-Evangeliums' [1958], pp. 58).

64. 'Mark 4.10-12 and Marcan Epistemology' (1984), pp. 562, 566.

65. E.E. Lemcio, 'External Evidence for the Structure and Function of Mark iv. 1-20, vii. 14-23 and viii. 14-21' (1978), p. 324.

66. Discussions of 'discipleship failure' sometimes do not distinguish between a failure to understand and a failure to follow faithfully. It has been suggested that the disciples' failure to understand remains unrelieved throughout the Gospel and that there is no progress and gradual illumination. It is much rather the case that their understanding *does* grow, but with greater understanding there is a greater reluctance to *follow* in the direction Jesus is leading them. This is confirmed by the fact that whenever they receive eye-opening insights into what messiahship and discipleship mean, they find their willingness to follow most severely tested (cf. esp. 8.31, 32b, and the Passion account).

67. Cf. 'The Messianic Secret and the Enemies of Jesus' (1980), esp. pp. 42f.

68. Mark 12.12 is thought to be a key piece of evidence that the religious leaders *do* understand. However, there is in 12.1-12 no indication that they understood the real point of the parable (that the rejection of the Son would serve to hasten the demise of the misappropriating tenants and lead to their

replacement by Jesus, the new temple, and the new tenants). What they understood was that the parable was 'against them' (12.12). The only time the religious leaders are particularly perceptive is when they quite rightly perceive that Jesus is stripping them of their authority and power, the very thing that was so crystal clear to the demons ('You have come to destroy us' [1.24]). Does this tell us anything about their source of 'revelation?' (Cf. T.A. Burkill, 'The Cryptology of Parables' [1956], p. 246). See the view developed by W. Swartley that 'In the drama of this gospel, *heaven* knows and *hell* knows, but *humans* do not know. The divine voices and the demonic voices tell the reader, but the disciples are struggling, struggling, and struggling to understand' [emphasis his] (*Mark: The Way for All Nations* [1981], pp. 72f).

69. *The Hidden Kingdom* (1972), p. 79. It is a fundamental error of H. Räisänen's study of Mark's parable theory that the distinction is not observed. Cf. Ambrozic, *ibid.*, p. 137.

70. *Mark as Story* (1982), p. 49.

71. It may well be that Mark knew that he was writing a piece of literature that would appear to the unsympathetic reader as 'ordinary human clumsiness'. (Cf. J.C. Meagher, *Clumsy Construction in Mark's Gospel* [1980]). He hoped that the sympathetic reader would understand, or would at least consider the text an ongoing challenge to understand with growing clarity.

72. 'Modern Theology and Biblical Criticism' (1967), quoted by J.W. Sider, 'Nurturing our Nurse' (1982), p. 15.

73. Greek mythology has bequeathed to us many vivid personifications. Unfortunately, some of these have fallen into relative obscurity. Scylla and Charybdis were two sea-monsters dwelling on opposite sides of a narrow strait (possibly the Strait of Messina) representing its dangerous rocks and eddies. Odysseus survived a journey through the dangerous strait but not without losing six men to Scylla.

74. *The Problem of History in Mark* (1957), p. 12.

75. *The Gospel According to St. Mark* (1948), p. 86.

76. Cf. Q. Quesnell, *The Mind of Mark* (1969), pp. 239f.

77. This is confirmed by the fact that the two following pericopes make exactly the same point in relation to giving and to the temple. An impressive outward appearance hides nothing from Jesus who can penetrate beneath externals. The next usage of βλέπω to be analysed makes precisely the same point.

78. Cf. J.A. Baird, *Audience Criticism and the Historical Jesus* (1969), p. 134, for similar conclusions about the historical Jesus.

79. Or to use the Old Testament formulation: 'He does not judge by what he sees with his eyes, or decide by what he hears with his ears' (Isa. 11.3).

80. Cf. E.S.Johnson, 'Mark viii. 22-26' (1979), pp. 375-83 for an analysis of various terms. Especially significant is the 'seeing' terminology in 15.32, 36

and 39. Donald Senior probably assesses it most succinctly in his comments that 'The chief priests and the bystanders had mockingly offered to believe in Jesus if they could "*see*" him "come down from the cross"' (cf. 15.32, 36). Their brand of sight, which the Gospel has already labeled as 'blind' (4.11-12), is countered by another "seeing" which the evangelist fully endorses. "*Seeing* ... how he expired", the Roman centurion pronounces the first unqualified confession of Jesus' identity in the entire Gospel. ... The centurion is standing facing the *dead* Jesus (15.39). In this moment the evangelist has pushed his christology to its most eloquent and radical expression' [emphasis his] (The Passion of Jesus [1984], p. 129). We would add that in this moment Mark also gives his epistemology its most eloquent expression. The Jewish leaders wanted 'signs' (15.32, 36) and were not obliged; a foreigner was willing to change his mind about Jesus and was given a divine revelation of the truth. (O.A. Piper, 'God's Good News' [1955], p. 180).

81. Cf. also H.C. Kee, *Community of the New Age* (1977), p. 40. Kee comes part way towards our conclusions about βλέπω as a technical term.

82. Cf. e.g., M.D. Hooker, 'Trial and Tribulation in Mark 13' (1982), pp. 96f., and P. Vassiliadis, 'Behind Mark: Towards A Written Source' (1974), pp. 156-59.

83. *Naherwartungen* (1968), p. 107.

84. It is almost exactly parallel to 4.24 where it functions as a call to understand what is heard.

85. Cf. Q. Quesnell, *The Mind of Mark* (1969), p. 239.

86. It is possible that the disciples are being called to discern in the very presence of deceivers an indication that God's eschatological promises are being fulfilled. M. Hooker attempts to find different meanings in the βλέπετε of 13.5 and that of 13.23 (cf. 'Trial and Tribulation in Mark xiii' [1982], pp. 86, 91). There are not, however, adequate grounds for claiming that the first calls believers to conclude that the end is *not* near, and the second calls them to conclude that now it *is*. The two warnings against deception bracket the entire section and function in a parallel way to warn against the deceptions of those who imagine that they can discern, perform or fulfill apocalyptic functions which guarantee the nearness of the end.

87. The only time in Mark as a whole and Mark 13 in particular where there is any suggestion that Jesus' hearers are to take careful thought for their own safety is 13.14a, and even there the thought of safety is secondary. As we shall argue, 13.14b with its call to flee Jerusalem (and Judea?) is not primarily a call to protect one's self, but an urgent appeal to disassociate from those who imagine that in the temple there is either immunity from punishment or divine protection from danger.

88. M.D. Hooker, 'Trial and Tribulation in Mark xiii' (1982), p. 86. If there is any emphasis to be put on the reflexive pronoun βλέπετε ... ἑαυτούς, it is to call disciples to be careful about their own propensities to move blindly

into situations with no discernment of the meaning or implications of those situations. (Cf. G.R. Beasley-Murray, *A Commentary on Mark 13* [1957], p. 40).

89. Cf. e.g., J. Marcus, 'Mark 4.10-12 and Marcan Epistemology' (1984), pp. 558f.

90. Cf. B. Englezakis, 'Markan Parable' (1974), p. 355.

91. Cf. e.g., M. Boucher, *The Mysterious Parable* (1977), p. 60, for a good summary.

Notes to Chapter 4

1. *History and Interpretation in the Gospels* (1935), p. 94.

2. Cf. *Naherwartungen* (1968).

3. *The Formation of the Gospel According to Mark* (1975).

4. Cf. *The Gospel Message of St. Mark* (1950), pp. 48-59. Lightfoot was building on and supplementing suggestions by Austin Farrer, later published by Farrer in *A Study of St. Mark* (1951); see esp. pp. 140f. Cf. J.M. Robinson, *The Problem of History in Mark* (1957), p. 62 n. 1, for a list of scholars who have argued for, and analysed, links between Mark 13 and various other texts in Mark including the Passion narrative.

5. *TDNT* II, pp. 333-39.

6. It is possible, of course, that the limitation of the term γρηγορέω to these two pericopes is coincidental, that Mark had no other occasion to use the term. However, the fact that Luke manages to report the Gethsemane account without use of γρηγορέω, despite Mark's precedent, should caution us against assuming that the parallel usage of the term in the two Markan texts is accidental.

7. 'The Hour of the Son of Man and the Temptation of the Disciples' (1976), p. 48.

8. Among numerous examples, we could mention: F. Dewar, 'Chapter 13 and the Passion Narrative in St Mark' (1977), p. 100; J. Kallikuzhuppil, 'The Glorification of the Suffering Church' (1983), pp. 256f.; T.A. Burkill, *New Light on the Earliest Gospel.* (1972), p. 258.

9. R.P. Martin correctly notes that 'In the biblical tradition, the mark of a trusting man whose confidence reposes in God is that he sleeps in the midst of peril because he is sure of the sustaining and protecting care of God (Ps. 4.8; Prov. 3.23-24; Job 11.18-19; Lev. 26.6)' (*Mark: Evangelist and Theologian* [1972], p. 111). This motif is the controlling one in 4.38 and probably in 4.27, but is clearly set aside in the two texts under present consideration. There are exceptions to the general rule in the Old Testament as well (e.g., Jonah).

10. In the article quoted above, Kelber's goal was to analyse Mark's intended meaning in the Gethsemane account, not in Mark 13.33-37. Not

surprisingly therefore, he lets the interpretative clues flow from 13.33-37 into 14.32-42. There are also interpretative clues flowing in the opposite direction.

11. Cf. also E. Lövestam, 'Spiritual Wakefulness in the New Testament' (1963), pp. 78f.; J. Dupont 'La parabole du maître qui rentre dans la nuit' (1970), pp. 95-99.

12. *The Rediscovery of Jesus' Eschatological Discourse* (1984), p. 45.

13. *Ibid.*, p. 46.

14. *Ibid.*, p. 18.

15. R. Bauckham points out instances where 'deparabolization' has taken place, with parabolic imagery being absorbed into ordinary Christian discourse. Cf. 'Synoptic Parousia Parables and the Apocalypse' (1977), p. 170. We might well use the term 'reparabolization' for what we think is happening here..Alternatively we might say that the 'parable' in 13.33-37 is tailored to fit the fact that it has two intended meanings and fulfilments, not just the one fulfilment most in focus in the Mark 13 context.

16. This in turn might help with another frequently posed question: Does the doorkeeper in particular have a special watch-care responsibility, thus representing (perhaps) apostolic responsibility over the church (the servants)? (So, e.g., R. Wolff, *The Gospel According to Mark* [1969], p. 107). Surely all are *called* to be faithful servants, but Mark knows that in fact only one *succeeds* in being a faithful watchman. All servants are *called* to obey the command γρηγορεῖτε in the manner in which they serve. Mark knows that not all will do so.

17. It can hardly be objected that to picture Jesus first as the doorkeeper and then as the master is a forced reading. Is that not just the kind of 'role reversal' that one expects to find as Jesus goes faithfully through the passion? The principle (even if not the imagery) is paralleled frequently in Mark (cf. 12.10, 14.62).

18. 'The Hour of the Son of Man and the Temptation of the Disciples' (1976), p. 42.

19. *The Gospel Message of St. Mark* (1950), p. 53.

20. Cf. especially L. Gaston, *No Stone on Another* (1970), p. 478.

21. This point would be securely based if we could be certain that Mark has adapted his material in part from the parable that Luke retains in 12.35-38, where the three Jewish watches are referred to. It is of course possible that the Roman usage had penetrated Jewish usage to the extent that the four watches may have been original. Cf. Mark 4.48 and G.R. Beasley-Murray, *A Commentary on Mark 13* (1957), p. 117.

22. Several people have suggested that this is the origin of the time notes throughout the Passion account; cf. e.g., J. Navone, 'Mark's Story of the Death of Jesus' (1984), p. 125.

23. Cf. e.g., E. Schweizer, 'Mark's Theological Achievement' (1985), p. 56; W. Harrington, *Mark* (1979), p. 247; J.J. Kilgallen, 'The Messianic Secret and Mark's Purpose' (1977), p. 64.

24. Cf. D. Rhoads, and D. Michie, *Mark as Story* (1982), p. 99; G.B. Caird, *The Language and Imagery of the Bible* (1980), p. 267.

25. Cf. esp., B.M.F. van Iersel, 'The gospel according to St. Mark—written for a persecuted community?' (1982).

26. *Loaves and Fishes* (1981), p. 147.

27. Cf. V.K. Robbins, 'Last Meal' (1976), p. 34.

28. Cf. R.P. Martin, *Mark: Evangelist and Theologian* (1972), pp. 199f.

29. *The Passion of Jesus in the Gospel of Mark* (1984), p. 49.

30. P.J. Achtemeier, 'Mark as Interpreter of the Jesus Traditions' (1978), p. 349.

31. *Studien zur Passionsgeschichte des Markus* (1971), p. 282. ('Zwar ist nur *einer* aus diesem Kreis der Verräter, aber alle könnten dieser 'Eine' sein'). Cf. also K. Stock, *Boten aus dem Mit-Ihm-Sein* (1975), p. 154.

32. *Ibid.*, p. 62.

33. Cf. G.B. Caird, *The Language and Imagery of the Bible* (1980), p. 267. Caird mentions that in the first watch, Judas was 'caught napping'.

34. L.W. Hurtado, *Mark* (1984), p. 212.

35. *Gospel Criticism and Christology* (1935), p. 60. Cf. also the comment by D. Senior: 'The threefold indictment of the disciples' sleep is in stark contrast to Jesus' repeated prayer' (*The Passion of Jesus in the Gospel of Mark* [1984], p. 78).

36. D. Senior, *The Passion of Jesus in the Gospel of Mark* (1984), p. 39.

37. A. Stock, *Call to Discipleship* (1982), pp. 178f.

38. Cf. D. Brady, 'The Alarm to Peter in Mark's Gospel' (1979), pp. 54–57.

39. Cf. esp., W.J.P. Boyd, 'Peter's Denials' (1956), p. 341; G. Schneider, 'Gab es eine vorsynoptische Szene "Jesus vor dem Synedrium"?' (1970), pp. 38f.

40. Cf. K.E. Dewey 'Peter's Curse and Cursed Peter' (1976), pp. 109f. A. Stock comments, 'Debate has centered on whether this is to be understood as Peter's cursing himself (if he lies) or his cursing Jesus. But the effect is the same in either case. Peter utters a series of curses designed to disassociate himself publicly from Jesus. The ambiguity over the object of the curse is perhaps best understood as intentional on the part of Mark who creates the highly ironic situation in which Peter either directly curses himself or indirectly does so by cursing Jesus, and by attempting to save himself in this situation in reality loses himself and is placed in even greater jeopardy' (*Call to Discipleship* [1982], p. 190).

41. Peter is not technically blaspheming according to the norms of Jewish religion, but the term is not inappropriate in terms of the teaching of Jesus (cf. 8.38). Concerning 14.72, T.A. Burkill says, 'This tearful denoument (sic) signifies that he is finally ashamed of his having been ashamed of an erstwhile allegiance to the prisoner now being charged with the very crime he himself has just committed' ('Blasphemy' [1975], p. 72).

42. J.R. Donahue, 'Temple, Trial, and Royal Christology' (1976), p. 78.

43. D. Senior comments: 'Two contradictory promises—Jesus' and Peter's [cf. 14.27-31]—hang in the air, and now the reader will see the outcome' (*The Passion of Jesus in the Gospel of Mark* [1984], p. 87).

44. J.N. Birdsall may well be correct that 14.72 means more than Peter's remembrance of Jesus' prophecy. It may well signify that he remembered the whole situation in which the prophecy was made, the willingness of Jesus to be struck down, the assurance of re-gathering afterwards, maybe even the redemptive significance of Jesus' predicted suffering, made clear in 10.45 and alluded to in the account of the Last Supper. Cf. 'τό ῥῆμα ὡς εἶπεν αὐτῷ ὁ Ἰησοῦς' (1958), pp. 274f.

45. Those who imagine that an analysis of 10.45 is sufficient to determine whether or not Mark holds the view that Jesus' suffering is redemptive, fail to appreciate the wholeness of his Gospel and the fact that his deepest convictions will leave traces throughout the narrative, not only in isolated texts where particular words are utilized.

46. 'Mark's Contribution to the Quest of the Historical Jesus' (1964), p. 430.

47. *The Passion and Resurrection of Jesus Christ* (1969), p. 80.

48. Except for Judas, none, significantly, joins the enemies. The remaining disciples, are therefore still defined as officially 'for' Jesus (9.40). The renewal of their discipleship, however, now depends on the faithfulness of Jesus alone, who will stand faithfully right through the eschatological Night and bring in the eschatological Day.

49. C.M. Martini, 'La confessione messianica di Pietro a Cesarea e l'inizio del nuovo popolo di Dio secondo il Vangelo di S. Marco' (1967), p. 551.

50. 'The Hour of the Son of Man and the Temptation of the Disciples' (1976), pp. 49, 53. Cf. also D.E. Nineham, *The Gospel of St Mark* (1963), p. 392.

51. If fullness of knowledge were the goal in Gethsemane, Jesus' own praying would have to be negatively evaluated. It is precisely his willingness to carry out the divine will *without* full knowledge of what that might entail, which constitutes Jesus' model praying in the garden. He was praying 'in the dark'. If insight came concerning the plans of God, the insight followed his faithfulness; it did not constitute it. When the captors appear on the scene, he can affirm that this is not just any hour, or any watch of the night; 'The Hour has come' (ἦλθεν ἡ ὥρα 14.41). The fact that Mark is describing, not just any night, but a Passover night, adds eschatological colouring to the statement, for it was widely held that eschatological fulfilment was to be expected during the Passover night, perhaps even specifically at the midnight hour; cf. E. Lövestam, 'Spiritual Wakefulness in the New Testament' (1963), p. 83. In the Synoptic tradition, 'midnight' had very strong eschatological overtones of its own, quite apart from being the name of one of the night watches (cf. Matt. 25.6). Perhaps the reason 'midnight' is not specified as the

time of the Gethsemane 'watch' is that Mark does not want to over-stress the eschatological significance of the Gethsemane scene itself. After all, it is the whole passion, not only the midnight arrest in the garden, which constitutes 'the hour' that has arrived and that fulfills, on one level at least, eschatological expectations. Cf. V. Taylor, *The Gospel According to St. Mark* (1953), p. 557.

52. Cf. C.E.B. Cranfield, *The Gospel According to St. Mark* (1977), p. 411.

53. It is frequently asserted that Mark 13.33-37, with its urgent call to preparedness, obviously presupposes that the End is exceedingly close. Why the urgent call for alertness if the event may well be delayed a long time? (Cf. A.M. Ambrozic, *The Hidden Kingdom* [1972], p. 212f). Nothing in 13.33-37 (however one might interpret other parts of the chapter) lends any support to this sentiment. It is gratuitous to imagine that the Doorkeeper parable is saying, 'Watch closely, the End may be closer than you think'. There is at least as much reason to read it as saying, 'Keep watching faithfully, the End may be delayed longer than you expect'. More precisely it says that the urgency of the call to faithful discipleship rests in the very fact that there is no way of knowing whether the End is near or far away. The disciple is not called to *eliminate* his ignorance of the timing of the End, he is called to *cope* with it, and respond to it appropriately.

54. E. Lövestam insists that we must not focus on *either* ensuring the safety of the house *or* on readiness to receive the master. 'It is not a matter of "either-or", but of "both-and"' ('Spiritual Wakefulness in the New Testament' [1963], pp. 81f).

55. The intruder might of course take various forms. Surely the imposters who deceive the undiscerning (13.5, 22) would be intruders in the master's house. Satan who snatches away the good seed (4.15) would be one. Even the 'rocks' and the 'thorns' (i.e., wrong responses in times of persecution, concerns with the affairs of this life, the deceitfulness of wealth, misplaced desires, etc. [cf. 4.16-19], i.e., weaknesses of the flesh [cf. 14.38]), could be the intruders. Clearly not all enemies are external. After all, in Gethsemane the disciples were called to 'watch', not for an external enemy, but against their own propensities to fail and flee. Jesus did not position them as lookouts and bodyguards against the external enemy. He admonished vigilant prayer lest, giving in to the weakness of the flesh, they should fall into temptation. Failure to resist the inner enemies constituted their unpreparedness, their 'sleep'.

56. *Die Passion Jesu als Verhaltensmodell* (1974), p. 283; cf. also K.E. Dewey, 'Peter's Curse and Cursed Peter' (1976), p. 109 n. 41. ('During the night watches Jesus is pictured not as a master in the end time [13.32-37], but as passive, obedient, and powerless'.)

57. It might be countered that the presence of apocalyptic phenomena both in Mark 13 and in the passion is evidence that Mark expects his readers

to be on the lookout for such. However, it is significant that the 'apocalyptic' signs accompanying the first fulfilment of 'the day and hour' happen when Jesus is already on the cross (e.g., the darkness at noon [15.33]), *after* all those called to follow him have fallen away. If any apocalyptic signs are to appear, they will be part of the very fulfilment of God's promises, not advance indicators that the fulfilment is near. (Cf. D. Senior, *The Passion of Jesus in the Gospel of Mark* [1984], p. 122; F.H. Milling, 'History and Prophecy in the Marcan Passion Narrative' [1967], p. 50). This correlates well with our view that Mark 13 contains no apocalyptic signs by which the near arrival of the end can be calculated, but apocalyptic signs only as accompaniments of the end itself (13.24f.). For Mark, apocalyptic phenomena are not the objects of the required 'watching'. They indicate the character of the event when it happens.

58. E. Best, *Mark: The Gospel as Story* (1983), p. 90.

59. Cf. esp. the arguments of C.B. Cousar in 'Eschatology and Mark's *Theologia Crucis*' (1970), pp. 333f. E. Lövestam argues that both here and in the New Testament generally, 'The admonition to "keep awake" means an exhortation to the Christians not to let themselves be spiritually stupified and choked by absorption in the present age of night, but to realize their position as sons of light and sons of the day, living in such a way as agrees with the day to come and being thus ready for the parousia of the Lord' ('Spiritual Wakefulness in the New Testament' [1963], p. 58; cf. also p. 143). It may well be true, as C. Breytenbach argues, that for Mark future expectation is the ultimate motivation for discipleship (*Nachfolge und Zukunftserwartung nach Markus* [1984], p. 279; cf. also R. Pesch, *Naherwartungen* [1968], p. 242). It is equally true that discipleship is the ultimate definition of eschatological preparedness.

60. Cf. e.g., V. Taylor, *The Gospel According to St. Mark* (1953), p. 523. Amazingly, even those who think they are a perfect fit sometimes do so only because they misunderstand *both* the main discourse and the conclusion. J. Schmid, for example, is convinced the final call for watchfulness (i.e., watching for signs) is appropriate since Mark 13 is entirely about signs and the early end! (*The Gospel According to Mark* [1969], p. 233).

61. Cf. W. Schmithals, *Das Evangelium nach Markus II* (1979), p. 569.

62. At this point we must draw attention to the excellent article by K. Brower ('Mark 9.1' [1980]) in which he argues persuasively that Mark frequently speaks with double messages, transmitting viewpoints to his readers in various ways that 'go over the heads' of characters within the story. Moreover, one of the crucial points which Mark makes in relation to his readers is that various of Jesus' statements can have meanings on several levels, and that promises can have different levels of fulfilment. Brower argues that statements like Mark 9.1, in the context of Mark's thought, are deliberately multi-meaningful, and that the promise therein contained finds at least proleptic fulfilment in the passion of Jesus.

63. 'St. Mark's Philosophy of History' (1957), p. 144.

64. Cf. F. Kermode, *The Genesis of Secrecy* (1979), p. 127.

65. Cf. the arguments of G.R. Osborne that Mark's use of 'hour' (ὥρα) in his Gospel evidences a deliberate correlating of the final Hour with the hour of the passion ('Redactional Trajectories in the Crucifixion Narrative' [1979], p. 92). Not to be overlooked is the fact that 'the hour' (ἡ ὥρα) in 14.35 is directly paralleled with 'the cup' (τὸ ποτήριον) in 14.36, which clearly has eschatological significance as a comparison with 10.39 and 14.23-25 makes plain. The term 'the hour' (ἡ ὥρα) appears three times in the Gethsemane pericope, once symbolically (14.35), once literally (14.37), and once, we claim, ambivalently (14.41). Both chronological time and eschatological time is being 'measured' in Gethsemane.

66. Cf. H. Anderson, *The Gospel of Mark* (1976), p. 301.

67. It is surprising that C.E.B. Cranfield, normally so attuned to Mark's paradoxical and ambiguous means of communication, should state categorically, 'By "that day" the Day of the Parousia and last Judgment is clearly intended. In the OT "that day" is an eschatological technical term' ('St. Mark 13' [1954], p. 294). Does he imagine that Jesus' disciples will fast on *that* day? It is an impossible suggestion, especially in the light of Mark 14.25, Mark's only other use of 'that day' (ἐκείνη ἡ ἡμέρα).

68. That even the Son did not fully know 'concerning that Day and the Hour' (περὶ τῆς ἡμέρας ἐκείνης ἤ τῆς ὥρας) emerges in the story (especially in Gethsemane and in the cry from the cross).

69. *According to Mark* (1960), pp. 296f.

70. *The Gospel According to St. Mark* (1953), p. 116.

71. It is interesting to note that in David Wenham's reconstructed eschatological discourse, Mark's own contributions to 13.32-37 consist specifically in introducing the four Roman watches and generalizing the ignorance reference from 'because you do not know in which watch' (ὅτι οὐκ οἴδατε ποία φυλακῇ) to 'for you do not know when the time will come' (οὐκ οἴδατε γὰρ πότε ὁ καιρός ἐστιν), the very changes he would have had to make if it was his purpose to highlight the four watches, yet keep the statements ambivalent enough to fit both the passion night and a period of unknown length before the coming of the Son of Man. (Cf. *The Rediscovery of Jesus' Eschatological Discourse* [1984], pp. 39-41).

72. Mark 1.2 prophesies John's coming by revalidating a prophecy that had been fulfilled already with the return of the Babylonian exiles. Moreover even Mark's *source* (Isa. 40.3) is the incorporation of a prophecy that had seen a fulfilment centuries before (Isa. 40.3; cf. Ex. 23.20) (W. Lane, *The Gospel According to Mark* [1974], pp. 45f.). It is characteristic of Old Testament prophetic poetry to run together allusions from various moments of God's mighty works, past and future. Creation motifs, exodus motifs, delivery-from-captivity motifs, and final Day-of-the-Lord motifs can be run together in one great recital of the working of God (cf. esp. Isa. 51.9b, 10).

73. *History and Interpretation in the Gospels* (1935), p. 94.

74. *The Gospel Message of St. Mark* (1950), p. 51.

75. Cf. e.g., *Locality and Doctrine in the Gospels* (1938), p. 75.

76. *The Gospel Message of St. Mark* (1950), pp. 48-59, 106-16.

77. Cf. P.J. Achtemeier, 'Mark as Interpreter of the Jesus Traditions' (1978), p. 344.

78. Cf. e.g., M.D. Hooker, 'Trial and Tribulation in Mark XIII' (1982), pp. 94f.

79. Cf. esp. G.B. Caird, *The Language and Imagery of the Bible* (1980), pp. 121, 251f.; C.E.B. Cranfield, *The Gospel According to St. Mark* (1977), pp. 388f.

Notes to Chapter 5

1. 'The Cross as Power in Weakness' (1976), p. 121.

2. J.C. Meagher, *Clumsy Construction in Mark's Gospel* (1980), p. 58.

3. C.F. Evans, *The Beginning of the Gospel* (1968), p. 81.

4. Cf. R.A. Culpepper, 'The Passion and Resurrection in Mark' (1978), p. 591; D. Juel, *Messiah and Temple* (1977), p. 128; J.R. Donahue, *Are You the Christ?* (1973), pp. 202f.

5. Cf. esp. D. Juel, *Messiah and Temple* (1977), pp. 55-57.

6. R.J. McKelvey suggests: 'How much weight one should give this secondary and deeper meaning is not clear, but Mark's cryptic way of writing (cf. 15.38) and the interpretative words "made with hands . . . not made with hands" and "in three days" rather suggests that he invites his readers to read between the lines' (*The New Temple* [1968], p. 71).

7. Cf. H.L. Chronis, 'The Torn Veil' (1982), p. 97.

8. The most frequently cited are Hos. 9.15f., Zech. 14.20f. and Mal. 3.1.

9. Cf. G.W. Buchanan, 'Mark 11.15-19: Brigands in the Temple' (1959), p. 177; 'An Additional Note to "Mark 11,11-15: Brigands in the Temple"' (1960), p. 105.

10. Cf. J.D.M. Derrett, 'The Zeal of the House and the Cleansing of the Temple' (1977), pp. 85f.; D.E. Nineham, *The Gospel of St Mark* (1963), p. 301.

11. Cf. C. Roth, 'The Cleansing of the Temple and Zechariah xiv 21' (1960), p. 175; R.H. Hiers, 'Purification of the Temple' (1971), pp. 82-90.

12. A. Caldecott, 'The Significance of the "Cleansing of the Temple"' (1923), p. 385. The idea is that λῃσταί really means 'butchers'. Cf. W.H. Kelber, *Mark's Story of Jesus* (1979), p. 60.

13. P.J. Achtemeier, *Mark* (1975), p. 24; A. Stock, *Call to Discipleship* (1982), pp. 167f.

14. Cf. C.E.B. Cranfield, *The Gospel According to St. Mark* (1977), p. 358.

15. Cf. esp. C.K. Barrett, 'The House of Prayer and the Den of Thieves' (1978), pp. 14f.; J.M. Ford, 'Money "Bags" in the Temple' (1976), p. 17.

16. Cf. R.J. McKelvey, *The New Temple* (1968), p. 63; J.R. Donahue, *Are You The Christ?* (1973), pp. 120-27; J. Lambrecht, *Parables of Jesus* (1978), p. 189.

17. The fact that the religious leaders knew the parable was against them (πρὸς αὐτοὺς 12.12) implies by the same token that it was in support of Jesus and his authoritative action.

18. For our present purposes it is enough to view Jesus' counter-question as a test of their sincerity, since in fact it reveals their hypocrisy. The passage, however, has deeper levels than this. Jesus' enemies reject his authority precisely because they have rejected John's. And because 'Elijah' has been rejected, it becomes inevitable that the Son of Man will have to suffer (9.12f.). .

19. J.R. Donahue, *Are You The Christ?* (1973), p. 127.

20. If they would not accept his authority to forgive (2.1-12), how can they be expected to accept his authority to condemn? If they reject him when he takes on himself the rights of temple and cult, how much more surely will they be rejected when he claims authority to take those rights from them!

21. Cf. the references given in K. Snodgrass, *The Parable of the Wicked Tenants* (1983), p. 77 n 20. Cf. also M.D. Hooker, *The Message of Mark* (1983), p, 87; E. Best, *Mark: The Gospel as Story* (1983), p. 71.

22. Cf. C.H. Giblin, *The Destruction of Jerusalem According to Luke's Gospel* (1985), p. 66.

23. Cf. L. Gaston, *No Stone on Another* (1970), p. 476.

24. D. Juel speaks of 'a group within Israel' (*Messiah and Temple* [1977], p. 131). Both H.C. Kee (*Community of the New Age* [1977], p. 113) and K. Snodgrass (*The Parable of the Wicked Tenants* [1983], pp. 77, 91) are careful to point out that the tenant replacement focuses on replacement of Israel's *leadership*, not on replacement of Israel with Gentiles.

25. Cf. L.W. Hurtado, *Mark* (1984), p. 179.

26. H.C. Kee, *Community of the New Age* (1977), p. 113. That the people as a whole do not here stand condemned should be clear enough from the fact that at this point in the story, the role of the Jewish crowd is precisely one of *hindering* the leaders in their attempt to do away with Jesus (11.18, 32). When the crowds eventually cease to block the way, the blame is laid squarely on the shoulders of the chief priests. Only because they stir up the people, do the crowds side with Barabbas and against Jesus (15.11). Moreover, as we shall see, Mark uses 12.41-44 to help make the point that what is under divine scrutiny is not the piety of the people but rather the leaders whose corruption prevents the fruit from reaching the 'owner'.

27. Contra E. Lohmeyer (cf. *Lord of the Temple* [1962], pp. 43-45) and many others.

28. Targumic tradition subsequent to the Babylonian exile understood Isa.

5.1-7 as a prediction of the temple's destruction. Cf. C.A. Evans, 'On the Vineyard Parables of Isaiah 5 and Mark 12' (1984), p. 83.

29. To rob people is bad enough, and according to the Psalmist it disqualifies one from living on God's holy hill (Ps. 15.1, 5), but it hardly warrants labels like λῃσταί (D. Juel, *Messiah and Temple* [1977], pp. 132f.). It is only because they rob *God*, and because of the things they do as a result, that the term is appropriate.

30. Contra E. Schweizer, *The Good News According to Mark* (1970), p. 239. If there is an underlying play on words between 'Son' and 'Stone' (see a summary of scholarship on this point in K. Snodgrass, *The Parable of the Wicked Tenants* [1983], pp. 94-98), that might betray the brilliance of the allusion, but it certainly does not exhaust its meaning.

31. A. Suhl is correct that the main focus is on reversal, but it is hard to agree with him. that therefore the Christological focus can be eliminated from the quotation altogether. Cf. *Die Funktion der alttestamentlichen Zitate* (1965), pp. 138-42; Snodgrass, *Ibid.*, p. 97.

32. Lightfoot, Dodd, McKelvey, Telford and Kelber are among those who accept the allusion. Others think the idea is far-fetched.

33. This is the error of D. Juel (*Messiah and Temple* [1977], p. 133.) and A. Stock (*Call to Discipleship* [1982], pp. 183-85).

34. Cf. N.M. Flanagan, 'Mark and the Temple Cleansing' (1972), pp. 982f. To call their beloved temple a 'den of robbers' would be as abrasive as calling Jerusalem, Israel's 'high place' (Mic. 1.5).

35. In this respect the Isa. 56.7 quotation is more suited to the 'cleansing' account than the Jeremiah allusion, for there it is clearly stated that Israel's watchmen are blind and have turned 'each to his own gain' (56.10f).

36. This does not mean that 'Gentile inclusion' is not a concern of Mark. Clearly it is. Certainly one of the misdeeds of the corrupt Jewish leadership was their exclusion of Gentiles. And Gentile *inclusion* is clearly an important element in the reversal of fortunes that is sealed by the death of Jesus (cf. Mark 15.37-39). It is, however, part of a larger concern. When the issue of leadership and temple replacement is settled, then the renewed faithful Israel under the leadership of Jesus will fulfil the highest ideals of the old covenant, to bring the Gospel to all nations. Mark's perspective is that Gentiles will be incorporated into a renewed Israel; they will not displace a nation that is rejected.

37. A great deal has been written about the historical basis (or lack thereof) for the story of the fig tree cursing. For useful summaries and evaluations of the various views, see W.R. Telford, *The Barren Temple and the Withered Tree* (1980), pp. 22-25; L.A. Losie, 'The Cursing of the Fig Tree' (1977).

38. Jeremias argues that the use of the fig tree cursing as a frame around the 'cleansing' disturbs an original connection between the triumphal entry, the 'cleansing' and the question of Jesus' authority (cf. *The Eucharistic*

Words of Jesus [1976], p. 91). However, if the fig tree cursing is intimately tied to the 'cleansing' account, then the expanded unit (11.12-25) can still be directly related to the material preceding (11.1-11) and following (11.27-33).

39. If it be thought that the imagery (leaves, no fruit, withered from the root) is so apt for the temple (beautiful exterior, no fruit, destined to perish) that it must refer to it, what of the perfect match with the Jewish leaders (splendidly robed on the outside [12.38], failing to deliver fruit to the owner [12.1-12], and destined to be destroyed [12.9, 40])?

40. It is less likely that Mic. 7.1 stands in the background, but the suggestion is not impossible. Cf. J.N. Birdsall, 'The Withering of the Fig Tree' (1962), p. 191.

41. It might be thought that Mark intends the fig tree and the vineyard to be viewed as a matching pair since fruit could be obtained from neither. However, an unproductive fig tree and a productive vineyard are not very similar. A better comparison is between the fig tree and the vineyard *tenants*. A fig tree investing all its energies into leaf production with no fruit to deliver to the one seeking is a better parallel to a group of gardeners investing all their energies in their vineyard but yielding none of its produce to the owner. Both are excellent symbols of an official hierarchy maintaining a splendid religious system but usurping for personal gain everything that rightfully belonged to God.

42. W. Cotter's suggestion is attractive. She suggests that the phrase in question is a slightly misplaced explanatory clause (like 'for it was very great' [ἦν γὰρ μέγας σφόδρα] in 16.4) explaining not why there was no fruit, but why Jesus did not really think there would be ('For It Was Not the Season for Figs' [1986], pp. 62-66). Such an explanation still leaves room for Mark to intend more for the phrase in terms of the *application* of the event at a symbolic level.

In some ways at least the fig tree cursing is most emphatically 'non-eschatological'. Those who argue that Jesus cursed the fig tree because it failed to produce the 'wonder-crops' that haggadists expected in the eschatological age, would do well to apply their theory to a reconstructed historical event behind (and different from) Mark's version of it. The theory is impossible on the level of Mark's meaning. If, as one can safely assume, Mark was not himself enjoying the super-productivity some thought they had a right to expect in the coming age, then clearly he does not believe that Jesus' life, his passion, his resurrection, the advent of the Spirit or anything else prior to Mark's day, inaugurated the final age, *in that sense*. Mark cannot possibly believe that Jesus cursed the fig tree because it did not oblige him out of season with crops utterly inappropriate for the natural seasons, but appropriate for the eschatological age. Cf. J.D.M. Derrett, 'Figtrees in the New Testament' (1973), p. 254; R.H. Hiers, 'Not the Season for Figs' (1968), p. 395.

43. J.D. Crossan is not persuasive when he argues that Mark has redacted the material to draw attention away from, rather than in the direction of, judgment. Cf. 'Redaction and Citation in Mark 11.9-10 and 11.17' (1972).

44. When Jesus 'cleansed all foods' (καθαρίζων πάντα τὰ βρώματα [7.19]), he did so by drawing attention away from visible external cultic concerns and toward the inner recesses of the heart. The external boundary lines are not re-drawn, they are erased. One need make no distinction in the matter of externals as long as the springs of one's thoughts and actions are pure. The Isaiah passage quoted in Mark 11.17 has precisely the same focus. No longer must the foreigner be kept separate. No longer will the eunuch be considered [note well] 'a dry tree' (Isa. 56.3). They will no longer be excluded from holy places if they 'keep justice and do righteousness' (Isa. 56.1). For his time, Isaiah is radical in his re-definition of such righteousness (Isa. 56.4, 6). Mark is more radical still, drawing attention away from temple and cult altogether. In a sense the temple is disqualified. In another sense 'all places are declared clean'.

45. There are many studies of the 'cleansing' which over-focus on the Gentile question. Cf. e.g., G.H. Boobyer, 'Galilee and Galileans in St. Mark's Gospel' (1953), p. 342; F. Hahn, *Mission in the New Testament.* (1965), p. 115; E. Lohmeyer, *Lord of the Temple* (1962), p. 39; R.H. Lightfoot, *The Gospel Message of St. Mark* (1950), pp. 63f.

46. *Clumsy Construction in Mark's Gospel* (1980), p. 67.

47. Cf. W.R. Telford, *The Barren Temple and the Withered Tree* (1980), p. 260.

48. Telford notes that Jesus' call for faith (11.23) might almost be an equivalent to a call for understanding. Given the way 'faith' functions in Mark's Gospel, the suggestion is not impossible. *Ibid.* p. 82.

49. Cf. R.A. Culpepper, 'The Passion and Resurrection in Mark' (1978), p. 591. Various scholars have attempted to make a distinction between the two terms in Markan usage. The variation is probably not significant.

50. If the prophecy is considered substantially true, then perhaps there is a special nuance in the words '*and even so*' (καὶ οὐδὲ οὕτως) their testimony did not agree' (14.59). The verse would mean, 'Even when they got it right, they got it wrong!'

51. Despite the contrary claim by A. Ambrozic (*The Hidden Kingdom* [1972], p. 38), irony is very characteristic of Mark, especially in Mark 11-16. J.R. Donahue and D. Senior have demonstrated particular adeptness in identifying and evaluating it.

52. Cf. R.J. McKelvey, *The New Temple* (1968), pp. 68-71.

53. In 12.1-12, both the son and the stone are passive. It is the vineyard owner who acts in judgment, and it is 'the Lord' who raises up the rejected stone. The passivity of Jesus in relation to the temple's destruction and rebuilding is highlighted at the death scene when Jesus refuses to act on his own behalf (15.29f.).

54. *Messiah and Temple* (1977), pp. 55-57, 122-24; cf. also D. Senior, *The Passion of Jesus in the Gospel of Mark* (1984), p. 91.
55. *The New Temple* (1968), p. 182.
56. Cf. G. Biguzzi, 'Mc. 14, 58: un tempio ἀχειροποίητος' (1978), pp. 235f.
57. Cole, Chronis and Kazmierski defend the former; Donahue, Juel and Pesch the latter. There are still a few scholars who hold that Mark 16.7 is a direct reference to the Parousia and some of these imagine that the rebuilding of the temple will take place when the Son of Man gathers his elect (13.27). Because we will argue against the foundation of this view, we will not spend time dealing with its implications.
58. Cf. D. Juel, *Messiah and Temple* (1977), pp. 204ff.
59. D.Senior, *The Passion of Jesus in the Gospel of Mark* (1984), p. 92.
60. *Ibid.*, p. 46.
61. It is surprising that those who have examined Mark's references to women have not made more of these pericopes, especially of the way Mark contrasts the scribes robbing widows with the widow giving all, and the way he contrasts the woman who was willing to give a fortune to honour Jesus with Judas who was willing to betray him for (presumably) much less. Cf. E.S. Malbon, 'Fallible Followers: Women and Men in the Gospel of Mark' (1983), p. 28ff.
62. Cf. A. Stock, *Call to Discipleship* (1982), p. 180. The argument is that the woman who gave 'all her livelihood/life' (ὅλον τὸν βίον αὐτῆς 12.44) foreshadows Jesus who gave his life, and the woman who anointed for burial is brought into relation with the good news of the resurrection.
63. It may also be intended as a comment on the dual functions of Christian piety, honouring God and helping the poor. Cf. T.A. Burkill, 'St. Mark's Philosophy of the Passion' (1958), p. 253.
64. J.R. Donahue, *Are You the Christ?* (1973), p. 116.
65. Only a few have noted that if the main point is a contrast with the scribes, then we have here further indication that Mark does not imagine Jesus replacing Jews with Gentiles, but rather giving Israel new leaders to replace the corrupt old leaders. Cf. W. Harrington, *Mark.* (1979), p. 195.
66. R. Schnackenburg, *The Gospel According to St. Mark, II* (1971), pp. 89f.
67. Cf. e.g., P.J. Achtemeier, *Mark* (1975), p. 102.
68. Cf. e.g., W. Lane, *The Gospel According to Mark* (1974), p. 442.
69. 'Jesus as the Parable of God in the Gospel of Mark' (1978), p. 374.
70. 'Double-entendre in Mark XIII 9' (1968), p. 163.
71. 'Eschatology in Mark's Gospel' (1969), p. 115.
72. *The Gospel of St. Mark* (1883), p. 202. P.S. Minear comments: 'Having deflated the value of the currency, Jesus turned to the deflation of the most sacred building itself. . . . ' (*The Gospel According to Mark* [1962], p. 115).
73. 'The Widow's Mites' (1982), p. 262.

74. Preying on widows is, of course, proverbially associated with those who abuse power (cf. Isa. 10.1f.). The fact that the 'purification' predicted by Malachi specifically indicated that widow-oppressors (Mal. 3.5) would be judged seems to argue that a concern for the poor is more pervasive here than is often noted. 'Robbing God' is the topic to which Malachi turns (3.8ff.) immediately after the mention of widow oppressing! The temple's 'purification' and the widow-oppressors' judgment are conveniently combined in a single act of God.

75. Mark 11.15 may be an attempt to highlight oppression against the poor. Those selling doves (the offering of the poor) are given special mention. (Cf. W. Swartley, *Mark: The Way for all Nations* [1981], p. 170).

76. 'Das Liebeswerk rangiert vor dem Almosen, und Jesus—als der Armste—vor den Armen' (R. Pesch, *Das Markusevangelium, II* [1977], p. 333).

77. D. Senior rightly notes that 'This sense of proportion—the love command as more fundamental than ritual—echoes the sabbath conflicts of 1.23-28 and 3.1-6 and is the key to Mark's critique of the temple. . . . ' (*The Passion of Jesus in the Gospel of Mark* [1984], pp. 26f).

78. Cf. H.B. Swete, *The Gospel According to St. Mark* (1927), pp. 309, 313.

79. Walter Wessel contends that Mark must have regarded this as a supernatural act, but does not assign any theological significance to it; cf. 'Mark' (1984), p. 783.

80. Frequently interpreters appear to be selecting one of these, but a closer inspection shows they really (perhaps unwittingly) include two or three more as explicit or implicit implications of the one they selected.

81. Cf. J.R. Michaels, 'The Centurion's Confession and the Spear Thrust' (1967), pp. 107f.

82. Cf. R.H. Lightfoot, *The Gospel Message of St. Mark* (1950), pp. 55f.; for a contrary view see H.C. Kee, *Jesus in History* (1977), p. 151.

83. H.L. Chronis, 'The Torn Veil' (1982), p. 108.

84. We should take this as an ablative of separation, not a genitive of place.

85. Cf. P. Carrington, *According to Mark* (1960), p. 331.

86. Ezekiel's vision of the re-built temple is accompanied with the words, 'Son of man, look with your eyes and hear with your ears and pay attention to everything I am going to show you' (Ezek. 40.4).

87. Cf. J. Drury, 'The Sower, the Vineyard, and the Place of Allegory in the Interpretation of Mark's Parables' (1973).

Notes to Chapter 6

1. L. Gaston, *No Stone on Another* (1970), p. 469.
2. See especially arguments by B.M.F. van Iersel, in 'The gospel

according to St. Mark—written for a persecuted community?' (1980), pp. 20ff.; cf. also N. Perrin, *What is Redaction Criticism?* (1970), p. 52; P.S. Minear, *The Gospel According to Mark* (1962), pp. 7-19.

3. Cf. J.D. McCaughey, 'Three "Persecution Documents" of the New Testament' (1969), p. 40.

4. Cf. G.G. Bilezikian, *The Liberated Gospel* (1977), p. 125; E.S. Malbon, 'Galilee and Jerusalem' (1982), p. 248.

5. The interpretation of Mark 16.7f. which we will adopt is vigorously rejected by a group of literary-critics (mostly American) who argue that the disciples never heard the post-resurrection call to Galilee, and never went. Cf. W.H. Kelber, *The Kingdom in Mark* (1974), p. 146.

6. 'The Church has linked the suffering of a disciple with the passion of Jesus by the conception of discipleship in the sense of walking behind Jesus' (E. Schweizer, *Lordship and Discipleship* [1960], p. 77).

7. 'As we shall see, the scope of the journey is far wider than the few kilometers from Galilee to Jerusalem. Mark will use the journey as a basic theological symbol' (D. Senior, *The Passion of Jesus in the Gospel of Mark* [1984], p. 30).

8. Cf. D.C. Duling, 'Interpreting the Markan "Hodology"' (1974), p. 8.

9. To identify precisely what is intended by discipleship 'cross-carrying' (8.34), either in the words of Jesus, in the understanding of the tradition, or in the context of Mark's Gospel, is notoriously difficult. Taking one's stand alongside Jesus, and therefore being rejected with him and suffering with him, is certainly implied, as the immediate context (8.31-37) makes clear enough. Self-sacrifice in a more general sense is also obviously implied. It is highly unlikely that any Christian in the first century imagined one could live a life of Christian discipleship and avoid persecution entirely. For a summary of views on the connotations of 'cross-bearing', see M.P. Green, 'The Meaning of Cross-Bearing' (1983), pp. 118-20.

10. B. Englezakis, 'Markan Parable: More than Word Modality' (1974), p. 349.

11. 'The Heart of the Gospel of Mark' (1956), p. 79.

12. J. Marcus, following H. Räisänen (*Parabeltheorie* 119) reaches the same conclusion and correlates it with a suggested reconstruction of the social situation of Mark's community. 'The opposition that the Marcan community is experiencing is no cause either for alarm or for questioning the presence of the kingdom. It rather means that God's purpose is working itself out in a mysterious manner that involves triumph in apparent defeat' ('Mark 4.10-12 and Marcan Epistemology' [1984], p. 573).

13. When demonic opposition first rises up against Jesus and calls forth Jesus' authoritative rebuke (1.23-25), immediately we read that his fame spreads far and wide (1.27f.). When the teachers of the law first take issue with Jesus (2.6f.), Jesus' fame attracts great multitudes (2.12f.) and he immediately has great success with precisely those people he came to call

(2.14-17). When the death plot is first mentioned (3.6), Jesus finds himself surrounded by people from virtually every region in Palestine (3.6f.). When the legal teachers attempt to draw the battle lines (3.22ff.) and the family of Jesus attempts to restrict his movement (3.21, 31), we immediately read of some of the largest crowds to date (4.1), the secrecy (4.10-12) and unstoppability (esp. 4.30-32) of the kingdom's advance, and of Jesus' first move into Gentile territory (4.35-5.1). (Cf. D. Senior, 'The Struggle to be Universal' [1984], p. 79, and W.H. Kelber, *The Kingdom in Mark* [1974], pp. 48ff.). When his home townspeople reject him (6.1-6), he initiates an expanded ministry through the twelve (6.7). When the Pharisees again come on the attack (7.1f.), he opens the door theologically (7.17-23) and then moves out geographically (7.24) into his closest contact with Gentiles (7.24-8.10).

14. F. Hahn rightly notes the parallelism between 14.8f. and 15.37-39. 'The announcement of Jesus' death and the proclamation of the gospel in the whole world belong indissolubly together' (*Mission in the New Testament* [1965], p. 118).

15. H.C. Kee, *Jesus in History*, p. 158.

16. For a contrary view see J.C. Meagher, *Clumsy Construction in Mark's Gospel* (1980), p. 43.

17. This sets the stage for the highly ironic scene at the cross where Jesus is misunderstood as calling for Elijah to take him down. The fact is that Elijah does not fail to aid Jesus in his time of need. He has done precisely that by preceding him, as it was necessary for him to do, in the 'way' they were both to travel. See the masterful article by K.Brower outlining the dramatic irony Mark incorporates in his reporting of the relationship between John/Elijah and the death of Jesus; 'In Mark's view, the Day of the Lord has arrived in the cross of Jesus and Elijah's function in the messianic drama has been completed by definition. Just as Jesus has reversed popular expectation and has been a suffering messiah, so the Baptist has overturned popular legend about Elijah and has been a suffering figure' ('Elijah in the Markan Passion Narrative' [1983], p. 95).

18. Cf. A. Stock, *Call to Discipleship* (1982), p. 198; F. Matera, *The Kingship of Jesus* (1982), pp. 98f.; A. Farrer, *St Matthew and St Mark* (1954), pp. 5f., 14; W.J. Bennett, 'The Herodians of Mark's Gospel' (1975), pp. 12f.; D. Losada, 'La muerte de Juan el Bautista' (1977), p. 154; C. Wolff, 'Zur Bedeutung Johannes des Täufers im Markusevangelium' (1977), p. 863.

19. Cf. E. Schweizer, *The Good News According to Mark* (1970), p. 44.

20. C.E.B. Cranfield, *The Gospel According to St. Mark* (1977), p. 62.

21. P.J. Achtemeier, 'Mark as Interpreter of the Jesus Traditions' (1978), p. 342.

22. U. Luz, 'The Secrecy Motif and the Marcan Christology' (1983), p. 84.

23. See M.D. Hooker, *The Message of Mark* (1983), pp. 78f. for a very

tentative acceptance of the suggestion that Mal. 3.1 in Mk. 1.2 is a deliberate linking of John/Elijah with the temple issue. Had she considered 'the way' as the road through suffering, it would seem that a more whole-hearted acceptance would have been quite consistent with her thesis, and especially with her study of *The Son of Man in Mark* (1967).

24. Is it Mark's clumsy way of making up for a deficiency when he finds himself speaking of John's resurrection (6.14) and suddenly remembers that the reader does not even know he has died? (Cf. E. Schweizer, *The Good News According to Mark* [1970], p. 45). Is it a convenient time-filler to give the impression of time lapse from the disciples' departure on their mission assignment until their return? (Cf. V. Taylor, *The Gospel According to St. Mark* [1953], p. 307). Is it a hint that when the disciples (or the readers) go out on mission, they can expect no better treatment than John received? (Cf. D. Senior, *The Passion of Jesus in the Gospel of Mark* [1984], p. 19).

25. Cf. e.g., G.G. Bilezikian, *The Liberated Gospel* (1977), p. 58; cf. also comment by E. Stegemann in W. Schottroff, and W. Stegemann, eds *God of the Lowly* (1984), p. 105.

26. Ironically even John's executioner believes in the ultimate triumph of the man he beheads (6.16)! (D. Senior, *The Passion of Jesus in the Gospel of Mark* [1984], p. 19).

27. Is not 13.26f. a silver lining appearing beyond the persecution clouds of Mark 13?

28. Cf. H.E. Tödt, *The Son of Man in the Synoptic Tradition* (1965), p. 248.

29. Cf. 'The Social World of Mark's Gospel' (1978), pp. 56f.

30. Cf. W. Swartley, *Mark: the Way for All Nations* (1981), p. 112.

31. Cf. e.g., S.G.F. Brandon, *The Fall of Jerusalem and the Christian Church* (1951), p. 197; J.B. Tyson, 'The Blindness of the Disciples in Mark' (1961), p. 268; S. Sandmel, 'Prolegomena to a Commentary on Mark' (1963), pp. 294-300; T.J. Weeden, *Mark—Traditions in Conflict* (1971), p. 164; J.D. Crossan, 'Mark and the Relatives of Jesus' (1973), p. 111; W.H. Kelber, *The Kingdom in Mark* (1974), p. 82; E. Trocmé, *The Formation of the Gospel According to Mark* (1975), p. 136.

32. A useful article summarizing various views in F.J. Moloney, 'The Vocation of the Disciples in the Gospel of Mark' (1981), pp. 487-516.

33. W.H. Kelber provides a useful list of texts in which this is done, cf. 'Conclusion: From Passion Narrative to Gospel' (1976), p. 156.

34. R.P. Meye, *Jesus and the Twelve* (1968), p. 224.

35. J. Lambrecht appeals to this 'argument by default' (cf. 'The Relatives of Jesus in Mark' (1974), p. 255).

36. T.J. Weeden, *Mark—Traditions in Conflict* (1971), p. 50.

37. Cf. C. Focant, 'L'incompréhension des disciples dans le deuxième évangile' (1975), pp. 161f., 184f.

38. D.O. Via, *Kerygma and Comedy in the New Testament* (1975), p. 75.

39. H.-J. Klauck has argued that when the various narrative levels are carefully distinguished, the polemical approach to the disciples is exposed as untenable ('Die erzählerische Rolle der Jünger im Markusevangelium' [1977], p. 26). Cf. also N.R. Petersen's arguments that if the disciples are really repudiated and rendered ultimately unreliable, then logical consistency demands that both Jesus and the narrator must be as well ('When is the End not the End?' [1980], pp. 161f.).

40. N.R. Petersen, *Literary Criticism for New Testament Critics* (1978), pp. 79f.; A. Stock, *Call to Discipleship* (1982), p. 204.

41. S. Sandmel is wrong when he compares the disciples with the Pharisees, Sadducees and chief priests and concludes: 'The disciples are worse, for they are the epitome of disloyalty' ('Prolegomena to a Commentary on Mark' [1963], p. 298).

42. When the disciples sleep in the garden, they do so out of weakness, not indifference. When they strike out with swords in the garden, they are misguided, not wrongly aligned. When they flee, they do so out of cowardice, not changed allegiances. When Peter denies Jesus, he is not choosing to be detached from Jesus, he is telling lies in an attempt to hide a real and ongoing allegiance to him.

43. 'The historical reconstruction of early Christianity which some of these essays imply seems to hang in mid-air' (L.E. Keck, 'Mark and the Passion' [1977], p. 434).

44. Cf. esp E. Best, 'Peter in the Gospel According to Mark' (1978), p. 558.

45. Cf. esp. Mark 16.7 where the separate mention of Peter can hardly be an indication that the speaker no longer includes him under the designation 'his disciples' (οἱ μαθηταὶ αὐτοῦ). More likely it 'specifies him among the disciples as the one whose faith, having been most shaken, needs most the restoring effect of this announcement' (E.P. Gould, *A Critical and Exegetical Commentary on the Gospel According to St. Mark* [1896], p. 300).

46. Cf. e.g., T.A. Burkill, *Mysterious Revelation* (1963), pp. 186f.; E. Schweizer, 'Towards a Christology of Mark?' (1977), p. 33; W. Wrede, *The Messianic Secret* (1971), p. 235.

47. It is amazing that Kelber can countenance a reversal of positions for Joseph of Arimathea who voted against Jesus and for the Centurion who executed him, but not for the disciples who have been told they will be made into fishers of men! Cf. W.H. Kelber, 'Conclusion: From Passion Narrative to Gospel' (1976), p. 175.

48. We think the evidence is incontrovertible that Mark has far more than historical concerns in mind in portraying the disciples. One does not need to over-allegorize the story to see motifs and emphases that are aimed directly at the readers of the Gospel for warning and instruction. Mark is no trailblazer if he uses this methodology, for we can see in the desert community in Deuteronomy features of seventh century Israel (A.M. Ambrozic, *The*

Hidden Kingdom [1972], p. 30) and according to Paul, even the lineaments of the first century church (1 Cor. 10.11).

49. D.J. Hawkin, 'The Incomprehension of the Disciples in the Marcan Redaction' (1972), p. 500.

50. W.R. Farmer in *The Last Twelve Verses of Mark* (1974), presented all the plausible arguments for the authenticity of 16.9-20, and even he considered the outcome inconclusive. The fact that his study did not persuade many is probably an indication that we can safely set the longer ending aside as spurious.

51. The arguments by A.E. Haefner ('The Bridge Between Mark and Acts' [1958]) and E. Linnemann ('Der [wiedergefundene] Markusschluβ' [1969] have not stood the test of scholarship any better than Farmer's.

52. Cf. R.R. Ottley, '*ephobounto gar* Mark xvi 8' (1926); P.W. van der Horst, 'Can a Book End With *GAR?*' (1972); F.C. Synge, 'Mark 16.1-8' (1975); T.E. Boomershine and G.L. Bartholomew, 'The Narrative Technique of Mark 16.8' (1981).

53. F. Kermode is correct about the present ending (assuming it was the intended one): 'The conclusion is either intolerably clumsy; or it is incredibly subtle' (*The Genesis of Secrecy* [1979], p. 609). We are given a fair choice: Mark is a very subtle writer.

54. V. Taylor, R. Bultmann and a whole host of other scholars notwithstanding, we believe that Mark 16.8 makes a very appropriate narrative ending to the kind of book Mark has written.

55. The fact that the burden of proof is now clearly on those who would insist a lost ending needs to be postulated has turned the tide of opinion in the direction we are advocating. Already in 1963, W.G. Kümmel could say that 'scholarship in increasing measure is inclining toward the view that Mark reached his intended end with 16.8'. Today that conclusion is very widely accepted indeed. For Kümmel quotation, cf. Evans, *Resurrection and the New Testament* (1970), p. 72. Cf. pp. 70-81 for a broad survey of the various views advocated.

56. Cf. e.g., G. Hebert, 'The Resurrection-Narrative in St. Mark's Gospel' (1962), pp. 66-73; M.D. Goulder, 'The Empty Tomb' (1976), pp. 206-14. If Mark meant what Goulder says he meant, the women's fear and silence would be not only understandable but appropriate!

57. Cf. C.F. Evans, 'I Will Go Before You Into Galilee' (1954), p. 13. Sodom and Gomorrah (cf. Isa. 1.9f.) and Shiloh (cf. Jer. 26.6-9) are examples that come immediately to mind.

58. Cf. C.E.B. Cranfield, *The Gospel According to St. Mark* (1977), p. 469.

59. The celebrated defenders of the Galilee-Parousia link are Loymeyer, Lightfoot (in his earlier material), Marxsen and Kelber, though there have also been others (F.C. Grant, N. Perrin, etc.).

60. The structural similarity between 14.27-29 and 16.6f. strongly suggests

that 14.28 and 16.7 are not alien intrusions into an otherwise coherent narrative. Note the parallelism:

	Promise		Fulfilment
14.27	'I will smite the Shepherd'	16.6	'Jesus of Nazareth who was crucified'
14.28	'after I have risen'	16.6	'he is risen'
14.28	'I will go before you into Galilee'	16.7	'he goes before you into Galilee'
14.29	Special reference to Peter's anticipated failure.	16.7	Special reference to Peter, who failed.

(Cf. W.L. Lane, 'From Historian to Theologian' [1978], p. 610).

61. Cf. R.H. Smith, 'New and Old in Mark 16.1-8' (1972), p. 524.

62. H.-D. Knigge, 'The Meaning of Mark' (1968), p. 65f.

63. W.L. Lane, 'From Historian to Theologian' (1978), p. 609.

64. For additional counter-arguments to the theory, see E. Schweizer, 'Eschatology in Mark's Gospel' (1969), pp. 114-18.

65. One of the best current defenders of the view is D. Senior; cf. 'The Struggle to be Universal' (1984), p. 78; *The Passion of Jesus in the Gospel of Mark* (1984). While Senior defends the 'mission' interpretation, almost all his arguments seem logically to entail a different conclusion—the one we shall defend.

66. Cf. W. Au, 'Discipleship in Mark' (1973), pp. 1249-51, for an analysis of how the two parallel requirements influence the telling of various stories in Mark.

67. Cf. J.-M. van Cangh, 'La Galilée dans l'évangile de Marc' (1972), pp. 74ff.

68. Cf. C.F. Evans, 'I Will Go Before You Into Galilee' (1954), p. 13. Frequently 'Galilee of the Gentiles' is substituted for 'Galilee' without any attempt at defending the substitution.

69. *Mark: The Gospel as Story* (1983), pp. 132f.

70. Cf. e.g., G. Hebert, 'The Resurrection-Narrative in St. Mark's Gospel' (1962), p. 71; R.P. Meye, *Jesus and the Twelve* (1968), pp. 80-87; R.C. Tannehill, 'The Disciples in Mark' (1977), p. 403f.; J. Ernst, *Das Evangelium nach Markus* (1981), p. 489; M.D. Hooker, *The Message of Mark* (1983), p. 120.

71. Tannehill, *Ibid.*, pp. 403ff.

72. It is probable that 'he is going ahead' (προάγει) in 16.7 means Jesus will get to Galilee first, not that he will lead them on the road to Galilee. B.M.F. van Iersel's tentative suggestion that 16.7 means Jesus will lead the disciples around in Galilee, rather than precede them to Galilee ('"To Galilee" or "in Galilee" in Mark 14,28 and 16,7?' [1982]), is probably not to be accepted.

73. It is quite impossible to hold simultaneously that the discipleship-journey section (8.27-10.45) is a paradigm for discipleship in the post-

resurrection situation and that mission is virtually the only concern of the disciples after the resurrection. The mission question is not dominant in 8.27–10.45 at all.

74. *The Message of Mark* (1983), p. 120.

75. Cf. e.g., D. Senior, *The Passion of Jesus in the Gospel of Mark* (1984), p. 151. He speaks as though the disciples have, by the time of 16.7, 'pass[ed] through the experience of the passion'. That is precisely what they have *not* done.

76. In addition to Best and Hooker (quoted above), several scholars have interpreted the 'Galilee symbolism' in ways similar to our suggestion, or have at least defended positions which seem to point in the direction indicated above. Cf. S. Freyne, 'At Cross Purposes: Jesus and the Disciples in Mark' (1982), p. 339; E.L. Schnellbächer, 'The Temple as Focus of Mark's Theology' (1983), p. 96; B.M.F. van Iersel, 'Locality, Structure, and Meaning in Mark' (1983), p. 53; A. Stock, 'Hinge Transitions in Mark's Gospel' (1985), p. 27.

77. 'By placing all this material in the setting of a journey, Mark creates a profound metaphor for the meaning of Christian discipleship. Following Jesus, then and now, means leaving behind Galilee and setting out for Jerusalem—a painful but life-giving process of putting aside our blindness and experiencing a gradual conversion based on the gospel of Jesus' (D. Senior, 'The Gospel of Mark' [1979], p. 2101 [sic]).

78. F.F. Bruce, 'The Book of Zechariah and the Passion Narrative' (1961), p. 345.

79. W.M. Swartley insists on the importance of retaining this literal level even while interpreting the theology Mark implies by the symbolic use of the journey motif. Cf. *Mark: The Way for All Nations* (1981), p. 212, and especially his unpublished dissertation, *A Study in Markan Structure* (1973), p. 229.

80. P.O.G. White, 'The Resurrection and the Second Coming of Jesus in Mark' (1973), p. 616, and more recently A. Lindemann, 'Die Osterbotschaft des Markus (1980), p. 317.

81. M.D. Goulder, 'The Empty Tomb' (1976), pp. 206-14.

82. D. Catchpole uses this line of argument, comparing 16.8 with 1.44, and insisting that a general instruction to keep silence does not prevent disclosure to a specified individual; cf. 'The Fearful Silence of the Women at the Tomb' (1977), p. 6; cf. also C.F.D. Moule, 'St. Mark XVI.8 Once More' (1956), pp. 58f.

83. F.C. Synge, 'Mark 16.1-8' (1975), p. 73.

84. E.A. LaVerdiere, 'The End, A Beginning' (1984), p. 488.

85. In Mark's Gospel fear is always reprehensible, even when it is a response to the divine power in Jesus. It signifies 'defective faith and understanding'. Cf. A.M. Ambrozic, *The Hidden Kingdom* (1972), p. 65. To say that 'for they were afraid' (ἐφοβοῦντο γάρ) is an appropriate narrative

ending to the Gospel is not the same thing as to say that fear is an appropriate response to the resurrection message. Not all commentators have made the distinction carefully. Cf. W.L. Lane, *The Gospel According to Mark* (1974), pp. 591f.

86. R.H. Lightfoot, *The Gospel Message of St. Mark* (1950), pp. 96f. Cf. also E. Schweizer, *The Good News According to Mark* (1970), p. 373.

87. *Literary Criticism for New Testament Critics* (1978), p. 78.

88. R.A. Culpepper takes this approach, interpreting 16.8 as a direct appeal to the readers: 'The reader is shocked; how could the women who had witnessed the death of Jesus (15.40) and who could testify to the kernel of the kerygma, 'He is risen' (16.6), go and not tell anyone? Mark was a skilful writer. Perhaps shock and surprise were the reaction he intended for the church to have, for now it knew everything the women knew. So, the question comes home to haunt those who hear Mark's Gospel. How *could* they, how can *we*, hear these words, go, and tell no one?' [emphasis his] ('The Passion and Resurrection in Mark' [1978], p. 597). Similarly, T.E. Boomershine argues that Mark is appealing to his reader to condemn the women's actions (cf. 'Mark 16.8 and the Apostolic Commission' [1981], p. 229).

89. M.D. Hooker makes the point well: 'And how typical of the Markan Jesus that message is: "Go and you will see him". Not "You will see him, and then you must go". The message *demands* a response. "Stretch out your hand", says Jesus to the man with a shrivelled hand. How *can* he stretch out a hand which is shrivelled? But he does. "Go", runs the message to the disciples—to men paralyzed with fear; it is only as they go that they will see him' (*The Message of Mark* [1983], p. 119).

90. A. Stock in his analysis of the Bartimaeus story, makes the suggestion, 'Whoever does not see Jesus, cannot follow him, and whoever does not follow him, cannot see him (16.7). This is one of the paradoxes of Mark' ('Hinge Transitions in Mark's Gospel' [1985], p. 30). Recall also the point we sought to demonstrate in Chapter 2: 'Adequate proofs do not lead to insight or obedience: Obedience, however, leads to insight and adequate bases for believing' (cf. pp. 40ff.).

91. Cf. L.A. Whiston, *Through Suffering to Victory* (1976), p. 157.

92. Existentialist interpretations misconstrue this in their insistence that faith and obedience are induced by the mere hearing of the resurrection message. Cf., A. Lindemann, 'Die Osterbotschaft des Markus' (1980), p. 317.

93. Mark obviously believed that both finally obeyed. The implied future story guarantees the disciples were renewed. Simple logic requires that the women finally told. Mark was not so careless as to imagine that their silence was perpetual. Somehow the story got out; they must eventually have reported it.

94. It is of course widely held that since the message was never delivered

through the women, the disciples never got the signal to go. This is to ignore completely 14.28 in which the invitation is given even before the death of Jesus and final defection of the disciples. They know in advance that neither of those events will cancel the promise. Indeed 'Jesus' prediction about meeting his disciples in Galilee was made with full foreknowledge of the Twelve's imminent defection' (A. Stock, *Call to Discipleship* [1982], p. 204). If they are not on their way to Galilee, they cannot lay all the blame on the women. They have been invited.

95. Cf. N.R. Petersen, 'When is the End not the End?' (1980), p. 153. 'The end of the text is not the end of the work when the narrator leaves unfinished business for the reader to complete, thoughtfully and imaginatively, not textually'. We would add 'volitionally and existentially'. Mark's concern is to produce disciples, not graduates in theology. Cf. also B.M.F. van Iersel, 'Locality, Structure, and Meaning in Mark' (1983), p. 53.

96. W. Kelber notes that 'The synchronization of John's death with the disciples' mission becomes intelligible as an analogy to Jesus' death and the beginnings of the apostolic mission. As John's death coincided with the sending out of the disciples-apostles, so will Jesus' death usher in the mission' (*Mark's Story of Jesus* [1979], p. 34). The analogy is even clearer in 1.14 where John's 'handing over' is coincided with the beginning of Jesus' proclamation.

97. M.D. Hooker makes the point that Mark's use of Son of Man strongly suggests the theological point made in 4 Maccabees that the suffering of the saints of God has redemptive significance. While she hesitates to broaden the application beyond the Son of Man as a single individual Jesus (in Mark's usage), there might well be a limited application of this also for the Baptist and the disciples, at least in so far as God transmutes their 'defeat' into ultimate victory and opportunity for others. Scholars debate whether or not Mark 10.45 points to suffering that has redemptive value. If it does, would it not follow that so also does the disciples' suffering? The verse implies Jesus is the model servant. The 'cup' that Jesus' followers are called to drink may not quite be the cup of God's wrath (14.36) or the eucharistic cup of salvation (14.23f.) (cf. E. Best, *The Temptation and the Passion* [1965], p. 156) but it is Jesus' cup nevertheless. To identify 10.39 too closely with the celebration of the eucharist is to read too little into it. Post-resurrection disciples were drinking the cup not only when they identified with Christ's suffering, and not only when they committed themselves to die with him. They drank the cup most fully when they were being impaled on crosses, lashed with the flagellum, or thrown to the lions.

98. It would not be amiss to suggest that in Mark's prologue John is pictured preparing 'the way' for Jesus. In Mark's narrative, Jesus is pictured preparing 'the way' for the apostles. In the implied future of Mark's story (as indicated by Mark 13), i.e., up to the time of Mark's writing, the apostles are preparing 'the way' for those to whom Mark writes, and in the genuine

future for Mark, the readers of the Gospel are to be preparing 'the way' for those still to come, until the race is finished when the Son of Man appears.

99. Cf. C.R. Kazmierski, *Jesus, the Son of God* (1979), pp. 22f.; R.H. Lightfoot, *The Gospel Message of St. Mark* (1950), p. 52; B.M.F. van Iersel, 'The gospel according to St. Mark—written for a persecuted community?' (1980), p. 33.

100. L. Hartman, citing Cullmann, cautions against inadvertent incorporation of a 'cyclical view of history' into the 'teleological' Biblical view (*Prophecy Interpreted* [1968], p. 24).

101. See the argument by B.M.F. van Iersel that both the desert and the tomb in their own way are the beginning of the Gospel of Jesus Christ ('Locality, Structure, and Meaning in Mark' [1983], p. 52).

102. Cf. D. Ewert, *And Then Comes the End* (1980), p. 35.

103. M. Hengel, *Studies in the Gospel of Mark* (1985), p. 24. If D. Wenham is correct, Mark has deliberately reached into a mission discourse for the appropriate event concomitant to the suffering which post-resurrection disciples will experience (*The Rediscovery of Jesus' Eschatological Discourse* [1984], p. 219). It is even possible that this 'passion paradigm' sheds light on the significance of 15.34, the cry of dereliction. The question is 'why?'—λεμα;—εἰς τί;—'for what?' The answer is supplied in 15.39 ... for this! ... for its effect in bringing others into the kingdom!

Notes to Chapter 7

1. Cf. M. Hengel, 'Probleme des Markusevangeliums' (1983), p. 221.

2. J.L. Bailey, 'Perspectives on the Gospel of Mark' (1985), p. 24.

3. Cf. D.A. Carson, 'Hermeneutics: A brief assessment of some recent trends' (1980), p. 16.

4. E.S. Malbon rightly notes: 'The complex relations of characters within the text should prepare us for the complex relations of the text to realities beyond it. Perhaps Markan fallible followers have something to say to Markan historians and hermeneuts: interpretation, like followership, is never easy and never perfect, and never ending' ('Fallible Followers' (1983), pp. 47f.). We would add that 'interpretation' and 'followership' are not only alike, they are interrelated.

5. F. Kermode, *The Genesis of Secrecy* (1979), p. 59. It has been argued that the book of Daniel had a very significant influence on Mark (cf. studies by L. Hartman, *Prophecy Interpreted* [1966], and M.D. Hooker, *The Son of Man in Mark* [1967]). If it did, this fact may well be evidenced more by the theory of knowledge they share than by putative similarities in their dealings in apocalyptic portents. Daniel believed, 'He [God] gives wisdom to the wise and knowledge to the discerning. He reveals deep and hidden things' (Dan.

2.21f.). 'None of the wicked will understand, but those who are wise will understand' (Dan. 12.10). The Markan Jesus and Mark himself apparently share this view.

6. *Studies in the Gospel of Mark* (1985), p. 41. For an excellent treatment of the relationship between history and theology in Mark, see M.E. Glasswell, 'St. Mark's Attitude to the Relationship between History and the Gospel' (1980), pp. 115-27.

7. 'It is necessary to recognize that Mark was a Christian thinker who reflected theologically on the event of Jesus' life, death, and resurrection and on its significance for his own community' (W.L. Lane, 'From Historian to Theologian' [1978], p. 614); 'In the last resort this evangelist's purpose is theological, rather than merely historical; or, to put the matter in another way, the historical material is being used for a theological purpose' (R.H. Lightfoot, *The Gospel Message of St. Mark* [1950], p. 16).

8. Cf. J.R. Donahue, 'Jesus as the Parable of God in the Gospel of Mark' (1978), pp. 369-86; W.H. Kelber, *The Oral and the Written Gospel* (1983), pp. 120-29; J.G. Williams, *Gospel Against Parable* (1985), p. 211.

9. K. Snodgrass is not correct when he says 'In the New Testament the method of teaching in parables is confined to the earthly Jesus. The early church dropped the parabolic form and spoke openly and propositionally' (*The Parable of the Wicked Tenants* [1983], p. 108).

10. Cf. C.H. Giblin, *The Destruction of Jerusalem According to Luke's Gospel* (1985), p. 99: 'Historicity in the sense of facticity ... is not by any means at odds with symbolic representation, especially in the dimension of typological thinking'.

11. 'One could say that the mysteriousness comprises the two levels of meaning *plus* the hearer's failure to grasp the second level' (*The Mysterious Parable* [1977], p. 24).

12. Cf. E. Richard, 'Expressions of Double Meaning and their Function in the Gospel of John' (1985), pp. 97, 103f.

13. Cf. *The Destruction of Jerusalem According to Luke's Gospel* (1985), p. 106ff.

14. N.R. Petersen, '"Point of View" in Mark's Narrative' (1978), pp. 102, 118; D. Rhoads and D. Michie, *Mark as Story* (1982), p. 39.

15. Cf. G.R. Beasley-Murray, *A Commentary on Mark 13* (1957), p. 6. C.H. Turner suggested that there are as many as nineteen such instances of narrator 'asides' to the reader in Mark's Gospel. That is probably an over-estimation ('Markan Usage' [1925], pp. 145-56).

16. It would be our judgment that one of the reasons Mark so frequently leaves out chronological or topographical links between pericopes is that the real connection that concerns him resides in the fact that the two events are *recorded* next to each other. Cf. E.S. Malbon, 'Mythic Structure and the Meaning in Mark' (1980), p. 120; P.J. Achtemeier, 'Mark as Interpreter of the Jesus Traditions' (1978), p. 340.

17. 'Polyvalence' or 'amphibole' are strictly more accurate than 'ambiguity', though we shall not avoid the latter designation in our discussion since it is widely used. John's Gospel employs a similar technique, sometimes without explicitly indicating the same (e.g., the 'departure - return' language of chs. 13-17), sometimes reporting the errors of those who took a statement the wrong way (e.g., John 2.19-22). (Cf. A.L. Moore, *The Parousia in the New Testament* [1966], p. 161; C.L. Blomberg, 'New Horizons in Parable Research' [1982], p. 17.)

18. *Call to Discipleship* (1982), pp. 33, 44.

19. *The Gospel of Mark* (1976), pp. 22f.

20. *The Problem of History in Mark* (1957), p. 27.

21. 'Jesus' Audiences in the Gospels of St Mark and St Luke' (1963), pp. 144f. The theory is that Jesus never delivered the private explanations. The reference to privacy is a literary device Mark uses to introduce post-resurrection interpretations into the authentic tradition. Cf. also J. Lambrecht, *Parables of Jesus* (1978), p. 161.

22. Cf. A.M. Ambrozic, 'New Teaching With Power' (1975), p. 146.

23. Cf. L. Williamson, *Mark, Interpretation* (1983), p. 8; D.Juel, *Messiah and Temple* (1977), pp. 207ff.

24. *Mark: The Gospel as Story* (1983), p. 139. Cf. also M.E. Boring, 'The Christology of Mark' (1985), p. 141.

25. Cf. J.D. Crossan, *In Parables* (1973), pp. 49f.

26. 'Paul and Mark' (1955), pp. 89f.

27. Cf. W.H. Kelber, 'Conclusion: From Passion Narrative to Gospel' (1976), p. 179. ('A major requirement of any Gospel model is that it does justice to the text as an *undivided* whole and to all the elements which compose it'.)

28. Exact placement often depends on the relative weight that is placed on geographical, topographical, and chronological factors, on whether or not one accepts the idea of transitional or 'hinge' pericopes, and on whether one gives more weight to the narrative plot development or the theological messages accompanying it. (Cf. C.W. Hedrick, 'What is a Gospel?' [1983], pp. 255ff.)

29. Other events could also be added: the anticipated reporting of the transfiguration after the resurrection (9.9), the coming 'salting with fire' (9.49), the hundred fold return on things given up in this life (10.30), etc. Cf. D. Rhoads, and D. Michie, *Mark as Story* (1982), pp. 97f.

30. Cf. J. Delorme, 'Aspects doctrinaux du second Evangile' (1967), pp. 98f.

31. Cf. N.R. Petersen, 'When is the End not the End?' (1980), pp. 163f.

32. In the passion narrative we have a great deal of the sort of two-level communication that Donald Juel and Kent Brower analyse so brilliantly, in which both the 'inter-character' level and the 'narrator-addressee' level are designed to help the reader understand what is really going on *in the Jesus*

story. But we also have the sort of 'meta-message' communication we are discussing here, most notably in 15.27-39 and 16.7f.

33. *The Gospel Message of St. Mark* (1950), pp. 48-59.

34. We accept 1.15 rather than 1.13 as the dividing line, though perhaps to call 1.14f. as transitional would be the best solution of all. 'The close of the passage, vv. 14-15, requires rather more careful thought. On the one hand, these verses join what follows to what has gone before, thus functioning as a kind of hinge' (B.M.F. van Iersel, 'Theology and Detailed Exegesis' [1971], p. 82). The arguments for and against each option are readily available.

35. R.A. Guelich, '"The Beginning of the Gospel"' (1982), p. 5.

36. 'The idea that a word may mean two opposite things should not come amiss to a generation in which stoppage of work is called "industrial action"' (G.B. Caird, *The Language and Imagery of the Bible* [1980], p. 149).

37. R.A. Guelich does a superb job of recreating the first option in '"The Beginning of the Gospel"' (1982). His mistake is his assumption that the ambiguity of 1.1 is 'unfortunate' and that it is the exegete's task to eliminate it. W. Marxsen (cf. *Mark the Evangelist* [1969], pp. 149f.) and most others who downplay Mark's interest in the history of the earthly Jesus, do a superb job of recreating the second option. No one seems to have suggested that Mark intended it both ways, though some have suggested that Mark 1.1 (alone) is intentionally polyvalent.

38. If we can accept that Mark was deliberately ambiguous, we can examine the text for additional examples. Is it possible that the evangelist's adaptation of the Malachi quotation in 1.2 ('who will prepare *your* way') is designed to address the *reader*? The *reader's* way is prepared by God's messenger (Jesus), just as Jesus' way is prepared by God's messenger, John. The wilderness/tomb correspondence would suit this model perfectly.

39. It is interesting to note which disciples are recipients of the eschatological discourse. It is the *four* who were originally called to discipleship at the beginning of the Gospel (1.16-20), not the threesome (Peter, James and John) who are usually present at revelatory events (5.37; 9.2; 14.33). Is Mark 13.3 the evangelist's way of assuring the reader that these four men who originally left work and family at the beginning of the Gospel, who were there with Jesus when he began his ministry (1.29), are now there again when it is their turn to take up the baton? (Cf. L. Williamson, *Mark, Interpretation* [1983], p. 237). They have learned their lessons this time. They will now defend the truth, preach the Gospel and endure trials 'to the end'.

40. For example he uses the narrative flashback device to foster his 'passion paradigm' theme in 6.6b-30 (see Chapter 6), and he uses prediction to foster his 'data-significance' distinction in Mark 8.29-31 (see Chapter 3).

41. If an example is needed for clarification, let it be this: Mark 13.10 in its relation to 13.9, 11f. is such a perfect example of Mark's 'passion paradigm'

(see Chapter 6), that we should judge the link between Mark 13.10 and Mark 13.9, 11f. to be dictated primarily by that fact. (Cf. J. Dupont, 'La Persécution comme situation missionaire' [1977], p. 97). We should be reluctant to draw any chronological conclusions other than the one made explicit in 13.10 itself. World mission precedes the return of the Son of Man. We have no warrant for assuming that it necessarily precedes the crisis events in Judea which are reported thereafter (13.14ff.).

42. *Mark the Evangelist2* (1969), pp. 85, 198 n. 177.

43. Cf. E. Schweizer, 'Towards a Christology of Mark?' (1977), p. 39.

Notes to Chapter 8

1. Cf. P. Vielhauer, 'Erwägungen zur Christologie des Markusevangeliums' (1964), pp. 158ff.; W.R. Telford, *The Barren Temple and the Withered Tree* (1980), p. 257; cf. also J.D. Kingsbury, *The Christology of Mark's Gospel* (1983), pp. ix, x.

2. Cf. W.H. Kelber's cogent refutations of the strictly 'Christological' formulations of the secrecy motifs (*The Kingdom in Mark* [1974], pp. 5f.).

3. 'The kind of imagery used in the three parables is significant. Not that of marching armies, heroic deeds, and valorous exploits, but the humble, homely imagery of sowing, tilling, and harvest. The seed is scattered, falls, and lies on the ground, and meets a variety of fates. Instead of striking out, defiant and aggressive, the Kingdom of God appears lowly and vulnerable. The seed is subject to adversity, rejection, delays, and loss. The parables contain no promise of instant and universal triumph' (A. Stock, *Call to Discipleship* [1982], p. 94).

4. Many puzzles in Mark's text are solved when the link between kingdom secrecy and passion Christology is seen. It explains why Peter's messianic confession is muzzled in order that Jesus can teach about the necessity of the passion. It explains why the centurion's 'Son of God' confession is inseparably tied to Jesus' death. It explains why God's affirmation to Jesus of his divine Sonship is made as part of a statement that inaugurates him into his ministry and his passion. It explains why God's declaration of Jesus' divine Sonship to the disciples is made in a pericope bounded on both sides by teaching about the necessity of the passion for any who would 'see the kingdom', etc.

5. 'The parable gives some knowledge of the kingdom of God without completely unveiling it. The complete unveiling will come not so much by way of added revelation, as of added perception gained through faith, so that the hearers may comprehend what they have already heard' (R.E. Brown, 'The Semitic Background of the New Testament *Mysterion*' [1958], p. 431).

6. Cf. K. Haacker, 'Erwägungen zu Mc IV 11' (1972), p. 219.

7. Cf. H.C. Kee, *Community of the New Age* (1977), p. 172.

8. Cf. H.A. Kelly, 'The Devil in the Desert' (1964), p. 218.

9. Is this why it is important to Jesus that those who cast out demons are not divided among *themselves* (9.38-41)?

10. Cf. P. Patten, 'The Form and Function of Parable in Select Apocalyptic Literature' (1983), pp. 256f.

11. Cf. I.H. Marshall, 'Slippery Words: I. Eschatology' (1978), p. 266.

12. N.R. Petersen, *Literary Criticism for New Testament Critics* (1978), pp. 69f. A.M. Ambrozic's otherwise excellent study of Mark is marred when he reaches Mark 13 precisely because he fails to take this into account. He imagines that in order to understand the answer given by the Markan Jesus in Mark 13, we must understand the question that occasioned it. 'For this reason we must examine vs. 4 more closely' (*The Hidden Kingdom* [1972], p. 225). Are we following the most reliable guides when we ask the Markan disciples to help us understand what the Markan Jesus really meant?

13. 8.34-38 and 13.33-37 confirm that this is the Markan perspective, and together they make any 'post-millennialism' difficult to harmonize with the perspective of Mark.

14. It is not hard to hear echoes of the interpretation of the sower parable (4.14-20).

15. W.G. Kümmel, *Promise and Fulfilment* (1957), p. 98.

16. A.L. Moore says, 'Although the End event is to be of a different texture from the events prior to it, it will be a real presence of Christ in the context of history and the total cosmic structure—i.e., it is a further phase in salvation history' (*The Parousia in the New Testament* [1966], p. 91).

17. It may happen in the external world or in one's subjective experience (e.g., 2.8). It may be reported (or predicted) in literal or symbolic language. Its significance can be evaluated at different levels and communicated in different ways. Its causation can be evaluated at different levels (cf. 14.21). Its outcomes can be varied. But little is gained by modern conceptions of history and imagining Mark was privy to them.

18. There is no need to look to apocalyptic literature to explain the use of ciphers, symbols and ambiguous speech in Mark 13; it is adequately explained by observing the characteristic teaching method of Jesus in Mark. And there is no need to look to apocalyptic literature for the idea that God controls events, that he reveals his plans in advance, and that he enables those who experience them to understand their significance. If an Old Testament prophet can say, 'When disaster comes to a city, has not the Lord caused it? Surely the Sovereign Lord does nothing without revealing his plan to his servants the prophets' (Amos 3.6f.), we have no need to look to Jewish apocalyptic for Mark's emphasis both on divine sovereignty (even in a 'disaster') and discipleship discernment. For a helpful survey of views on the similarities and differences between Mark 13 and Jewish apocalyptic, see L. Morris, *Apocalyptic* (1972), pp. 74-77; L. Gaston, *No Stone on Another* (1970), pp. 50f.

19. Recall how the framework around it (12.41-44 and 14.1-9) encouraged us to see Mark 13 as the fulfilment of Jesus' predictions that a temple without hands would replace the physical building (see Chapter 5).

20. Surprisingly, none of the major recent studies of Mark 13 give any notice of Ezek. 33 and 34. These chapters are absent from the Biblical indices of the major studies by Lambrecht, Pesch, Wenham and Brandenburger. Hartman includes passing references to Ezek. 34 but not in the ways suggested here.

21. While it is clear that the actual phrase used in Mark 13.14 (τὸ βδέλυγμα τῆς ἐρημώσεως) derives from Daniel, it is quite possible that Mark intends it to be read in Mark 13 in the light of Ezek. 33.29 (and not impossible that the author of Daniel intended the same for his text). The connections between Ezek. 33 and Mark's temple theology, and especially the crucial terms ἐρημωθήσεται . . . βδελύγματα add weight to the idea that it is not the Romans but the Jews who abominate the temple and therefore bring it to the brink of its destruction.

22. He draws on Isaiah (29.13; Mark 7.6f.), Daniel (9.27; 11.31; 12.11; Mark 13.14), and Zechariah (13.7; Mark 14.27) for material paralleling Ezekiel's material.

23. 'God's Good News' [1955], p. 168.

24. C.E.B. Cranfield lists the following as reasons why Jesus predicted the temple's destruction: it would no longer be needed with his coming; it was a stumbling block to Israel; it was a stumbling block to the disciples; the political situation in relation to Rome looked threatening (*The Gospel According to St. Mark* [1977], pp. 392f.). Surely he has missed the main one for Mark: God is judging Israel's leaders for rejecting Jesus.

25. We will deal briefly in the next chapter with the question whether or not Mark 13.24-27 alludes to judgment.

26. Interestingly, it also has similar effects on the location of the proclamation. Both the resurrection and the destruction of the temple move the disciples out of Jerusalem, first to be regathered and recommissioned in Galilee for their discipleship and their mission, then much later to evangelize the world after their work in Jerusalem was done.

27. A. Jones says graphically: 'The Destruction of the Temple was the nativity of Christianity—the severance of the umbilical cord . . . Jerusalem has died in child-birth and a new order is born' ('Did Christ Foretell the End of the World in Mk XIII' [1951], p. 270).

28. See T.M. Lindsay, *The Gospel According to St. Mark* (1883), p. 203, for details of wars, famines, and earthquakes in the period from 30-70 A.D.

29. It is not certain whether the warning is against agitation that messianic pretenders and apocalyptic speculators would stir up, or against the distress that the events themselves might occasion. Cf. L. Hartman, *Prophecy Interpreted* (1966), pp. 176, 197. If it is the latter, one hears echoes of Jesus'

words to the disciples on the lake: 'Why are you so afraid?' (4.40).

30. R. Pesch, *Naherwartungen* (1968), p. 125.

31. Cf. C.E.B. Cranfield, *The Gospel According to St. Mark* (1977), pp. 9-11. G.D. Kilpatrick's ingenious re-punctuating of the verses has not proven persuasive (cf. 'The Gentile Mission in Mark and Mk 13.9-11' [1955]).

32. Cf. D. Wenham, *The Rediscovery of Jesus' Eschatological Discourse* (1984), p. 280.

33. 'Trial and Tribulation in Mark XIII' (1982), p. 86.

34. 'Whether this testimony is a blessing or curse to those who hear will depend on their response' (Wenham, *Ibid.*, p. 278). Cf. also C.E.B. Cranfield, *The Gospel According to St. Mark* (1977), p. 397.

35. A. Stock, *Call to Discipleship* (1984), p. 87.

36. R. Schnackenburg's attempt to make 'flee' mean its very opposite does not work (cf. *The Gospel According to St. Mark, II* [1971], p. 99). The reason for the flight is surely not the one that W. Marxsen suggested, namely that haste was required since the parousia would take place in Galilee shortly (cf. *Mark the Evangelist* [1969], p. 182). It is hard to imagine a less appropriate way of urging immediate and decisive flight to Galilee than to speak in riddles and insert the wrong destination into the command.

37. See C.E.B. Cranfield, *The Gospel According to St. Mark* (1977), p. 403, for Old Testament references in support of this.

38. L. Hartman, *Prophecy Interpreted* (1966), p. 153.

39. G.R. Beasley-Murray, *A Commentary on Mark 13* (1957), pp. 14, 74.

40. Cf. J. Schreiber, *Theologie des Vertrauens* (1967), pp. 143f.

41. See D. Wenham, *The Rediscovery of Jesus' Eschatological Discourse* (1984), p. 178, for a discussion of the question whether or not the false prophets are thought to be operating concurrently with the events described in 13.14-21.

42. Cf. A.M.Ambrozic, *The Hidden Kingdom* (1972) pp. 89-91 and p. 244: 'The community is asked to trust, in the teeth of outward appearances, that the kingdom will not remain hidden forever'.

Notes to Chapter 9

1. Cf. ὅταν (13.4, 7, 11, 14, 28f.), οὔπω (13.7), τέλος (13.7, 13), ἀρχή (13.8, 19), πρῶτον (13.10), αἱ ἡμέραι ἐκεῖναι (13.17, 19, 24, 32; cf. also 13.20), ἐγγύς (13.28f.), ἡ γενεὰ αὕτη (13.30), ἡ ὥρα (13.11, 32), ποτέ (13.4, 33, 35), (καὶ) τότε (13.14, 21, 26f.), ἢ ὀψὲ ἢ μεσονύκτιον ἢ ἀλεκτοροφωνίας ἢ πρωΐ (13.35).

2. Mission is, of course, also to be a preoccupation of disciples in the earlier time periods of the post-resurrection age (cf. 13.9, 11).

3. R. Pesch is a prime defender of the position that judgment is in view

(cf. *Naherwartungen* [1968], pp. 158-62; *Das Markusevangelium, II* [1977], pp. 302-304). His view is criticized by L. Hartman (Review of *Naherwartungen* [1969], p. 579), and G.R. Beasley-Murray ('The Parousia in Mark' [1978], pp. 577f.). W.H. Kelber lists about a dozen scholars who would agree with Hartman and Beasley-Murray (*The Kingdom in Mark* [1974], p. 123 n. 43).

4. According to D. Wenham, Mark has here omitted from his tradition references to further distresses on earth (cf. *The Rediscovery of Jesus' Eschatological Discourse* [1984], pp. 321ff.). Mark seems to have made the cosmic disturbances an integral part of the final intervention of God, not a series of signs which might serve to warn people that the End is near (see Chapter 2 of this study).

5. Cf. E. Schweizer, *The Good News According to Mark* (1970), p. 102; G.R. Beasley-Murray, *Jesus and the Kingdom of God* (1986), p. 126.

6. H.B. Swete, *The Gospel According to St. Mark* (1927), p. 311.

7. 'The Parousia in Mark' (1978), p. 578.

8. From the perspective of a modern reader, a statement like 'in those days after that distress' is perhaps subconsciously interpreted like this: 'The End is not in *these* days (i.e., in the twentieth century), it is in *those* days (i.e., much nearer 70 A.D'. Naturally, viewed in this way, the two events seem quite inseparably linked to each other. But what we must keep clearly in mind is that from the only relevant vantage point, that of the Markan Jesus, 'following that distress' projects the End beyond the events previously prophecied. All it says is that the End is more distant in time than the events of 13.5-23.

This would be true even if Mark wrote after the destruction of the temple, for it is not Mark but the Markan Jesus who speaks the words of 13.24a. From *his* perspective, the events of 13.5-23 constitute *future time* and 13.24-27 plots a great event somewhere in future time beyond the events of 13.5-23. Viewed from *that* perspective, it is much less certain that a close temporal link between the two events is indicated.

9. There is clearly no scholarly consensus, but many of the major studies of the past few decades argue for a major time gap between 13.23 and 13.24. Conzelmann, Pesch, Lambrecht, Brandon and Ambrozic have all argued thus. (Cf. A. Ambrozic, *The Hidden Kingdom* [1972], pp. 228f.).

10. *Prophecy Interpreted* (1966), p. 152.

11. *The Rediscovery of Jesus' Eschatological Discourse* (1984), p. 361.

12. Cf. e.g., W.L. Lane, *The Gospel According to Mark* (1974), p. 472. This view of course requires that the description of the tribulation accompanying the destruction of the temple is hyperbolic. Cf. Lane, *Ibid.*, p. 471.

13. 'The parousia is so close as to virtually fall into "those days", but it will be an event distinct from the "tribulation". It arrives in connection with, but is not itself part of the present crisis. It is thus a tenuous borderline which separates the Markan present from the parousia' (W.H. Kelber, *The*

Kingdom In Mark [1974], p. 123). 'In Mark, the desecration of the Tempel (sic) is interpreted as a sign of the Temple's destruction, and though this is of course firmly linked with the End, the two apparently take place at different times' (M.D. Hooker, 'Trial and Tribulation in Mark XIII' [1982], p. 98). The logic of Hooker's whole argument really supports greater *dis*continuity but she is prevented from accepting that option by her initial assumption that 13.4 establishes the correct agenda.

14. *Invitation to Mark* (1978), p. 187.

15. V. Taylor, 'The Apocalyptic Discourse of Mark xiii' (1949), p. 98.

16. A.M. Ambrozic, *The Hidden Kingdom* (1972), p. 229.

17. Cf. D. Wenham, *The Rediscovery of Jesus' Eschatological Discourse* (1984), p. 294.

18. Cf. W. Hendriksen, *New Testament Commentary: Mark* (1975), p. 526.

19. *The Language and Imagery of the Bible* (1980), p. 258.

20. Can we really argue that Amos knew the fall of Samaria was not the Day (Amos 8.9)? That Isaiah knew the Messiah would not come in the context of the Assyrian army's overthrow (Isa. 7-11)? That Habakkuk knew the End would not follow on the destruction of Babylon (Hab. 2.2f.)? That Jeremiah (Jer. 29-31), Ezekiel (Ezek. 36) and Deutero-Isaiah (Isa. 49, 51) all knew the kingdom of God would not be established with the return from exile? That Haggai knew the temple then under construction would not be the glorious end-time temple (Hag. 2)? (Cf. G.R. Beasley-Murray, 'The Eschatological Discourse of Jesus' [1960], pp. 160f.) That Malachi knew the Day would not arrive when the Lord came to his temple to 'cleanse' it (Mal. 3.1f.)? (Cf. A. Jones, 'The Eschatology of the Synoptic Gospels' [1950], p. 224; J.K. Howard, 'Our Lord's Teaching Concerning His Parousia' [1966], p. 153).

21. *The Hidden Kingdom* (1972), pp. 220f.

22. Cf. G.R. Beasley-Murray, 'The Eschatological Discourse of Jesus' (1960), pp. 160f.

23. This view entails the conclusion that the Gospel was written any time before the Roman-Jewish war, or during it, or *immediately* after it; few scholars would deny that it is one of these. It does not demand a Palestinian provenance for the Gospel. The Roman-Jewish war was not a private affair. Christians, especially Jewish Christians, would have been well aware and vitally concerned about affairs in Judea, wherever they lived. This would be all the more true if the writer of the Gospel was a native of Jerusalem.

24. A. Jones, 'Did Christ Foretell the End of the World in Mark XIII?' (1951), p. 266.

25. It might well be that secondary meanings for πρῶτον would include 'first', before persecution sets in (13.9), or 'first', before being delivered up to trial (13.11). It is left unspecified. (Cf. L. Gaston, *No Stone on Another* [1970], p. 20).

26. J.W. Thompson, 'The Gentile Mission as an Eschatological Necessity' (1971), pp. 23-25; G.R. Beasley-Murray, *A Commentary on Mark 13* (1957), pp. 41f.

27. W. Hendriksen suggests that 'the end' for the individual is death, but for the church is Christ's return (*New Testament Commentary: Mark* [1975], p. 522f.).

28. Cf. G.R. Beasley-Murray, *A Commentary on Mark 13* (1957), p. 56. He claims that the prophecy of 13.14 was perhaps not intended to have a precisely defined fulfilment. Both Jer. 7.30, 34 and Ezek. 33.29 use the two terms βδελύγματα and ἐρήμωσιν / ἐρημωθήσεται to describe *Jewish* abominations which result in desolation. Mark likely believed that 13.14 pointed to a *Jewish* defilement of the temple (as Josephus believed). If there were to be an additional future fulfilment of the 13.14 prophecy, τὸ βδέλυγμα τῆς ἐρημώσεως would represent an Antichrist figure of some sort.

29. V. Taylor, *The Gospel According to St. Mark* [1952], p. 499.

30. M.D. Hooker, 'Trial and Tribulation in Mark XIII' (1982), p. 78.

31. For a useful summary and evaluation of the various views see C.E.B. Cranfield, *The Gospel According to St. Mark* (1977), pp. 408f.; A.M. Ambrozic, *The Hidden Kingdom* (1972), pp. 229-31 (including notes). Jan Lambrecht in his earlier work defends the view that the parousia is not included (cf. *Die Redaktion der Markus-Apokalypse* [1967], pp. 207f. Note that in *Parables of Jesus* [1978], pp. 196-99, he defends the opposite conclusion!). Rudolf Pesch defends the alternative view (cf. *Naherwartungen* [1968], pp. 179-87).

32. Cf. A.L. Moore, *The Parousia in the New Testament* (1966), pp. 132f.

33. 'The ἡ γενεὰ αὕτη Eschatology in Mk 13,30 parr' (1980), pp. 408-13.

34. *Ibid.*, p. 411.

35. Lövestam draws precisely the opposite conclusion because he does not view the destruction of the temple as God's judgment on those who rejected Jesus, tempted him by seeking signs, and finally crucified him.

36. Cf. G.R. Beasley-Murray, *Commentary on Mark 13* (1957), p. 97.

37. Mark's unspecified chronology of pre-parousia events does not permit us to decide. Does 13.11 double back after a reference to a mission that follows the destruction of the temple or does it not? Does 13.14 double back after a reference to 'the end' or not?

38. C.E.B. Cranfield asks us to consider whether 'the eschatological is seen as it were through the medium of an approaching historical crisis, the historical catastrophe being regarded as foreshadowing the final convulsion (*without necessarily implying that there will not be other such crises before the End*)' [emphasis mine] ('St. Mark 13' [1953], p. 297).

39. Cf. H. Anderson, *The Gospel of Mark* (1976), p. 298.

40. Cf. E.F Siegman, 'Teaching in Parables' (1961), p. 181 (taken from Lagrange).

41. G.R. Beasley-Murray, *Commentary on Mark 13* (1957), p. 99.

42. Cf. H.B. Swete, *The Gospel According to St. Mark* (1927), p. 315; C.B. Cousar, 'Eschatology and Mark's *Theologia Crucis*' (1970), pp. 324-26; C.B. Clark, *A Reinvestigation of Mark 13 as a Possible Key to the Structure of the Gospel* (1981), pp. 155f., 182-89.

43. For surveys of studies concerning its meaning, see M. Künzi, *Das Naherwartungslogion Mk 9.1 par* (1977). For a helpful summary of redactional interpretations of Mark 9.1 see E. Nardoni, 'A Redactional Interpretation of Mark 9.1' (1981), pp. 365-84.

44. Cf. e.g., P.J. Achtemeier, *Mark* (1975), p. 55.

45. Cf. A.A. Trites, 'The Transfiguration of Jesus' (1979), p. 78.

46. Trites, *Ibid.*, p. 67.

47. Cf. G. Bornkamm, 'Die Verzögerung der Parusie' (1968), p. 49; E. Nardoni, 'A Redactional Interpretation of Mark 9.1' (1981), p. 380.

48. Cf. esp. K. Brower, 'Mark 9.1: Seeing the Kingdom in Power' (1980), pp. 17-41.

49. The fact that both terms ἡ ἡμέρα ἐκείνη (cf. 2.20) and ἡ ὥρα (cf. 14.35, 41) are used by Mark as technical terms for the passion (for Mark a foreshadowing of the final eschatological victory) confirms that these terms do more to specify the event under discussion than to focus on the day or hour of its arrival.

50. Cf. W.L. Lane, *The Gospel According to Mark* (1974), pp. 481f.; K. Brower, 'Mark 9.1: Seeing the Kingdom in Power' (1980), p. 38.

51. Those who would argue that 13.30 specifies the time of the arrival of the Son of Man within narrow scope, whereas 13.32 denies only that the precise day and hour can be identified, have greater difficulty with 13.33 than with 13.32.

52. The Markan Jesus confesses his ignorance by the inclusion of 'nor the Son'; the implied narrator confesses his ignorance by allowing the Markan Jesus to include him by means of 'no one knows'.

53. 'The Apocalyptic Discourse of Mark xiii' (1949), p. 95.

54. Cf. C.R. Kazmierski, *Jesus the Son of God* (1979), pp. 141f. D. Wenham seems to have missed the point of the γάρ when he considers it unnecessary after 13.32. It does not serve to explain further the fact of timing ignorance. It serves to establish the fact that the need for watching is a direct consequence of that ignorance. Cf. *The Rediscovery of Jesus' Eschatological Discourse* (1984), p. 26.

55. Cf. G. Neville, *The Advent Hope* (1961), p. 56: '. . . it does not fit. For it is used to teach that the coming of the Son of Man can be detected in advance, which is not the teaching of Mark 13, verses 5-27'.

56. *A Commentary on Mark 13* (1957), p. 10.

57. By 'spatial nearness' we do not mean to imply necessarily that he/it is already present but unseen. We wish to imply rather that he/it stands ready to make his/its entry onto the stage without any more advance indications, but also without guaranteeing it will be temporally soon.

58. J. Dupont, 'La parabole du figuier qui bourgeonne' (1968), pp. 546-48.

59. One does not have to agree with J. Drury that 'Mark has already told the reader how to understand parables in iv: they are allegories or riddles which he has to decode' ('The Sower, the Vineyard and the Place of Allegory in the Interpretation of Mark's Parables' [1973], p. 371) in order to agree with him that parables for Mark are much more complex and subtle communicators than is often suspected, certainly more so than Jeremias and his followers have argued they are.

60. θέρος ('summer') and θερισμός ('harvest') are related etymologically, by means of their associations with the crop cycles, and also by their eschatological connections. It is even possible that the Hebrew pun operative in Amos 8.1-2 links the idea of fruit bearing with the End. Cf. J. Dupont, 'La parabole du figuier qui bourgeonne' (1968), p. 542; W.R. Telford, *The Barren Temple and the Withered Tree* (1980), p. 213.

61. *The Barren Temple and the Withered Tree* (1980), p. 213.

62. J.W. Sider in his otherwise excellent article on parable interpretation seems to have overlooked this in analysing this parable. Cf. 'Proportional Analogy in the Gospel Parables' (1985), pp. 1-4.

63. J.D.M. Derrett, 'Figtrees in the New Testament' (1973), p. 259. Derrett believes it is 'the Age' which is near. This would fit in well in Mark's Gospel where 'That Day' and 'The Hour' already arrive (in one sense) in the passion of Jesus.

64. Cf. Mark 13.33-37 and especially James 5.7-9 where it is affirmed that the Judge stands by the door, but the implication is that patience is needed, just as a farmer needs it while waiting through the seasons for the expected crops.

65. Cf. W.R. Telford, *The Barren Temple and the Withered Tree* (1980), p. 213.

66. We are not of course suggesting that the two 'parables' have their origin in the same place within the ministry of Jesus. The arguments in favour of this suggestion are not impressive. Cf. G.R. Beasley-Murray, *A Commentary on Mark 13* (1957), p. 98. Luke obviously does not take the fig tree symbolism seriously, for he adds 'and all the trees'. The fact that Mark does not relate the fig tree to 'other trees' might suggest that the associations of the tree itself are important. Wenham thinks the pre-Markan tradition was without Luke's added words (cf. *The Rediscovery of Jesus' Eschatological Discourse* [1984], pp. 328f.).

67. This is especially surprising in the light of W.R. Telford's persuasive evidence that in Old Testament and inter-testamental literature the withering of a fig tree and its blossoming are used respectively as images for God's judgment on Israel and his blessings (cf. *The Barren Temple and the Withered Tree* [1980], p. 162).

68. Cf. *The Barren Temple and the Withered Tree* (1980), p. 218.

69. Cf. F. Dewar, 'Chapter 13 and the Passion Narrative in St Mark' (1961), p. 105.

70. It is significant that in Hag. 2.18f. being without a temple is correlated with fig trees not bearing fruit, while the laying of foundations for a re-built temple signals the return of God's blessing (presumably in making crops fruitful).

71. 'The discourse has described (a) the events that will lead up to the parousia and then (b) the parousia itself, and the natural way to take the parable in its context is as relating (a) to (b). There is no problem with this' (D.Wenham, *The Rediscovery of Jesus' Eschatological Discourse* [1984], p. 327). Cf. I.H. Marshall, *Eschatology and the Parables* (1963), p. 26.

72. This of course does not mean that 'mission' is 'at the door'. It means that mission is the appropriate and required concern of believers in the time of waiting and serving while they stand faithfully and expectantly on one side of the door and their master stands, waiting for His Father's signal, on the other. Cf. L. Gaston, *No Stone on Another* (1970), pp. 36f.

73. Cf. G.B. Caird's helpful discussion of 'mixed metaphors' (*The Language and Imagery of the Bible* [1980], p. 150).

74. Cf. J. Dupont, 'La parabole du maître qui rentre dans la nuit' (1970), p. 111; J. Lambrecht, *Parables of Jesus* (1978), p. 200.

75. If Mark 4 is our guide, we might be tempted to expect a long delay, but the reader of Mark must resist that temptation. After all the new temple does not begin to replace the old temple only when that latter is destroyed. It replaced it already when the Jewish authorities disqualified themselves and their temple by rejecting Jesus, and when God vindicated his Son by raising up the rejected stone to the key position in a rebuilt temple. If the actual destruction of the temple becomes an eye-opener which helps believers to 'see' the fig tree in leaf, then the destruction of the temple functions as an encouragement to take seriously the *ongoing* task; it does not function as a belated signal for it to *begin*.

76. In fact, no possible course of events after 70 AD could falsify anything in that chapter, unless the Son of Man never came back. As long as history goes on, the chapter retains whatever validity it had when composed. If the chapter were designed to provide an apologetic for Christianity on the basis of someone's ability to make accurate predictions, this unfalsifiability would be a fatal flaw. Its present paranetic purposes, however, are totally unaffected by its unfalsifiability.

77. Very closely tied to this is the difficulty of relating 13.30 with 13.32.

78. G.R. Beasley-Murray (quoted in: F. Dewar, 'Chapter 13 and the Passion Narrative in St Mark' [1961], p. 99).

79. C.E.B. Cranfield, criticizing the idea that Jesus' eschatological predictions were unambiguous and have been subsequently falsified, rightly notes: 'Jesus' paradoxes are far too lively to be successfully caught and confined in so simple and rectilinear a strait-jacket' ('St. Mark 13' [1954], p. 287).

BIBLIOGRAPHY

Achtemeier, P.J., '"And he followed him": Miracles and Discipleship in Mark 10.46-52', *Semeia* 11 (1978), pp. 115-45.

—'An Apocalyptic Shift in Early Christian Tradition: Reflections on Some Canonical Evidence', *CBQ* 45 (1983), pp. 231-48.

—'An Exposition of Mark 9.30-37', *Int* 30 (1976), pp. 178-82.

—'"He Taught Them Many Things": Reflections on Marcan Christology', *CBQ* 42 (1980), pp. 465-81.

—*Invitation to Mark: A Commentary on the Gospel of Mark with Complete Text from the Jerusalem Bible*, Garden City, NY: Doubleday, 1978.

—'Mark as Interpreter of the Jesus Traditions', *Int* 32 (1978), pp. 339-52.

—*Mark*, Philadelphia: Fortress Press, 1975.

—'Miracles and the Historical Jesus: A Study of Mark 9.14-29', *CBQ* 37 (1975), pp. 471-91.

—'Person and Deed: Jesus and the Storm-Tossed Sea', *Int* 16 (1962), pp. 169-76.

Ambrozic, A.M., *The Hidden Kingdom: A Redaction-critical Study of the References to the Kingdom of God in Mark's Gospel*, Washington, DC; Catholic Biblical Association of America, 1972.

—'Mark's Concept of the Parable', *CBQ* 29 (1967), pp. 220-27.

—'New Teaching with Power (Mk 1.27)', in *Word and Spirit: Essays in Honor of David Michael Stanley, S.J. on his 60th Birthday*, ed. J. Plevnik, Willowdale, Ont.: Regis College, 1975, pp. 113-49.

Anderson, H., *The Gospel of Mark*, London: Oliphants, 1976.

—'The Old Testament in Mark's Gospel', in *The Use of the Old Testament in the New and Other Essays: Studies in Honor of William Franklin Stinespring*, ed. J.M. Efird, Durham, NC: Duke University, 1972, pp. 280-306.

Anthonysamy, S.J., 'The Gospel of Mark and the Universal Mission', *Biblebhashyam* 6 (1980), pp. 81-96.

Anzalone, V., 'Il fico maledetto (Mc. XI, 12-14 e 20-25)', *PalCler* 37 (1958), pp. 257-64.

Au, W., 'Discipleship in Mark', *TBT* 67 (1973), pp. 1249-51.

Aune, D.E., 'The Problem of the Messianic Secret', *NovT* 11 (1969), 1-31.

Bacon, B.W., *The Gospel of Mark: Its Composition and Date*, New Haven, CT: Yale University Press, 1925.

Bailey, J.L., 'Perspectives on the Gospel of Mark', *CurTM* 12 (1985), pp. 15-25.

Baird, J.A., *Audience Criticism and the Historical Jesus*, Philadelphia: Westminster, 1969.

Barbour, R.S., 'Gethsemane in the Tradition of the Passion', *NTS* 16 (1970), pp. 231-51.

—'Recent Study of the Gospel According to St. Mark', *ExpTim* 79 (1968), pp. 324-29.

Barr, D.L., 'Speaking of Parables: A Survey of Recent Research', *TSF Bulletin* (Madison, Wi) 6 (1983), pp. 8-10.

Barrett, C.K., 'The House of Prayer and the Den of Thieves', in *Jesus und Paulus: Festschrift für Werner Georg Kümmel zum 70. Geburtstag* (2nd ed.) ed. E.E. Ellis and E. Gräßer, Göttingen: Vandenhoeck & Ruprecht, 1978, pp. 13-20.

—*Jesus and the Gospel Tradition*, London: SPCK, 1967.

Bartsch, H.-W., 'Early Christian Eschatology in the Synoptic Gospels', *NTS* 11 (1965), 387-97.

—'Die "Verfluchung" des Feigenbaums', *ZNW* 53 (1962), pp. 256-60.

Bassler, J.M., 'The Parable of the Loaves', *JR* 66 (1986), pp. 157-72.

Bauckham, R., 'Synoptic Parousia Parables Again', *NTS* 29 (1983), pp. 129-34.

—'Synoptic Parousia Parables and the Apocalypse', *NTS* 23 (1977), pp. 162-76.

Beardslee, W.A., *Literary Criticism of the New Testament*, Philadelphia: Fortress Press, 1970.

Beasley-Murray, G.R., *The Coming of God*, Exeter: Paternoster, 1983.

—*A Commentary on Mark 13*, London: MacMillan, 1957.

—'The Eschatological Discourse of Jesus', *RevExp* 57 (1960), pp. 153-66.

—'Eschatology in the Gospel of Mark' *SWJournTheol* 21 (1978), pp. 37-53.

—'Jesus and Apocalyptic: With Special Reference to Mark 14,62', in *L'Apocalypse johannique et l'Apocalyptique dans le Nouveau Testament*, ed. J. Lambrecht, Leuven: Leuven University Press, 1980, pp. 415-29.

—*Jesus and the Future: An Examination of the Criticism of The Eschatological Discourse, Mark 13, with Special Reference to the Little Apocalypse Theory*, London: MacMillan, 1954.

—*Jesus and the Kingdom of God*, Exeter: Paternoster, 1986.

—'The Parousia in Mark', *RevExp* 75 (1978), pp. 565-81.

—'Second Thoughts on the Composition of Mark 13', *NTS* 29 (1983), pp. 414-20.

Beauvery, R., 'La guérison d'un aveugle à Bethsaïde (Mc 8, 22-26)', *NRT* 90 (1968), 1083-91.

Beck, N.A., 'Reclaiming a Biblical Text: The Mark 8.14-21 Discussion About Bread in the Boat', *CBQ* 43 (1981), pp. 49-56.

Bennett, W.J., Jr., 'The Herodians of Mark's Gospel', *NovT* 17 (1975), pp. 9-14.

Benoit, P., *The Passion and Resurrection of Jesus Christ*, New York: Herder & Herder, 1969.

Best, E., 'Discipleship in Mark: Mark 8.22-10.52', *SJT* 23 (1970), pp. 323-37.

—*Following Jesus: Discipleship in the Gospel of Mark*, Sheffield: JSOT Press, 1981.

—*Mark: The Gospel as Story*, Edinburgh: T. & T. Clark, 1983.

—'Mark's Preservation of the Tradition', in *L'Evangile selon Marc: Tradition et rédaction*, ed. M. Sabbe, Louvain: Leuven University Press, 1974, pp. 21-34.

—'The Miracles in Mark', *RevExp* 75 (1978), pp. 539-54.

—'Peter in the Gospel According to Mark', *CBQ* 40 (1978), pp. 547-58.

—'The Purpose of Mark', *ProcIrBibAssoc* 6 (1982), pp. 19-35.

—'The Role of the Disciples in Mark', *NTS* 23 (1977), pp. 377-401.

—*The Temptation and the Passion: The Markan Soteriology*, Cambridge: Cambridge University Press, 1965.

Betz, O., 'The Concept of the So-called "Divine Man" in Mark's Christology', in *Studies in New Testament and Early Christian Literature: Essays in Honor of Allen P. Wikgren*, ed. D.E. Aune, Leiden: E.J. Brill, 1972, pp. 229-40.

Biguzzi, G., 'Mc. 14,58: un tempio ἀχειροποίητος', *RevistB* 26 (1978), pp. 225-40.

Bilezikian, G.G., *The Liberated Gospel: A Comparison of the Gospel of Mark and Greek Tragedy*, Grand Rapids, MI: Baker Book House, 1977.

Birdsall, J.N., 'τὸ ῥῆμα ὡς εἶπεν αὐτῷ ὁ Ἰησοῦς: Mk xiv 72', *NovT* 2 (1958), pp. 272-75.

—'The Withering of the Fig-Tree (Mark xi. 12-14, 20-22)', *ExpTim* 73 (1962), p. 191.

Bishop, J., '*Parabole* and *Parrhesia* in Mark', *Int* 40 (1986), pp. 39-52.

Blair, E.P., 'Mark, John', *IDB* (1962), III, pp. 277-78.

Blatherwick, D., 'The Markan Silhouette?' *NTS* 17 (1971), pp. 184-92.

Blevins, J.L., *The Messianic Secret in Markan Research, 1901-1976*, Washington, DC: University Press of America, 1981.

—'Seventy-Two Years of the Messianic Secret', *PerspRelStud* 1 (1974), pp. 187-94.

Bligh, J., 'The Gerasene Demoniac and the Resurrection of Christ', *CBQ* 31 (1969), pp. 383-90.

Blomberg, C.L., 'New Horizons in Parable Research', *TrinJourn* 3 (1982), pp. 3-17.

Boobyer, G.H., 'Galilee and Galileans in St. Mark's Gospel', *BJRL* 35 (1953), pp. 334-48.

—'The Miracles of the Loaves and the Gentiles in St. Mark's Gospel', *SJT* 6 (1953), pp. 77-87.

—*St. Mark and the Transfiguration Story*, Edinburgh: T. & T. Clark, 1942.

—'The Secrecy Motif in St. Mark's Gospel', *NTS* 6 (1960), pp. 225-35.

Boomershine, T.E., 'Mark 16.8 and the Apostolic Commission', *JBL* 100 (1981), pp. 225-39.

—and G.L. Bartholomew, 'The Narrative Technique of Mark 16.8', *JBL* 100 (1981), pp. 213-23.

Boring, M.E., 'The Christology of Mark: Hermeneutical Issues for Systematic Theology', *Semeia* 30 (1985), pp. 125-53.

Bornkamm, G., 'μυστήριον', *TDNT*, IV, pp. 802-28.

—'Die Verzögerung der Parusie: Exegetische Bemerkungen zu zwei synoptischen Texten', in *Geschichte und Glaube* (Bornkamm), München: C. Kaiser, 1968, pp. 46-55.

Boucher, M., *The Mysterious Parable: A Literary Study*, Washington, DC: Catholic Biblical Association of America, 1977.

Bouttier, M., 'Commencement, force et fin de l'évangile', *ETR* 51 (1976), pp. 465-93.

Bowker, J.W., 'Mystery and Parable: Mark iv. 1-20', *JTS* 25 (1974), pp. 300-17.

Bowman, J., *The Gospel of Mark: The New Christian Jewish Passover Haggadah*, Leiden: E.J. Brill, 1965.

Boyd, W.J.P., 'Peter's Denials—Mark xiv. 68, Luke xxii. 57', *ExpTim* 67 (1956), p. 341.

Bracht, W., 'Jüngerschaft und Nachfolge: Zur Gemeindesituation im Markusevangelium', in *Kirche im Werden: Studien zum Thema Amt und Gemeinde im Neuen Testament*, ed. J. Hainz, Munich: Ferdinand Schönigh, 1976, pp. 143-65.

Brady, D., 'The Alarm to Peter in Mark's Gospel', *JSNT* 4 (1979), pp. 42-57.

Brandenburger, E., *Markus 13 und die Apokalyptik*, Göttingen: Vandenhoeck & Ruprecht, 1984.

Brandon, S.G.F., *The Fall of Jerusalem and the Christian Church*, London: SPCK, 1951.

Braumann, G., '"An jenem Tag" Mk 2,20', *NovT* 6 (1963), pp. 264-67.

Breytenbach, C., *Nachfolge und Zukunftserwartung nach Markus*, Zürich: Theologischer Verlag, 1984.

Brower, K., 'Elijah in the Markan Passion Narrative', *JSNT* 18 (1983), pp. 85-101.
—'Mark 9.1: Seeing the Kingdom in Power', *JSNT* 6 (1980), pp. 17-41.
Brown, C.,*Miracles and the Critical Mind*, Grand Rapids, MI: Eerdmans, 1984.
Brown, R.E., 'The Semitic Background of the New Testament *mysterion*', *Bib* 39 (1958), pp. 426-48.
Brown, S.,'"The Secret of the Kingdom of God" (Mark 4.11)', *JBL* 92 (1973), pp. 60-74.
Bruce, F.F., 'The Book of Zechariah and the Passion Narrative', *BJRL* 43 (1961), pp. 336-53.
Buchanan, G.W., 'An Additional Note to "Mark 11.11-15: Brigands in the Temple"', *HUCA* 31 (1960), pp. 103-105.
—'Mark 11.15-19: Brigands in the Temple', *HUCA* 30 (1959), pp. 169-77.
Budesheim, T.L.,'Jesus and the Disciples in Conflict with Judaism', *ZNW* 62 (1971), pp. 190-209.
Bultmann, R., *The History of the Synoptic Tradition* (2nd ed.), Oxford: Basil Blackwell, 1968.
—'Die Interpretation von Mk 4.3-9 seit Jülicher', in *Jesus und Paulus: Festschrift für Werner Georg Kümmel zum 70. Geburtstag* (2nd ed.), ed. E.E. Ellis; and E. Grässer (Gottingen: Vandenhoeck & Ruprecht, 1978), pp. 30-34.
Bundy, W.E., 'Dogma and Drama in the Gospel of Mark', in *New Testament Studies*, ed. E.P. Booth, New York: Abingdon-Cokesbury, 1942, pp. 70-94.
Burchard, C., 'Markus 15.34', *ZNW* 74 (1983), pp. 1-11.
Burkill, T.A., 'Anti-Semitism in St. Mark's Gospel', *NovT* 3 (1959), pp. 34-53.
—'Blasphemy: St. Mark's Gospel as Damnation History', in *Christianity, Judaism and Other Greco-Roman Cults: Studies for Morton Smith at Sixty*, ed. J. Neusner, Leiden: E.J. Brill, 1975, pp. 51-74.
—'The Cryptology of Parables in St. Mark's Gospel', *NovT* 1 (1956), pp. 246-62.
—*Mysterious Revelation: An Examination of the Philosophy of St. Mark's Gospel*, Ithaca, NY: Cornell University Press, 1963.
—*New Light on the Earliest Gospel*, Ithaca, NY: Cornell University Press, 1972.
—'St. Mark's Philosophy of History', *NTS* 3 (1957), pp. 142-48.
—'St. Mark's Philosophy of the Passion', *NovT* 2 (1958), pp. 245-71.
Busch, F., *Zum Verständnis der synoptischen Eschatologie; Markus 13 neu untersucht*, Gütersloh: C. Bertelsmann, 1938.
Buse, I., 'The Cleansing of the Temple in the Synoptics and in John', *ExpTim* 70 (1959), pp. 22-24.
Caird, G.B., *The Language and Imagery of the Bible*, London: Duckworth Press, 1980.
Caldecott, A., 'The Significance of the "Cleansing of the Temple"', *JTS* 24 (1923), pp. 382-86.
Cangh, J.-M., van, 'La Galilée dans l'evangile de Marc: un lieu théologique?' *RB* 79 (1972), pp. 59-75.
Carrington, P., *According to Mark: A Running Commentary on the Oldest Gospel*, Cambridge: Cambridge University Press, 1960.
—*The Primitive Christian Calendar: A Study in the Making of the Markan Gospel*, Cambridge: Cambridge University Press, 1952.
Carson, D.A., 'Hermeneutics: A brief assessment of some recent trends', *Themelios* 5 (1980), pp. 12-20.
Catchpole, D., 'The Fearful Silence of the Women at the Tomb: A Study in Markan Theology', *JournTheolSAfr* 18 (1977), pp. 3-10.
Chilton, B.D., 'The Transfiguration: Dominical Assurance and Apostolic Vision', *NTS* 27 (1980), pp. 115-24.

Chronis, H.L., 'The Torn Veil: Cultus and Christology in Mark 15.37-39', *JBL* 101 (1982), pp. 97-114.

Clark, C.B., *A Reinvestigation of Mark 13 as a Possible Key to the Structure of the Gospel*, Th. D. Thesis. (Unpublished), Ft. Worth, TX: Southwestern Baptist Theological Seminary, 1981.

Cole, R.A., *The Gospel According to St. Mark: An Introduction and Commentary*, London: Tyndale, 1961.

—*The New Temple: A Study in the Origins of the Catechetical 'Form' of the Church in the New Testament*, London: Tyndale, 1950.

Collins, A.Y., 'The Early Christian Apocalypses', *Semeia* 14 (1979), pp. 61-121.

Conzelmann, H., 'Geschichte und Eschaton nach Mc 13', *ZNW* 50 (1959), pp. 210-21.

—'History and Theology in the Passion Narratives of the Synoptic Gospels', *Int* 24 (1970), pp. 178-197.

Cook, M.J., *Mark's Treatment of the Jewish Leaders*, Leiden: E.J. Brill, 1978.

Cosby, M.R., 'Mark 14.51-52 and the Problem of Gospel Narrative', *PerspRelStud* 11 (1984), pp. 219-231.

Cotter, W.J., 'For It Was Not the Season for Figs', *CBQ* 48 (1986), pp. 62-66.

Countryman, L.W., 'How Many Baskets Full? Mark 8.14-21 and the Value of Miracles in Mark', *CBQ* 47 (1985), pp. 643-655.

Cousar, C.B.,'Eschatology and Mark's *Theologia Crucis*: A Critical Analysis of Mark 13', *Int* 24 (1970), pp. 321-35.

Coutts, J.,'The Authority of Jesus and of the Twelve in St. Mark's Gospel', *JTS* 8 (1957), pp. 111-18.

—'The Messianic Secret and the Enemies of Jesus', *Studia Biblica 1978: II. Papers on the Gospels*, ed. E.A. Livingstone, Sheffield: JSOT Press, 1980, pp. 37-46.

—'"Those Outside" (Mk 4.10-12)', in *Studia Evangelica II: Papers Presented to the Second International Congress on New Testament Studies held at Christ Church, Oxford, 1961*, ed. F.L. Cross, Berlin: Akademie-Verlag, 1964, pp. 155-57.

Crane, T.E., 'Redaction-criticism and *MARK*', *Essays in Faith and Culture* 3 (1979): pp. 157-72.

Cranfield, C.E.B., 'The Baptism of our Lord—A Study of St. Mark 1.9-11', *SJT* 8 (1955), pp. 53-63.

—*The Gospel According to St. Mark: An Introduction and Commentary*, (5th ed.), Cambridge: Cambridge University Press, 1977.

—'Mark, Gospel of', *IDB* (1962), Vol. III, pp. 267-77.

—'St Mark 4.1-34', *SJT* 5 (1952), pp. 49-66.

—'St. Mark 13', *SJT* 6 (1953), pp. 189-96, 287-303; 7 (1954), pp. 284-303.

Crawford, B.S., 'Near Expectation in the Sayings of Jesus', *JBL* 101 (1982), pp. 225-44.

Crossan, J.D., *Cliffs of Fall: Paradox and Polyvalence in the Parables of Jesus*, New York: Seabury Press, 1980.

—'Empty Tomb and Absent Lord (Mark 16.1-8)', in *The Passion in Mark*, ed. W. Kelber. Philadelphia: Fortress Press, 1976, pp. 135-52.

—*Finding is the First Act: Trove Folktales and Jesus' Treasure Parable*, Philadelphia: Fortress Press, 1979.

—*In Parables: The Challenge of the Historical Jesus*, London: Harper & Row, 1973.

—'Mark and the Relatives of Jesus', *NovT* 15 (1973), pp. 81-113.

—*Raid on the Articulate: Comic Eschatology in Jesus and Borges*, New York: Harper & Row, 1976.

—'Redaction and Citation in Mark 11.9-11 and 11.17', *BR* 17 (1972), pp. 33-50.

Cullmann, O., 'ὁ ὀπίσω μου ἐρχόμενος', in *Vorträge und Aufsätze, 1925—1962*, ed. K. Fröhlich, Tübingen: Mohr/Siebeck, 1966, pp. 169-75.

Culpepper, R.A., 'The Passion and Resurrection in Mark', *RevExp* 75 (1978), pp. 583-600.

Dahl, N.A., 'The Purpose of Mark's Gospel', in *The Messianic Secret*, ed. C. Tuckett, London: SPCK, 1983, pp. 29-34.

Danker, F.W., 'The Demonic Secret in Mark: A Reexamination of the Cry of Dereliction (15.34)', *ZNW* 61 (1970), pp. 48-49.

—'Double-entendre in Mark XIII 9', *NovT* 10 (1968), pp. 162-63.

Daube, D., *The New Testament and Rabbinic Judaism*, London: Athlone, 1956.

Davies, W.D., 'Reflections on Archbishop Carrington's "The Primitive Christian Calendar"', in *The Background of the New Testament and its Eschatology: In Honour of Charles Harold Dodd*, ed. W.D. Davies and D. Daube, Cambridge: Cambridge University Press, 1956, pp. 124-52.

Delorme, J., 'Aspects doctrinaux du second Evangile', *ETL* 43 (1967), 74-99.

Denis, A. -M., 'Une théologie de la Rédemption: La Transfiguration chez saint Marc'. *VSpir* 41 (1959), pp. 136-49.

Derrett, J.D.M., 'Figtrees in the New Testament', *HeyJ* 14 (1973), pp. 249-65.

—'Leek-beds and Methodology', *BZ* 19 (1975), pp. 101-103.

—*The Making of Mark: The Scriptural Bases of the Earliest Gospel, I–II*, Shipston-on-Stour, Eng.: P. Drinkwater, 1985.

—'The Zeal of the House and the Cleansing of the Temple', *DownRev* 95 (1977), pp. 79-94.

Dewar, F., 'Chapter 13 and the Passion Narrative in St Mark', *Theology* 64 (1961), pp. 99-107.

Dewey, J.B., *Disciples of the Way: Mark on Discipleship*, Cincinnati: Women's Division, Board of Global Ministries, United Methodist Church, 1976.

—'The Literary Structure of the Controversy Stories in Mark 2.1—3.6', *JBL* 92 (1973), pp. 394-401.

—*Markan Public Debate: Literary Technique, Concentric Structure and Theology in Mark 2.1—3.6*, Chico, CA: Scholars Press, 1980.

Dewey, K.E.,'Peter's Curse and Cursed Peter', in *The Passion in Mark*, ed. W. Kelber, Philadelphia: Fortress Press, 1976 pp. 96-114.

Dibelius, M., *From Tradition to Gospel*, London: Ivor Nicholson & Watson, 1934.

—*Gospel Criticism and Christology*, London: Ivor Nicholson & Watson, 1935.

Dillon, R.J.,'Mark and the New Meaning of "Gospel"', *DunRev* 7 (1967), 131-61.

Dodd, C.H., 'The Fall of Jerusalem and the "Abomination of Desolation"', *JRS* 37 (1947), pp. 47-54.

Dombois, H., 'Juristische Bemerkungen zum Gleichnis von den bösen Weingärtnern (Mk 12,1-12)', *Neue Zeitschrift für Systematische Theologie und Religionsphilosophie* 8, (1966), pp. 360-73.

Donahue, J.R., *Are You the Christ? The Trial Narrative in the Gospel of Mark*, Missoula, MT: Society of Biblical Literature, 1973.

—'Introduction: From Passion Traditions to Passion Narrative', in *The Passion in Mark*, ed. W. Kelber, Philadelphia: Fortress Press, 1976, pp. 1-20.

—'Jesus as the Parable of God in the Gospel of Mark', *Int* 32 (1978), pp. 369-86.

—'Temple, Trial, and Royal Christology (Mark 14.53-65)', in *The Passion in Mark*, ed. W. Kelber, Philadelphia: Fortress Press, 1976 pp. 61-79.

Donaldson, J., '"Called to Follow": A Twofold Experience of Discipleship in Mark', *BIB* 5 (1975), pp. 67-77.

Dormeyer, D., *Die Passion Jesu als Verhaltensmodell: Literarische und theologische Analyse der Traditions- und Redaktionsgeschichte der Markuspassion*, Münster: Verlag Aschendorff, 1974.

—*Der Sinn des Leidens Jesu: Historisch-kritische und textpragmatische Analysen zur Markuspassion*, Stuttgart: Katholisches Bibelwerk, 1979.

Doughty, D.J., 'The Authority of the Son of Man (Mk 2.1–3.6)', *ZNW* 74 (1983), pp. 161-81.

Drury, J., 'The Sower, the Vineyard, and the Place of Allegory in the Interpretation of Mark's Parables', *JTS* 24 (1973), pp. 367-79.

Duling, D.C., 'Interpretation the Markan "Hodology": Biblical Criticism in Preaching and Teaching', *Nexus* 17 (1974), pp. 2-11.

Dunn, J.D.G., 'The Messianic Secret in Mark', *TynBull* 21 (1970), pp. 92-117.

—*Unity and Diversity in the New Testament*, London: SCM Press, 1977.

Dupont, J., 'La parabole du figuier qui bourgeonne (Mc xiii, 28-29 et par.)', *RB* 75 (1968), pp. 526-48.

—'La parabole du maître qui rentre dans la nuit (Mc 13,34-36)', in *Mélanges bibliques: en hommage au R.P. Béda Rigaux*, ed. A. Descamps and A. de Halleux, Gembloux: Editions J. Duculot, 1970, pp. 89-116.

—'La Persécution comme situation missionaire (Marc 13, 9-11)', in *Die Kirche des Anfangs: Festschrift für Heinz Schürmann zum 65. Geburtstag*, ed. R. Schnackenburg, J. Ernst and J. Wanke, Leipzig: St. Benno, 1977, pp. 97-114.

—'La Ruine du Temple et la Fin des Temps dans le Discours de Marc 13', in *Apocalypses et Théologie de l' Espérance*, ed. L. Monloubou, Paris: Editions du Cerf, 1977, pp. 207-69.

Eakin, F., 'Spiritual Obduracy and Parable Purpose', in *The Use of the Old Testament in the New and Other Essays*, ed. J. Efird, Durham: Duke University, 1972, pp. 87-109.

Edwards, R.A., 'A New Approach to the Gospel of Mark', *LQ* 22 (1970), pp. 330-35.

—'The Redaction of Luke', *JR* 49 (1969), pp. 392-405.

Egger, W., *Nachfolge als Weg zum Leben: Chancen neuer exegetischer Methoden dargelegt an Mk 10, 17-31*, Klosterneuburg: Osterreichisches Katholisches Bibelwerk, 1979.

Elliott, J.H., Review of Lambrecht, J., *Die Redaktion des Markus-Apokalypse*, *CBQ* 30 (1968), pp. 267-69.

Englezakis, B., 'Markan Parable: More than Word Modality, a Revelation of Contents', *DeltBibMel* 2 (1974), pp. 349-57.

Enslin, M.S., 'A New Apocalyptic', *RelLife* 44 (1975), pp. 105-110.

Entrevernes Group, The, *Signs and Parables: Semiotics and Gospel Texts*, Pittsburgh: Pickwick Press, 1978.

Ernst, J., *Das Evangelium nach Markus: Übersetzt und erklärt*, Regensburg: F. Pustet, 1981.

—'Noch einmal: Die Verleugnung Jesu durch Petrus (Mk 14, 54.66-72)', *Catholica* 30 (1976), pp. 207-26.

Evans, C.A., 'The Function of Isaiah 6.9-10 in Mark and John', *NovT* 24 (1982), pp. 124-38.

—'On the Isaianic Background of the Sower Parable', *CBQ* 47 (1985), pp. 464-68.

—'On the Vineyard Parables of Isaiah 5 and Mark 12', *BZ* 28 (1984), pp. 82-86.

Evans, C.F., *The Beginning of the Gospel: Four Lectures on St. Mark's Gospel*, London: SPCK, 1968.

—'"I Will Go Before You Into Galilee"', *JTS* 5 (1954), pp. 3-18.

—*Resurrection and the New Testament*, London: SCM Press, 1970.

Ewert, D., *And Then Comes the End*, Scottdale, PA: Herald Press, 1980.

Falusi, G.K., 'Jesus' Use of Parables in Mark with Special Reference to Mark 4.10-12', *IndJournTheol* 31 (1982), pp. 35-46.

Farmer, W.R., *The Last Twelve Verses of Mark*, London: Cambridge University Press, 1974.

—*The Synoptic Problem: A Critical Analysis*, New York: MacMillan, 1964.

Farrer, A., 'An Examination of Mark XIII. 10', *JTS* 7 (1956), pp. 75-79.

—*A Study of St Mark*, London: Dacre Press, 1951.

—*St Matthew and St Mark*, London: A. & C. Black, 1954.

Fascher, E., 'Jesus und die Tiere', *TLZ* 90 (1965), pp. 561-570.

Faw, C.E., 'The Heart of the Gospel of Mark', *JBR* 24 (1956), pp. 77-82.

—'The Outline of Mark', *JBR* 25 (1957), pp. 19-23.

Feneberg, W., *Der Markusprolog: Studien zur Formbestimmung des Evangeliums*, München: Kösel-Verlag, 1974.

Fenton, J.C., 'Destruction and Salvation in the Gospel According to St.Mark', *JTS* 3 (1952), pp. 56-58.

—'Paul and Mark', in *Studies in the Gospels: Essays in Memory of R.H. Lightfoot*, ed. D.E. Nineham, Oxford: Basil Blackwell, 1955, pp. 89-112.

Feuillet, A., 'Le Baptême de Jésus', *RB* 71 (1964), pp. 321-52.

—'Le discours de Jésus sur la ruine du temple d'après Marc XIII et Luc XXI, 5-36', *RB* 55 (1948), pp. 481-502; 56 (1949), pp. 61-92.

—'Le logion sur la rançon', *RSPT* 51 (1967), pp. 365-402.

—'La signification fondamentale de Marc XIII: Recherches sur l'eschatologie des Synoptiques', *RevThom* 80 (1980), pp. 181-215.

Flanagan, N.M., 'Mark and the Temple Cleansing', *TBT* 63 (1972), pp. 980-84.

Fleddermann, H., 'And He wanted to Pass by Them' (Mark 6.48c)', *CBQ* 45 (1983), pp. 389-95.

—'The Discipleship Discourse (Mark 9.33-50)', *CBQ* 43 (1981), pp. 57-75.

Fletcher, D.R., 'Condemned to Die. The Logion on Cross-Bearing: What Does It Mean?' *Int* 18 (1964), pp. 156-64.

Flückiger, F., 'Die Redaktion der Zukunftsrede in Mark. 13', *TZ* 26 (1970), pp. 395-409.

Focant, C., 'L'incompréhension des disciples dans le deuxième évangile. Tradition et rédaction', *RB* 82 (1975), pp. 161-85.

Ford, D., *The Abomination of Desolation in Biblical Eschatology*, Washington, DC: University Press of America, 1979.

Ford, J.M., 'Money "Bags" in the Temple (Mk 11,16)', *Bib* 57 (1976), pp. 249-53.

—*My Enemy is My Guest: Jesus and Violence in Luke*, Maryknoll, NY: Orbis Books, 1984.

Fowler, R.M., *Loaves and Fishes: The Function of the Feeding Stories in the Gospel of Mark*, Chico, CA: Scholars Press, 1981.

France, R.T., *Jesus and the Old Testament: His Application of Old Testament Passages to Himself and His Mission*, London: Tyndale Press, 1971.

Freyne, S., 'At Cross Purposes: Jesus and the Disciples in Mark', *Furrow* 33 (1982), pp. 331-39.

Gaide, G., 'De l'admiration à la foi, Mc 1, 29-39, *AsSeign* 36 (1974), pp. 39-48.

Gärtner, B.E., *Markus Evangelium*, Stockholm: Verbum, 1970.

Gaston, L., *No Stone on Another: Studies in the Significance of the Fall of Jerusalem in the Synoptic Gospels*, Leiden: E.J. Brill, 1970.

Gennarini, S., 'Le principali interpretazioni postliberali della pericope della tras-figurazione di Gesu', *RevistStorLettRel* 8, (1972), pp. 80-132.

Giblin, C.H., *The Destruction of Jerusalem According to Luke's Gospel: A Historical-Typological Moral*, Rome: Biblical Institute Press, 1985.

Gibson, J.B., 'The Rebuke of the Disciples', *JSNT* 27 (1986), pp. 31-47.

Giesen, H., 'Mk 9,1—ein Wort Jesu über die nahe Parusie?' *TTZ* 92 (1983), pp. 134-48.

—'Der verdorrte Feigenbaum—Eine symbolische Aussage? Zu Mk 11,12-14.20f.' *BZ* 20 (1976), pp. 95-111.

Glasson, T.F., 'Mark xiii and the Greek Old Testament', *ExpTim* 69 (1958), pp. 213-15.

Glasswell, M.E., 'The Beginning of the Gospel: A Study of St. Mark's Gospel with Regard to its First Verse', in *New Testament Christianity for Africa and the World: Essays in Honour of Harry Sawyerr*, ed. M.E. Glasswell and E.W. Fasholé-Luke, London: SPCK, 1974, pp. 36-43.

—'The Relationship Between John and Mark', *JSNT* 23 (1985), pp. 99-115.

—'St. Mark's Attitude to the Relationship between History and the Gospel', in *Studia Biblica 1978*, II. *Papers on the Gospels, Sixth International Congress on Biblical Studies, Oxford, 3-7 April 1978*, ed. E.A. Livingstone, Sheffield: JSOT Press, 1980, pp. 115-127.

—'The Use of Miracles in the Markan Gospel', in *Miracles: Cambridge Studies in their Philosophy and History*, ed. C.F.D. Moule, London: A.R. Mowbray, 1965, pp. 149-62.

Gnilka, J., *Das Evangelium nach Markus, Mk 1-8,26*, Zürich: Benziger Verlag, 1978.

—*Das Evangelium nach Markus, Mk 8,27-16,20*, Zürich: Benziger Verlag, 1979.

Gould, E.P., *A Critical and Exegetical Commentary on the Gospel According to St. Mark*, Edinburgh: T&T Clark, 1896.

Goulder, M.D., 'The Empty Tomb', *Theology* 79 (1976), pp. 206-14.

Graham, H.H., 'The Gospel According to St. Mark: Mystery and Ambiguity', *ATR Supp.* 7 (1976), pp. 43-55.

Grant, F.C., *The Earliest Gospel*, New York: Abingdon Press, 1943.

—'The Gospel According to St. Mark', in *The Interpreter's Bible, VII*, New York: Abingdon Press, 1951, pp. 629-917.

Gräßer, E., *Die Naherwartung Jesu*, Stuttgart: Katholisches Bibelwerk, 1973.

—*Das Problem der Parusieverzögerung in den synoptischen Evangelien und in der Apostelgeschichte* (2nd ed.), Berlin: Verlag Alfred Töpelmann, 1960.

Grassi, J.A., '*Abba*, Father (Mark 14.36): Another Approach', *JAAR* 50 (1982), pp. 449-58.

Grayston, K., 'The Study of Mark XIII', *BJRL* 56 (1974), pp. 371-87.

Green, M.P., 'The Meaning of Cross-Bearing', *BSac* 140 (1983), pp. 117-33.

Greenwood, D.S., 'Poststructuralism and Biblical Studies: Frank Kermode's *The Genesis of Secrecy*', in *Gospel Perspectives: Studies in Midrash and Historiography, Vol. III*, ed. R.T. France and D. Wenham, Sheffield: JSOT Press, 1983, pp. 263-288.

Grundmann, W., *Das Evangelium nach Markus* (3rd ed.), Berlin: Evangelische Verlagsanstalt, 1968.

Guelich, R.A., '"The Beginning of the Gospel"—Mark 1.1-15', *BR* 27 (1982), pp. 5-15.

Gundry, R.H., *The Church and the Tribulation*, Grand Rapids, MI: Zondervan, 1973.

Haacker, K., 'Erwägungen zu Mc IV 11', *NovT* 14 (1972), pp. 219-25.

Haefner, A.E., 'The Bridge Between Mark and Acts', *JBL* 77 (1958), pp. 67-71.

Haenchen, E., 'Die Komposition von Mk viii 27—ix 1 und Par', *NovT* 6 (1963), pp. 81-109.

—*Der Weg Jesu: Eine Erklärung des Markus-Evangeliums und der kanonischen Parallelen*, (2nd ed.), Berlin: de Gruyter, 1968.

Hahn, F., 'Die Rede von der Parusie des Menschensohnes Markus 13', in *Jesus und der Menschensohn: Für Anton Vögtle*, ed. R. Pesch and R. Schnackenburg, in collaboration with O. Kaiser, Freiburg: Herder & Herder, 1975, pp. 240-66.

—*Mission in the New Testament*, London: SCM Press, 1965.

Hallbäck, G., 'Der anonyme Plan. Analyse von Mk 13, 5-27 im Hinblick auf die Relevance der apokalyptischen Rede für die Problematik der Aussage', *LingBib* 49 (1981), pp. 38-53.

Hamilton, N.Q., 'Resurrection Tradition and the Composition of Mark', *JBL* 84 (1965), pp. 415-21.

—'Temple Cleansing and Temple Bank', *JBL* 83 (1964), pp. 365-72.

Hamilton, R., 'The Gospel of Mark: Parable of God Incarnate', *Theology* 86 (1983), pp. 438-41.

Harder, G., 'Das eschatologische Geschichtsbild der sogenannten kleinen Apokalypse Markus 13', *ThViat* 4 (1948-49), pp. 71-107.

Harrington, W., *Mark*, Wilmington, DE: Michael Glazier, 1979.

Harrisville, R.A., *The Miracle of Mark: A Study in the Gospel*, Minneapolis, MN: Augsburg, 1967.

Hartman, L., *Prophecy Interpreted: The Formation of Some Jewish Apocalyptic Texts and of the Eschatological Discourse, Mark 13 par*, Lund: CWK Gleerup, 1966.

—Review of Pesch, R., *Naherwartungen*, *Bib* 50 (1969), pp. 576-80.

Hawkin, D.J., 'The Incomprehension of the Disciples in the Marcan Redaction', *JBL* 91 (1972), pp. 491-500.

—'The Symbolism and Structure of the Marcan Redaction', *EvQ* 49 (1977), pp. 98-110.

Hay, L.S., 'The Son of Man in Mark 2.10 and 2.28', *JBL* 89 (1970), pp. 69-75.

Hebert, G., 'The Resurrection-Narrative in St. Mark's Gospel', *SJT* 15 (1962), pp. 66-73.

Hedrick, C.W., 'The Role of "Summary Statements" in the Composition of the Gospel of Mark: A Dialogue with Karl Schmidt and Norman Perrin', *NovT* 26 (1984), pp. 289-311.

—'What Is a Gospel? Geography, Time, and Narrative Structure', *PerspRelStud* 10 (1983), pp. 255-68.

Hendriksen, W., *New Testament Commentary: Exposition of the Gospel According to Mark*, Grand Rapids, MI: Baker Book House, 1975.

Hengel, M., 'Das Gleichnis von den Weingärtnern Mc 12.1-12 im Lichte der Zenonpapyri und der rabbinischen Gleichnisse', *ZNW* 59 (1968), pp. 1-39.

—'Probleme des Markusevangeliums', in *Das Evangelium und die Evangelien*, ed. by P. Stuhlmacher, Tübingen: JCB Mohr, 1983, pp. 221-65.

—*Studies in the Gospel of Mark*, London: SCM Press, 1985.

Hiebert, D.E., *Mark: A Portrait of the Servant*, Chicago: Moody Press, 1974.

Hiers, R.H., *The Kingdom of God in the Synoptic Tradition*, Gainesville, FL: University of Florida P., 1970.

—'"Not the Season for Figs"', *JBL* 87 (1968), pp. 394-400.

—'Purification of the Temple: Preparation for the Kingdom of God', *JBL* 90 (1971), pp. 82-90.

Hirsch, E.D., Jr. *Validity in Interpretation*, New Haven, CT: Yale University Press, 1967.

Hooker, M.D., *The Message of Mark*, London: Epworth Press, 1983.

—Review of Hartman, L., *Prophecy Interpreted*, *JTS* 19 (1968), pp. 263-65.

—*The Son of Man in Mark: A Study of the Background of the Term 'Son of Man' and Its Use in St. Mark's Gospel*, London: SPCK, 1967.

—'Trial and Tribulation in Mark XIII', *BJRL* 65 (1982), pp. 78-99.

Horst, P.W., van der, 'Can a Book End With *GAR*? A Note on Mark xvi. 8', *JTS* 23 (1972), pp. 121-24.

Hoskyns, E.C., and Davey F.N., *The Riddle of the New Testament*, (3rd ed.), London: Faber & Faber, 1947.

Howard, J.K., 'Men as Trees, Walking: Mark 8.22-26', *SJT* 37 (1984), pp. 163-70.

—'Our Lord's Teaching Concerning His Parousia: A Study in the Gospel of Mark', *EvQ* 38 (1966), pp. 52-58; 68-75; 150-57.

Hunter, A.M., *The Gospel According to St. Mark*, London: SCM Press, 1948.

Hurtado, L.W., *Mark: A Good News Bible Commentary*, Basingstoke, Hants: Pickering & Inglis, 1984.

Iersel, B.M.F., van, 'The Gospel according to St Mark—written for a persecuted community?', *NedTTS* 34 (1980), pp. 15-36.

—'Locality, Structure, and Meaning in Mark', *LingBib* 53 (1983), pp. 45-54.

—'Theology and Detailed Exegesis', in *Theology, Exegesis and Proclamation*, ed. R. Murphy, New York: Herder & Herder, 1971, pp. 80-89.

—'"To Galilee" or "in Galilee" in Mark 14.28 and 16.7?' *ETL* 58 (1982), pp. 365-70.

—'Die wunderbare Speisung und das Abendmahl in der synoptischen Tradition (Mk vi 35-44 par., viii 1-20 par.)', *NovT* 7 (1964). pp. 167-94.

—and Linmans, A.J.M., 'The Storm on the Lake, Mk iv 35-41 and Mt viii 18-27 in the Light of Form Criticism, "Redaktionsgeschichte" and Structural Analysis', in *Miscellanea Neotestamentica, II*, ed. T. Baarda, A.F.J. Klihn and W.C. van Unnik. Leiden: E.J. Brill, 1978, pp. 17-48.

Jeremias, J., *The Eucharistic Words of Jesus*, London: SCM Press, 1976.

—*New Testament Theology*, New York: Charles Scribner's Sons, 1971.

—*The Parables of Jesus*, (2nd English ed.), London: SCM Press, 1963.

Johnson, S.E., 'Mark viii. 22-26: The Blind Man from Bethsaida', *NTS* 25 (1979), pp. 370-83.

Johnson, S.E. *A Commentary on the Gospel According to St. Mark*, London: A. & C. Black, 1960.

Jones, A., 'Did Christ Foretell the End of the World in Mark XIII?', *Scr* 4 (1951), pp. 264-73.

—'The Eschatology of the Synoptic Gospels', *Scr* 4 (1950), pp. 222-30.

Juel, D., *Messiah and Temple: The Trial of Jesus in the Gospel of Mark*, Missoula, MT: Scholars Press, 1977.

Kallikuzhuppil, J., 'The Glorification of the Suffering Church (Mk 13.1-37)', *Biblebhashyam* 9 (1983), pp. 247-57.

Kazmierski, C.R., *Jesus, the Son of God: A Study of the Markan Tradition and its Redaction by the Evangelist*, Würzburg: Echter-Verlag, 1979.

Kealy, S.P., *Mark's Gospel: A History of Its Interpretation. From the Beginning until 1979*, New York: Paulist Press, 1982.

Keck, L.E., 'Mark and the Passion', *Int* 31 (1977), pp. 432-34.

Kee, H.C., *Community of the New Age: Studies in Mark's Gospel*, London: SCM Press, 1977.

—*Jesus in History: An Approach to the Study of the Gospels*, (2nd ed.), New York: Harcourt Brace Jovanovich, 1977.

328   *Watchwords*

—'Mark as Redactor and Theologian: A Survey of Some Recent Markan Studies', *JBL* 90 (1971), pp. 333-36.

—'Mark's Gospel in Recent Research', *Int* 32 (1978), pp. 353-68.

—'Scripture Quotations and Allusions in Mark 11-16', in *Society of Biblical Literature 1971 Seminar Papers II*, ed. L.C. McGaughy, Atlanta, GA: Society of Biblical Literature, 1971, pp. 475-502.

Kelber, W.H., 'Conclusion: From Passion Narrative to Gospel', in *The Passion in Mark*, ed. W. Kelber, Philadelphia: Fortress Press, 1976, pp. 153-80.

—'The History of the Kingdom in Mark—Aspects of Markan Eschatology', in *Society of Biblical Literature 1972 Seminar Papers I*, ed. L.C. McGaughy, Los Angeles: Society of Biblical Literature, 1972, pp. 63-95.

—'The Hour of the Son of Man and the Temptation of the Disciples (Mark 14.32-42)', in *The Passion in Mark*, ed. W.H. Kelber, Philadelphia: Fortress Press, 1976, pp. 41-60.

—*The Kingdom in Mark: A New Place and a New Time*, Philadelphia: Fortress Press, 1974.

—*Mark's Story of Jesus*, Philadelphia: Fortress Press, 1979.

—*The Oral and the Written Gospel*, Philadelphia: Fortress Press, 1983.

—(Editor), *The Passion in Mark: Studies in Mark 14-16*, Philadelphia: Fortress Press, 1976.

Keller, J., 'Jesus and the Critics: A Logico-Critical Analysis of the Marcan Confrontations', *Int* 40 (1986), pp. 29-38.

Kelly, H.A., 'The Devil in the Desert', *CBQ* 26 (1964), pp. 190-220.

Kermode, F., *The Genesis of Secrecy: On the Interpretation of Narrative*, London: Harvard University Press, 1979.

Kernaghan, R., 'History and Redaction in the Controversy Stories in Mark 2.1—3.6', *Studia Biblica et Theologica* 9 (1979), pp. 23-47.

Kertelge, K., 'The Epiphany of Jesus in the Gospel (Mark)', in *The Interpretation of Mark*, ed. W.R. Telford, Philadelphia: Fortress Press, 1985, pp. 78-94.

—*Die Wunder Jesu im Markusevangelium: Eine redaktionsgeschichtliche Untersuchung*, München: Kösel-Verlag, 1970.

Kiddle, M., 'The Death of Jesus and the Admission of the Gentiles in St Mark', *JTS* (OS) 35 (1934), pp. 45-50.

Kilgallen, J.J., 'The Messianic Secret and Mark's Purpose', *BTB* 7 (1977), pp. 60-65.

Kilpatrick, G.D., 'The Gentile Misson in Mark and Mk 13, 9-11', in *Studies in the Gospels: Essays in Memory of R.H. Lightfoot*, ed. D.E. Nineham, Oxford: Basil Blackwell, 1955, pp. 145-58.

—'Mark XIII 9-10', *JTS* 9 (1958), pp. 81-86.

Kingsbury, J.D., *The Christology of Mark's Gospel*, Philadelphia: Fortress Press, 1983.

—'The Gospel of Mark in Current Research', *RelStudRev* 5 (1979), pp. 101-107.

Klauck, H.-J., 'Die erzählerische Rolle der Jünger im Markusevangelium. Eine narrative Analyse', *NovT* 24 (1982), pp. 1-26.

Knigge, H.-D., 'The Meaning of Mark. The Exegesis of the Second Gospel', *Int* 22 (1968), pp. 53-70.

Koch, K., *The Rediscovery of Apocalyptic*, London: SCM Press, 1972.

Kolenkow, A.B., 'Beyond Miracles, Suffering and Eschatology', *Society of Biblical Literature 1973 Seminar Papers, II*, ed. G. MacRae, Cambridge, MA: Society of Biblical Literature, 1973, pp. 155-202.

Kosmala, H., 'The Time of the Cock-Crow, II', *ASTI* 6 (1968), pp. 132-34.

Kremer, J., 'Jesu Antwort auf die Frage nach seiner Vollmacht. Eine Auslegung von Mk 11, 27-33', *BibLeb* 9 (1968), pp. 128-36.

Kuby, A., 'Zur Konzeption des Markus-Evangeliums', *ZNW* 49 (1958), pp. 52-64.

Kümmel, W.G., *Promise and Fulfilment*, London: SCM Press, 1957.

Künzi, M., *Das Naherwartungslogion Mk 9.1 par: Geschichte seiner Auslegung, mit einem Nachwort zur Auslegungsgeschichte von Markus 13, 30 par*, Tübingen: J.C.B. Mohr, 1977.

Ladd, G.E., *Jesus and the Kingdom: The Eschatology of Biblical Realism*, New York: Harper & Row, 1964.

—*The Presence of the Future: The Eschatology of Biblical Realism*, Grand Rapids, MI: Eerdmans, 1974.

Lagrange, M.-J., *Evangile selon Saint Marc*, (4th ed.), Paris: J. Gabalda, 1966.

Lamarche, P., 'La mort du Christ et le voile du temple selon Marc', *NRT* 106 (1974), pp. 583-99.

Lambrecht, J., 'The Christology of Mark', *BTB* 3 (1973), pp. 256-73.

—'A Man to Follow: The Message of Mark', *Revue Africaine de Théologie* 4 (1980), pp. 37-53.

—'Parables in Mc. 4', *TijdTheol* (1975), pp. 26-43.

—*Parables of Jesus: Insight and Challenge*, Bangalore, India: Theological Publications in India, 1978.

—'Redaction and Theology in Mk. IV', in *L'Evangile selon Marc: Tradition et rédaction*, ed. M. Sabbe, Leuven: Leuven University Press, 1974, pp. 269-307.

—*Die Redaktion Der Markus-Apokalypse: Literarische Analyse und Structuruntersuchung*, Rome: Päpstliche Bibelinstitut, 1967.

—'The Relatives of Jesus in Mark', *NovT* 16 (1974), pp. 241-58.

—'De vijf parabels van Mc. 4, Structuur en theologie van de parabelrede', *Bijdragen* 29 (1968), pp. 25-53.

Lane, W.L., 'From Historian to Theologian: Milestones in Markan Scholarship', *RevExp* 75 (1978), pp. 601-17.

—*The Gospel According to Mark: The English Text with Introduction, Exposition and Notes*, Grand Rapids, MI: Eerdmans, 1974.

LaVerdiere, E.A., 'The End, a Beginning', *Emmanuel* 90 (1984), pp. 484-91.

Lee, J.A.L., 'Some Features of the Speech of Jesus in Mark's Gospel', *NovT* 27 (1985), pp. 1-26.

Leitch, J.W., 'The Injunctions of Silence in Mark's Gospel', *ExpTim* 66 (1955), pp. 178-82.

Lemcio, E.E., 'External Evidence for the Structure and Function of Mark iv. 1-20, vii. 14-23 and viii. 14-21', *JTS* 29 (1978), pp. 323-38.

—'The Intention of the Evangelist, Mark', *NTS* 32 (1986), pp. 187-206.

Lescow, T., 'Jesus in Gethsemane', *EvT* 26 (1966), pp. 141-59.

Lightfoot, R.H., *The Gospel Message of St. Mark*, London: Oxford University Press, 1950.

—*History and Interpretation in the Gospels*, London: Hodder & Stoughton, 1935.

—*Locality and Doctrine in the Gospels*, London: Hodder & Stoughton, 1938.

Lindemann, A., 'Die Osterbotschaft des Markus. Zur theologischen Interpretation von Mark 16.1-8', *NTS* 26 (1980), pp. 298-317.

Lindeskog, G., 'The Veil of the Temple', *ConNT* 11 (1948), pp. 132-37.

Linton, O., 'The Demand for a Sign from Heaven (Mk 8, 11-12 and Parallels)', *ST* 19 (1965), pp. 112-29.

Lindsay, T.M., *The Gospel According to St. Mark*, Edinburgh: T. & T. Clark, 1883.

Linnemann, E., *Studien zur Passionsgeschichte*, Göttingen: Vandenhoeck & Ruprecht, 1970.

330   *Watchwords*

—'Der (wiedergefundene) Markusschluß', *ZTK* 66 (1969), pp. 255-87.

Lohmeyer, E., *Das Evangelium des Markus. übersetzt und erklärt* (17th ed.), Göttingen: Vandenhoeck & Ruprecht, 1967.

—*Galiläa und Jerusalem*, Göttingen: Vandenhoeck & Ruprecht, 1936.

—*Lord of the Temple: A Study of the Relationship Between Cult and Gospel*, Richmond, VA: John Knox Press, 1962.

Lohse, E., *Mark's Witness to Jesus Christ* (2nd ed.), London: Lutterworth Press, 1955.

Longenecker, R.N., 'The Messianic Secret in the Light of Recent Discoveries', *EvQ* 41 (1969), pp. 207-15.

Losada, D., 'La muerte de Juan el Bautista. Mc 6, 17-29', *RevistB* 39 (1977), pp. 143-54.

Losie, L.A., 'The Cursing of the Fig Tree: Tradition Criticism of a Marcan Pericope (Mark 11.12-14, 20-25)', *Studia Biblica et Theologica* 7 (1977), pp. 3-18.

Lövestam, E., 'The ἡ γενεά αὕτη Eschatology in Mk 13, 30 parr', in *L'Apocalypse johannique et l'Apocalyptique dans le Nouveau Testament*, ed. J. Lambrecht, Leuven: Leuven University Press, 1980, pp. 403-13.

—'Spiritual Wakefulness in the New Testament', *Lunds Universitets Arsskrift* 55 No. 3 (1963), pp. 1-170.

Luz, U., 'The Secrecy Motif and the Marcan Christology', in *The Messianic Secret*, ed. C. Tuckett, London: SPCK, 1983, pp. 75-96.

McCasland, S.V., 'Signs and Wonders', *JBL* 76 (1957), pp. 149-52.

McCaughey, J.D., 'Literary Criticism and the Gospels—A Rumination', *AusBR* 29 (1981), pp. 16-25.

—'Three "Persecution Documents" of the New Testament', *AusBR* 17 (1969), pp. 27-40.

McCombie, F., 'Jesus and the Leaven of Salvation', *NewBlackfr* 59 (1978), pp. 450-62.

McCowen, A., *Personal Mark*, London: Fount, 1985.

McKelvey, R.J., *The New Temple: The Church in the New Testament*, London: Oxford University Press, 1968.

Malbon, E.S., 'Disciples/Crowds/Whoever: Markan Characters and Readers', *NovT* 28 (1986), pp. 104-30.

—'Fallible Followers: Women and Men in the Gospel of Mark', *Semeia* 28 (1983), pp. 29-48.

—Galilee and Jerusalem: History and Literature in Marcan Interpretation', *CBQ* 44 (1982), pp. 242-55.

—'Mythic Structure and Meaning in Mark: Elements of Lévi-Straussian Analysis', *Semeia* 16 (1980), pp. 97-132.

Malley, E.J., 'The Gospel According to Mark', in *The Jerome Bible Commentary, II*, ed. R.E. Brown, J.A. Fitzmyer, and R.E. Murphy, London: Geoffrey Chapman, 1968, pp. 21-61.

Manek, J., 'Mark viii 14-21', *NovT* 7 (1964), pp. 10-14.

Manson, T.W., 'The Cleansing of the Temple', *BJRL* 33 (1951), pp. 271-82.

—'The Purpose of the Parables: A Re-Examination of St. Mark iv. 10-12', *ExpTim* 68 (1957), pp. 132-35.

Marcus, J., 'Mark 4.10-12 and Marcan Epistemology', *JBL* 103 (1984), pp. 557-74.

Marshall, I.H., *Eschatology and the Parables*, London: Tyndale, 1963.

—*The Gospel of Luke: A Commentary on the Greek Text*, Grand Rapids, MI: Eerdmans, 1978.

—(Editor), *New Testament Interpretation: Essays on Principles and Methods*, Grand Rapids, MI: Eerdmans, 1977.

—'St. Mark', in *The Daily Commentary*, ed. A.E. Cundall, London: Scripture Union, 1974, pp. 104-66.

—'Slippery Words: I. Eschatology', *ExpTim* 89 (1978), pp. 264-69.

Martin, R., 'The Messianic Secret in Mark', *CurTM* 11 (1984), pp. 350-52.

Martin, R.P., *Mark: Evangelist and Theologian*, Exeter: Paternoster, 1972.

Martini, C.M., 'La confessione messianica di Pietro a Cesarea e l'inizio del nuovo popolo di Dio secondo il Vangelo di S. Marco (8, 27-33)', *CivCatt* 118/2 (1967), pp. 544-51.

Martyn, J.L., *History and Theology in the Fourth Gospel*, New York: Harper & Row, 1968.

Marxsen, W., *Mark the Evangelist: Studies on the Redaction History of the Gospel*, Nashville: Abingdon Press, 1969.

Matera, F.J., 'Interpreting Mark—Some recent theories of Redaction Criticism', *LouvStud* 2 (1968), pp. 113-31.

—*The Kingship of Jesus: Composition and Theology in Mark 15*, Chico, CA: Scholars Press, 1982.

Mauser, U.W., *Christ in the Wilderness: The Wilderness Theme in the Second Gospel and Its Basis in the Biblical Tradition*, Naperville, IL: Allenson, 1963.

Meagher, J.C., *Clumsy Construction in Mark's Gospel: A Critique of Form- and Redaktionsgeschichte*, New York: Edwin Mellen Press, 1980.

Menzies, A., *The Earliest Gospel*, London: MacMillan, 1901.

Meye, R.P., *Jesus and the Twelve: Discipleship and Revelation in Mark's Gospel*, Grand Rapids, MI: Eerdmans, 1968.

—'Mk 4.10; "Those about Him with the Twelve"', in *Studia Evangelica II: Papers Presented to the Second International Congress on New Testament Studies held at Christ Church, Oxford, 1961*, ed. F.L. Cross, Berlin: Akademie-Verlag, 1964, pp. 211-18.

—'Mark 16.8—The Ending of Mark's Gospel', *BR* 14 (1969), pp. 33-43.

—'Psalm 107 as "Horizon" for Interpreting the Miracle Stories of Mark 4.35—8.26', in *Unity and Diversity in New Testament Theology: Essays in Honor of George E. Ladd*, ed. R.A. Guelich, Grand Rapids, MI: Eerdmans, 1978, pp. 1-13.

Michaelis, W., ὁράω, *TDNT* V, pp. 315-82.

Michaels, J.R., 'The Centurion's Confession and the Spear Thrust', *CBQ* 29 (1967), pp. 102-109.

Milling, F.H., 'History and Prophecy in the Marcan Passion Narrative', *IndJournTheol* 16 (1967), pp. 42-53.

Minear, P.S., 'Audience Criticism and Markan Ecclesiology', in *Neues Testament und Geschichte: Historisches Geschehen und Deutung im Neuen Testament: Oscar Cullmann zum 70. Geburtstag*, ed. H. Baltensweiler and B. Reicke, Zürich: Theologischer Verlag, 1972.

—*The Gospel According to Mark*, Richmond: John Knox Press, 1962.

Minnette de Tillesse, G., *Le secret messianique dans l'évangile de Marc*, Paris: Editions du Cerf, 1968.

Mitton, C.L., *The Gospel According to St. Mark*, London: Epworth Press, 1957.

Mohn, W., 'Gethsemane (Mk 14.32-42)', *ZNW* 64 (1973), pp. 194-208.

Moloney, F.J., 'The Vocation of the Disciples in the Gospel of Mark', *Salesianum* 43 (1981), pp. 487-516.

Montefiore, C.G., *The Synoptic Gospels, I*, New York: KTAV Publishing House, 1968.

Moore, A.L., *The Parousia in the New Testament*, Leiden: E.J. Brill, 1966.

Moore, C.A., 'Mark 4.12: More Like the Irony of Micaiah than Isaiah', in *A Light unto my Path: Old Testament Studies in honor of Jacob M. Meyers*, ed. H.N. Bream, R.D. Heim and C.A. Moore, Philadelphia: Temple University Press, 1974, pp. 335-44.

Mora, V., *Le signe de Jonas*, Paris: Editions du Cerf, 1983.

Morris, L., *Apocalyptic*, Grand Rapids, MI: Eerdmans, 1972.

Mosley, A.W., 'Jesus' Audiences in the Gospels of St Mark and St Luke', *NTS* 10 (1963), pp. 139-49.

Moule, C.F.D., *The Gospel According to Mark*, Cambridge: Cambridge University Press, 1965.

—'Mark 4.1-20 Yet Once More', in *Neotestamentica et Semitica*, ed. E.E. Ellis and M. Wilcox, Edinburgh: T. & T. Clark, 1969, pp. 95-113.

—(Editor), *Miracles: Cambridge Studies in Their Philosophy and History*, London: A.R. Mowbray, 1965.

—'On Defining the Messianic Secret in Mark', in *Jesus und Paulus: Festschrift für Werner Georg Kümmel zum 70. Geburtstag*, (2nd ed.), ed. E.E. Ellis and E. Grässer, Göttingen: Vandenhoeck & Ruprecht, 1978, pp. 239-52.

—'St. Mark XVI.8 Once More', *NTS* 2 (1956), pp. 58-59.

Muddiman, J.B., 'Jesus and Fasting: Mark ii. 18-22', in *Jesus aux origines de la christologie*, ed. J. Dupont, Leuven: Leuven University Press, 1975, pp. 271-81.

Münderlein, G., 'Die Verfluchung des Feigenbaumes (Mk. xi.12-14)', *NTS* 10 (1963), pp. 89-104.

Murray, D.J., 'Mark's Theology of Baptism', *Dimension* 8 (1976), pp. 92-97.

Mußner, F., 'Die Bedeutung von Mk 1, 14f. für die Reichgottesverkündigung', *TTZ* 66 (1957), pp. 257-75.

—*Christ and the End of the World: A Biblical Study in Eschatology*, Notre Dame, IN: University of Notre Dame P., 1965.

—'Gleichnisauslegung und Heilsgeschichte: Dargetan am Gleichnis von der wachsenden Saat (Mc 4,24-29)', *TTZ* 64 (1955), pp. 257-66.

Nardoni, E., 'A Redactional Interpretation of Mark 9.1', *CBQ* 43 (1981), pp. 365-84.

Navone, J., 'Mark's Story of the Death of Jesus', *NewBlackfr* 65 (1984), pp. 123-35.

Negoïtă, A., and Daniel, C., 'L'énigme du levain. Ad Mc. viii 15; Mt. xvi 6; et Lc. xii 1', *NovT* 9 (1967), pp. 306-14.

Neil, W., 'Expounding the Parables: II, The Sower (Mk 4.3-8)', *ExpTim* 77 (1965), pp. 74-77.

Neirynck, F., *Duality in Mark: Contributions to the Study of the Markan Redaction*, Leuven: Leuven University Press, 1972.

—*L'Evangile de Marc. A propos du commentaire de R. Pesch*, Leuven: Editions Peeters, 1979.

—'The Redactional Text of Mark', in *Evangelica: Gospel Studies—Etudes d'évangile: Collected Essays*, ed. F. van Segbroeck. Leuven: Leuven University Press, 1982, pp. 618-36.

Neville, G., *The Advent Hope: A Study of the Context of Mark 13*, London: Darton, Longman & Todd, 1961.

Newell, J.E., and R.R., 'The Parable of the Wicked Tenants', *NovT* 14 (1972), pp. 226-37.

Nickelsburg, G.W.E., 'The Genre and Function of the Markan Passion Narrative', *HTR* 73 (1980), pp. 153-84.

Niederwimmer, K., 'Johannes Markus und die Frage nach dem Verfasser des zweiten Evangeliums', *ZNW* 58 (1967), pp. 172-88.

Nineham, D.E., *The Gospel of St Mark*, Middlesex: Penguin Books, 1963.
—'St. Mark's Gospel', *Theology* 60 (1957), pp. 267-72.
Nützel, J.M., 'Hoffnung und Treue: Zur Eschatologie des Markusevangeliums', in *Gegenwart und kommendes Reich: Schülergabe Anton Vögtle zum 65. Geburtstag*, ed. P. Fiedler and D. Zeller, Stuttgart: Verlag Katholisches Bibelwerk, 1975, pp. 79-90.
Oepke, A., 'ἐγείρω', *TDNT* II, pp. 333-39.
O'Mahony, G., 'Mark's Gospel and the Parable of the Sower', *TBT* 98 (1978), pp. 1764-68.
Osborne, G.R., 'Redactional Trajectories in the Crucifixion Narrative', *EvQ* 51 (1979), pp. 80-96.
Ottley, R.R., *'ephobounto gar* Mark xvi 8', *JTS* 27 (1926), pp. 407-09.
Parker, P., 'The Authorship of the Second Gospel', *PerspRelStud* 5 (1978), pp. 4-9.
Patte, D., (Editor), *Semiology and Parables: Exploration of the Possibilities Offered By Structuralism for Exegesis*, Pittsburgh: Pickwick Press, 1976.
Patten, P., 'The Form and Function of Parable in Select Apocalyptic Literature and Their Significance for Parables in the Gospel of Mark', *NTS* 29 (1983), pp. 246-58.
Paul, A., 'Guérison de Bartimée. Mc 10,46-52', *AsSeign* 61 (1972), pp. 44-52.
Paulsen, H., 'Mk xvi 1-8', *NovT* 22 (1980), pp. 138-75.
Pedersen, S., 'Is Mark 4,1-34 a Parable Chapter?' in *Studia Evangelica 6: Papers presented to the Fourth International Congress on New Testament Studies held at Oxford, 1969*, ed. E.A. Livingstone, Berlin: Akademie-Verlag, 1973, pp. 408-16.
Pérez Fernández, M., '"prope est aestas" (Mc 13,32; Mt 24,32; Lc 21,29)', *VD* 46 (1968), pp. 361-69.
Perrin, N., 'The Christology of Mark: a Study in Methodology', in *The Interpretation of Mark*, ed. W.R. Telford, Philadelphia: Fortress Press, 1985, pp. 95-108.
—'The Composition of Mark ix, 1', *NovT* 11 (1969), pp. 67-70.
—'Gospel of Mark', *The Interpreter's Dictionary of the Bible Supplementary Volume*, Nashville: Abingdon Press, 1976, pp. 571-73.
—'The High Priest's Question and Jesus' Answer (Mark 14.61-62)', in *The Passion in Mark*, ed. W. Kelber, Philadelphia: Fortress Press, 1976, pp. 80-95.
—'The Interpretation of the Gospel of Mark', *Int* 30 (1976), pp. 115-24.
—*Jesus and the Language of the Kingdom. Symbol and Metaphor in New Testament Interpretation*, Philadelphia: Fortress Press, 1976.
—*A Modern Pilgrimage in New Testament Christology*, Philadelphia: Fortress Press, 1974.
—*Rediscovering the Teaching of Jesus*, New York: Harper & Row, 1976.
—*The Resurrection According to Matthew, Mark and Luke*, Philadelphia: Fortress Press, 1977.
—'Towards an Interpretation of the Gospel of Mark', in *Christology and a Modern Pilgrimage: A Discussion with Norman Perrin*, ed. H.D. Betz, Claremont, CA: New Testament Colloquium, 1971, pp. 1-78.
—*What is Redaction Criticism?* London: SPCK, 1970.
—and Duling, D.C., 'The Gospel of Mark: The Apocalyptic Drama', in *The New Testament: An Introduction*, (2nd ed.), ed. N. Perrin and D.C. Duling, New York: Harcourt Brace Jovanovich, 1982, pp. 233-62.
Perrot, C., 'Essai sur la Discours eschatologique (*Mc. XIII*, 1-37; *Mt. XXIV*, 1-36; *Lc. XXI*, 5-36)', *RSR* 47 (1959), pp. 481-514.
Pesch, R., 'Anfang des Evangeliums Jesu Christi: Eine Studie zum Prolog des Markusevangeliums (Mk. 1,1-15)', in *Die Zeit Jesu: Festschrift für Heinrich*

Schlier, ed. G. Bornkamm and K. Rahner, Freiburg: Herder & Herder, 1970, pp. 108-44.

—*Das Markusevangelium. I. Teil: Einleitung und Kommentar zu Kap. 1,1-8,26*, Freiburg: Herder & Herder, 1976.

—*Das Markusevangelium. II. Teil: Kommentar zu Kap. 8,27-16,20*, Freiburg: Herder & Herder, 1977.

—*Naherwartungen: Tradition und Redaktion in Mk. 13*, Düsseldorf: Patmos-Verlag, 1968.

Petersen, N.R., 'The Composition of Mark 4.1-8.26', *HTR* 73 (1980), pp. 185-217.

—*Literary Criticism for New Testament Critics*, Philadelphia: Fortress Press, 1978.

—'"Point of View" in Mark's Narrative', *Semeia* 12 (1978), pp. 97-121.

—'The Reader in the Gospel', *Neot* 18 (1984), pp. 38-51.

—'When is the End not the End? Literary Reflections on the Ending of Mark's Narrative', *Int* 34 (1980), pp. 151-66.

Piper, O.A., 'God's Good News: The Passion Story According to Mark', *Int* 9 (1955), pp. 165-82.

Pryke, E.J., *Redactional Style in the Markan Gospel: A Study of Syntax and Vocabulary as Guides to Redaction in Mark*, Cambridge: Cambridge University Press, 1978.

Pryor, J.W., 'Markan Parable Theology: An Inquiry into Mark's Principles of Redaction', *ExpTim* 83 (1972), pp. 242-45.

Quesnell, Q., *The Mind of Mark. Interpretation and Method Through the Exegesis of Mark 6.52*, Rome: Pontifical Biblical Institute, 1969.

Räisänen, H., 'The "Messianic Secret" in Mark's Gospel', in *The Messianic Secret*, ed. C. Tuckett, London: SPCK, 1983, pp. 132-40.

—*Das 'Messiasgeheimnis' Im Markusevangelium: Ein redaktionskritischer Versuch*, Helsinki: Finnish Exegetical Society, 1976.

—*Die Parabeltheorie im Markusevangelium*, Helsinki: Finnish Exegetical Society, 1973.

Rawlinson, A.E.J., *St. Mark* (7th ed.), London: Methuen, 1949.

Reedy, C.J., 'Mk 8.31-11.10 and the Gospel Ending: A Redaction Study', *CBQ* 34 (1972), pp. 188-97.

Reicke, B., 'Synoptic Prophecies on the Destruction of Jerusalem', in *Studies in New Testament and Early Christian Literature: Essays in Honor of Allen P. Wikgren*, ed. D.E. Aune, Leiden: E.J. Brill, 1972, pp. 121-34.

Rengstorf, K.H., 'σημεῖον', *TDNT*, VII, pp. 200-69.

Reploh, K.-G., *Markus—Lehrer der Gemeinde. Eine redaktionsgeschichtliche Studie zu den Jüngerperikopen des Markus-Evangeliums*, Stuttgart: Katholisches Bibelwerk, 1969.

Rhoads, D., 'Narrative Criticism and the Gospel of Mark', *JAAR* 50 (1982), pp. 411-34.

—and Michie, D., *Mark as Story: An Introduction to the Narrative of a Gospel*, Philadelphia: Fortress Press, 1982.

Richard, E., 'Expressions of Double Meaning and their Function in the Gospel of John', *NTS* 31 (1985), pp. 96-112.

Richardson, A., 'The Feeding of the Five Thousand: Mark 6.34-44', *Int* 9 (1955), pp. 144-49.

—*The Miracle-Stories of the Gospels*, (2nd ed.), London: SCM Press, 1942.

Riesner, R., *Jesus als Lehrer: Eine Untersuchung zum Ursprung der Evangelienüberlieferung*, Tübingen: Mohr/Siebeck, 1981.

Rigaux, B., *The Testimony of St. Mark*, Chicago: Franciscan Herald Press, 1966.

Robbins, V.K., 'Dynameis and Semeia in Mark', BR 18 (1973), pp. 5-20.
—Jesus the Teacher: A Socio-Rhetorical Interpretation of Mark, Philadelphia: Fortress Press, 1984.
—'Last Meal: Preparation, Betrayal, and Absence (Mark 14.12-25)', in The Passion in Mark, ed. W. Kelber, Philadelphia: Fortress Press, 1976, pp. 21-40.
Roberts, R.E., The Message of the Parables, London: Epworth Press, 1935.
Robertson, A.T., Studies in Mark's Gospel, rev. and ed. H.F. Peacock, Nashville: Broadman Press, 1958.
—Word Pictures In The New Testament. Vol. I. Matthew Mark, New York: Richard R. Smith, 1930.
Robey, D. (Editor), Structuralism: An Introduction: Wolfson College Lectures 1972, Oxford: Clarendon Press, 1973.
Robinson, J.A.T., Jesus and His Coming, (2nd ed.), London: SCM Press, 1979.
—'The Second Coming—Mark xiv. 62', ExpTim 67 (1956), pp. 336-40.
—Twelve New Testament Studies, London: SCM Press, 1962.
Robinson, J.M., 'Kerygma and History in the New Testament', in The Bible in Modern Scholarship, ed. J.P. Hyatt, Nashville: Abingdon Press, 1965.
—'The Literary Composition of Mark', in L'Evangile selon Marc: Tradition et rédaction, ed. M. Sabbe, Leuven: Leuven University Press, 1974, pp. 11-19.
—'On the Gattung of Mark (and John)', Perspective 11 (1970), pp. 99-129.
—The Problem of History in Mark, London: SCM Press, 1957.
—'The Problem of History in Mark, Reconsidered', USQR 20 (1965), pp. 131-47.
Robinson, W.C., Jr., 'The Quest for Wrede's Messianic Secret', in The Messianic Secret, ed. C. Tuckett, London: SPCK, 1983, pp. 97-115.
Rohde, J., Rediscovering the Teaching of the Evangelists, Philadelphia: Westminster, 1968.
Romaniuk, K.,'"Car ce n'était pas la saison des figues ... " (Mk 11.12-14 parr)', ZNW 66 (1975), pp. 275-78.
Roth, C., 'The Cleansing of the Temple and Zechariah xiv 21', NovT 4 (1960), pp. 174-81.
Rousseau, R.P., 'John the Baptist: Jesus' Forerunner in Mark's Christology', TBT 77 (1975), pp. 316-22.
Russell, D. S., Apocalyptic: Ancient and Modern, London: SCM Press, 1978.
—The Method and Message of Jewish Apocalyptic, Philaldephia: Westminster, 1964.
Sabbe, M. (Editor), L'Evangile selon Marc: Tradition et rédaction, Leuven: Leuven University Press, 1974.
Sandmel, S., 'Prolegomena to a Commentary on Mark', JBR 31 (1963), pp. 294-300.
Schenke, L., Glory and the Way of the Cross: The Gospel of Mark, Chicago: Franciscan Herald Press, 1972.
—Studien zur Passionsgeschichte des Markus: Tradition und Redaktion in Markus 14,1-42, Würzburg: Echter-Verlag, 1971.
—Die Wundererzählungen des Markusevangeliums, Stuttgart: Katholisches Bibelwerk, 1974.
Schmahl, G., Die Zwölf im Markusevangelium, Trier: Paulinus-Verlag, 1974.
Schmid, J., The Gospel According to Mark: A Version and Commentary, Staten Island, NY: Alba House, 1969.
Schmidt, K.L., Der Rahmen der Geschichte Jesu, Darmstadt: Wissenschaftliche Buchgesellschaft, 1969.
Schmithals, W., Das Evangelium nach Markus, I-II, Gütersloh: G. Mohn, 1979.
Schnackenburg, R., '"Das Evangelium" im Verständnis des ältesten Evangelisten', in

Orientierung an Jesus: Zur Theologie der Synoptiker: Für Josef Schmid, ed.
P. Hoffman, N. Brox and W. Pesch, Freiburg: Herder, 1973, pp. 309-24.

—*The Gospel According to St. Mark I-II*, London: Sheed & Ward, 1971.

Schneider, G.,'Gab es eine vorsynoptische Szene "Jesus vor dem Synedrium"?' *NovT* 12 (1970), pp. 22-39.

Schnellbächer, E.L., 'The Temple as Focus of Mark's Theology', *HorBibTheol* 5 (1983), pp. 95-112.

Schniewind, J., *Das Evangelium nach Markus: übersetzt und erklärt*, (5th ed.), Göttingen: Vandenhoeck & Ruprecht, 1949.

Schottroff, W., and Stegemann, W. (Editors), *God of the Lowly: Socio-Historical Interpretations of the Bible*, Maryknoll, NY: Orbis Books, 1984.

Schreiber, J., *Die Markuspassion; Wege zur Erforschung der Leidensgeschichte Jesu*, Hamburg: Furche-Verlag, 1969.

—*Theologie des Vertrauens: Eine redaktionsgeschichtliche Untersuchung des Markus-evangeliums*, Hamburg: Furche-Verlag, 1967.

Schrenk, G., 'ἱερός' *TDNT* Vol. III, pp. 221-83.

Schulz, S., 'Mark's Significance for the Theology of Early Christianity', in *The Interpretation of Mark*, ed. W.R. Telford, Philadelphia: Fortress Press, 1985, pp. 158-66.

—'Markus und das Alte Testament', *ZTK* 58 (1961), pp. 184-97.

Schweitzer, A., *The Quest of the Historical Jesus: A Critical study of Its Progress from Reimarus to Wrede*, London: A. & C. Black, 1948.

Schweizer, E., 'Eschatology in Mark's Gospel', in *Neotestamentica et Semitica: Studies in honour of Matthew Black*, ed. E.E. Ellis and M. Wilcox, Edinburgh: T. & T. Clark, 1969, pp. 114-18.

—*The Good News According to Mark*, Atlanta, GA: John Knox Press, 1970.

—*Lordship and Discipleship*, London: SCM Press, 1960.

—'Mark's Contribution to the Quest of the Historical Jesus', *NTS* 10 (1964), pp. 421-32.

—'Mark's Theological Achievement', in *The Interpretation of Mark*, ed. W.R. Telford, Philadelphia: Fortress Press, 1985, pp. 42-63.

—'The Portrayal of the Life of Faith in the Gospel of Mark', *Int* 32 (1978), pp. 387-99.

—'The Question of the Messianic Secret in Mark', in *The Messianic Secret*, ed. C. Tuckett, London: SPCK, 1983, pp. 65-74.

—'Towards a Christology of Mark?', in *God's Christ and His People: Studies in honor of Nils Alstrup Dahl*, ed. J. Jervell and W.A. Meeks, Oslo: Universitetsforlaget, 1977, pp. 29-42.

Scott, M.P., 'Chiastic Structure: A Key to the Interpretation of Mark's Gospel', *BTB* 15 (1985), pp. 17-26.

Scroggs, R., and Groff, K.I., 'Baptism in Mark: Dying and Rising with Christ', *JBL* 92 (1973), pp. 531-48.

Senior, D., 'The Eucharist in Mark: Mission, Reconciliation, Hope', *BTB* 12 (1982), pp. 67-72.

—'The Gospel of Mark', *TBT* 103 (1979), pp. 2096-104.

—*The Passion of Jesus in the Gospel of Mark*, Wilmington, DE: Michael Glazier, 1984.

—'The Struggle to be Universal: Mission as Vantage Point for New Testament Investigation', *CBQ* 46 (1984), pp. 63-81.

Shaw, A., 'The Marcan Feeding Narratives', *CQR* 162 (1961), pp. 268-78.

Sibinga, J.S., 'Text and Literary Art in Mark 3.1-6', in *Studies in New Testament and Text: Essays in Honour of George D. Kilpatrick on the Occasion of his Sixty-fifth Birthday*, ed. J.K. Elliott. Leiden: E.J. Brill, 1976, pp. 357-65.

Sider, J.W., 'The Meaning of *Parabole* in the Usage of the Synoptic Evangelists', *Bib* 62 (1981), pp. 453-70.

—'Nurturing our Nurse: Literary Scholars and Biblical Exegesis', *Christianity and Literature* 32 (1982), pp. 15-21.

—'Proportional Analogy in the Gospel Parables', *NTS* 31 (1985), pp. 1-23.

Siegman, E.F., 'Teaching In Parables (Mk 4, 10-12; Lk 8, 9-10; Mt 13, 10-15)', *CBQ* 23 (1961), pp. 161-81.

Smith, C.W.F., 'No time for Figs', *JBL* 79 (1960), pp. 315-27.

Smith, G.D., *Mark 13.9-13: Misson in Apocalyptic, With Special Reference to Jesus' Gentile Mission in Mark*, (Unpublished Ph. D. Thesis), Louisville, KY: Southern Baptist Theological Seminary, 1981.

Smith, M., *Clement of Alexandria and a Secret Gospel of Mark*, Cambridge, MA: Harvard University Press, 1973.

Smith, R., 'Thy Kingdom Come: Some Recent Work on Mark's Gospel', *CurTM* 8 (1981), pp. 371-76.

Smith, R.H., 'New and Old in Mark 16.1-8', *CTM* 43 (1972), pp. 518-27.

Snodgrass, K., *The Parable of the Wicked Tenants: An Inquiry into Parable Interpretation*, Tübingen: Mohr/Siebeck, 1983.

Snoy, T., 'Les miracles dans l'évangile de Marc: Examen de quelques études récentes', *RTL* 3 (1972), pp. 449-66; 4 (1973), pp. 58-101.

Sowers, S., 'The Circumstances and Recollection of the Pella Flight', *TZ* 26 (1970), pp. 305-20.

Standaert, B., *L'Evangile selon Marc: Commentaire*, Paris: Editions du Cerf, 1983.

Steichele, H.-J., *Der Leidende Sohn Gottes*, Regensburg: Verlag Friedrich Pustet, 1980.

Stein, R.H., 'The Proper Methodology for Ascertaining a Markan Redaction History', *NovT* 13 (1971), pp. 181-98.

—'A Short Note on Mark xiv. 28 and xvi. 7', *NTS* 20 (1974), pp. 445-52.

—'What is Redaktiongeschichte?' *JBL* 88 (1969), pp. 45-56.

Stock, A., *Call to Discipleship: A Literary Study of Mark's Gospel*, Wilmington, DE: Michael Glazier, 1982.

—'Chiastic Awareness and Education in Antiquity', *BTB* 14 (1984), pp. 23-27.

—'Hinge Transitions in Mark's Gospel', *BTB* 15 (1985), pp. 27-31.

Stock, K., *Boten aus dem Mit-Ihm-Sein*, Rome: Biblical Institute Press, 1975.

Strecker, G., 'The Passion- and Resurrection Predictions in Mark's Gospel (Mark 8.31; 9.31; 10.32-34)', *Int* 22 (1968), pp. 421-42.

—'The Theory of the Messianic Secret in Mark's Gospel', in *The Messianic Secret*, ed. C. Tuckett, London: SPCK, 1983, pp. 49-64.

Stuhlmann, R., 'Beobachtungen und Überlegungen zu Markus iv. 26-29', *NTS* 19 (1973), pp. 153-62.

Suhl, A., *Die Funktion der alttestamentlichen Zitate und Anspielungen im Markusevangelium*, Gütersloh: Gerd Mohn, 1965.

Suriano, T., 'Eucharistic Reveals Jesus: The Multiplication of the Loaves', *TBT* 58 (1972), pp. 642-51.

Swartley, W., *Mark: The Way for All Nations*, (2nd ed.), Scottdale, PA: Herald Press, 1981.

—*A Study in Markan Structure: The Influence of Israel's Holy History Upon the Structure of the Gospel of Mark* (Unpublished Ph.D. Thesis), Princeton: Princeton Theological Seminary, 1973.

Swete, H.B., *The Gospel According to St. Mark* (3rd ed.), London: Macmillan, 1927.

Swetnam, J., 'No Sign of Jonah', *Bib* 66 (1985), pp. 126-30.

Synge, F.C., 'Mark 16.1-8', *JournTheolSAfr* 11 (1975), pp. 71-73.

Tagawa, K., Marc 13. La tâtonnement d'un homme réaliste éveillé face à la tradition apocalyptique', *FoiVie* 76 (1977), pp. 11-44.

Talbert, C.H., *What is a Gospel? The Genre of the Canonical Gospels*, Philadelphia: Fortress Press, 1977.

Tannehill, R.C., 'The Disciples in Mark: The Function of the Narrative Role', *JR* 57 (1977), pp. 386-405.

Taylor, V., 'The Apocalyptic Discourse of Mark xiii', *ExpTim* 60 (1949): pp. 94-98.

—*The Gospel According to St. Mark; The Greek Text with Introduction, Notes, and Indexes*, London: MacMillan, 1953.

Telford, W.R., *The Barren Temple and the Withered Tree*, Sheffield: JSOT Press, 1980.

—(Editor), *The Interpretation of Mark*, Philadelphia: Fortress Press, 1985.

Thiering, B.E., '"Breaking of Bread" and "Harvest" in Mark's Gospel', *NovT* 12 (1970), pp. 1-12.

Thomas, J.C., 'A Reconsideration of the Ending of Mark', *JETS* 26 (1983), pp. 407-19.

Thompson, J.W., 'The Gentile Mission as an Eschatological Necessity', *RestorQuart* 14 (1971), pp. 18-27.

Thrall, M.E., 'Elijah and Moses in Mark's Account of the Transfiguration', *NTS* 16 (1970), pp. 305-17.

Tinsley, E.J., 'The Sign of the Son of Man (Mk 14,62)', *SJT* 8 (1955), pp. 297-306.

Tödt, H.E., *The Son of Man in the Synoptic Tradition*, (2nd ed.), London: SCM Press, 1965.

Towner, W.S., 'An Exposition of Mk 13.24-32', *Int* 30 (1976), pp. 292-96.

Trites, A.A., 'The Tranfiguration of Jesus: The Gospel in Microcosm', *EvQ* 51 (1979), pp. 67-79.

Trocmé E., *The Formation of the Gospel According to Mark*, London: SPCK, 1975.

—'Is there a Markan Christology?', in *Christ and the Spirit in the New Testament: In Honour of Charles Francis Digby Moule*, ed. B. Lindars and S.S. Smalley, Cambridge: Cambridge University Press, 1973, pp. 3-13.

Trotti, J.B., 'Mark 13.32-37', *Int* 32 (1978), pp. 410-13.

Trueblood, E., *Confronting Christ*, Waco, TX: Word Books, 1960.

Tuckett, C. (Editor), *The Messianic Secret*, London: SPCK, 1983.

Turner, C.H., 'Marcan Usage: Notes, Critical and Exegetical, on the Second Gospel', *JTS* (OS) 25 (1924), pp. 377-86; 26 (1925), pp. 12-20, 145-56, 225-40; 27 (1926), pp. 58-62; 28 (1927), pp. 9-30, 349-62; 29 (1928), pp. 275-89, 346-61.

Tyson, J.B., 'The Blindness of the Disciples in Mark', *JBL* 80 (1961), pp. 261-68.

Vassiliadis, P., 'Behind Mark: Towards a Written Source', *NTS* 20 (1974), pp. 155-60.

Via, D.O., Jr., *Kerygma and Comedy in the New Testament: A Structuralist Approach to Hermeneutics*. Philadelphia: Fortress Press, 1975.

Vielhauer, P., 'Erwägungen zur Christologie des Markusevangeliums', in *Zeit und Geschichte: Dankesgabe an Rudolf Bultmann zum 80 Geburtstag*, ed. E. Dinkler and H. Thyen, Tübingen: JCB Mohr, 1964, pp. 155-69.

Vo, T.A.N., 'Interpretation of Mark's Gospel in the Last Two Decades', *Studia Biblica et Theologica* 2 (1972), pp. 37-62.

Vorster, W.S., 'Kerygma/History and the Gospel Genre', *NTS* 29 (1983), pp. 87-95.

—'Mark: Collector, Redactor, Author, Narrator?' *JournTheolSAfr* 31 (1980), pp. 46-61.

Walker, G., 'The Blind Recover Their Sight', *ExpTim* 87 (1975), pp. 23.

Walter, N., 'Tempelzerstörung und synoptische Apokalypse', *ZNW* 57 (1966), pp. 38-49.

Watson, F., 'The Social Function of Mark's Secrecy Theme', *JSNT* 24 (1985), pp. 49-69.

Weber, J.C., 'Jesus' Opponents in the Gospel of Mark', *JBR* 37 (1966), pp. 214-22.

Weeden, T.J., 'The Cross as Power in Weakness (Mark 15.20b-41)', in *The Passion in Mark*, ed. W. Kelber, Philadelphia: Fortress Press, 1976, pp. 115-34.

—'The Heresy That Necessitated Mark's Gospel', *ZNW* 59 (1968), pp. 145-58.

—*Mark—Traditions in Conflict*, Philadelphia: Fortress Press, 1971.

Weinacht, H., *Die Menschwerdung des Sohnes Gottes im Markusevangelium: Studien zur Christologie des Markusevangeliums*, Tübingen: Mohr-Siebeck, 1972.

Wenham, D., *Gospel Perspectives: The Jesus Tradition Outside the Gospels, V.*, Sheffield, JSOT Press, 1985.

—'The Interpretation of the Parable of the Sower', *NTS* 20 (1974), pp. 299-319.

—'Paul and the Synoptic Apocalypse', in *Gospel Perspectives: Studies of History and Tradition in the Four Gospels II*, ed. R.T. France and D. Wenham, Sheffield: JSOT Press, 1981, pp. 345-75.

—'Recent study of Mark 13', *TSFBull* 71 (1975), 6-15; 72 (1975), pp. 1-9.

—*The Rediscovery of Jesus' Eschatological Discourse*, Sheffield: JSOT Press, 1984.

—'"This generation will not pass . . . "; A Study of Jesus' Future Expectation in Mark 13', in *Christ the Lord: Studies in Christology Presented to Donald Guthrie*, ed. H.H. Rowdon, Leicester: Inter-Varsity Press, 1982, pp. 127-50.

Wenham, J., *Easter Enigma: Do the Resurrection Stories Contradict One Another?* Exeter: Paternoster, 1985.

Wessel, W.W., 'Mark', in *The Expositors Bible Commentary, VIII*, Grand Rapids, MI: Zondervan, 1984, pp. 601-93.

Whiston, L.A., *Through Suffering to Victory: Relational Studies in Mark [10.1—16.8]*, Waco, TX: Word Books, 1976.

White, P.O.G., 'The Resurrection and the Second Coming of Jesus in Mark', in *Studia Evangelica 6: Papers Presented to the Fourth International Congress on New Testament Studies Held at Oxford, 1969*, ed. E.A. Livingstone, Berlin: Akademie-Verlag, 1973, pp. 615-18.

Wikgren, A., 'ΑΡΧΗ ΤΟΥ ΕΥΑΓΓΕΛΙΟΥ', *JBL* 61 (1942), pp. 11-20.

Wilde, J.A., 'The Social World of Mark's Gospel. A Word about Method', in *Society of Biblical Literature 1978 Seminar Papers*, Edited by P.J. Achtemeier, Missoula, MT: Scholars Press, 1978, pp. 47-70.

Wilder, A.N., *Early Christian Rhetoric: The Language of the Gospel*, Cambridge, MA: Harvard University Press, 1971.

Williams, J.G., *Gospel Against Parable: Mark's Language of Mystery*, Sheffield: JSOT Press, 1985.

Williamson, L., *Mark, Interpretation: A Bible Commentary for Teaching and Preaching*, Atlanta: John Knox Press, 1983.

Winandy, J., 'Le logion de l'ignorance (Mc, XIII, 32; Mt., XXIV, 36)', *RB* 75 (1968), pp. 63-79.

Wolff, C., 'Zur Bedeutung Johannes des Täufers im Markusevangelium', *TLZ* 102 (1977), pp. 857-65.

Wolff, R., *The Gospel According to Mark*, Wheaton, IL: Tyndale, 1969.

Wrede, W., *The Messianic Secret*, Cambridge: James Clarke & Co., 1971.

Wretlind, D.O., 'Jesus' Philosophy of Ministry: A Study of a Figure of Speech in Mark 1.38', *JETS* 20 (1977), pp. 321-23.

Wright, A.G., 'The Widow's Mites: Praise or Lament?—A Matter of Context', *CBQ* 44 (1982), pp. 256-65.

Ziener, G., 'Das Bildwort vom Sauerteig Mk 8,15', *TTZ* 67 (1958), pp. 247-48.

Zmijewski, J., *Die Eschatologiereden des Lukas-Evangeliums. Eine traditions- und redaktionsgeschichtliche Untersuchung zu Lk 21,5-36 und Lk 17,20-37*, Bonn: Peter Hanstein, 1972.

INDEXES

INDEX OF BIBLICAL REFERENCES

OLD TESTAMENT

Exodus			308n22	33–34	210, 211
23.20	285n72	34.4	227	33	210, 211
		40.3	285n72	33.1-20	242
Leviticus		42.18f.	271n23	33.6-9	210
26.6	279n9	46.6	132	33.12f.	210
		49	311n20	33.21	210
Deuteronomy		51	311n20	33.29	210, 211,
13.1f.	34, 262n19	51.9f.	285n72		308n21,
		56.1	290n44		312n28
Job		56.3	290n44	33.30-32	211
11.18f.	279n9	56.4	290n44	33.33	211, 213, 221
		56.6	290n44	34	211, 212
Psalms		56.7	288n35	34.10f.	211
4.8	279n9	56.10f.	288n35	34.23-29	211
15.1	288n29			34.23	211
15.5	288n29	*Jeremiah*		34.25-30	221
27.12	131	5.21	271n23	34.30f.	212
35.11	131	7.2	121, 125	36	311n20
41.9	96	7.4	124	40.4	292n86
115.4	132	7.6	124		
118.22f.	123	7.7	125	*Daniel*	
		7.8	125	2.21f.	302n5, 303n5
Proverbs		7.9f.	124	2.35	138
3.23f.	279n9	7.10	124	9.27	308n22
		7.11	117, 121	11.31	308n22
Isaiah		7.14	125, 210	12.10	303n5
1.9f.	297n57	7.30	312n28	12.11	308n22
3.14	121	7.34	312n28		
5.1-7	287n28,	26.6-9	297n57	*Hosea*	
	288n28	29–31	311n20	9.10–10.2	125
5.7	120	38.2	219	9.10	125, 126
6.10	74			9.15f.	286n8
7–11	311n20	*Lamentations*		9.15	127
10.1f.	292n74	1.1	137	9.16	126
11.3	277n79			10.1f.	126
13.10	107, 227	*Ezekiel*			
13.17	232	12.2	271n23	*Joel*	
29.13	107, 274n47,	32.7	227	2.10	227

Amos
3.6f.   307n18
8.1f.   314n60
8.9   311n20

Micah
1.5   288n34
7.1   289n40

Habakkuk
2.2f.   311n20

Haggai
2   311n20
2.18f.   315n70

Zechariah
2.3-6   219
10.3f.   123
13.7   308n22
14.20f.   286n8

Malachi
3.1f.   311n20
3.1   175, 286n8, 295n23
3.3   156, 175
3.5   292n74
3.8ff.   292n74
3.12   175

NEW TESTAMENT

Matthew
12.39   35
15.31   60
16.4   35
24.29-35   35
24.30   32, 35, 36, 260n11
25.6   282n51
26.48   31, 37, 260n11

Mark
1.1-12.44   185
1.1-16   276n63
1.1-15   185, 189, 191, 238
1.1-14   156
1.1-13   189
1.1   54, 156, 174, 182, 189, 190, 305n37
1.2f.   156, 174
1.2   190, 285n72, 295n23, 305n38
1.5   74
1.9   151, 166
1.13   33, 305n34
1.14-20   275n63
1.14f   276n63, 305n34
1.14   151, 155-57, 166, 301n96
1.15   185, 252, 305n34
1.16-12.44   185-88, 191

1.16-20   46, 305n39
1.16   187
1.17   46
1.21-3.6   266n56
1.21-39   193
1.21-28   265n55, 266n56
1.21   265n54, 266n56
1.23-28   292n77
1.23-25   293n13
1.24   50, 277n68
1.27f.   293n13
1.29   305n39
1.35-39   44
1.35   202
1.36   261n14
1.39   265n54
1.44   42, 299n82
2.1-3.6   41-43, 47, 68, 193, 210, 265n49, 266n60
2.1-12   42, 120, 264n39,47, 265n49, 287n20
2.6f.   293n13
2.8   47, 307n17
2.10   42, 44, 119, 264n47
2.12f.   293n13
2.13-17   210
2.14-17   294n13
2.16f.   265n49
2.17   42

2.19-22   42
2.19f.   265n49
2.20   108, 313n49
2.22   138
2.23-28   43
2.25f.   42, 44
2.27   138, 265n49
2.28   119, 264n47
3.1-6   266n56, 292n77
3.1-4   42
3.1   265n54, 266n56
3.2   42
3.5   44, 47, 68, 69, 73, 74
3.6f.   294n13
3.6   32, 33, 40-47, 73, 78, 79, 119, 120, 185, 201, 265nn48,49, 54, 266nn55, 56, 272n30, 294n13
3.7-19   275n63
3.7-12   44, 276n63
3.7   44
3.11f.   259n18
3.13-19   44, 193, 276n63
3.14   45, 78, 79, 102, 165
3.20-35   45
3.20f   45, 193
3.21   266n58,

Mark (cont.)

	294n13	4.29	227	7.6-13	210, 211
3.22-30	45, 193,	4.30-32	152, 294n13	7.6f.	120, 211,
	270n11	4.34	72, 74		308n22
3.22ff.	294n13	4.35-8.26	76, 199	7.6	138
3.22	50, 265n48,	4.35-5.1	294n13	7.14	43
	275n59	4.35-41	75	7.17-23	294n13
3.23-26	201	4.38	279n9	7.17f.	75
3.25	201	4.40	309n29	7.19-23	138
3.27	73, 201	4.41	75	7.19	182
3.31-35	45, 193	4.48	280n21	7.24-8.10	193, 294n13
3.31	294n13	5.1-20	75	7.24-30	76
3.32	261n14	5.7	50	7.24	294n13
3.34f.	45, 274n44	5.21-24	75	7.30	75
3.34	74, 78	5.21	49	7.31-8.26	64, 70, 71,
4.1-34	46, 71, 74,	5.24	49		73-77, 110
	75, 199,	5.27	49	7.31-37	70, 76, 78
	268n85	5.30	49	8.1-21	70-72, 78
4.1-20	71, 72	5.31	49, 83, 84	8.1-10	68, 69, 72,
4.1-9	72	5.35-43	75		75
4.1	294n13	5.37	305n39	8.11-21	26
4.3-8	73, 152	6.1-6	294n13	8.11-13	29, 30, 32,
4.3ff.	110	6.2ff.	49		34, 40, 42,
4.10-12	272n30,	6.2	44, 49		60, 67, 68,
	276n64,	6.3	45		72, 256,
	279n89,	6.5	44, 49		261nn14,15,
	293n12,	6.6-30	305n40		265n48,
	294n13	6.6	44, 276n63		270n11
4.10	74, 78	6.7ff.	44	8.11f.	44, 241
4.11-13	45	6.7	276n63,	8.11	33, 241,
4.11f.	44, 72, 74,		294n13		261n15
	278n80	6.12f.	157	8.12	57, 241
4.11	54, 76, 152,	6.14-29	157	8.14-21	35, 54, 57,
	154, 200,	6.14-16	50, 69		60-68, 70-72,
	202, 269n90	6.14	49, 69,		77, 78, 80,
			265n48,		81, 129, 244,
4.12	69, 74, 82,		295n24		269n3,
	271n23,	6.16	275n59		270nn8,11,
	274n45,46	6.18	69		272n24
4.13-20	72, 73	6.20	69		
4.13	72	6.30-44	75	8.14-16	66
4.14-20	71, 72, 146,	6.30	157	8.14	67
	307n14	6.34	44	8.15	61-64, 67, 68,
4.15-19	80	6.39-44	202		70, 75, 81-
4.15	283n50	6.45-56	76		83, 269n6,
4.16-19	283n50	6.49-52	75		272n30
4.17	157	6.49	75, 202	8.16	66
4.21-23	53	6.50	76	8.17-21	68, 268n78
4.22	200	6.52	54, 66, 68,	8.18	34, 66, 67,
4.24	82, 278n84		69, 268n78		69, 82,
4.27	200, 279n9	7.1f.	294n13		271n23
4.28	157, 174	7.5-13	43	8.19-21	66
				8.19f	67

Mark (cont.)

8.19	67
8.20	67
8.21	81
8.22-26	60, 70, 76, 78, 103, 152, 272n32, 276n63, 277n80
8.23	82
8.24	82
8.27-10.52	266n60, 275n53
8.27-10.45	78, 103, 152, 156, 164, 298n73, 299n73
8.27-30	40, 46, 71
8.27	46
8.28	275n59
8.29-31	200, 305n40
8.30	52, 76, 185
8.31-10.45	78
8.31-37	293n9
8.31f.	276n63
8.31	78, 266n60
8.32	201
8.33	80, 152, 201
8.34-9.1	29, 186
8.34-38	98, 150, 153, 260n2, 307n13
8.34	293n9
8.35	87
8.36f.	152
8.38	152, 245, 281n41
9.1	48, 176, 201, 245, 284n62, 313nn43,47, 48,50
9.2	305n39
9.9-13	193
9.9	52, 53, 304n29
9.11-13	155
9.12f.	287n18
9.13	155
9.23	138
9.28f	138
9.30-37	275n61
9.33-37	152
9.38-41	307n9
9.39	49
9.40	282n48
9.49	304n29
10.1	151
10.2	33
10.17-21	153
10.28-31	153
10.30	304n29
10.32	202
10.35-45	193
10.35-40	152
10.37f.	153
10.37	75
10.38f.	150
10.39f.	186
10.39	99, 285n65, 301n97
10.40	153
10.42-45	201
10.42-44	152
10.43f.	153
10.45	96, 143, 282nn44,45, 301n97
10.46-52	50, 78, 103, 152, 275n63, 276n63
10.52	185
11.1-11	289n38
11.9f.	290n43
11.11-12.40	137
11.11-12.12	120
11.11-15	286n9
11.11	84, 129
11.12-13.2	126
11.12-12.44	208
11.12-12.40	193
11.12-25	289n38
11.12-21	127, 210, 219
11.12-14	114, 125, 249
11.13	253
11.14	129
11.15-19	286n9
11.15-17	114, 122, 125, 201
11.15	124, 292n75
11.16	118
11.17	114, 117, 121, 122, 124, 128, 138, 214, 290n43
11.18	116, 261n14, 287n26
11.20f.	114, 249
11.20	126, 129, 251
11.21f.	125
11.21	120, 129
11.23-25	143
11.23	290n48
11.27-12.44	43
11.27-33	43, 155, 261n15, 289n38
11.30	261n15
11.32	287n26
12.1-12	114, 115, 119-21, 125, 127, 208, 210, 212, 276n68, 289n39, 290n53
12.1-9	210
12.1	43
12.7-12	209
12.7-9	123, 128
12.8-12	145
12.8	124
12.9	129, 208, 289n39
12.10f.	123
12.10	133, 208, 280n17
12.12	201, 261n14, 276n68, 277n68, 287n17
12.13-44	135
12.13-17	122, 208, 272n30
12.13	124
12.14	82-84, 86
12.15	33
12.17	83
12.24	48
12.28-34	122, 123, 208
12.33	135, 138
12.34	128, 264n41,

Mark (cont.)

	265n52		250, 251, 310n8		169, 176, 193, 207, 210, 218-20, 236, 237, 242, 278n87, 308n21,22, 309n1, 312nn28,37
12.35-38	280n21	13.5-8	215, 216, 218		
12.35	43, 208	13.5ff	215		
12.36	209	13.5f.	193, 221		
12.38-44	208	13.5	34, 85, 86, 90, 204, 278n86, 283n55		
12.38-40	122, 134, 135			13.15-23	226
12.38	43, 82, 86, 126, 136, 289n39	13.7f	215	13.17	309n1
12.39	44	13.7	44, 216, 235, 236, 309n1	13.18	274n47
12.40	122, 124, 135-38, 211, 289n39	13.8	193, 236, 309n1	13.19f.	193
				13.19	220, 225, 230, 309n1
12.41-44	122, 134-39, 145, 287n26, 308n19	13.9-14	210	13.20	113, 237, 309n1
		13.9-13	158, 174, 175, 188, 216-18, 220	13.21-23	230
12.42	135, 136			13.21f.	193, 221
12.44	135, 185, 186, 291n62	13.9-12	209	13.21	229, 309n1
		13.9-11	193, 309n11	13.22	30, 32-34, 40, 48, 256, 261n16, 263n33, 283n55
13.1-37	185, 187, 188, 191	13.9	34, 44, 86, 87, 193, 305n41, 306n41, 309n2, 311n25		
13.1-4	21, 23, 24, 203-205, 207				
13.1ff.	135			13.23	34, 85, 86, 195, 229-31, 235, 239, 240, 278n86, 310n9
13.1f.	137				
13.1	126, 135, 136, 207	13.10	146, 172, 174, 193, 216, 225, 236, 243, 251, 305n41, 306n41, 309n1		
13.2	85, 86, 113, 117, 125, 128, 131, 136, 201, 207, 208			13.24-37	242
				13.24-31	35
				13.24-27	178, 226-28, 242-44, 308n25, 310n8
13.3	146, 305n39	13.11f.	305n41, 306n41		
13.4-23	196			13.24-26	227, 231
13.4	22, 24, 39, 57, 59, 116, 146, 204, 206, 212, 224, 226, 234, 240, 309n1, 311n13	13.11	216, 217, 309nn1,2, 311n25, 312n37	13.24ff.	193, 226, 228, 239
				13.24f.	227-29, 235, 262n31, 284n57
		13.12	193, 237	13.24	228-31, 235, 239, 309n1, 310nn8,9
		13.13	87, 209, 236, 309n1		
		13.14-27	230	13.25	48
13.5-37	21, 23, 203, 204, 206, 246	13.14-21	309n41	13.26f.	228, 295n27, 309n1
13.5-33	59	13.14-20	230, 237		
13.5-31	116	13.14ff.	206, 207, 214, 218, 226, 228, 236, 306n41	13.26	48, 242, 243
13.5-27	313n55			13.27	138, 242, 252, 253, 291n57
13.5-23	111, 113, 116, 195, 235, 242,	13.14	36, 138, 146, 164,		

Mark (cont.)

				313n51		308n22
13.28-37	238	13.34-36	92		14.28	16, 64, 97,
13.28-32	239	13.34f.	93			101, 160,
13.28f.	128, 147,	13.34	91, 105			163-66, 172,
	230, 251,	13.35	89, 91, 93-			189, 270n14,
	309n1		95, 102, 105,			298nn60,72,
13.28	242, 248,		309n1			301n94
	249, 251,	13.36	242		14.29-31	101
	252	13.37	90, 91, 93,		14.29	298n60
13.29	240, 242,		185, 195,		14.30	97, 100
	248, 249		196, 221,		14.31	99
13.30	24, 57, 147,		238, 242,		14.32-42	90, 91, 94,
	176, 195,		244, 247			106, 280n10
	230, 232,	14.1-16.8	185-88, 191		14.33	102, 305n39
	237, 239-46,	14.1-11	134		14.34-36	202
	249, 257,	14.1-9	134, 138,		14.34	99
	309n1,		139, 145,		14.35	285n65,
	313n51,		308n19			313n49
	315n77	14.1f.	134		14.36	285n65,
13.31	240, 244	14.1	137, 261n14			301n97
13.32-37	85, 91, 243,	14.3-9	134, 137, 139		14.37	91, 99, 100,
	255, 283n51,	14.5	138			285n65
	285n71	14.8f	294n14		14.38	99, 215, 227,
13.32ff.	22, 127	14.9	138, 172,			283n50
13.32f.	246		174, 189		14.40	91, 99
13.32	91, 107, 108,	14.10-12	96, 264n45		14.41	91, 99, 107,
	234, 239,	14.11	261n14			201, 282n51,
	242, 244,	14.14f.	134			285n65,
	246, 247,	14.14	102			313n49
	252, 254,	14.17-15.15	93			100
	309n1,	14.17-31	93		14.43-52	100
	313nn51,54,	14.17	95, 98, 102		14.44	37, 38
	315n77	14.18-21	97		14.50	170
13.33-37	89-92, 94-96,	14.18	96, 102		14.52	170
	99, 103,	14.19	97		14.54	102
	174, 176,	14.20	102		14.55	261n14
	188, 194,	14.21	97, 307n17		14.57-64	212
	195, 210,	14.22-24	97, 202		14.57-59	115
	225, 235,	14.22	97		14.57f.	130
	243, 279n10,	14.23-25	285n65		14.58	115
	280nn10,15,	14.23f.	301n97		14.59	290n50
	283n53,	14.24	96, 160		14.62	48, 189, 208,
	307n13,	14.25	97, 189,			212, 227,
	314n64		285n67			280n17
13.33-36	195	14.26-31	97		14.67	102
13.33	34, 85-87,	14.26	96		14.72	100, 160,
	90, 93, 107,	14.27-31	164			281n41,
	110, 221,	14.27-29	297n60			282n44
	242, 246,	14.27f.	166, 195		15.1	102
	247, 253,	14.27	97, 98,		15.11	103, 287n26
	309n1,		298n60,		15.13	151
					15.14f.	124

Mark (cont.)

15.18	189
15.20	152
15.22	152
15.26	189
15.27-39	305n32
15.29f.	115, 290n53
15.29	115, 130
15.32	277n80, 278n80
15.33-36	189
15.33	107, 215, 284n57
15.34	202, 302n103
15.35f.	155
15.36	277n80, 278n80
15.37-39	288n36, 294n14
15.37	140, 142-44
15.38f.	201
15.38	115, 141, 143-45, 189, 209, 286n6
15.39	133, 140, 144, 278n80, 302n103
15.40	300n88
15.43	264n41, 265n52
15.47	185
16.1-8	161, 202, 287n52, 298n61
16.1-7	170, 275n63
16.4	289n42
16.6f.	297n60
16.6	154, 298n60, 300n88
16.7f.	158, 172, 176, 178, 187, 188, 194-96, 238, 293n5, 305n32
16.7	16, 64, 101, 109, 133, 151, 158, 161-66, 169-71, 176, 195, 213, 261n14, 270n14, 291n57, 296n45, 298nn60,72, 299n75, 300n90
16.8	158, 162, 163, 169-72, 297nn52,54, 55, 299n82, 300n88
16.9-20	161, 297n50
16.10	170
16.17	260n10
16.20	260n10

Luke

2.12	260n11, 263n34
2.34	263n34
11.29	35
12.36	105
17.28f.	230
21.1	37
21.11-25	32
21.11	37, 260n11
21.12	263n32
21.25	37, 260n11
22.48	37
23.8	263n34
24.12	60

John

2.19-22	304n17
20.5	60

Acts

2.22	263n33
2.43	261n12, 263n33
4.16	31
4.30	261n12, 263n33
5.12	261n12, 263n33
6.8	261n12, 263n33
13.13	160
14.13	261n12, 263n33
15.12	261n12, 263n33

Romans

1.5	236
15.19	261n12

1 Corinthians

1.22	261n12
10.11	297n48

2 Corinthians

4.18	60
12.12	261n12

Ephesians

5.2	137

2 Thessalonians

2.6	57

Hebrews

2.4	261n12
11.3	60

James

5.7-9	314n64

Revelation

9.20	60

INDEX OF AUTHORS

Achtemeier, P.J. 51, 230, 269n7, 275n61, 276n63, 281n30, 286nn77,13, 291n67, 294n21, 303n16, 313n44

Ambrozic, A.M. 80, 184, 233, 234, 259n20, 268n81, 273n35,36, 275n53, 277n69, 283n53, 290n51, 296n48, 299n85, 304n22, 307n12, 309n42, 310n9, 311n16, 312n31

Anderson, H. 66, 184, 268n82, 270n10, 272n30, 273n32, 285n66, 312n39

Au, W. 298n66

Bacon, B.W. 268n87

Bailey, J.L. 275n61, 302n2

Baird, J.A. 277n78

Bartholomew, G.L. 297n52

Barrett, C.K. 287n15

Bauckham, R. 280n15

Beardslee, W.A. 268n76

Beasley-Murray, G.R. 16, 36, 228, 247, 262n24, 273n40, 274n50, 279n88, 280n21, 303n15, 309n39, 310nn3,5, 311nn20,22, 312nn26,28,36, 313n41, 314n66, 315n78

Beauvery, R. 275n56

Beck, N.A. 61, 62, 269n3

Bennett, W.J., Jr 294n18

Benoit, P. 101

Best, E. 51, 77, 166, 275nn53,54, 284n58, 287n21, 296n44, 299n76, 301n97

Biguzzi, G. 291n56

Bilezikian, G.G. 293n4, 295n25

Birdsall, J.N. 282n44, 289n40

Blomberg, C.L. 304n17

Boobyer, G.H. 271n24, 290n45

Boomershine, T.E. 297n52, 300n88

Boring, M.E. 304n52

Bornkamm, G. 313n47

Boucher, M. 71, 73, 181, 273n39, 275n60, 279n91

Boyd, W.J.P. 281n39

Brady, D. 281n38

Brandenburger, E. 18, 308n20

Brandon, S.G.F. 295n31, 310n9

Breytenbach, C. 284n59

Brower, K. 284n62, 294n17, 304n32, 313nn48,50

Brown, C. 52, 260n9

Brown, R.E. 306n5

Bruce, F.F. 299n78

Buchanan, G.W. 286n9

Budesheim, T.L. 264n41

Bultmann, R. 81, 115, 261n13, 297n54

Burkill, T.A. 53, 107, 160, 277n68, 279n8, 281n41, 291n63, 296n46

Busch, F. 29

Caird, G.B. 232-34, 259n17, 262n19, 263n35, 273n40, 281nn24,33, 286n79, 305n36, 315n73

Caldecott, A. 286n12

Cangh, J.-M. van 298n67

Carrington, P. 108, 260n22, 292n85

Carson, D.A. 302n3

Catchpole, D. 299n82

Chilton, B.D. 269n89

Chronis, H.L. 286n7, 291n57, 292n83

Clark, C.B. 313n42

Cole, R.A. 291n57

Conzelmann, H. 78, 310n9

Cotter, W.J. 289n42

Countryman, L.W. 272n24

Cousar, C.B. 284n59, 313n42

Coutts, J. 79

Cranfield, C.E.B. 55, 262nn17,23, 271n21, 283n52, 285n67, 286nn79,14, 294n20, 297n58, 308n24, 309nn31,34,37, 312nn31,38, 315n79

Crossan, J.D. 290n43, 295n31, 304n25

Cullmann, O. 302n100

Culpepper, R.A. 286n4, 290n49, 300n84

Danker, F.W. 135

Daube, D. 273n40

Davey, F.N. 268n86

Delorme, J. 304n30

Derrett, J.D.M. 271n16, 286n10, 289n42, 314n63
Dewar, F. 279n8, 315nn69,78
Dewy, J.B. 42, 276n63
Dewey, K.E. 281n40, 283n56
Dibelius, M. 98
Dodd, C.H. 288n32
Donahue, J.R. 135, 282n42, 286n4, 287nn16,19, 290n51, 291nn57,64, 303n8
Dormeyer, D. 106
Doughty, D.J. 266n56
Drury, J. 292n87, 314n59
Duling, D.C. 266n60, 272n31, 293n8
Dupont, J. 280n11, 306n41, 314nn58,60, 315n74

Edwards, R.A. 275n60
Englezakis, B. 279n90, 293n10
Ernst, J. 298n70
Evans, C.A. 288n28
Evans, C.F. 286n3, 297nn55,57, 298n68
Ewert, D. 302n102

Farmer, W.R. 260n10, 297n50
Farrer, A. 279n4, 294n18
Faw, C.E. 153
Fenton, J.C. 185, 265n55
Flanagan, N.M. 288n34
Focant, C. 295n37
Ford, D. 259n21
Ford, J.M. 287n15
Fowler, R.M. 96
Freyne, S. 299n76

Gaide, G. 265n54
Gaston, L. 17, 280n20, 287n23, 292n1, 307n18, 311n25, 315n72
Giblin, C.H. 182, 287n22, 303n10
Glasswell, M.E. 42, 267nn66,74, 271n20, 303n6
Gould, E.P. 296n45
Goulder, M.D. 297n56, 299n81
Graham, H.H. 273n39
Grant, F.C. 297n59
Green, M.P. 293n8
Guelich, R.A. 305nn35,37

Haacker, K. 306n6
Haefner, A.E. 297n51
Hahn, F. 290n45, 294n14

Harrington, W. 280n23, 291n65
Hartman, L. 17, 229, 302nn100,5, 308nn20,29, 309n38, 310n3
Hawkin, D.J. 275nn57,61, 297n49
Hebert, G. 261n14, 297n56, 298n70
Hedrick, C.W. 276n63, 304n28
Hendriksen, W. 270n12, 311n18, 312n27
Hengel, M. 180, 182, 302nn103,1
Hiebert, D.E. 67
Hiers, R.H. 286n11, 289n42
Hirsch, E.D., Jr 259n17
Hooker, M.D. 46, 166, 167, 216, 230, 259n16, 260n2, 271n24, 275n62, 278nn82,86,88, 286n78, 287n21, 294n23, 298n70, 299n76, 300n89, 301n97, 302n5, 311n13, 312n30
Horst, P.W. van der 297n52
Hoskyns, E.C. 268n86
Howard, J.K. 275n55, 311n20
Hunter, A.M. 81
Hurtado, L.W. 281n34, 287n25

Iersel, B.M.F. van 64, 281n25, 292n2, 298n72, 299n76, 301n95, 302nn99,101, 305n34

James, W. 57
Jeremias, J. 273n38
Johnson, E.S. 272n31, 277n80
Jones, A. 308n27, 311n24
Juel, D. 131, 286nn4,5, 287n24, 288nn29,33, 291nn57,58, 304nn23,32

Kallikuzhuppil, J. 279n8
Kazmierski, C.R. 291n57, 302n99, 313n54
Keck, L.E. 30, 296n43
Kee, H.C. 52, 65, 115, 261n16, 268nn76,77, 271n18, 278n81, 287nn24,26, 292n82, 294n15, 307n7
Kelber, W.H. 90, 91, 94, 104, 230, 259n10, 266n57, 279n10, 286n12, 288n32, 293n5, 294n13, 295nn31,33, 296n47, 297n59, 301n96, 303n8, 304n27, 306n2, 310nn3,13
Kelly, H.A. 307n8
Kermode, F. 270n16, 273n42, 285n64, 297n53, 302n5
Kertelge, K. 260n4, 261n12
Kierkegaard, S. 31
Kilgallen, J.J. 280n23
Kilpatrick, G.D. 309n31

Kingsbury, J.D. 306n1
Klauck, H.-J. 296n39
Knigge, H.-D. 298n62
Kolenkow, A.B. 269n92
Kremer, J. 265n51
Kuby, A. 276n63
Kümmel, W.G. 297n55, 307n15
Künzi, M. 313n43

Lagrange, M.-J. 312n40
Lambrecht, J. 17, 74, 273n40, 287n16, 295n35, 304n21,308n20, 310n9, 312n31, 315n74
Lane, W.L. 263n11, 270n11, 273n37, 285n72, 291n68, 298nn60,63, 300n85, 303n7, 310n12, 313n50
LaVerdiere, E.A. 2992n84
Lemcio, E.E. 79, 276n65
Lewis, C.S. 81
Lightfoot, R.H. 77, 89, 94, 95, 108, 109, 163, 188, 267n66, 274n51, 279n4, 288n32, 290n45, 292n82, 297n59, 300n86, 302n99, 303n7
Lindemann, A. 299n80, 300n92
Lindsay, T.M. 135, 308n28
Linnemann, E. 297n51
Linton, O. 260n7
Lohmeyer, E. 163, 287n27, 290n45, 297n59
Lohse, E. 52
Losada, D. 294n18
Losie, L.A. 288n37
Lövestam, E. 240, 241, 280n11, 282n51, 283n54, 284n59, 312n35
Luz, U. 30, 51, 264n42, 267n72, 294n22

McCasland, S.V. 30, 260n6
McCaughey, J.D. 293n3
McCowen, A. 267n73
McKelvey, R.J. 131, 133, 286n6, 287n16, 288n32, 290n52
Malbon, E.S. 291n61, 293n4, 302n4, 303n16
Malley, E.J. 270n10
Manson, T.W. 267n73
Marcus, J. 79, 272n30, 279n89, 293n12
Marshall, I.H. 264n43, 307n11
Martin, R.P. 261n14, 262n18, 263n39, 264n48, 268n84, 279n9, 281n28
Martini, C.M. 282n49
Marxsen, W. 16, 164, 195, 297n59, 305n37, 309n36

Matera, F.J. 273n32, 294n18
Mauser, U.W. 274n49
Meagher, J.C. 61, 129, 270n8, 271n17, 277n71, 286n2, 294n16
Menzies, A. 269n2
Meye, R.P. 261n17, 268n84, 272n27, 275n57, 295n34, 298n70
Michaelis, W. 59
Michaels, J.R. 292n81
Michie, D. 80, 265n48, 281n24, 303n14, 304n29
Milling, F.H. 284n57
Minear, P.S. 273n44, 291n72, 293n2
Mitton, C.L. 269n6
Moloney, F.J. 295n32
Moore, A.L. 16, 304n17, 307n16, 312n32
Moore, C.A. 274n45
Mora, V. 262n21
Morris, L. 307n18
Mosley, A.W. 184
Moule, C.F.D. 261n15, 268n76, 269n91, 274n44, 299n82
Muddiman, J.B. 264n44

Nardoni, E 313nn43,47
Navone, J. 280n22
Neville, G. 313n55
Nineham, D.E. 272n32, 273n36, 282n50, 286n10

Oepke, A. 90
O'Mahony, G. 273n33
Osborne, G.R. 285n65
Ottley, R.R. 297n52

Patten, P. 274n46, 307n10
Paul, A. 275n63
Perrin, N. 262n22, 272n31, 293n2, 297n59
Pesch, R. 17, 84, 89, 187, 259nn2,11, 284n59, 291n57, 308n20, 309nn30,3, 310n9, 312n31
Petersen, N.R. 170, 204, 296nn39,40, 301n95, 303n14, 304n31, 307n12
Piper, O.A. 212, 278n80

Quesnell, Q. 261n15, 277n76, 278n85

Räisänen, H. 51, 264n47, 277n69, 293n12
Rawlinson, A.E.J. 262n23
Ramsey, A.M. 163

Rengstorf, K.H. 31, 36, 48, 260nn7,8
Rhoads, D. 80, 265n48, 281n24, 303n14, 304n29
Richard, E. 303n12
Richardson, A. 51, 52, 65, 76, 77, 264n47, 272n32, 275n52
Robbins, V.K. 30, 48, 68, 281n27
Robey, D. 269n90
Robinson, J.M. 21, 81, 184, 262n20, 264n48, 279n4
Roth, C. 286n11

Sandmel, S. 295n31, 296n41
Schenke, L. 51, 97, 267n72
Schmid, J. 284n60
Schmithals, W. 284n61
Schnackenburg, R. 272n29, 291n66, 309n36
Schneider, G. 281n39
Schnellbächer, E.L. 299n76
Schottroff, W. 295n25
Schreiber, J. 309n40
Schweizer, E. 51, 135, 160, 262n22, 263n38, 270n10, 280n23, 288n30, 293n6, 294n19, 295n24, 296n46, 298n64, 299n77, 300n86, 306n43, 310n5
Senior, D. 97, 271n24, 278n80, 281nn35,36, 282n43, 284n57, 290n51, 291nn54,59, 292n77, 293n7, 294n13, 295nn24,26, 298n65, 299n75
Sider, J.W. 269n88, 273n40, 277n72, 314n62
Siegman, E.F. 312n40
Smith, R.H. 298n61
Snodgrass, K. 287nn21,24, 288nn30,31, 303n9
Snoy, T. 261n12, 267n75
Stegemann, E. 295n25
Stegemann, W. 295n25
Stock, A. 183, 276n63, 281nn37,40, 286n13, 288n33, 291n62, 294n18, 296n40, 299n76, 300n90, 301n94, 306n3, 309n35
Stock, K. 281n31
Strecker, G. 268n80

Suhl, A. 288n31
Suriano, T. 272n31, 274n48
Swartley, W. 265nn48,53, 277n68, 292n75, 295n30, 299n79
Swete, H.B. 292n78, 310n6, 313n42
Swetnam, J. 262n22
Synge, F.C. 297n52, 299n83

Tannehill, R.C. 298nn70,71
Taylor, V. 64, 108, 247, 273n38, 283n51, 284n60, 295n24, 297n54, 311n15, 312n29
Telford, W.R. 248, 250, 288nn32,37, 290n47, 306n1, 314nn60,65,67
Thiering, B.E. 271n24
Thompson, J.W. 312n26
Tinsley, E.J. 268n76
Todorov, T. 269n90
Tödt, H.E. 295n28
Trites, A.A. 313nn45,46
Trocmé, E. 89, 187, 295n31
Turner, C.H. 61, 303n15
Tyson, J.B. 295n31

Vassiliadis, P. 278n82
Via, D.O., Jr 295n37
Vielhauer, P. 306n1

Walker, G. 275n55
Weber, J.C. 264n41
Weeden, T.J. 29, 51, 114, 115, 260n3, 295nn31,36
Wenham, D. 18, 37, 39, 92, 93, 230, 259n1, 260n21, 262n25, 285n71, 302n103, 308n20, 309nn32,34,41, 310n4, 311n17, 313n54, 314n66
Wessel, W.W. 292n79
Whiston, L.A. 300n91
White, P.O.G. 299n80
Wilde, J.A. 267n68
Williams, J.G. 303n8
Williamson, L. 304n23, 305n39
Wolff, C. 294n18
Wolff, R. 272n29, 280n16
Wrede, W. 52, 61, 76, 160, 200, 268n80, 296n46
Wright, A.G. 135, 136, 166

DATE DUE